THE LOST BOYS OF ZETA PSI

Laurie A. Wilkie   ·   THE LOST BOYS
OF ZETA PSI

*A Historical Archaeology of Masculinity
at a University Fraternity*

University of California Press

Berkeley   Los Angeles   London

University of California Press, one of the most distinguished university presses in the United States, enriches lives around the world by advancing scholarship in the humanities, social sciences, and natural sciences. Its activities are supported by the UC Press Foundation and by philanthropic contributions from individuals and institutions. For more information, visit www.ucpress.edu.

University of California Press
Berkeley and Los Angeles, California

University of California Press, Ltd.
London, England

Library of Congress Cataloging-in-Publication Data

Wilkie, Laurie A.
  The lost boys of Zeta Psi : a historical archaeology of masculinity at a university fraternity / Laurie A. Wilkie.
    p.   cm.
  Includes bibliographical references and index.
  ISBN 978-0-520-26059-7 (cloth : alk. paper)—ISBN 978-0-520-26060-3 (pbk. : alk. paper)
  1. Zeta Psi Fraternity—History.   2. University of California, Berkeley—History.   3. Greek letter societies—California—Berkeley—History.   4. Male college students—California—Berkeley—Conduct of life.   5. Male college students—California—Berkeley—Psychology.   6. Male college students—California—Berkeley—Sexual behavior.   7. Masculinity—California—Berkeley—History.   8. Gender identity—California—Berkeley—History.   I. Title.
  LJ75.Z735W55 2010
  378.18'550979467—dc22   2009030993

Manufactured in the United States of America

19 18 17 16 15 14 13 12 11 10
10 9 8 7 6 5 4 3 2 1

This book is printed on Cascades Enviro 100, a 100% post consumer waste, recycled, de-inked fiber. FSC recycled certified and processed chlorine free. It is acid free, Ecologo certified, and manufactured by BioGas energy.

To Dad, the frat boy in my life

CONTENTS

FIGURES

TABLES

ACKNOWLEDGMENTS

No matter how we archaeologists cloak ourselves in the protective garb of science, the reality is that archaeological interpretation is 80 percent random bursts of creative wonder and 20 percent evidentiary justification. In the introduction to the published version of *Peter Pan*, James Barrie proclaims that he cannot remember writing the play, that it conjured itself. I feel that Barrie's spirit must have whispered in my ear as I conducted this analysis, because once the random notion that *Peter Pan* was the story of early-twentieth-century gender relations flitted through my mind, I could see the archaeology of the Zeta Psi fraternity in no other way. In attempting to convince myself that using the play to interpret the site was an act of intellectual silliness, I only managed to see more and more levels of connection between the two.

While Barrie may have claimed innocence in the authorship of his work, I will make no such claim. This was written neither in a dream nor without the help of many people. Just as interpretive inspiration comes from many sources, so does the will and energy to complete the writing task. I am unable to thank by name all my sources of inspiration and encouragement—and many may not even know of the role they played in creating this manuscript. Nameless members of lecture audiences, Zeta Psi alumni, friends, colleagues, students, family members, and archive and library staff, and even random strangers on cross-country flights, all provided inspiration, feedback, and support of various kinds. I will thank as many as I can, but also hope those not mentioned here by name will know their contributions to this project were invaluable to me.

Given the admittedly novel, or should I say theatrical, nature of this work, I was concerned that perhaps in this manuscript I was crossing the line that separates "quirky" from "downright bizarre." Even my eleven-year-old daughter, a Peter Pan fan herself, was skeptical when I described the concept to her. As a result, I recruited a number of people for the literary equivalent of hand-holding, for reading multiple versions of the text and reassuring me that the concept worked. Let me thank Dan Hicks for inviting me to give the 2006 keynote address at the Contemporary and Historical Archaeology in Theory conference (CHAT) in Bristol. The participants of the conference were first subjected to my ravings during that lecture—I figured that if I could not sell the Pan connection in Peter's homeland, all was lost. That audience's enthusiasm and encouragement provided the momentum I needed to write the manuscript during my sabbatical the following semester.

Rosemary Joyce, Paul Farnsworth, Sabrina Agarwal, Kim Christensen-Schwarz, Stacy Kozakavich, John Chenoweth, Kat Howlett-Hayes, and Mike Way all read portions of the manuscript as it was being written and provided helpful suggestions for how to strengthen it, rather than encouraging me to abandon it. Mike Way, and particularly, Stacy Kozakavich, were instrumental in assuring that the artwork in this book is tidy and professional.

Writing is but a small part of the archaeological enterprise. Before I ever reached that stage, a large number of graduate and undergraduate students had already been involved in the project. The initial salvage excavations in 1995 were assisted by Meredith Chesson, Ian Kuijt, Mark Hall, Jason Bass, Peter Mills, Cyndi Van Guilder, and others, whose faces have become foggy in the jumble of time. A number of undergraduate papers were produced on the site in 1996, and I have cited many of them in this work. Geoff Hughes, Lorinda Miller, Carolyn Luong, Kira Blaisdell-Sloan, Samantha Holcamp, Persephone Hintlin, Trushna Parekh, and Kim Glitch wrote particularly helpful papers. I am pleased to note that a number of these individuals have now completed advanced degrees in anthropology and are working in the discipline.

In 2000, a new set of graduates and undergraduates undertook excavation and lab work related to Zeta Psi. In particular, David Palmer, Cheryl Lintner-Smith, Bill Whitehead, Xena Phillips, Angela Smith, Victoria Zetterquist, Erica Roberts, and an active member of Zeta Psi, Matthew Hammond, were important members of that field and lab team. Their hours of work (including jackhammering) made this work possible.

The University of California's Capital Projects crew worked around the archaeological field school during the beginning of the retrofit. The construction company in charge of the retrofit kindly helped us remove flooring and provided jack-hammers for our use—and, undoubtedly, their amusement.

Many, many, many, people have contributed to my understanding of fraternity culture—both from within Zeta Psi and from outside. Geoff Hughes, an archaeology student and fraternity member, should be credited with igniting my willingness to consider fraternities a legitimate avenue of research. It was his indignation with media coverage of the site that prompted me to evaluate my own biases about fraternities. In 1995, a number of active Zetes were very helpful, providing access to fraternity archives. In 2000, Matthew Hammond, who served as the Delta, or chapter historian, at the time, was an outstanding source of insight into the fraternity. Many generations of Zeta Psi brothers, from both the Iota chapter and the national chapter, generously gave their time, stories, and even photographs, yearbooks, and letters. In particular, I thank brothers John Beales, Orrin Hyde, Dwight Barker, Jim Galitan of the Iota chapter, and many representatives of the national chapter were very encouraging. It could be disconcerting to have an archaeologist dig through the trash of your youth and your organization, but never did I experience anything but enthusiasm and encouragement from the national fraternity and its local brothers. In the fall of 2007, I had the opportunity to present a number of my findings and interpretations to a large assembly of Iota alumni attending a pre-football-game party. One always faces descendant groups with trepidation—what if the archaeological narrative tells a story they would prefer not to hear—but I was pleased to find that the brothers retained the ability to laugh at themselves and were genuinely interested in the ways that fraternity life adapted to changing social movements and time periods. They are a fascinating group of men.

The Bancroft Library was my temporary home during the spring of 2007. The staff was extremely helpful, despite having to endure temporary lodgings on Allston Avenue. I had been concerned that it would be difficult to access all the collections I needed due to circumstances related to the library's retrofit; my worries were unfounded. Likewise, the staff overseeing the University of California, Berkeley, microfilm and newspaper collections, and the staffs at the Berkeley Historical Society and the Berkeley History Room of the Berkeley Public Library, were all extremely friendly and helpful. Steve Finacom, local historian extraordinaire and a walking archive, was helpful during this project, as he has been during all of my campus research.

Blake Edgar, my editor at University of California Press, was supportive during this process (and patient—a virtue I sometimes lack, but respect in others). I am particularly indebted to the two readers for the press, who were kind enough to identify themselves to me, Mary Beaudry and Matthew Johnson. Both of these extraordinary scholars provided much appreciated guidance for the final version of this work.

I want to thank the Abigail Reynolds Hodgen Publication Fund for a grant that enabled me to complete the illustrations and obtain the necessary permissions to reproduce the historic photographs and illustrations included here. Stacy Kozakavich helped me with the paperwork for the permissions, something I greatly appreciate.

Of course, I thank my family for their patience while I completed this manuscript. They dealt with my bouts of hogging the coffee table as I typed, and they navigated through endless piles of books and listened endlessly as I hashed out various ideas and recounted odd tidbits of campus history that I am sure were not nearly as interesting to them as to me.

Peering into the Rooms of
a Fraternity's Far Past

> Some say that we are different people at all different
> periods of our lives, changing not through effort of will,
> which is a brave affair, but in the easy course of nature
> every ten years or so. . . . I think one remains the
> same person throughout, merely passing, as it were, in
> these lapses of time from one room to another, but all in
> the same house. If we unlock the rooms of the far past
> we can peer in and see ourselves, busily occupied in the
> beginning to become you and me.
>
> JAMES BARRIE, in the dedication to *Peter Pan, or the Boy
> Who Would Not Grow Up*

In June of 1907, San Francisco was still reeling from the ongoing impacts of the
great earthquake and fire that had physically and psychically gutted the city in April
1906. While electricity, telephone, and car service had been restored, and the
sounds of rebuilding echoed in every corner of the city, residents could not help but
be exhausted and overwhelmed by the tasks still to be faced. The reopening of the-
aters and cultural life became an important marker of the city's revival, and in the
months following the earthquake, established vaudeville acts and theater greats like
Sandra Bernhardt toured the area. On June 11, 1907, at the Van Ness Theater, beloved
actress Maude Adams starred in the West Coast premiere of James Barrie's newest
hit play, *Peter Pan*.

Under the headline "Sane Adults Unblushingly Tell Peter Pan They Believe in
Fairies," James Crawford, critic for the *San Francisco Call*, proclaimed, "The play's
purity appeals to our best nature, it imbues us with yearning to acquire an idealism
that may lighten our load of sordidness. And this subtle appeal of *Peter Pan* was never
more needed than at this time, in this community." San Franciscans were not the only
Americans to embrace *Peter Pan*. In New York, the play broke the audience attendance records of the Empire Theater, running there for two years. What drew American audiences to this play? In his review, Crawford attempts to explain the appeal:

It grips and holds your interest with the intensity of the most intense drama ever
staged. Its author's intention, evidently, was to sketch a fantasy of youth and to

revive youth's impressions in adult minds. In this he succeeded so marvelously that the audience last night unanimously declared its belief in fairies when Maude Adams anxiously inquired if it did believe in them. Every man who sees "Peter Pan" recognizes in him the romantic restlessness of youth—the desire to "try one's wings" on the flight of this or that mad fancy—and every woman perceives in Wendy that awakening of that maternal instinct that led to the adoption of dolls as playthings.[1]

And, for me, therein lies the heart of Peter's popularity. While San Francisco may have been recovering from a geological quake, the nation was in the grip of a mighty social seismic wave, one that was shaking and rupturing the foundations of what it was to be a man or woman in American society. This work focuses on how young men on the cusp of adulthood responded to these changes.

This is not a book about *Peter Pan,* but it is a work that depends on Peter to guide us through a particular corner of Never Land and help us understand a particular community of Lost Boys. The setting of this story is the late-nineteenth- and early-twentieth-century campus of the University of California, and the Lost Boys in question are the brothers of the Iota chapter of the Zeta Psi fraternity. Although I focus on this specific place and group, the social transformations that each generation of Zeta Psi fraternity members faced were met by all men and women of their generation. The fraternity's particular history, however, allows us to look closely at these massive societal changes and how they shaped a single community. Like all microscale history, by focusing on the scale of the intimate my study illuminates larger social trends.

As one of the first coeducational public universities in the United States, the University of California was on the front lines of the gender skirmishes that shaped racial, social, political, and economic life at the turn of the twentieth century. Although generally ignored in academic research of late, Greek letter societies, or social fraternities, hold an extraordinary place in this history. In an increasingly sexually integrated campus world, fraternities became enclaves where men could, under the guidance of tradition and alumni, navigate and respond to the changing social landscape while actively creating new masculine identities.[2]

James Barrie, in envisioning *Peter Pan,* was able to articulate for many living in this same period the essence of the masculine identity that came to be valued by white men—both in England and in the United States. Barrie's insights and his immortal boy, Peter, will lead us into fraternal and campus history.

Zeta Psi, the first fraternity chapter formed west of the Rocky Mountains, has existed as a social fraternity at the University of California since 1870. When Zeta Psi was founded, there was only one University of California campus, the one in Berkeley. The fraternity built its first house on the edge of campus in 1876; they replaced that house with a finer one on the same site in 1910, and the fraternity remained at that address until 1957, when a university expansion claimed their house and resulted in the fraternity's relocation to a third house.[3] The experiences of Zeta Psi members at their first two houses are the focus of this work.

The fraternity's residence at 2251 College Avenue spanned a period of just over eighty years. During this time, remarkable changes took place in American society. While technological innovations, like electricity, plumbing, radio, film, television, automobiles, and airplanes, appeared at an astonishing rate, social changes were just as breathtaking. The frontier was closed, the United States became a superpower, and white men's social, economic, and political dominance was questioned to a degree unprecedented in American history.

College fraternal societies developed as an outgrowth of fraternal orders such as the Freemasons. Many scholars have come to understand fraternal orders as ritual organizations designed to allow men to escape the tedium of management level positions in the new industrial society and the emasculating effects of home life in the female-dominated domestic sphere. But while fraternal orders focused on the experience of shared ritual over interpersonal relationships,[4] Greek letter societies focused on the shared experience of daily life. Through living together, the brothers came to embody the shared values and traditions of the organization. These daily practices naturalized the experience of the fraternity and had an enduring influence on members' adult lives.

Due to the nature of the fraternal experience, which occurred at a particularly important period in a man's social and emotional development, Greek letter societies were important spaces where elite, white, masculine identities were constructed in the late nineteenth and early twentieth centuries. Within fraternities, groups of similarly minded and positioned men made the transition to young adulthood. They left the university and the fraternity with an extended network of fictive brothers who could be called upon in a variety of settings—literally, a good-young-boy network. Zeta Psi was a prestigious fraternity with many prestigious alumni—among them were governors, university professors, capitalists, railroad barons, politicians, lawyers, judges. Many of them gave generously to their alma mater, and a number of the university's buildings bear the names of Zeta Psi brothers. The brothers held important economic, educational, political, and social positions in their postgraduate lives (table 1). They were men positioned to influence Californian and American society at the highest levels. As such, Zeta Psi specifically, and fraternities like it, deserve our consideration.[5]

TABLE 1　Examples of prominent alumni from the Iota chapter of Zeta Psi

Alumnus name	Year of graduation	Postgraduate achievement(s)
George Ainsworth	1873	President, Oregon Railroad and Navigation Co., University of California regent
James Budd	1873	Governor of California
John Budd	1874	State representative, Stockton, UC Regent
Howard Stillman	1874	Professor of chemistry, vice president, Stanford University
Phillip Bowles	1882	Founder, Bank of Oakland
O. K. McMurray	1890	Dean, law school, University of California, Berkeley
John Nesbitt LeConte	1891	Professor of engineering, University of California, Berkeley
Dean Witter	1909	Founder, Witter and Blythe
Jean Witter	1916	Cofounder, Dean Witter and Co., University of California regent

THE NOT-SO-NICE REPUTATION OF COLLEGE FRATERNITIES

A number of fraternity men I met during this project were suspicious to find a woman interested in the history of fraternity life. Perhaps this is justified, since Greek letter societies are rarely presented in a positive light in such works. Today, as has happened over the last 150 years, newspaper articles, books, movies, and other media that focus on fraternities discuss mainly the evils of fraternal life. Hazing deaths, the prevalence of sex (including many forms of rape), drug use, and alcohol abuse have all drawn widespread attention. Hazing, or the systematic taunting and sometimes torturing, of new fraternity initiates, too, receives media attention every year in the United States. The film *Borat* features a particularly memorable representation of the mind-set that can be nurtured by fraternal life. In fact, the term *frat-boy behavior* has come to describe any idiotic, juvenile, and dangerous behavior. When a participant in a contest held by a Sacramento-area morning radio show died from water intoxication (the ingestion of too much water), a *San Francisco Chronicle* columnist referred to the disk jockeys as "the Bay Area kings of frat-boy broadcasting."[6]

Alexandra Robbins, in her popular undercover account of contemporary sorority life, *Pledged,* paints an ugly portrait of fraternity men as rapists, pimps, drug pushers, and general misogynists. In scholarly circles, Peggy Reeves Sanday's 1990 book, *Fraternity Gang Rape,* remains one of the most damning scholarly studies of fraternity life. Understandably outraged by a gang rape that occurred in a fraternity house on her college campus, Sanday used her anthropological and feminist research skills to understand the culture of fraternity life that created and nurtured this behavior. In interviewing brothers from a number of fraternities, she was shocked to discover that the men refused to recognize many forms of nonconsensual sex as rape. Her analysis ultimately focused on the role of initiation practices within the fraternity in creating a corporate identity that trumped whatever individual value systems had been instilled in the young men before they joined the fraternity. Sanday writes, "The misogyny evident in some fraternity group rituals raises the question of the legal status of groups of men on campus who train incoming students to demean and disparage their female peers, attitudes that may well lead to breaking the law in cases of gang rape or date rape. The silencing effect of sexist practices and institutions on a college campus also places their legality in question because by blocking women's achievement they deny women equality of educational opportunity."[7] As a result, Sanday calls for the abolition of fraternities on college campuses.

Scholars studying Greek letter societies founded by minority groups have, moreover, portrayed predominantly white fraternities as the evil twins of the institutions they study. A number of recent academic studies of black letter societies assert that African American letter societies are more community-service-centered, encourage respectful relationships between the sexes, and in general, should be seen as institutions that do not engage in the sexual violence and "depredations" that can occur in white fraternity life.[8]

Much of the literature on contemporary Greek organizations also emphasizes that these are organizations in which racism and racist ideologies are nurtured. Marianne Sanua, in a history of Jewish fraternities, touches on the anti-Semitism of traditionally white fraternities. In their comparative study of sexism in white and black fraternities, Tyra Black and colleagues write, "We found a Greek and campus system where white privilege runs rampant, and black students and fraternity members face countless forms of racism." Although racism is not the focus of her study, Sanday, too, recounts instances of racism—toward black men and women—that she encountered during the interview process for her research.[9]

In the popular media, only two movies have been released that focus on black Greek letter organizations. The 2007 release *Stomp the Yard* emphasizes the positive, transformative, nature of black fraternal bonds and support. In 1988, Spike Lee released *School Daze*, a film depicting such organizations, which he says are "politically (a)pathetic, are presented as a mimicry of white fraternal members, and spend the majority of their time engaging in unproductive hazing and pledging rituals."[10] In many ways, this is a typical representation of white fraternity life in movies. Compare Lee's movie with movies like the National Lampoon classics *Animal House* and *Revenge of the Nerds*, and more recent offerings like *Old School* and *Sorority Boys*, in which the seemingly mindless excesses of (white) fraternal life are simultaneously glorified and critiqued. Moreover, sexualized murders in white fraternities and sororities have become staples on popular crime shows like *CSI* and *Law and Order* series. I am unaware of any uplifting representations of white fraternal organizations in recent popular films or television shows.

WHY STUDY FRATERNITIES?

I point out the negative image of fraternities intentionally. I think current hostile opinions of fraternities have created a lacuna in the academic literature. The literature I have discussed focuses on issues related to contemporary fraternities; there is a paucity of scholarly literature focusing on the history of white Greek letter societies. While predominantly white fraternal organizations like labor unions and Masonic societies have received a wide range of scholarly attentions,[11] this consideration has generally not extended to the college social fraternities. In fact, Mark Carnes, a noted expert on nineteenth-century fraternal lodges, dismisses college fraternities as being of no historical relevance since they involved such a small number of men: "Fewer than 70,000 men belonged to college fraternities in 1883, a tiny figure compared to the millions in the orders."[12] Most of the works that do discuss the history of white letter organizations are either publications by the individual fraternities or by the Interfraternity Conference (the self-governing body for Greek letter societies).[13] Needless to say, such publications are unlikely to be self-reflective or critical of their organizations.

Movements to dismantle college fraternities and their elder brothers, the fraternal orders, are not a recent phenomenon but have a nearly two-hundred-year-old history in this country.[14] Accusations of abuse and misconduct have long plagued these institutions, and their enduring popularity indicates that membership in these societies creates clear social advantages for members. As the Interfraternity Conference's own publications point out, nearly every president of the United States belonged to a Greek letter society.[15] If college fraternities are sites where young white men can be instilled with both racist and sexist ideologies that, paradoxically, allow them to move in the highest circles of American society, then perhaps these institutions deserve further scholarly consideration; perhaps we need to understand their origins and histories in order to understand how they came to be. To paraphrase James Barrie, we need to peer backward to see how fraternities were in the beginning of being themselves.

College fraternities are products of their particular histories and historical contexts. They are institutions that favor conservatism—through the maintenance of rituals and symbols that often originated in mid-nineteenth-century Masonic practices, and though selection processes that favor the membership of former members' kin. The popularity of fraternal organizations, whether college fraternities or fraternal orders drawing on adult male membership, has been a product of broader dialogues about gender, race, and power in the United States. As a result, we cannot understand modern fraternities without understanding the social and political cultures from which they sprang. The conservatism of these organizations should not be taken as evidence of stagnation. They have experienced change—from influences internal and external to the fraternity. We cannot simply graft our understandings of modern fraternities onto the past or vice versa. I propose that we must take a diachronic, or across-time, perspective to these institutions if we are to understand them. These are institutions that have maintained their social relevance to millions of young college men (and women), and as such, deserve serious scholarly attention. This work is not intended to speak to all fraternities at all times. This is a starting point in what I hope will lead to a larger academic discourse.

The work before you is a microhistory—an attempt to illuminate larger scales of history through the intimate understanding of a smaller slice of the past. The small slice of history I am exploring is the history of the Zeta Psi fraternity at the University of California, from the period of 1870 to 1956. I have drawn on the traditional sources utilized by historians—personal papers, university publications and archives, newspaper accounts, oral histories, and papers and publications available through the fraternity itself. In this last category, my access to materials was tempered by my status as an outsider.[16]

Had these documents been my sole sources, it would be difficult to justify focusing on such a narrow slice of society. However, I also draw on two additional sources less utilized by historians. Because I was trained as an anthropologist with a specialty in historical archaeology, I have made use of evidence of the fraternity's material life drawn from two seasons of archaeological research. Finally, still standing on the University of California campus is a particularly compelling artifact—the house that

Zeta Psi built and then occupied from 1910 to 1956, and which had remained remarkably unaltered by the university until its seismic retrofit in 2000. Even now, much of the important symbolic content of the fraternity's occupation remains preserved within this structure.

I gained access to the mundane and routine rituals of everyday life within the fraternity, and this provided me with a different window of understanding into the Zeta Psi brothers' lives. Sanday and Carnes both focus on the importance of high ritual (initiation and movement from one fraternal level to another) in their studies of the fraternity experience.[17] In the college fraternity life cycle, initiation is an annual event. Dining, studying, spending time with one's brothers—these are daily occurrences that have enduring impacts on members' attitudes and practices. Unlike the initiation, around which a shroud of secrecy is maintained, these everyday happenings are also the visible face of fraternity life that ultimately attracts new members.

WHY DID I STUDY THIS FRATERNITY?

Most of my scholarly work has focused on using historical archaeology to understand the lives of enslaved and recently freed African Americans.[18] In such an academic context, my interest in the lives of privileged white men may seem like an abrupt shift. I have been studying the experiences of individuals who historically did not have full access to the opportunities to acquire wealth and prestige offered by this country. In contrast, many of the fraternity men were about to embark on adult lives of comfort, prestige, and achievement.

Hayden White argues that historians, no matter how scrupulous their evidentiary practices, rely on modes of thought that are not empirical. They adopt distinctive forms of argument and employ different types of emplotment, or storytelling, in creating historical narratives. Most histories, he says, have one of four tropes: "romance," "tragedy" "comedy," or "satire," and he categorizes the history of historical writing according to the popularity of certain tropes.[19] I think that much of historical archaeology today, my own work included, follows a romantic trope. It is easy to see the experiences of oppressed peoples as they struggle through their material lives as heroic, and the interpretive narratives that result are characterized by White's romantic trope. In such narratives, there must be a hero. In my writing, the heroes are typically the people who inhabited the archaeological site I studied. There must also be a villain or villains—typically those actors who created the landscape of inequality that my subjects traveled. For me, the fraternity project represents a unique challenge, the opportunity to write about subjects who may not elicit the natural sympathies of the modern reader in the same manner.[20]

I consider myself a feminist, and as such I find that many aspects of modern fraternity life concern me. As I studied the history of the men of Zeta Psi, I encountered individuals whose values and opinions ran contrary to my own. It would be easy to write about the fraternity as a negative space—I have a narrow body of data that I could spin as evidence of the inevitable evolution of fraternities into the kinds of institutions where alcohol abuse, racism, and sexual violence reign. I could take Sanday's work as an end point for this study and shape this work as a great tragedy— here, the human potential of these young men was twisted and ruined by the unfathomable rituals of fraternal initiation! In fact, such a work would probably have much broader marketability—after all, fraternity men have already been established as popular villains.

I cannot write that particular book. The material evidence considered more broadly does not support this narrative but instead tells a range of very different stories. Just as I have evidence of fraternity life shaping individual men, I have evidence of individual men shaping the fraternity. The men of Zeta Psi and the people they interacted with, and yes, sometimes harassed and abused, were three-dimensional human beings with all the endearing and frustrating qualities that exemplify our species. We currently live in a society that is polarized socially by issues painted as pro or con, leaving little room for recognizing the vast spaces between. This work is about the gray space between "fraternities should be abolished" and "fraternities must always be allowed to exist." yes!

I have other reasons to be evenhanded with the men of Zeta Psi. I had a range of personal experiences with fraternities, both negative and positive. First, I should admit that I am fraternity spawn: my parents met at a fraternity party. My father was a post-GI-bill-era fraternity brother, a member of Lambda Chi Alpha, at Drexel University in Pennsylvania. He was the first generation of college-goers among the Wilkies, and the fraternity gave him a community and housing away from home. The fraternity figured little in his postcollege days, beyond his keeping touch with a few brothers. My sister and I grew up around some obvious artifactual material associated with the fraternity period of his life—his Greek letters emblazoned on his college ring, a souvenir glass from a fraternity "Playboy party," and a tattered fraternity T-shirt. I also have a vague notion that perhaps there was a fraternity paddle somewhere in the garage at some time.

Due in part to my father's experiences in Greek life, I did briefly consider rushing while an undergraduate at Syracuse University. A friend from my dorm and

I attended the rush meeting for sororities in our freshman year. "Rushing" is the period when prospective members visit houses they might join. While rush procedures give the impression that selection is a two-way process between prospective members and houses, the reality is that all control over the process and selection lies with the organizations. We were appalled at the convoluted and bizarre paperwork system that organized sorority rush and that contrasted so starkly with the more casual and welcoming fraternity rushes that my male friends explored. We didn't participate further. Ultimately, only one of my close college friends entered the Greek system, so most of the interaction I had with fraternities as a college student in the late 1980s was as an outsider. These experiences were varied; many were negative.[21]

As a college instructor and faculty member at two universities, I find that my views of Greek life continue to be ambivalent. Perhaps age has also tempered them with a sense of amusement. I now know students of all ranges of intellect and personality involved in Greek life. I have come to know sororities better through "favorite professor dinners," events that have demonstrated to me some of the positive aspects of sorority life (if you can get beyond the extraordinarily cruel psychological hazing that happens in some of these organizations).[22] I admit to being amused by "hell week," the week before initiation. During hell week, pledges are most likely to suffer public hazing, when fraternity pledges can be seen on campus walking around in housecoats, wearing clothing backwards, or sometimes toting piles of bricks decorated with their fraternal letters (figure 1).

I have not found that Greeks cheat any more or less than other students on exams, or that they generally do any better or worse in my large introductory or upper-division breadth courses. In general, at the four universities where I did my training and teaching, anthropology rarely attracts Greek students, so my overall exposure remains limited.

Given that there has been little reason for me to be particularly pro– or anti– Greek letter societies, you may again wonder why I have come to do this particular research project. The answer is fairly simple: the project literally popped up in my backyard, or should I say my office's backyard? Today, the Archaeological Research Facility of the University of California, and the faculty offices of the archaeologists of the Anthropology Department, are housed in 2251 College Avenue, which served as the second chapter house of the Zeta Psi fraternity.

My first office in this building was in the back, situated in what once served as the guest room for the fraternity. In the fall of 1995, Boalt Law School, our expansive neighbor to the south, embarked on an extension of its building, which wrapped

Decorated fraternity bricks. Bricks courtesy of Geoff Hughes.

around the back of ours. I was able to look out my window and watch the backhoe clearing the asphalt lot where we used to park. Given that the noisy demolition made it nearly impossible to work, watching the activity outside became a favorite pastime, and I idly wondered whether the project might hit archaeological remains. It did.

Construction workers were observed by one of my colleagues filling and hiding buckets with bottles. We confronted them (nicely), demanded that they hand over the artifacts (also nicely), and called the project manager and several people in the Capital Projects section of the university (decidedly not nicely), ultimately resulting in a work stoppage. The materials uncovered were from a Prohibition-period dumpsite dating to about the mid-1920s. At that point, much of the archaeological feature had been destroyed. We were given two days (after a number of archaeologists yelled at the administration about abiding by cultural preservation laws) to salvage what information we could from the site to determine whether any remains were a hundred years old or older, which would therefore require additional archaeological work under California's Environmental Quality Act. I had learned that the men of Zeta Psi had built their first house on the same site as their second, and at that point I became concerned about whether any deposits associated with that occupation remained.

I quickly established that the construction crew had disturbed only one dump, which had been used for only a short time. The dump seemed to be a large, backfilled pit containing many bottles, ceramics—including examples bearing Zeta Psi's crest—jars, inkwells, animal bones, buttons, pipe pieces, Mazda lightbulbs (including two remarkable intact examples), cans, and a range of other household trash. I was able to take a stratigraphic profile from the remaining edge of the pit, excavate a small unit in a remnant of intact soil, and then give the university permission to continue on its destructive way.

A great deal of media attention focused on the discovery of the site, and I quickly learned why little scholarly attention is given to college fraternities—scholars studying fraternities get no respect. Media coverage focused on the fact that a large number of alcohol bottles were recovered from a Prohibition-period fraternity site. "Archaeologist Finds Ancient Animal House," was a common theme of all the stories. I was frustrated with the coverage, particularly since, among the substantial remains found, there was evidence that fraternity life in the early twentieth century was very different from fraternity life in the late twentieth century. A second wave of media coverage in the same vein followed in the spring of 1996, when I had students from an undergraduate course study the artifacts from the site. On campus, I went from being the "new historical archaeologist" to being "the one who found that fraternity site," an introduction that brought both instant recognition and a chuckle. The perceived trivial nature of the project even led some of my colleagues to debate during reviews of my performance whether studying this material was the proper thing for an untenured faculty member to be doing. Some of my students jokingly called me the "party archaeologist."[23]

Despite the general hilarity, and sometimes disgust, that the site provoked among a number of my peers, I realized that the project had a number of interesting contributions to make to scholarship. The fraternity assemblage offered the opportunity to look at constructions of gender among male communities—a rarity in the historical archaeological literature. A brief and relatively obscure proceedings paper I wrote about the site in 1998 is still highly cited today, simply because there are so few published accounts that look at constructions of manhood with archaeological data.[24]

Within archaeology over the last twenty years, work focusing on issues of gender and sexuality has increased.[25] For the most part, however, these topics have become almost synonymous with studies of women. Indeed, one of the major critiques put forth by archaeologists calling for considerations of masculinities in our work is that "manhood," if not rendered completely invisible in our writings, has been constructed as an essential and unchanging category. In contrast, womanhood is seen as fluid and existing within a particular social-historical context.[26] Central to this work is a consideration of how changing notions of manhood and masculinity result in changing social dynamics and practices within the fraternity.

The nature of my archaeological assemblage—basically, a limited excavation of a bulldozed dump—made me cautious about trying to interpret too much from this single assemblage. What I needed was more archaeological evidence and, preferably, evidence drawn from the first Zeta Psi house. I had my opportunity in 2001, when 2251 College Avenue was slated for earthquake retrofitting. The archaeology faculty was relocated from the building for two years.

The house was originally designed as a C-shaped building with an open courtyard. After taking over the building, the university added a wall that enclosed the courtyard and created a large atrium with a raised plank floor. According to my calculations from available historic maps, there was a strong possibility that remains from the first fraternity house were preserved in the atrium. I negotiated with the university and got permission to run an archaeological field school in the building during the summer of 2001 (figure 2).

That summer, my students and I accomplished several important things. First, we found a layer of asphalt under the plank floor of the atrium Believe it or not, this was a positive development. Valiant students removed this layer using jackhammers. Underneath, we discovered areas that had been undisturbed by the university's later uses of the building: an archaeological layer associated with the use of the second house's courtyard; a layer associated with the construction of the second house; and, below that, a layer that contained a portion of the original house's foundation and domestic trash associated with the fraternity's occupation of that house (figure 3). In other words, instead of knowing about only a short moment in the fraternity's history (the prohibition dump), I now had material evidence of life within the house from 1876 until 1956.

My archaeological evidence falls into three time categories: 1876–1909; 1910–1956; and about 1923, the date of the dump. These dates are significant because they correspond to times when significant shifts were taking place in the conceptualization of masculinity in the United States. The existence of two distinct house assemblages allowed me to study how a community of men changed their fraternal life in significant ways as a result of changes in attitudes about manhood in the world around them.

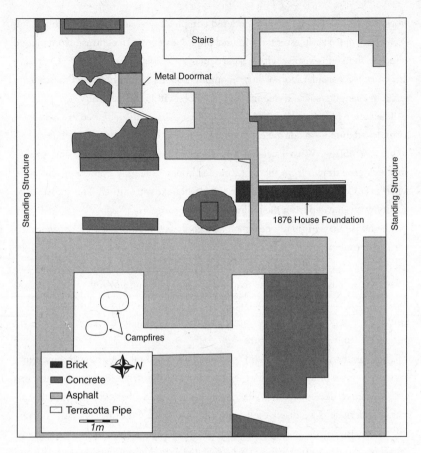

FIGURE 2

Map of 2001 excavations in the atrium of 2251 College Avenue.

A second, unanticipated body of evidence was "unearthed" by my field school. During the early stages of the retrofit, portions of several wooden wall panels were removed from a basement room that had served as the fraternity's party room. One panel was taken down to so that engineers could inspect the foundation. Upon splitting and removing a plank, the construction workers found that the interior of the plank was completely carbonized—there had been an electrical fire inside the wall at some point that had smoldered away, carbonizing the wood but not igniting the building. They showed the Archaeological Research Facility's lab manager, who in turn, decided I should be shown it as well. I admit, I was a nonplussed at seeing a charred wood panel, until I looked at it closely. Visible on the top of the plank was

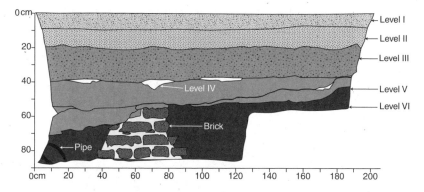

FIGURE 3

Example of the soil profile from the 2001 excavations. Level I is
associated with recent university activities, levels II and III with
the occupation of the 1910–1956 house. Level IV is a shallow lens
associated with the completion of construction of the second
house; some earlier materials were pressed into this level. Levels V
and VI are associated with the occupation of the 1876–1910 house.

an impressed "09" and what appeared to be a list of partial names under it. I realized the wood must be one of the mythical pledge panels described to me by Zete alumni.

In 1995, following the first archaeological discoveries, a number of Zeta Psi alumni had asked if the old Zete "name panels" were still in the house. They described these as redwood panels with the names of Zetes carved into them. I had looked through the building for the panels, but for whatever reason, it had never occurred to me that the panels had been flipped over and painted an institutional color. I had the construction workers remove the other half of the split panel, and when we put them together, sure enough, we had a complete panel showing the names of the brothers of Zeta Psi in the class of 1909.

During the field school, I had students do vertical excavations of the walls of the party room, removing, mapping, and recording the location of panels in the room. Unfortunately, it appeared that the panels had been flipped and replaced on the walls randomly, and that at some point a number of panels had been lost or destroyed. Still, there are fifty-three years of brothers, and nearly four hundred names, represented on the panels we recovered. The earliest entry dates to 1873, and the most recent dates to 1949 (figure 4). The panels are important artifacts and documents that tell us who the Iota chapter recognized as members. They

FIGURE 4

Example of the pledge panels recovered during the retrofit of 2251
College Avenue. Photograph by the author.

also provide a membership list to compare with those generated from official fraternity registers and membership lists as published in *The Blue and Gold*, the campus yearbook.[27]

WHAT WE CAN LEARN FROM THE EVIDENCE

The archaeological information we recovered, combined with insights from archival and oral historical sources and with information gleaned from the house itself, forms the basis for the interpretations in my study. Among archaeologists working in the deeper past, the ability to distinguish two occupation periods separated by a mere forty years is a fairly rare occurrence. My colleagues studying the deeper past often work in chunks of time extending for centuries or even millennia, not decades. In my field, however, forty-year periods are quite long. In urban areas, it is not unusual to find large features like privies that have been used and filled over relatively short periods, less than a decade. I have worked on sites where it was possible to pinpoint within a year or two when a deposit was created.[28]

Relatively speaking, the fraternity materials represent a significant stretch of time for study in a historical site. To put this in perspective, based on the fraternity's official register of members a minimum of 212 men lived at 2251 College Avenue between 1876, when the chapter house was built, and 1910, when the first house was abandoned. The community represented by the archaeological materials was dynamic, fluid, and forever changing in its specific membership. No more than 20 men ever lived in the house at a time.[29] While some men lived there for a full four years, most lived there two to three years before moving on. The archaeological materials present a portrait of these men's collective, not individual, actions. Their unique personalities and quirks, for the most part, are not represented in the archaeology. Fortunately, this level of texture can be derived from documentary sources.[30]

My goal is to understand more broadly the fraternity as a community and institution. The archaeological materials from the two houses demonstrate that the fraternal communities that occupied them, while sharing a number of practices and routines, were also profoundly different from one another. While I present these differences in stark terms, I also demonstrate through evidence from other sources that not all of these changes were sudden and abrupt, that some gradually insinuated themselves within the house. Although I am interested mainly in the community and institution, I haven't ignored the brothers' individual lived experiences. I cannot offer archaeological insights on particular, historically identified persons, but I can speak of generalized experiences of people within the house.[31]

At any time in its history, the fraternity community of Zeta Psi consisted of brothers of various ages and school levels, as well as domestic servants who were not part of the brotherhood. One's experiences of fraternity life differed radically over time, depending on whether one was a pledge or initiate, or a senior member. While it was a community founded on shared values, the fraternity was not a homogeneous community. By acknowledging the different types of persons that occupied the house at any time, we can ensure that we consider how they may have differently engaged with the house, its materials, and practices.

Because of the nature of fraternity life itself, multiple scales of time are at play in this work. First, there were the repeating annual cycles of the school year. Every year members were gained through pledging and initiation, and members were lost (or at least experienced a status change) due to graduation. During summers, the house was only minimally used, with few brothers staying between terms. Every year, current members moved up in the household hierarchy, both filling spaces vacated by graduating members and making room for new brothers. To maintain the health of the house, this cycle was necessary and ongoing.

There were also slightly longer cycles of cohabitation. Every fifth year, if all students progressed through the academy as planned (and many did not), there would be a complete replacement of the entire house population. In terms of communities of memory, a brother who was four years beyond his graduation could no longer expect anyone in his house to have direct memory of him, unless he had returned during that period—the men who were freshmen when he was a senior would have graduated as well. Potentially, a house could completely remake itself in a very short period of time.

There are longer cycles of time to consider as well. There is social time, the accumulation of years stacked one upon another. This scale of time, too, is a shaper of fraternity life and experience. The institution long outlives its individual members but is shaped by the collective generations of members' changing experiences and values. In theory, these many generations of brothers are united to one another through the shared, explicit values of the Zeta Psi fraternity, and though engaging in ritual practices passed down from previous generations. In practice, social time can bring such shifts that brothers may no longer be intelligible to one another. All these factors must be considered in Zeta Psi's history.

AT LAST, PETER PAN

Finally, I must return again to Peter Pan, who has been impatiently tugging at the edges of this discussion. In attempting to organize and situate this work, I have struggled to create a narrative that forces both the reader and me to reexamine the ways we think about fraternities. How do we discuss these communities of young men as they existed a hundred years ago, or longer, without tainting them with late-twentieth- and twenty-first-century associations? The image of John Belushi chanting, "Toga! Toga! Toga!" is a difficult demon to exorcise. Yet the men I studied are the cultural ancestors of the later communities. I found myself seeking an alternative image of fraternity men that could subvert the late-twentieth-century stereotypes and yet be equally powerful and time appropriate. To do this, I turned to the literature of the late nineteenth and early twentieth centuries.

ARCHAEOLOGISTS AND TEXTS

As a historical archaeologist, I use both materials and texts to understand past societies and cultures. Some people think of these as completely separate bodies of evidence, but archaeologists are reluctant to do so. Martin Hall observes, "Both artifacts and literary texts make use of images; those who read their meaning did not respect the disciplinary boundaries of the practitioners who would one day seek to understand their minds."[32]

John Moreland has critiqued historical archaeologists as falling in two camps: those who are too quick to embrace the authority of documents, and those too quick to dismiss their reliability. In both cases, he argues, archaeologists miss the role of writing as a tool of oppression and power. Moreland proposes that archaeologists need to see "the Object, the Voice and the Word" as tools that past societies used to create systems of power.[33] Like Hall and Moreland, I see texts and materials as pieces of the same pie. If anything, I would throw in more historical ingredients. In neither case do these authors seem to be explicitly including fictive literature in their discussions of texts. This is not surprising. There has been remarkably little consideration of contemporary literary and performing arts in archaeologists' discussions of social context.[34]

By *literary works*, I mean novels, poems, plays, operas, and similar works. Archaeologists have been very good at using textual genres such as autobiographies, travel accounts, proscriptive literature, and so on to aid in the interpretive venture, but for the most part we have not dipped our toes into literary texts.[35] I suspect there are several reasons for this, foremost being the baggage of our discipline's scientific heritage—a heritage that has sometimes smacked more of scientism than science. We tend to emphasize the use of documents that we see as more reliable, factual, or truthful. Literature at first glance appears to be none of these things.

My first forays into the use of literary sources in archaeological interpretation were in African American studies, where thinly disguised autobiographical writing has a long tradition. I sought out African American voices to provide insights into the multiple meanings and emotions specific materials evoked for these writers during the period of American history following Reconstruction. I drew on works that were clearly autobiographical in nature or clearly influenced by personal experiences.[36] Still, it was these works that led me to first think about the alternate meanings that the mass-produced goods found at archaeological sites held for African American consumers.[37]

If archaeologists accept Hall's and Moreland's points, however, that the artifacts we excavate are products of the same lifeworlds as the texts we interrogate, then it logically follows that all and any texts created by a society are potentially relevant to archaeologists' work. In revisiting early-twentieth-century literature, I found myself face-to-face with *Peter Pan*, and I realized that, if I dared to wade into (and perhaps even swim in) deeper literary waters, I might be able to look at the shore with greater interpretive insights than if I stayed on dry land.

PETER PAN AS GENDER SATIRE

James Barrie first released Peter Pan from his imagination in 1894, in a story called the "The Little White Bird." The boy so caught the fancy of the author and the British public that, in 1904, Peter, along with Wendy, starred as the subject of a play. Americans proved to be every bit as fascinated by Peter and Wendy's adventures, and when the play was introduced to the United States in 1906, they enthusiastically bought up tickets. So well known was the play shortly after its introduction that a June 9, 1907, announcement of the play's imminent opening in San Francisco led a writer for *The Call* to write, "The fame of this play is so widespread as to make description of it seem superfluous." The book version, *Peter and Wendy*, first appeared in 1911, and the boy who would not grow up firmly established himself in the literary and social landscape.[38]

Barrie has been the subject of much speculation, innuendo, and rumor. His relationship with Silvia Davies and her sons, George, Jack, Michael, and Peter, acknowledged by Barrie to be the inspiration for Peter and the Lost Boys, has inspired books and movies in which Barrie is portrayed in a wide range of roles from pedophile to romantic lead.[39] While many have looked to Barrie to understand Peter, I had a more basic question. Why was Peter such a phenomenon? In Peter, Wendy, the Lost Boys, Tiger Lily, Tinkerbell, the Darlings, and Captain Hook and his pirates, audiences must have seen something of *themselves* and *their social worlds*, something that clarified and commented on their lives and realities.

As part of the post–Disney Peter Pan generation, I must admit I did not read the original play, *Peter Pan*, until recently. While watching the latest cinematic incarnation, a 2003 live-action movie, I was struck by the delicious nastiness and tension between the genders not developed in the animated feature, and wondered whether it originated in the play. I justified hunting down an original copy of the play in our library based on a passing whim that Peter might bring me insight into the men of Zeta Psi.

The men of Zeta Psi were either members of the generation of fathers who took their children or grandchildren to the play or bought the book, or who had grown up with *Peter Pan* as part of their childhood fiction. What does *Peter Pan* have to say about these men and the world they navigated? Once I read the play and book, I was convinced that *Peter Pan* provided a powerful means for understanding gender tensions and shifting notions of masculinity and femininity at the turn of the twentieth century.

Social historians interested in masculinity in America have defined the period of the late nineteenth and early twentieth century as a time when expectations of manhood underwent profound shifts. Gail Bederman has described this transition as one from a Victorian manliness defined by civilization (whiteness) to an early-twentieth-century masculinity emphasizing innate male violence and primal urges.[40] For middle-class and elite Victorian and Edwardian men, the hegemonic world was divided into two clearly defined spheres: the public sphere, where men served as wage earners for their families; and the domestic sphere, where women served as protectors of the household and held the position of moral authority in the family. The abandonment of the civilized man, caged by etiquette and the demands of his household, was also a rejection of a certain kind of women's power.[41] Just as Peter Pan resisted Wendy's civilizing advances, the new primal man was not domesticated and had no intention of being so.

The embrace of this new imagery of maleness is evidenced in a number of ways in the early twentieth century. Boxing, a sport that displayed the embodied strength, agility, and ferocity of men, was wildly popular. Camping, hunting, and fishing, too, became popular, and boys in the United States and England were directed to movements like the Woodcraft Indians and the Boy Scouts.[42]

Perhaps nowhere were these shifts better presented than in the literature of the times. Robert Louis Stevenson wrote stories of swashbuckling pirates and lost treasure. Using Freud's notion of ego and id, he wrote *Dr. Jekyll and Mr. Hyde,* a fable documenting the total defeat of a civilized man at the hands of a primal brute. But while Stevenson mourned the end of civility—if we can take *Dr. Jekyll and Mr. Hyde* as evidence of his feelings—other authors reveled in it.[43] Jack London translated his adventures in Alaska into *White Fang* and *The Call of the Wild.* In the United States in 1902, Kipling's poems and stories about exotic India were sold through the Sears catalog alongside works like E. R. Shepherd's *True Manhood.* Zane Grey's literature glorified the Wild West, Edgar Rice Burroughs thrilled readers with the adventures of Tarzan, and Stevenson's *Treasure Island* and *Kidnapped* became staples of boyhood literature. The fiction of the British and American masses included stories focusing on war, pirates, and the American frontier. Art, literature, science, and pop culture of the early twentieth century were, metaphorically speaking, testosterone charged.[44]

Women were not complacent about these shifts, but were fighting their own social wars. Dress reformers in United States and Europe advocated the abandonment of the corset and participation in sports for women. In the United States, women struck against domestic violence and its believed cause, alcoholism. Women demanded education and entered universities at the undergraduate and graduate levels in numbers greater than ever before. They demanded access to birth control and agitated for the vote in the United States in most unseemly ways.[45] In the midst of these dramatic gender shifts Peter Pan was born, and he was clearly a boy of his times.

Peter Pan becomes a useful allegory for understanding the gender tensions and discourses of this time, with Barrie forcefully supporting, through Peter, the emancipation of men from the domestic sphere and all its responsibilities. Barrie has been described as a self-conscious writer and a fan of Robert Louis Stevenson, so it is not unreasonable to make the link between Barrie and masculinist writing.[46] Peter refuses to grow up and, in doing so, defies all attempts to civilize and domesticate him. His world, Never Land, is populated by "Red Indians" and pirates, and by mermaids and other feminine temptresses who fight for Peter's attention but never manage to hold it for long. Wendy is the only true threat to Never Land, for she alone represents the most cunning and alluring of female personas—the mother and her associated domesticity and civilizing influences. Peter may not be an adult, but he embraces the primal masculinity that came to characterize male gender ideologies in the early twentieth century. Barrie was an unlikely prophet for the masculinity movement, himself slight of build, unsuccessful with women, and plagued by insinuations in the press during his lifetime about both his sexual prowess and preferences.[47]

Let us then consider Peter, as he was committed to paper, a bit further, and then I will explain why this is relevant to understanding the Zeta Psi fraternity's archaeology. I draw from three of Barrie's works: the play *Peter Pan*, the storybook *Peter and Wendy*, and the epilogue to the play, *When Wendy Grew Up*.[48]

As Barrie created him, Peter Pan is an impossible child—large enough to be Wendy's size—yet eternally so young that he still possesses all his baby teeth. This attribute renders him irresistible to grown women, like Mrs. Darling, and young girls alike. Girls are said to hear him crowing outside their windows in their sleep. Peter lives in Never Land with the Lost Boys, formerly infants who fell from their prams and were not returned. Peter alone willfully abandoned reality upon hearing his parents discuss that he should one day become a man. He has none of the marks of civilization on him—he is the only boy in his band who cannot read a single letter. He is also the strongest, smartest, and wiliest member of the band. An accomplished fighter, he regularly outsmarts his foes, particularly his adult male nemesis, Captain Hook. In addition to fighting pirates and talking to mermaids, Peter wins the respect of Tiger Lily's Indian tribe. He has many unlikable characteristics. He is cocky, self-centered, forgetful, and, as one might expect of an uncivilized male, unmindful of time. Despite this, Wendy is entranced and easily flattered and manipulated by Peter. In essence, Peter Pan is very much the opposite of a civilized middle-class man.

The epitome of the middle-class man is present in *Peter Pan* and *Peter and Wendy* in the form of Mr. Darling. He is a clerk who thinks about stocks and worries about the opinions of the neighbors. He boasts that his wife is impressed with his work abilities; yet we are told that he won Mrs. Darling's hand by having the best transportation to her house—he arrived before his competitors. When the Darling children leave for Never Land, Mr. Darling blames himself for their disappearance, committing himself to living in the dog's house until they return. He makes such a spectacle of his remorse that his wife suspects he is enjoying it. On returning, the Darling sons are disappointed to see that their father is so small compared to the pirates. If there is any doubt about Barrie's opinion of such men, he makes it clear at the end of *Peter and Wendy*. Wendy and her mother basically agree to take the Lost Boys into the household, an idea at which Darling initially balks. Ultimately he breaks down and admits that he wanted to be asked so he didn't feel like a "cipher" in his own home.[49]

It is tradition in productions of *Peter Pan* to have the same actor play both Mr. Darling and Captain Hook. At first this may seem contradictory, since most pirates are presented in the period's literature as representatives of a fearsome masculinity. Alas, Hook is a less than fine specimen of pirate—he is an Eaton man and thus domesticated through education. Further, he lives in perpetual fear of a clock—at least the clock that signals the approach of the crocodile. Hook's character demonstrates that there is no room for civilized manhood in Never Land.

The ending of *Peter and Wendy* is perhaps the most revealing demonstration that Peter Pan's story is both a masculinist fantasy and cautionary tale. The Lost Boys return to London with Wendy and her brothers so that they too can have mothers. On entering school, they realize they have made a mistake, and all grow up to have unremarkable, middle-class careers. Peter's hold on Wendy remains strong. To keep her from leaving permanently, her mother agrees to let her return to Never Land annually to do "spring cleaning" for Peter. In the epilogue *When Wendy Grew Up*, we learn that, after Wendy has grown, she allows her daughter, Jane, to follow in this tradition. Peter Pan manages to have female company and labor strictly on his terms, without the responsibility of household and family that burdened middle-class men.

Peter Pan's success may have risen partly from the strongly defined characters who so clearly embodied recognizable archetypes in society. While anthropology has a well-defined body of theory related to identity formation and performance that is ultimately of great relevance to this study, in this instance I was interested specifically in how groups of people view other groups of people. I turned to social psychology and its approaches to understanding identity to further explore how literature might aid archaeological interpretation. Categorization theory proved a useful means of approaching this material. Richard Jenkins refers to categorization as the "internal and external moments of the dialectic of identification: how we identify ourselves, how others identify us, and the ongoing interplay of these in the process of identification."[50]

At the level of the self, people categorize groups in terms of prototypes. A prototype is "a subjective representation of the defining attributes of a social category which is actively constructed from relevant social information in the immediate or more enduring interactive context."[51] People who share similar contexts of interaction, therefore, come to share similar prototypes. In other words, audiences in England and America found that the satirical excesses in *Peter Pan* conformed to gender tensions and dynamics as they encountered them in their own experiences. They knew firsthand Hooks, Wendys, Peters, Lost Boys, and Mr. and Mrs. Darlings. This ability to speak to adults' and children's sensibilities alike gave the play its wide appeal.

Yes, there is an archaeological point to this treatise. If you will allow me this conceit, the character Peter Pan and his comrades provide a useful framework for understanding the social terrain in which the college men of Zeta Psi lived. Like the Lost Boys, the brothers of Zeta Psi created an all-male household where manly activities and culture could be created and replicated through multiple generations. Like the Lost Boys, the men of Zeta Psi shared secret rituals and practices that bound them together.

I have come to see the university campus as a Never Land where men attempted to flee the approach of adulthood by embracing primal masculinity. The fraternity house of Zeta Psi was a central place in this Never Land's geography, where the fictive brothers dined, hunted, and planned adventures together. In the 1930s, the men of Zeta Psi even had names for at least two of the bedrooms in the house—the cave and the ship, spaces highly evocative of masculinist action genres.

Just as in Pan's Never Land, women existed on the University of California campus, and in the classroom, athletics, and love, they sought to challenge the men of the university as equals or betters; and yes, some sought to domesticate their male coeds ultimately through love and marriage. Mermaids, Indian princesses, Tinkerbells, and Wendys were part of the university landscape and were potential obstacles to the achievement of the new masculinity.

The brothers of Zeta Psi shared something else with the Lost Boys. Ultimately, they all had to go to school and grow up. For Zetes, the challenge was to maintain their masculinity while simultaneously moving among the elite strata of their society. Unlike Barrie's Lost Boys, who became permanently banned from Never Land, the men's fraternity house and its young brothers remained accessible to the alumni after they left for adulthood. It was the elders' continued participation in the life of the fraternity house that enabled the younger brothers to make the transition from childhood to adulthood. If the spirit of fraternity during this time were to be personified, I think the result would be a character much like Pan.

It is also worth noting that the popularity of *Peter Pan* since its introduction has been cyclical, with great periods of interest in the 1950s and the early 2000s. While the more recent interest was in part related to the one-hundredth anniversary of the play, other social causes are at play as well. In each case, the period in question corresponds to upheavals in the gender status quo. In the 1950s, when Disney and Mary Martin put their individual stamps on the role of Peter, post–World War II families were attempting to renegotiate men's and women's roles as soldiers returned from the front. More recently, national debates have again focused attention on issues of reproductive rights and restrictions in the United States. Not only is Peter currently the star of several recent live-action and animated features, a new book series regarding his life has appeared. Using the prototypes delineated in Barrie's Peter Pan writings provides me with not only an entrée into the ways gendered identities were categorized but also a vehicle for presenting the research in a way that underscores the relevance of these issues to contemporary society.[52]

There are, of course, difficulties with using period texts. Great works of literature, like any other artifacts we study, can be imbued with new meanings by new generations; this is the basis of literary criticism. Contemporary literary criticism of *Peter Pan* has focused on the implications of Barrie's sexuality in the work or has explored, from a queer-theory perspective, the meanings of Peter being played by a female.[53] My own reading of both the materials and Barrie's biographical materials suggests to me that, while these avenues of interpretation are valid scholarly ponderings, they are decontextualized from the lifeworld that Barrie inhabited. Such is always a danger when reading any text. An archaeological approach to period literature must treat the text as a product of a particular social historical context and consider ways it is reused and reinvented by multiple consumers in different times and places.

PETER PAN'S ROLE IN THIS WORK

My embrace of this particular interpretive direction in my approach to the fraternity work has implications for the way that you, the reader, experience this research. I use the prototypes that peopled Never Land as an extended allegory to structure my consideration of the social life and practices of student and fraternity life at the University of California. While the individual actors may have constantly changed, the roles they played endured. There are multiple scales of time involved in this study. While an understanding of the characters in *Peter Pan* is a means of explaining the social categories that peopled the fraternity's world during the transition from a civilized manhood to a primal masculinity, the play's structure provides a means to understand the larger scale of social time that shaped the fraternity. As an institution, the fraternity moved from a Victorian kind of manhood shaped by the nursery (women's domestic sphere) to one shaped by its lived experience of Never Land's untamed masculinity and gender struggles. Finally, upon graduation or other separation from the university, all students returned to some sort of civilized life, or at least larger society, just as the Darlings returned to the nursery. As a way of shaping the narratives of both scales of fraternity time, I have borrowed shamelessly from Barrie's play and organized the chapters of my work by the acts of *Peter Pan*.

In the next section of the text, "Stage Directions," I set the scene for this work with a more detailed exploration of gender dynamics at the turn of the twentieth century and of how political and social conflicts between men and women shaped fraternal organizations and movements. I first discuss the national society of Zeta Psi as one of these fraternal groups, and I also present the historical origins of the University of California.

This takes us to the meat of our play, act 1, "The Nursery." In this chapter, I introduce the first house of Zeta Psi and the daily practices that shaped the private life of the fraternity during its early days. Ties of brotherhood within the fraternity during this time were created through a reliance on the practices of the female domestic sphere—brothers asserted brotherhood materially in a way that would have been familiar to their mothers. In other words, their manhood was defined in the vocabulary of the nursery.

While act 1 focuses on social relationships between brothers mainly inside of their chapter house, in act 2, "The Never Land," I consider how the fraternity presented itself to the broader nineteenth-century campus community. I show how ideas from the new masculinity began to enter both university and fraternity life during the end of the occupation of the first house. In this chapter I introduce some of Never Land's threats that the Lost Boys of Zeta Psi faced, and that ultimately lead to their creating a new chapter house.

Act 3, "The Mermaids' Lagoon," provides us with the opportunity to consider the women who populated the university in ever increasing numbers. Gender is a relational construct, and the new masculinity was a response to woman's entry into previously off-limits social, political, economic, and of course, educational arenas. In California, the period of 1890 to 1915 was particularly important for women's rights at the University of California. Women were not the only threat to the Lost Boys of Zeta Psi's Never Land. Pirates in the form of university administrators and anti-secret-society movements also set themselves against fraternities and their traditions and are introduced in this act.

The late nineteenth century also corresponds to the period when Zeta Psi redefined itself and its practices through the construction and occupation of a new fraternity house, the focus of act 4, "The House Underground." This chapter explores the ritualization of fraternity household life and looks at the explicit ways that the brothers shaped their second house into an exclusively male "sacred" space, rather than a female-derived one.

Act 5, "The Pirate Ship," finds us on a pirate ship and, ultimately, returned to the nursery where we began. In this chapter I discuss the ways that the brothers of the second house presented themselves to the university community. Finally, every play needs an epilogue. Here I consider final thoughts on how this study of Zeta Psi informs our broader understanding of fraternal communities. For readers who have not recently (or ever) read *Peter Pan,* I have included, before each act, a short summary of what happens in that particular act. This should help you see the connections I make between the play and the fraternal experiences.

I hope, that you, the reader, will not take my use of *Peter Pan* as flippant or see it as underplaying some of the darkness that characterizes some late-twentieth- and early-twenty-first-century fraternities. I am not a fraternity apologist but a fraternity anthropologist. To see these men and their institution clearly, we must distance ourselves from their late-twentieth- and early-twenty-first-century representatives; otherwise, we cannot judge them on their own merits and failures.

As I hope my brief introduction has indicated, Peter is not an entirely likeable fellow. He has certain misogynistic tendencies, is a braggart, and is not always a loyal companion. Yet he has a certain charm that has drawn generations of audiences to him. It is this mixed character that makes him the appropriate host to guide us through the complicated and fluid Never Land of fraternity life.

Stage Directions

Setting the Scene

Before the first boys and men of Zeta Psi can walk upon the stage, we must consider the world in which they lived. After all, every character has his history and motivations that propel him forward. It would be easy to get tangled in the vast reaches of history, so I have focused my attention on the period immediately leading up to the founding of Zeta Psi on the University of California campus in 1870. Just as Peter will later lead us to our first view of Never Land from a great height, so must we approach our stage.

From a high perch we must first consider the broad social landscape that our lads traversed. From this perspective we can see that they traveled in the midst of a great conflict between men and women. Not the type of conflict that involves swords and daggers, however: those are straightforward battles, where it is clear to observers who has drawn blood and who has escaped. No, these were battles that took place in parlors and libraries, against participants armed with terse body movements, coquettish glances, and longing sighs; they were campaigns fought over one's own impulses and desires, and were any number of small skirmishes that took place over forks and knives. While commentators may have weighed in with observations about the progress of this conflict, these gender wars were fought on the home front and involved many more combatants than even the great Civil War of the mid-nineteenth century.

If we fly in closer, we can see the institutions that came to house male refugees of the nineteenth-century gender conflicts: the dining club, the YMCA, the brothel, and perhaps the most important, the fraternal order. These places and their spaces provided opportunities for men to socialize with one another, to escape the perceived surveillance and tedium of their home lives. These spaces allowed them to shed the conventions of their confined and contained lives, giving them and their compatriots just the smallest taste of true freedom.

And finally, as we come ever closer to earth, we can spy the first major buildings of the University of California, one named for each of the winds. The campus, nestled on the rising slope of a ridge of mountains, overlooking the as-yet-bridgeless Golden Gate, surrounded by acres of barely developed farmland, is geographically isolated from both Oakland and San Francisco. It would be easy to mistake the campus for a remote island of civilization in this part of the East Bay. Just as the Spanish, the first Europeans to colonize this land, were mistaken to believe that California was an island, we would be mistaken to see the university campus as isolated. Like any good hub of research, the University of California is already at the center of things, tied to the rest of the state—and even the country—through a web of alliances, scholarly relationships, and students. This is the stage where most of the action of our play takes place, and while it is but a small space, relatively, the things that take place here are of no small import.

THE LANDSCAPES OF NINETEENTH-CENTURY GENDER DYNAMICS

The first brothers of Zeta Psi were born in the 1850s. They came to California via many different paths. As men of the Victorian era, they would have had certain ideas about how the social world was organized. Middle-class and elite white Victorian men saw the world as divided into two clearly defined ideological spheres: the public sphere, where men served as wage earners for their families; and the domestic sphere, where women served as protectors of the household and held the position of moral authority in the family. Men were supposed to rule the public domain; their affairs included politics, economics, and social movements. While there were men who resisted these divisions, and others whose economic realities made such arrangements impossible, there was a general sense that this was how things should be. All families were measured against this imaginary scale. But while the first brothers of Zeta Psi may have seen this as the natural order of the world, the home had been very differently organized not so many generations back.[1]

The late-eighteenth-century perception of manhood had been very different. Home and work had not yet been neatly spatially separated from one another. A man was the religious head of his household and presided over a house that may have contained not only his wife and children but also apprentices and journeymen who worked for him. Manhood was seen as synonymous with adulthood responsibility and, therefore, stood in contrast to childhood. A man's worth was grounded in his property ownership.[2]

By the 1830s, industrial capitalism was snaking its way into American life. Work became spatially separated from the home, and wives, who had formerly served as partners and helpmates in family enterprises, found themselves isolated at home. Men entered the work economy and, by the middle of the nineteenth century, a new model of manhood had become entrenched—"marketplace manhood"—in which a man demonstrated his identity by means of his success in the marketplace, through his accumulated wealth, power, and capital. The emerging middle-class, white, male managers became the unquestioned norm against whom all others— women, and men of all other races and ethnicities—were measured. Staking one's manhood on the market created a position less secure than that of property holder and religious authority of one's household.[3]

Through the active exclusion of women from the workplace, men created a homosocial arena where men competed against one another in business. These men were not bread makers or bread buyers; they were breadwinners, underscoring the competitive strand that ran through business dealings. Such success was, given the nature of the market, unstable and unpredictable, or in the words of Henry David Thoreau, "a site of humiliation." Manhood could be as easily lost as won.[4]

Such a construction of manhood had other costs. Participation in the marketplace required self-discipline. As Bederman puts it, "The mingled honor, high-mindedness, and strength stemming from powerful self-mastery were encapsulated in the term 'Manliness.'"[5] Self-mastery, too, required self-discipline, including regulation of the body. Self-help books directed at men offered advice on subjugating the less than manly drives and vices that endangered men. Onanism (masturbation)—and even marital sex—were activities that threatened to deprive men of their virile health. Self-pleasuring was to be avoided, and marital sex was to be engaged in no more than once a month to preserve men's health.[6] One's diet had to be watched so as not to throw off one's temperament. Eating flesh could turn one's mind to carnal thoughts. Food reformers like Sylvester Graham and James Kellogg encouraged diets high in fiber and low in animal protein.[7]

The spatial separation of home and work removed men's influence from their homes. Child rearing, home decorating, entertaining, managing servants, shopping: these made up the realm of middle-class women. Children were no longer perceived as "little adults" but were seen as mysterious creatures requiring particular kinds of attentions and nurturing throughout their development. The increased investment in child rearing demanded that mothers be fluent in a growing body of prescriptive literature. Among the middle and upper classes, an unintended consequence was the decrease in family size.[8] How could one properly mother more than three children? Women became interested in birth control; and, as Drew Gilpin Faust's study of antebellum southern women has demonstrated, abstinence was seen as a particularly effective means of preventing pregnancy.[9] Married men may have found their wives remarkably receptive to helping them retain their manly essences.

Along with their new focus on child rearing, women acquired the moral authority over the household that had once belonged to men. Within the home, women also became the face of the household for outsiders through social networking and entertaining other women. Men, who had willingly taken the workplace as their own sphere, excluding women, found that home had become a space where they were satellite presences. Excluded from the workplace, women could not completely understand the successes of the market place; but as keepers of the household, they bore the responsibility of enforcing the bodily disciplines—proper carriage, dining habits, manners—seen as essential to manly success.

As women competed against one another in their own homosocial sphere, they, too, turned to self-help guides and participated in a complicated and dynamic culture of etiquette that dictated which utensils could be used to consume which foods, how one should chew and swallow, where one's eyes could focus on the table, and how conversations should proceed in polite company. While women may have been shielded from the perceived evils of the workplace, men left work, where they were subjected to one form of management, only to return home and be subjected to another one. By the mid-nineteenth century, the separation of the spheres was well-established among the middle and upper classes and, in some cases, emulated, at least materially, by some in the working classes.[10]

Archaeologists and architects have demonstrated that the notion of the separation of the spheres had a clear material impact on home life during the nineteenth century. Women, no matter their particular economic (or working) position, were aware of the material manifestations of domesticity, and they used this knowledge to craft the appearance of respectability and gentility in their homes. The house was increasingly seen as a "sacred" space—one where children and women were to be protected from the corrupting influences of public life. Meals were times for families to join together in ritual celebration of their bonds to one another. Plain or simply decorated white dishes adorned the tables, which were quietly attended by ethnic servants or by African slaves or servants. Teapots and other ceramics bearing images that referred to biblical events were also popular in the mid-nineteenth century. As glass manufacturing processes made pressed glass readily available and affordable, this medium, too, came to communicate the sacred and wholesome values of the household using them. Self-help manuals on household management, written by famous women such as Catherine Beecher Stowe, showed women how to improve hygiene within their households. Toothbrushes, enema kits, cathartics, and an array of "germ-killing" medicines found in privy dumps all speak to women's attempts to protect their homes from physical threats to their families' health.[11]

New rooms, such as the parlor, became popular arenas for entertaining outsiders. These rooms could be easily cordoned off from the family's living spaces and their lavish décor displayed the family's wealth. Here, women entertained one another with delicate and ornately decorated dishes made of fine high-fired ceramics, like ironstone or porcelain, and watched one another for lapses in etiquette. These were also spaces where some women discussed matters of moral Christian concern, such as the horrors of African enslavement or how unfair it was that the protectors of morality should be denied participation in the vote. And it was in parlors where women met to hear visiting speakers on these issues and, increasingly, to raise money to support morally just causes.[12]

Home-based social action revolving around temperance, abolition, woman's suffrage, and a multitude of other charitable causes led to the blurring of lines between private and public spheres for women. If women were the moral authorities of their households, if they were the protectors of children and husbands, should not their moral guidance be sought in the public realm? Could not women help save society?

The Civil War and its aftermath only increased women's sense that the boundary between home and public life had become permeable. For their husbands returning home from war, however, the lines seemed more clearly defined than ever. The Civil War had demanded bloodlust and battlefield prowess. Stephen Kantrowitz suggests that, while African American men had ultimately been able to prove themselves as participants in slave rebellions and as soldiers on Civil War battlefields, such was not the same for women of any race.[13] While abolitionists and suffragists had worked together before the war, women found their quest for rights abandoned by men who had found their fraternity to one another on the battlefield. During Reconstruction, as women and African Americans struggled to achieve social and political equity, citizenship rights were increasingly framed by elite white males as belonging only to those who could die for them. But women who had run their family's farms, businesses, and households in the absence of military husbands no longer saw themselves as incapable of navigating the public realm, and attempts to isolate them in their houses would become increasingly difficult during the final thirty years of the nineteenth century.[14]

HOMOSOCIAL SPACES OF
THE NINETEENTH CENTURY

Away from the restrictions of the female-dominated household, men created spaces where they could spend time together. They gathered in saloons, where they could drink without concern about provoking a lecture on temperance. They gathered in barbershops, where they could read popular men's publications like the *Police Gazette*. They also gathered in brothels, where those willing and able to buy a night of entertainment could enjoy an inversion of the Victorian home, where men, not women, were the center of the household.[15]

Just as archaeology tells us of the materials and furnishings of the typical middle-class home, archaeology also tells how brothels intentionally played on that materiality in their establishments. At a brothel, men would be welcomed into a lavishly decorated parlor where they could purchase meals consisting of well-known aphrodisiacs like champagne, oysters, anchovies, dates, and olives. Little evidence of stemware or cutlery has been found in excavations of brothels, and it is not hard to imagine men simply drinking out of bottles and eating with their fingers. Yet even in these spaces, where men could thumb their noses at Victorian propriety with other men, they were still subjected to a certain degree of female rule. Accounts of visits to such places emphasize that the working women dictated the nature of the sexual contract. Prostitutes subjected a man to checks for venereal diseases, squeezing his penis and sanitizing it before the sexual act. Even in the brothel, where the women lived as well as worked, children often lurked in the back rooms and kitchens. The brothel household as a fantasy of patriarchal space was shallow, superficial, and only a temporary escape.[16]

Perhaps no space was more frequented in the nineteenth century than the fraternal order. While in the Americas fraternal orders like the Masons had roots extending into the colonial period, it was in the nineteenth century that they gained their greatest popularity and membership. According to Mark Carnes, in 1896 there were 5.5 million fraternal members frequenting more than seventy thousand fraternal lodges.[17] These numbers do not include the 140,000 young men participating in college fraternities at the same time.[18]

Fraternal societies, regardless of order, shared common features: members moved up in the order through a series of complicated initiations and rituals requiring specific regalia and paraphernalia. Advancement to each new level represented the attainment of a new "degree." Orders had as many as thirty-two different degrees. At each level, the initiation ritual revealed some new insight about the nature of life and men's role within it. Men could join multiple orders; therefore, creating new and unique rituals was an important industry surrounding the lodges. Biblical stories, Greek and Roman mythology, and even information from the new fields of ethnography and anthropology were sources of inspiration for rituals. So much time was spent by the orders engaged in ritual initiations that there was seemingly little time for men to form any sense of fraternity based on friendship. Instead, it was the experience of the shared participation in the rituals of lodge life that formed the bonds between lodge brothers.[19]

Carnes has argued that fraternal lodges were spaces where men retreated, not for the sake of socializing with other men, but because the complicated ritual life that the fraternal societies constructed filled an important emotional void in men. Fraternal orders relieved masculine anxieties about men's perceived changing status in the world. Rituals allowed men to face death, and ultimately rebirth, at the hands of other men within the fraternal structure. Men were removed from the seemingly pervasive presence of women—especially the most revered of women, the mother—in their ritual life. Carnes also argues that, ultimately, fraternal rituals (where men advanced through degrees or levels of the fraternal order) were moments in which men could safely express anxieties over the bifurcation of gender roles in their society. In Carnes's words, "All the final degrees . . . contradicted the assumption that men were innately impure, aggressive and unemotional. By affirming that men possessed traits socially defined as female, the symbols conveyed a message contained nowhere else in Victorian America."[20] Membership in fraternal orders that revolved around elaborate rituals declined in the early twentieth century as fewer young members joined. By then, the simple separation of the spheres among the middle class was hopelessly muddied, and the battlefield had shifted to a new arena.[21]

Histories of college fraternities show they had clear connections and parallels to the fraternal orders frequented by adult males. Both types of fraternal institution were founded on the notion of male fraternity, or brotherhood. Both had complex symbolic systems and secret ritual initiations. Yet there were important distinctions between the two. College fraternities had simpler and less involved ritual calendars. Rush and initiation constituted the entirety of the ritual calendar. Rush, the period when prospective members were screened and selected, was about finding brothers of suitable class and temperament. Initiation was the series of rituals through which pledges, or the chosen new brothers, formally entered the fraternity. In many instances, college fraternities were organizations that had their own, shared living spaces. Shared everyday interaction and friendship was an important element of creating a sense of brotherhood. While one could remain an active member of one's fraternal lodge for life, the ways in which a fraternity brother could interact with other brothers shifted during his course of life. The fraternity was an intensive part of one's daily lived experience for a time during the relatively short duration of one's college career. One could always return to one's fraternity after graduation, but in the role of honored visitor and alum. As an alumnus, one's responsibilities included ensuring that one's chapter remained active and healthy, which usually required financial support. Much of the ritual life association with the college fraternity ended after one's graduation. That said, while fraternal lodges were losing members in the 1900s, college fraternities were entering a golden period when many of the organizations controlled significant wealth through their collective landholdings, and recruited growing numbers. The historical origin of these institutions deserves some comment.

Writing in 1916, Hugh A. Moran described college fraternities: "The American College Fraternity is a *species Americana*, limited to the north temperate zone of the western Hemisphere—one may start out by saying that it is a cross between the *stedentenverein* of Germany and Oxford college, and that it favors neither of its progenitors."[22]

While the fraternities of the United States certainly have a historical debt to pay to each of these institutions, their most immediate ancestors were the literary societies popular in American universities in the mid-1700s. These societies provided students with opportunities to develop writing and speaking skills and encouraged intellectual debate in an educational system that focused on rote memorization and recitation. The societies competed for members, had secret initiations and mottoes, and served as primary intellectual influences in their student members' lives.[23]

Social fraternities emerged to replace the literary societies on campuses in the late 1700s and were a well-established part of college life by the early 1800s. These organizations sought to fill the social vacuum in college life, becoming places where drinking, socializing ,and friendship were emphasized as much as scholarship. Phi Beta Kappa, founded at the College of William and Mary in 1776, is credited as being the first American society bearing a Greek letter name. The letters were shorthand for mottos known only to members. Phi Beta Kappa extended to Harvard and Yale in 1779. These new chapters were distinguished from the original by an additional Greek letter. Although Phi Beta Kappa is known to us today as an honor society, this was not the case until 1881. Other letter societies followed, including Kappa Alpha at the University of North Carolina in 1812; Phi Beta Phi at

Union College in 1813; Chi Delta Theta, a local at Yale, in 1821, and Chi Phi at Princeton in 1824. Societies whose membership was limited to one campus only were called "locals," and societies that established multiple chapters at multiple universities were known as "nationals."[24] By the late 1820s, the practice of having a secret Greek name, a motto, badges, and named chapters was becoming standardized practice in all fraternities. These were, like many of the colleges at which they were founded, exclusively male institutions. In 1867 the first national women's fraternity was founded, Pi Beta Phi.[25] girl power x2

Many of the founders of the first fraternities were Masons, so there is little doubt that the ritual life of the early fraternities was rooted in Masonic tradition. Union College accelerated the fraternity movement in the late 1820s when in quick succession its students formed three fraternities: Kappa Alpha (1825), Sigma Phi (1827), and Delta Phi (1827).[26]

Chapter houses were not a regular part of fraternal life until the second half of the nineteenth century. The first fraternity house is said to have been a twenty-by-fourteen-foot log cabin erected by Chi Psi at Michigan in 1846; eight years later, in 1854, Delta Kappa Epsilon built a lodge at Kenyon. The first full-fledged residential fraternity chapter house was erected in 1864 by the Kappa Alpha Society at Williams. According to *Baird's Manual of American College Fraternities*, a chapter house is "a complete clubhouse containing public rooms, a lodge room or rooms, and sleeping rooms. In a few instances, the facilities of the chapter house are supplemented by a separate lodge, 'tomb,' or 'temple.'"[27] Fraternities have long drawn the suspicion of the public. Their activities are kept secret, allowing rumors and innuendoes about their practices to be circulated. Fraternities have suffered from waves of anti-Masonic sentiment that have swept the country, such as in 1827, following the murder of William Morgan, a Mason who had threatened to reveal the societies' secrets. Masons were blamed for the murder, and by association, all fraternal organizations were suspect.[28]

The Zeta Psi fraternity was founded in 1847 by John Bradt Yates Sommers, William Henry Dayton, and John Moon Skillman at New York University, which already had three chapters of other fraternities established there. Dayton died before the fraternity was officially established, leaving Sommers and Skillman to actually develop the young fraternity. The history of Zeta Psi recorded in the 1899 directory of the fraternity describes its ideals:

The Fraternity has never departed from the basal principles laid down by its founders. It has demanded character and culture as the first requisites for membership in Zeta Psi. Given character and culture, good-fellowship has been preferred to mere scholarship, although the Fraternity has always recognized that without scholarship the desired standing of member and of chapter could not be maintained in the college. It has been the policy of the Fraternity, inaugurated by its founders, never to choose men as members solely on account of attainment in restricted spheres of college activity. Scholarship or athletic ability alone, though highly prized when possessed by men of character and culture, were never sufficient qualifications for membership.[29]

The second chapter of Zeta Psi was founded through Sommers's efforts at Williams College in 1848, and the third at Rutgers in 1850. The fraternity grew quickly from that point, with chapters established at Princeton (1850), the University of Pennsylvania (1850), Colby (1850), Brown (1852), and Harvard (1852).

The original founders of Zeta Psi planned to have Drayton establish a chapter at the University of North Carolina. His death prevented this, but in 1858 the first southern chapter of the fraternity, the Upsilon chapter, was founded at this institution. This was its only southern chapter when the Civil War split the fraternity. The war presented particular problems for fraternities who found their members standing on opposite sides of the Mason-Dixon Line. The 1899 history of the Upsilon chapter describes this conflict: "In love of country Zeta Psi stood not behind the rest. The vast majority of her members hastened to the front, and nine, perhaps ten, lost their lives in behalf of the South. The bravery of the Southern Zetes was conspicuous on many a battlefield. . . . During the war, of course, correspondence was stopped entirely. The Upsilon was absolutely alone for four years, but it was not long after hostilities ceased until there was a reunion of Northern and Southern Zetes, the old relations were fully restored and correspondence was resumed."[30]

The first grand chapter meeting held after the war took place in late 1865 and was reported to be well attended by brothers from the North and South. Shortly after, financial troubles led to the temporary closure of the University of North Carolina, and brothers from Upsilon relocated to Virginia, where a chapter was founded in 1868.

When the Iota chapter was founded at the University of California in 1871, it was the first fraternity founded west of the Rocky Mountains. Before Iota, Zeta Psi had stretched as far west as Chicago and as far south as Chapel Hill, North Carolina. Most of its chapters were concentrated in New York, Pennsylvania, New Jersey, and Massachusetts (table 2). The University of California itself had been founded only two years earlier and was still housed at its temporary residence in Oakland. Both the Iota chapter of Zeta Psi and the University of California would grow together,

TABLE 2   Zeta Psi chapters and their founding, up to 1900*

Chapter name	Location	Date founded
Phi	New York University	1847
Zeta	Williams College (Massachusetts)	1848
Delta	Rutgers College (New Jersey)	1848
Omicron	Princeton University (New Jersey)	1850
Sigma	University of Pennsylvania	1850
Chi	Colby College (Maine)	1850
Epsilon	Brown University (Rhode Island)	1852
Rho	Harvard University (Massachusetts)	1852
Alpha	Dickinson College (Pennsylvania)	1852
Psi	Dartmouth College (New Hampshire)	1853
Kappa	Tufts College (Massachusetts)	1855
Theta	Union College (New York)	1856
Tau	Lafayette College (Pennsylvania)	1857
Upsilon	University of North Carolina	1858
Xi	University of Michigan	1858
Pi	Amherst College (Massachusetts)	1858
Eta	Pennsylvania College (Gettysburg)	1861
Omega	University of Chicago	1864
Lambda	Bowdoin College (Maine)	1867
Beta	University of Virginia	1868
Phi	Cornell University (New York)	1868
Iota	University of California	1870
Gamma	Syracuse University (New York)	1875
Theta Xi	University of Toronto (Canada)	1879
Alpha	Columbia University (New York)	1879
Alpha Psi	McGill University (Canada)	1883
Nu	Case School of Applied Science (Ohio)	1884
Eta	Yale University (Connecticut)	1889
Mu	Stanford University (California)	1892
Alpha Beta	University of Minnesota	1899

* SOURCE: Zeta Psi 1926.

with the latter becoming dependent on the former in ways that were probably unimaginable at the start.

THE UNIVERSITY OF CALIFORNIA

The people of California always intended to have a university. After all, the Spanish and Mexicans who had occupied the territory previously had never managed to establish a school system, and what better way to establish the clear superiority of the United States than to bring education to the Golden State? When California entered the union in 1850, much earlier than ever anticipated, the state constitution expressed the intention to create a university.[31]

In 1853, California was granted forty-six thousand acres of national land to sell to generate funding for a "seminary of learning."[32] The land market was vastly overestimated, and sale of the land generated only fifty-seven thousand dollars. Not surprisingly, there was little push from the gold miners and other adventurers who composed the overwhelming majority of California's population to establish a state university, so it was not until the Morrill Act of 1862 provided incentives that any progress was made toward this goal.

The Morrill Act, pushed by a Massachusetts congressman, called for the federal government to financially encourage, through a series of land grants to states, the development of public universities that would train men for "farm, factory, profession." Morrill first proposed his legislation in 1857, only to have it blocked by southern legislators. It was pushed through in July 1862 while the southern representatives were conveniently away from Congress. Each state, in accepting the federal scrip, was required to create or charter a school that would fulfill the act's mission. The act gave each state 30,000 acres for each legislator it had—California received 150,000 acres.[33]

The states had the option, under the Morrill Act, to either augment existing colleges or develop new ones. California legislators decided to found a new college that would be both public and secular. Most of the existing colleges in California had religious affiliations. One of these, the College of California, founded by former Yale professor Reverend Henry Durant, was located in the city of Oakland. Durant had plans to expand his small college and, in anticipation, had purchased a plot of land on Strawberry Creek in Berkeley, four miles north of the city of Oakland, on which to build his new campus.

As financial realities collided with his dreams, Durant approached California's superintendent of public education about merging the College of California with the land-grant institution to form a new, secular, University of California. He proposed that the College of California's facilities be used while the new university was constructed, and that his existing student body and faculty be absorbed into the new college. After much wrangling, a bill was passed in March 1868 creating the university and its governing board of regents, and in the autumn of 1869, eleven returning students from the College of California and twenty-nine new freshmen entered the University of California under the leadership of President John LeConte.[34]

On September 25, 1873, the entire student body and faculty of the university assembled for the first time at the site in Berkeley. Two buildings stood on the campus, North College and South College. The college, nestled on the side of gently sloping mountains overlooking the San Francisco Bay, occupied an extraordinary location. From the grounds, one could easily enjoy views of the Golden Gate (sans bridge, of course) and San Francisco to the west. Looking south along Telegraph Avenue, one saw the growing city of Oakland. While the first two buildings must have seemed strangely alone on that Berkeley hillside, they would soon be surrounded by university gardens and agricultural fields and a growing collection of new structures. Eventually, North and South College would become North and South halls, as East and West halls joined them on the campus.[35]

The students of the new university saw themselves as part of a generation that would civilize the young state of California. This 1858 passage from the *College Echo*, the student newspaper of the College of California, is instructive:

CALIFORNIA

A few years since, and scarce a trace of civilization could be discerned within her borders. She was literally *terra incognita*, to the people of Europe, and known but in name to her American neighbor. Her Mexican proprietors thought her fit for nothing but the rearing of herds, and scarcely worth protecting from the hostile Indian tribes that ravaged her frontiers, and but for the transfer to American owners, together with the subsequent discovery of her mines, she today would have been comparatively a desert waste. The first event drew a few hardy spirits within her territory, the second filled her with the most energetic of every nation.[36]

The young men of the college saw themselves as situated in the broader tapestry of history, drawn from the world's strongest and heartiest men to create a new civilization out of a neglected wilderness. While the men of the College of California had been surrounded only by students of their own sex, this was not to be the case at the new University of California. Among the students attending the opening of the

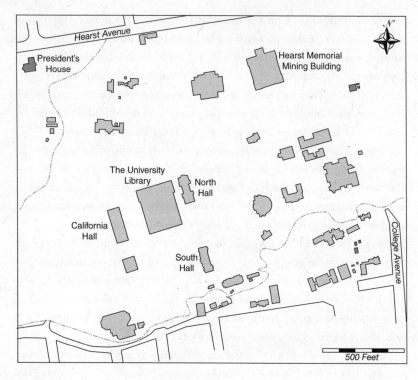

FIGURE 5

The campus and immediate vicinity, 1911. Based on Sanborn Fire
Insurance maps.

new campus were a small number of women. In its charter, the university had not
taken a stance on coeducation one way or the other. With the admission of 8 women
to the university in 1870 (representing 9 percent of the student body), the regents
reaffirmed the right of women to attend the university. In the 1875–76 school year, 42
of the 310 students enrolled were women.[37]

THE SOCIAL GEOGRAPHY OF CAMPUS

In his 1930 history of the university, William Ferrier paints a dismal portrait of
Berkeley at the time of the university's opening. "The business part of the town
consisted of a French restaurant at the end of the street car line on Telegraph avenue and Allston Way, and a hotel which could accommodate not more than twenty
persons."[38] Students found a housing shortage in Berkeley, so most lived in the
Temescal section of Oakland, located two miles or so south of campus (figure 5).

These students commuted to Oakland, mainly on foot to avoid the steep fares of horse cars that ran between the city and the university. Ferrier hypothesized that the muddy walk from Oakland to Berkeley during those first winters caused several of the coeds to drop out of the university. By 1874, new businesses emerged to cater to the young university. The Berkeley Hotel was founded on Shattuck Avenue, with an adjoining French restaurant. A Chinese laundry, butcher's shop, and grocery store quickly followed. Soon, more restaurants, boardinghouses, and coffeehouses followed. Still, Berkeley could not be accused of being a cosmopolitan place. When Mary Ritter arrived in Berkeley in 1887, she lived at 2223 Durant, just a few blocks from the university. In her memoir she describes the town:

> Berkeley when I first knew it was a straggling village clustered around the
> university. . . . Dwight Way Station was the center of the village. There were
> no public buildings, no paved streets, no sidewalks except rattling boards.
> Strawberry Creek meandered across Shattuck Avenue where Allston Way and
> the Hotel Whitecotton now are. . . . Southern Pacific trains made up of a decrepit
> engine and old red cars made hourly trips from the San Francisco Ferry to
> North Berkeley Station. A wheezing little engine of ancient vintage drawing a
> rattling old street car frightened the horses as it tooted its way out Telegraph
> Avenue to near the University entrance, which is now adorned by Sather Gate.[39]

Ritter remarked that the site of the university had been selected by "men who could envision the glory of the prospective campus."[40] Perhaps it was this sense of optimism and foresight that encouraged a small group of men to build a new fraternity house on the edge of the university campus. Now, the curtain is about to open, and the young men of the Iota chapter of Zeta Psi are about to make their entrance.

PROGRAM FOR ACT I

Act I finds us in the nursery of the Darling house. Three children, Wendy, John, and Michael Darling, sleep here. Wendy is the oldest. Their parents are not well-to-do but of the middle class. They call their maid "the servants"— so as to imply they have more staff than they do—and their Saint Bernard, Nana, serves as their governess. The young boys enjoy the stories that Wendy tells at bedtime, and their favorites involve the adventures of Peter Pan. Little do they know, Peter Pan himself travels to their home to hear the stories too. Once, Mrs. Darling catches him in the house, chases him out the window, and closes it behind him, causing his shadow to be severed from him. She carefully saves it and, subsequently, sees Peter's face outside the window of the nursery on several occasions, which makes her concerned for the children's welfare.

On a night when the Darling parents are going out for the evening, Mr. Darling, an insecure man, argues with his family and, in a moment of anger, sends the dog from the house, leaving the children without protection in the nursery. Peter, accompanied by the fairy Tinkerbell, enters the nursery in search of his shadow. Wendy finds him crying and offers to sew it back on for him. In return, he tells Wendy of his life in Never Land and invites her to come and tell stories to the Lost Boys, children who fell out of their prams and escaped to Never Land. Wendy wakes her brothers, and with the aid of fairy dust furnished by Tinkerbell, they fly out the nursery window. Nana, tied to the doghouse in the yard, tries to alert the Darlings, but they return only in time to see the children disappear.

ACT I · The Nursery

Brotherhood in the First House of Zeta Psi

> When in their daily business, and amid the cares and
> trials of life, [our graduates] look back upon their college
> days, which are to return no more, the happy hours
> which they have spent in their college societies, come up
> before them as their happiest memories.
>
> "ZETA PSI," *University Echo*, October 1871

> In the city, where he sits on a stool all day, as fixed as a
> postage stamp, he is so like all the others on stools that
> you recognize him not by his face but by his stool, but at
> home the way to gratify him is to say that he has a
> distinct personality.
>
> Mr. Darling as first described in *Peter Pan*

> The desperate man, who has not been out in the fresh air
> for days, has now lost all self-control.
>
> Mr. Darling just before he fires Nana, the Saint Bernard,
> in *Peter Pan*

On the 16th of July 1873, twelve men stood before President Daniel Coit Gilman in the still-unfinished North College (which soon became known as North Hall) to receive their degrees from the University of California.[1] The first building of the new university stood on a cleared, gently rising slope. With its single lonely building and empty surrounds, the campus was still a place of dreams and plans more than of reality—quite fitting for the site of a Never Land. These were the early days of the Never Land that would come to be known as "Cal." The young men of the campus had come from fine preparatory schools and, in many cases, had descended from old East Coast blood.

The dreams about the campus were not for these new graduates but for future generations of students. These twelve had completed their degree work on the campus of the former College of California in downtown Oakland, and Temescal and Oakland had been the sites of their adventures and trials. Their class had contained twenty-four people at the start, but their numbers had dwindled to half of that.

They were the first to have completed a full four years at the new University of California, and they are immortalized in university history as "the twelve apostles." While the twelve are bonded together in history by their shared achievement, seven of these men shared another bond—brotherhood. George Ainsworth, John Bolton, James Budd, George C. Edwards, Lester Hawkins, Clarence Wetmore, and Thomas Woodward were brothers in the Iota chapter of Zeta Psi fraternity.[2]

coincid-ence

Perhaps it is fitting that the original graduating class of Zetes contained the same number of persons as Peter's band of Lost Boys. These early Zetes still had the smell of the nursery on them: domesticity and civilization, not animal skins, were draped across their shoulders. There was a sense of wildness about them; they could not be part of the young state of California without it. This wild streak is part of even the civilized manhood of California, and its constant presence makes the historical transition from manliness to masculinity seem natural and inevitable.[3] While men of the East consciously remade themselves in the masculine model, the men of the West could amplify the things they were already doing and tweak the stories they told about themselves accordingly. Masculinity was born in the West.

The Iota chapter of Zeta Psi was founded in 1870, before the new campus was completed.[4] The October 1871 issue of the *University Echo* announced its founding. The anonymous newspaper article stated that the population of the University of California had grown to such an extent that it could now support the existence of a secret society like those that flourished on all the East Coast college campuses. The implication was that, to be a great university, California needed secret societies.[5] Being the first fraternity on campus has always been a source of pride for the Zeta Psi brothers. Their status as first translated into their position in the university yearbook, *The Blue and Gold,* where fraternities were listed by the order of their founding—not alphabetically—until the 1920s. Pride is already evident in the wording of the announcement: "This is, we believe, the first chapter, of any such organization, that has been established on the Pacific Coast." Over time, Zete histories expanded their colonial boundaries to declare themselves the first fraternity "West of the Rockies" or "West of the Mississippi."[6]

Those familiar with modern fraternities may be surprised to read how the article's author describes secret societies: "These societies are nearly all different in their objects, but almost all of them are to some extent literary in their character, requiring their members at stated times to meet and deliver essays and orations upon various subjects of interest to the student." This description of fraternal contributions to campus life shaped Zeta Psi's public face during the first decades of its existence. The author then justifies the need for fraternities: "In our secret societies we are bound together by sacred ties, as brothers. It is these societies which give tone and spirit to college life. The hour which we spend together in brotherly love is a pleasant recreation from our books and college duties."[7]

In an 1899 history of the chapter, William Scott Foster ('oo) describes the chapter's founding: "From the very start the qualifications for membership were of the very highest, the aim being to gather together into closer bonds of friendship a company of manly, congenial men whose union would promote zeal in study, the formation of warm and lifelong friendships, and whose combined influence in the college should ever be exerted in the direction of progress."[8] The reality of the founding and selection of members seems to have been less proscribed than indicated in this description. There is a strong correlation between the membership of the Durant Rhetorical Society and the original members of Zeta Psi. In April of 1871, before the fraternity was announced, the officers of the rhetorical society were published. Included were six future Zetes. Officers for the following term included six more Zetes, nearly all the officers. In later years, the fraternities would be accused of taking over student organizations like this one. However, it is clear from a chronological perspective that the Durant Rhetorical Society made Zeta Psi, not the reverse.[9]

The 1899 self-description of the organization is worth considering further for its language. The men of Zeta Psi were to be "manly" and "congenial," their contributions to the college should be "in the direction of progress." These ideas are in keeping with Gail Bederman's (and others') characterization of Victorian manhood as focusing on civility and civilization building.[10] The young men of Zeta Psi were living on what was still recognized as the American frontier. The massacre at Wounded Knee and Turner's declaration that the frontier had been closed were twenty-some years in the future. As noted earlier, the University of California itself was seen as evidence of the civilizing influences of American society on the former Spanish and Mexican colony. The United States was still a growing country, at a time when expansion was seen as a natural right of civilized (white) men.[11]

In other ways, the early members of Zeta Psi were on the forefront of the shifts in masculinity already beginning to occur. Other men at the turn of the twentieth century would come to dream about the great possibilities of the western frontier and its adventurous lifestyle while reading such authors as Zane Grey and Jack London, but the young men of Zeta Psi were already living on the frontier. Succeeding generations would idolize the wildness of the West, but these men saw its great potential for being civilized and ordered. Many of the brothers in their postgraduate lives became involved in building the railroad and steamship industries that connected California to the rest of the country; others were surveyors or naturalists, categorizing and charting the available resources. Still others worked in the lucrative industry of mining; and a significant number literally served as architects of the young state in a variety of elected and appointed positions in the California government. While later generations might see them as romantic frontiersmen, their activities and accomplishments mark these men as civilizers.

There was a racial dimension to this discourse as well. The Spanish, who had occupied California for nearly a hundred years before its absorption by the United States, had established a racial hierarchy that dictated social movement in the colony of Alta California. That hierarchy, however, was fluid and mobility was possible.[12] During the American period, some of this fluidity remained, yet there were also attempts to reassert the standards of eastern society in the new state. It was common for California pioneers to brag of their East Coast origins. Kevin Starr has called this an attitude of "Anglo-Saxonism," one advocated by such diverse men as author Jack London and David Starr Jordan, president of Stanford University. Anglo-Saxonism was a vision of whiteness that reified those whose roots were planted in England and Germany, but which also allowed for the admittance of wealthy persons of French and even Italian and Irish ancestry and, in the early twentieth century, eastern Europeans.[13] This whiteness was somewhat more inclusive than that of the East Coast, where Catholicism, like Judaism, was seen as a clear marker of "otherness."[14] The men of Zeta Psi's Iota chapter may have been more diverse than East Coast chapters, but all considered themselves to be their century's equivalent of "white."

This subject position came with certain assumptions about the world and their place in it. Through their actions, we can see how these young men created a persona of civility within the campus community. We can also see how a commitment to civility shaped, in ways that are clearly evident in the materials of their everyday life, how they expressed their loyalty and fraternity to one another. And herein lies the contradiction in life at the early Zete house: even in the homosocial space of the fraternity house, they depended on the vocabularies of domesticity used by their mothers. In their outlooks, goals, and self-images, these men were fundamentally different from the later men of Zeta Psi, who came to outgrow the first fraternity house. But this is only the first act of our play, and I do not wish to give away too much of the story.

In this act we will accomplish several tasks. First I introduce you more fully to the men of Zeta Psi: their backgrounds, their accomplishments, and how they created a sense of brotherhood. This act takes place mainly in the house, the nursery to be exact, the space where a sense of family was created and notions of gendered performances were instilled and nurtured. Together we will look more closely at the house and its materials, and at how the men became brothers. We also see in this act the seeds of discontentment and frustration with a household that drips with the rituals and practices of the female-dominated domestic sphere.

THE BROTHERS OF ZETA PSI

Who then, were, the men of Zeta Psi? They may have lived in an early Never Land, but it is important to recognize that the earliest among them were not Lost Boys. Instead, they were more like John and Michael Darling, young men ready to leave the nursery for the delights of Never Land. John and Michael are shaped by the civilizing influences of domesticity. They embrace a fierce nationalistic pride and disdain those who would question the empire as the pirates do. These boys are on their way to becoming like their father: mediocre, frustrated, and ostracized by the family. The opportunity to become Lost Boys offers them another possible future. The primary women in the Darling boys' lives are both mother figures: Wendy, who serves as a mother in the nursery; and their biological mother, Mrs. Darling. While Mr. Darling's work has removed him from most of their day-to-day affairs, the boys still have a clear sense of their natural superiority over women. Even as Wendy tries to make them play house, John makes the exercise into a discourse on male superiority:

JOHN (good naturedly).   I am happy to inform you, Mrs. Darling, that you are now a mother. (WENDY gives way to ecstasy) You have missed the chief thing; you haven't asked, "boy or girl?"

WENDY.   I am so glad to have one at all, I don't care which it is.

JOHN (crushingly).   That is just the difference between gentlemen and ladies. Now you tell me.

WENDY.   I am happy to acquaint you, Mr. Darling, you are now a father.

JOHN.   Boy or girl?

WENDY (presenting herself).   Girl.

JOHN.   Tuts.

WENDY.   You Horrid.

John then beams when Wendy tells him he has a son, provoking Wendy to call him hateful.[15]

While John and Michael have a sense that a world awaits them outside the nursery, for the time being the nursery, with its feminizing influences, is their primary world. The same was true for the first men of Zeta Psi. They entered college so they would become better equipped to conquer the public sphere they would soon enter, but were still young in the ways of the world. Most came to college directly from one of the limited number of prep schools in Oakland and San Francisco. Statistics reported in *The Blue and Gold* yearbook demonstrate that most seniors left the university at twenty-one or twenty-two years of age, much as today. Yet, a surprising number entered when they were as young as sixteen. So let us now consider more closely the actual men of Zeta Psi.[16]

IDENTIFYING THE MEN OF ZETA PSI

Providing a census of Zeta Psi brothers would seem to be a straightforward venture. After all, many available documents provide this information. The national chapter of Zeta Psi compiled comprehensive lists of its alumni that it published in 1899 and 1926. The 1899 publication is particularly interesting in that it provides brief biographies of the brothers' accomplishments while at the university and afterward. The biographies are clearly self-reports and, as such, have differing levels of detail. Historically speaking, this is the one time when being a braggart is a desirable personality trait. The most comprehensive of the biographies include place of birth, parents' names, high school attended, college activities, date of marriage, names of spouse and children, names of other family members who joined Zeta Psi, and significant life accomplishments.

The 1926 publication is significantly smaller and lists only the brothers' current addresses or years of death by class year. Similar information can be found in a series of alumni registers published by the University of California's Alumni Association. The alumni records are less useful for inventorying the population of Zeta Psi, since those registers list only persons who graduated, a feat a number of Zetes failed to achieve.[17]

A complementary source of demographic information is *The Blue and Gold*, which lists each fraternity's membership. The advantage of the *Blue and Gold* listings is that they allow one to determine house population on a year-by-year basis. One disadvantage, however, is that this source tends to slightly underestimate the population—pledging took place during the entire year, but submissions to *The Blue and Gold* were due in February. Since, in its early days, it was not unusual for the fraternity to admit men at any stage in their college career, seniors who rushed late in the year could conceivably never show up in any volume of the yearbook.

A final source of demographic information is Iota's membership planks recovered from the party room. As mentioned before, we did not recover a complete set of years, but what we do have represents a significant number of years. The existence of the complementary evidence from the Zeta Psi registers and *The Blue and Gold* yearbooks makes it possible to fully contextualize the planks' role in fraternity life. It is worth noting that, although I have three different sources detailing the membership of Zeta Psi, none of them completely agree with any of the others. For instance, suppose we use just the names listed on the planks for the period of 1876 through 1908: this gives us a population of 173 Zetes (see appendix 1). The 1926 register, however, lists 181 Zeta Psi members for this same period. The difference in these two populations is small; in contrast, *The Blue and Gold* for the same period lists only 127 seniors.

This phenomenon does not mean that one particular source of evidence is more reliable than another, just that they represent different moments of time and different kinds of measures. Some of these differences are a result of process—there was a high dropout rate among all students of the University of California. Not everyone recognized as a brother became an alumnus of the university, so counting seniors in *The Blue and Gold* should always result in a smaller count. Moreover, I found names on the planks that do not appear in Zeta Psi's register—clearly, house members saw these persons as part of their brotherhood, but for whatever reason they were never recognized by the national chapter.

For our purposes, we do not need the brothers to hold still at a particular moment so we can count them. The variations remind us that brotherhood was socially constructed and fluid—perception of brotherhood in one arena did not guarantee recognition of brotherhood in another. The institution was bigger than any of its individual members. However, in all discussions of population trends, I identify which source(s) of population evidence I am using.

So, given this lengthy introduction, what can I say in general about the men of Zeta Psi during the occupation of the first chapter house? First, in the original house, no more than twenty men lived together at a time. At times, this number was much smaller. A surprising number of brothers were California natives. Given that the state had been part of the United States only since 1850, the first Zetes were among the first generation of American-born Californians (table 3). Among the brothers in the house from 1870 to 1880; 34 percent had been born in California; from 1881 to 1890, this increased to 68 percent; and from 1900 to 1910, nearly 77

TABLE 3 Geographic origins of Zeta Psi Iota brothers

Place of birth	1870–1879		1880–1889		1890–1899	
	Number	Percentage	Number	Percentage	Number	Percentage
Alabama			1	1.5		
California	23	34.3	43	68.3	46	76.7
Idaho					1	1.6
Illinois	1	1.5			1	1.6
Indiana	7	10.4	1	1.5	1	1.6
Iowa					1	1.6
Maine	2	3.0				
Massachusetts	1	1.5	1	1.5		
Minnesota	1	1.5	1	1.5		
Mississippi	2	3.0				
Missouri	3	4.4				
Nevada					2	3.3
New Jersey	1	1.5				
New York	5	7.4	4	6.0	1	1.6
Oregon	4	6.0	1	1.5	4	6.7
Ohio	1	1.5				
Pennsylvania	2	1.5				
Rhode Island	1	1.5				
Virginia	1	1.5				
Washington	1	1.5	1	1.5		
Wisconsin	2	3.0	2	3.0		
Canada			1	1.5		
Ireland					1	1.6
Japan					1	1.6
Mexico			1	1.5		
Panama	1	1.5				
Unknown	9	13.4	5	8.0		

percent of the brothers had been born in California. The California-born brothers hailed from all over the state—from San Francisco, Los Angeles, and Sonoma, as well as, of course, from towns like Placer, Marysville, and Chico in the gold country of the Sierra Nevada.[18] During a time when more and more outsiders came to Cal, Zeta Psi brothers were increasingly likely to have been born in the state.

Still, as has always been the case in California, many of the brothers came to the state from other places. Not surprisingly, the first decade of Zeta Psi brothers was the most geographically diverse, with brothers hailing from seventeen other states (table I-1), and with New York, Indiana, Oregon, and Missouri contributing the greatest numbers. One brother had been born abroad, in Panama. From 1881 to 1890, brothers had come from nine states other than California, with several coming from New York and Wisconsin. Two internationally born brothers were now members—one born in Chihuahua, Mexico, the other, British Columbia, Canada. From 1891 to 1900, only seven additional states contributed brothers, with Oregon, Nevada, and New York being the only states to contribute multiple members. One brother had been born in Ireland, and another, in Japan.[19]

Zeta Psi suffered from accusations that it was an overly exclusive and undemocratic fraternity. The demographic shift from a relatively geographically diverse population to one more clearly biased toward native Californians may be a measure of some of the fraternity's exclusiveness—were they selecting members primarily from established California families? A number of the Zetes came from well-known families that had deep roots in East Coast genealogies. George Edwards was said to be a descendent of New England's fiery minister Jonathan Edwards.[20] Joseph Rowell was the son of a well-known minister whose family could be traced back to Thomas Rowell, who had come to the American colonies in 1658.[21] Other names from the Zeta Psi register have deep histories in California, names like LeConte, Hittell, Dwinelle, and Russell.[22] Through time, Zeta Psi drew many of its new members from legacies—relatives of other Zeta Psi brothers and alumni. Since legacies would be the nephews, cousins, sons or other relatives of earlier classes of Zetes, one would expect legacies to hail almost exclusively from California.

THE DOMESTIC SPACE OF ZETA PSI

Advocates for fraternities often wrote that one of the advantages of fraternity life was that it provided a substitute home for young men living away for the first time in their lives.[23] Living together was an important aspect of the fraternity's shared experience. That the university provided no housing for its students made sharing

FIGURE 6

The first Zeta Psi house, circa 1880. Photograph courtesy of
the Bancroft Library.

lodging as a group all the more desirable. After the fraternity's founding, the number of brothers grew quickly, and as early as the fall of 1873 the group secured a
home for itself in a place called the Berkeley Farm House. The following year, they
rented Humboldt Hall, in Oakland, about two miles from the university campus.
The fraternity attempted to purchase this property, and failing to secure it, moved
again, to a house on Dwight Way. In the summer of 1876, they purchased a plot of
land on the western edge of campus, on what would become College Avenue, and
built a modest three-story house.[24] According to fraternity history, the dedication
of the house was attended by elders; brothers I. T. Hinton, William Dargie, W. M.
Van Dyke, Horry Meek, and D. B. Fairbanks were cited as being "owed a heavy
debt in this matter."[25]

Early photographs of the house show that it was the first built on that portion of
what was then called Audubon Street (figure 6). The neighborhood was barely settled, and the block between Audubon and Piedmont had been subdivided into eighteen different plots with thirteen different owners. The Zeta Psi plot is listed under
the names of A. L. Whitney and D. B. Fairbanks, two of the founding members.[26]

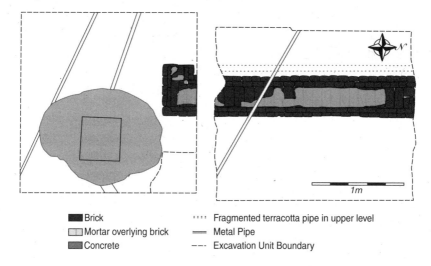

Brick
Mortar overlying brick
Concrete
:::: Fragmented terracotta pipe in upper level
=== Metal Pipe
--- Excavation Unit Boundary

FIGURE 7
Detail of the foundation of the 1876 Zeta Psi house, found in 2001.

Eventually, a neighborhood inhabited by college professors and staff, merchants, families, vocal feminists, and additional fraternities developed in the area. An 1880 article from the newspaper the *Berkeleyan* gives a detailed description of the first house.

> It is three stories in height, with a mansard roof and admirably arranged for the accommodation of the members of the society. On the first floor, there is a spacious entrance hall and on the right an elegant parlor, from which folding doors open into a spacious sitting-room; and when occasion requires the folding doors can be thrown back, and the two rooms, made one. Back on the sitting room is a small apartment, which can be used as a committee room. On the left of the entrance hall is the spacious dining room, and back of that a well-arranged kitchen with the necessary appurtenances. At the end of the hall is the linen room, and adjoining this is an elegant bath room. On the second floor are admirably arranged sleeping apartments, each provided with a grate, marble wash basin, closet for clothes, etc. The space on the third floor is devoted partly to sleeping and study rooms.[27]

During the 2001 archaeological excavations at the standing chapter house, we were able to locate a portion of the first house's foundation still preserved: part of the stairs and front porch (figure 7).

I should perhaps pause a moment to explain—you may wonder how we found a house that had been moved somewhere else, back at its original location. James Barrie describes Wendy's little house in Never Land as wandering about looking for anyone who needs it.[28] Nothing so whimsical is the explanation here. Although the house structure was picked up, turned, and moved back on the lot, the brick foundation that once supported the structure was left behind. Apparently, the value of the foundation's bricks did not justify the work it would have taken to dig them out. This is a boon for historical archaeologists—the foundation is really the only part of a structure we tend to find anyway. Foundations are places where trash tends to accumulate, and what we really hope to find is trash and some sort of feature—like remains of a building, fence post, drainage ditch, or something similar—that will help explain why the trash accumulated where it did.

Judging from photographs of other houses moved at the time, the first chapter house was probably moved using horse-powered labor, which is less detrimental to the ground surface than modern trucks and backhoes. As a result, not only do we have portions of the structure, but we also have parts of collapsed water drainage pipes and iron water pipes that ran in the front of the building, and yes, a respectable accumulation of trash.

If we were to find only a single portion of the house, this was one of the best locations to find. Corners, like the one at the intersection of the porch and stairs, are good places for trash to collect; corners also let us know exactly where on the house we are, something that would have been impossible had we uncovered only a straight length of wall.

As we worked on the dig, the shape of the foundation convinced me that we must be at the front porch, but the coup d'état came when, several meters away, students uncovered a strange iron artifact. It appeared to be some sort of rectangular object made out of woven iron wire. At first my students and I wondered if it was a strange interior of a cushion, but an Iota-scrapbook photograph taken of Zetes sitting on the porch steps solved the mystery—it was a heavy-duty welcome mat/foot scraper. Apparently it was left behind by the brothers when they abandoned the house. Other photographs from the same scrapbook show that the front steps and porch were popular social spaces for the brothers.[29] Given its elevation and relative lack of surrounding buildings, the porch would have featured a spectacular view of the Golden Gate.

Our understanding of the social space of this house is limited to what we gleaned from a few photographs showing some interior views, and a small number of descriptions of life at the fraternity house, as in the newspaper account mentioned earlier. Our archaeological finds provide further insights into the kinds of materials used within the house. In general, our understanding of life in this house comes from a relatively small number of sources. Still, when combined with photographic and documentary evidence, there is much we can say about life inside the first Zeta chapter house.

CREATING BONDS OF CLASS AND BROTHERHOOD

College life in the nineteenth century was extremely class oriented—in ways beyond socioeconomics. From their entry into the university until their graduation day, students were identified en mass by their class year and their class status. Freshmen, not surprisingly, occupied the lowest rung of the university social ladder. Newspaper accounts make it clear that they were targeted as the butts of jokes and hazing ranging from the informal to the formal, from gentle to brutal. A novel depicting life at Cal in the 1890s recounts how a freshmen straight off the train from the south is told by two sophomores that to register he must get back on the train and go to the university headquarters in Oakland. The young man is saved when an older woman familiar with sophomores' pranks intercedes.[30]

Class hazing was ritualized in annual events. The "Freshman Rush" was ultimately little more than a giant brawl between the freshman and sophomore classes. Class presidents were supposed to lead their respective classes into battle. Secret calls were devised to identify class members to one another—sophomores had the advantage of knowing their classmates, whereas freshmen did not. The two classes met in battle (women were delegated to the sidelines to cheer for their male brethren), *e wh* where the objective was to wrestle a member of the opposite class to the ground and tie his hands and feet so he could not escape. The captured men were carried to the opposite side's area and unceremoniously piled up. Some men were involved in trying to free captives while others were trying to capture opponents. The whole affair was not over until one entire class was tied up. It probably also goes without saying that these events attracted a fair number of observers from other classes and from outside the university.[31] An 1881 article in the student paper, the *Occident* provides an insightful description of the aftermath: "Soon the campus was deserted, and there was no sign of the recent carnage there, except the rags of various hues, remains of what had probably once been clothing, but was now mutilated beyond recognition. Those who had taken part in rush now looked like members of the Mayay race. The dry grass of the campus having been burned a few days before, the ground was left covered in black ashes. This made rolling about on Mother Earth more delightful than usual."[32]

In case our California students appear too barbaric, it is important to stress that hazing events were common at universities of the time. By the end of the nineteenth century, however—even at the University of California—these events were increasingly frowned on as juvenile and dangerous.[33]

Another festivity that marked the annual college cycle was the Bourdon Burial. This event was based on a similar ritual at Yale. Bourdon and Minto were authors of two particularly detested freshman primers. To celebrate their passage from freshmen to sophomores, the freshmen oversaw the cremation of the two primers (or stand-ins), enclosed the ashes in a small coffin, and led a funeral procession through the campus, stopping at Charter Hill to hold a mock funeral. Orators elected from the freshmen class served as memorialists for the deceased. In the early days, the procession was followed by a bust, or spree, as large parties featuring alcoholic beverages were called. Students set a subscription price that everyone was expected to pay to in order to cover the cost of the alcohol.[34] In *The Blue and Gold*, the class of 1876 took credit for introducing this burial tradition: " '76 was the first class on this coast to introduce the time honored practice of 'buying the Analytics.' Few were the eyes that grew not moist as with measured tread to the sound of a hundred toot horns we bore her to her last resting place."[35]

There was a competitive class element to this. Sophomores would do their best to intercept the coffin and disrupt the event. Sometimes these competitions became a little too extreme, with orators kidnapped and held hostage.[36] It was also a tradition for each class to present in the annual yearbook a history of their great achievements of the year and to describe what ongoing legacy(ies) they had created. The success or failure of the Bourdon Burial was often discussed by the hosting class's historian. The class of '79 was particularly proud of their Bourdon: a majority vote had determined it would be a dry affair, without the customary bust following. As noted in *The Blue and Gold*, "This, it is conceded by all, was the grandest class affair ever known to the University. What with music, stirring oratory, grand illumination, drinking, hallooing, and solemn reverential praying attending upon the funeral obsequies, an impression was made upon those present that neither time nor distance can ever efface. And we feel proud to add that, although beer and eggnog were supplied in abundance, it is to be mentioned as a most remarkable phenomenon that not one of all of those of '79 who were present became intoxicated."[37]

While certain events, like Junior Day, an annual day when the juniors celebrated their talents and accomplishments, and the Bourdon Burial, were moments in time that galvanized classes against one another, class status shaped everyday life at the university as well. At different times, freshmen were required to wear beanies.

Sophomore hat styles changed, but bowlers were popular for a time. The wearing of gray top hats was limited to junior men, and black top hats to senior men. To lose one's hat would be a sign of loss of status. Senior men could be seen with canes or smoking pipes, as fitting their status, but a freshman caught with such an affectation would be punished. Seniors' hats, while typically beat up to demonstrate seniors' lack of concern for social niceties, were not decorated. In contrast, the hats of the junior classmen might bear Greek fraternity letters or the familiar Cal cheer "Oski! Wow! Wow!" Senior men's status was also reinforced by their special study room, reserved for them in Senior Hall.[38]

Moving from one class level to another was not always automatic. Freshmen had to pass a series of exams in order to graduate to the next level. In an 1879 tirade against fraternities, a writer in the antifraternity paper the *Oestrus* noted, "Look at the records of the society-men, and you will see that an immense percentage has been successively remanded to the lower classes."[39] There may be some merit to this criticism. As we will see, a number of Zetes magically advanced from their second freshman year to junior or even senior status, and a surprising number did not graduate.

CLASS YEAR IN FRATERNAL LIFE

Given the class demarcations that shaped everyday life in the broader campus community, it is surprising that year rank was also a primary means of organizing life at the fraternity house. Interviews with brothers who had lived in the Iota chapter house in the 1920s and onward demonstrate this. Student class-year identities were much more important in the nineteenth-century, and this facet of fraternity life may have originated in the nineteenth century. As early as the 1920s, house life was structured by class. The seniors were the elders of the household and, as such, served as the symbolic house heads. They held the officers' positions, represented the house in public matters, and derived all benefits that came with seniority—the largest rooms, single rooms when available, and the privileges of having first food service at dinner, directing rush and initiation ceremonies, and commanding the labor and support of brothers who were lower classmen.[40]

For the Blue and Gold, a fictionalized account of life at Cal in the 1890s, describes the role of freshmen in a fraternity house.

" 'Phone, 'phone, wake up, there, freshman, step lively."

"Yes, it's his job to answer the 'phone," explained Boyce. "Each freshie has something special to do. I carved last year, and I tell you I was glad to graduate from it. Here, freshman, what sort of a slice is that to give to company? You couldn't carve a roll of butter."[41]

Later, freshmen are described bringing out the keg of beer and rushing back and forth in a sweat, serving steins of beer and listening to complaints about their ability to draw a proper mug of beer.

While the relegation of chores to the underclassmen could be seen as merely part of a larger culture of class-based hazing, it has greater significance than that. For men living together in a household, it was structurally important to define roles that would facilitate household management yet not symbolically feminize younger members. Remember, household management was seen as clearly part of the realm of women's work. Yet in a household full of men, it was work that still needed to be done. The structure of household relations within the fraternity house ensured that no brother was placed in the role of "symbolic woman." Since freshmen represented the future leaders of the fraternity, they could not be put in a position that would permanently undermine their relationship to the other brothers.

In the early twentieth century, a range of strategies and practices would be employed in the fraternity to constantly reaffirm all brothers' status as masculine, but during the early nineteenth century this seems to have been achieved through age-grade differentiations. Just as a freshman could look forward to burning Bourdon and Minto at the end of the year, the fraternity pledge could look forward to freedom from certain household chores.

RUSHING

The practice of rushing brought new members to the house. Few sources actually discuss what the processes of rushing and initiation entailed at this time. Ironically, an antifraternity column in the *Oestrus* provides some of the best descriptions of the rushing process in an 1879 warning to incoming freshmen. "Some of you, especially those who have considerable money to spend, will soon be approached, if you have not been approached already, by members of the upper classes. These men will be very friendly with you, they will be your constant companions; they will ask you to dine with them, they will treat you to the best things which the place affords, they will flatter and cajole you, till you will imagine to yourselves that you must be important persons." In particular, the authors were concerned about the bad influences of Zeta Psi:

The members of Zeta Psi, in addition to practicing upon you all the arts mentioned above, will take you to their house, the advantages of which will be pointed out, they will show you a Greek Letter Pin, set with any precious stones you may desire, the cost of which would make you feel deep into your pockets; they will doubtless tell you that the fraternities are the cream of university society, and promise you the best time in the world if you but join them. If you express a desire to spend a good part of your time in study, they will tell you how high their men have stood in their classes, because they had had the advantages of association, etc.[42]

By the time the *Oestrus* article was written, there was a total of four fraternities on campus: Zeta Psi (founded 1870), Chi Phi (founded 1875), Delta Kappa Epsilon (founded 1876), and Beta Theta Pi (1879). It may be that rushing was a competitive practice by that time, since more organizations were recruiting men. However, an examination of Zeta Psi's roles suggests that recruitment was a more organic social process than the *Oestrus* column might lead one to believe.

For instance, a review of the 1876 *Blue and Gold* shows that J. Mailliard, F. P. McLean, W. M. Van Dyke, and W. H. Nicholson were members of the Durant Rhetorical Society in the year before they became members of Zeta Psi. Their participation in the group would have made them known to the brothers before they were recruited by the fraternity. Likewise, Mailliard would have been known to a number of brothers from his participation in the Glee Club. Joseph Hutchinson, another future Zete, would have met Frank Solinsky and Vincent Hook through the Neolean Rhetorical Society, and any of eight other brothers through the Glee Club. In other words, there is evidence that recruitment was initially based on compatibility.[43]

Antifraternity newspapers in the late 1870s and early 1880s, suggested that the rushing process, or "roping in," as the process of trying to quickly secure the best members of the incoming class was called, made it too difficult for fraternities to realistically select compatible freshman members. These papers argued that fraternities should not rush until the second semester. By 1928, this was actually the official practice of the Greek organizations on campus.[44] In the case of Zeta Psi, while the fraternity added a number of freshmen each year, there is ample evidence that they also recruited men throughout their college careers. In particular, the fraternity recruited senior classmen during the years when, for whatever reason, that house would have otherwise lacked members of that class. For instance, the 1892 *Blue and Gold* showed that Zeta Psi had no senior members, but both Zeta Psi's registers and the panels show that Henry Beatty Denson and Walter Reno Hannah joined the fraternity that year as seniors.[45] Because of the age-grade hierarchy, having a house without senior members would have meant having a family without a symbolic head. Adding men at such a late date in their college career ensured the health of the house. Given seniors' high status both on campus and in the house hierarchy, these had to be men well thought of by the rest of the brotherhood.

An 1873 article about secret societies in the *University Echo* (presumably written by one or more of the Zete editors) states the philosophy of fraternal selection: "Through his fraternity he comes into intimate relations with those of congenial nature to himself, for if they were not, either he would not join them, or they would refuse to admit him."[46]

The book *For the Blue and Gold* describes rushing during the 1890s. After proving himself an able football player, the protagonist, James Rawson, is invited to "Gamma Delta Epsilon" on Bancroft. Though Rawson seems unaware of it, he is being rushed. He is shown the admirable house and its furnishings, and, as a guest, he is served first at the dinner table. He is shown the rooms of the house, including the bedrooms. Then the billiards table is moved out of the way and a keg of beer is rolled in. At the height of festivities, the house calls for a toast to Jim. He leaves the fraternity house with warm feelings of regard for the fraternity men. While the novel's author, Joy Lichtenstein, gives plenty of space to the popular antifraternity arguments of the time, he also clearly is taken with the romance of what fraternities are supposed to represent—. Rawson states, "They struck me as a mighty fine lot of boys—gentlemen, all of them. It's an ideal sort of life those fellows live there— they're just like brothers."[47]

While fraternities were to instill a sense of fictive brotherhood in their members, consanguineal brotherhood was also an important factor in the selection of fraternity brothers. While descending kin (fathers, sons, grandsons, uncles, nephews, cousins) become a contributing source of legacy members later, in the early days of Zeta Psi the most likely kinship relationship between fraternal brothers was blood brotherhood. The Whitworths, Mailliards, Budds, Fairbankses, Meeks, Stillmans, McGillivrays, and Sherwoods were families who contributed multiple brothers to the fraternity. George Ainsworth led extended-family members to the Zetes: his brothers-in-law, John and Albert Sutton. Joseph Mailliard brought both his brother, John, and his cousin Elliot McAllister into the fraternity.

Legacies of this type, while not forming the majority of the pledges, were a significant proportion of the fraternal population through time. Between the years of 1870 and 1880, out of sixty-eight fraternity members who graduated, twelve identified as having relatives in Zeta Psi (almost 18 percent). In the period from 1881 to 1890, sixteen of sixty-eight registered entrants to the fraternity (23.5 percent) listed relatives in Zeta Psi; and finally, during the period from 1891 to 1900, a period when membership in the fraternity was dropping, fifteen of fifty-eight graduates who were members of the fraternity had family members in the fraternity (26 percent). The numbers of brothers who had other family members in the fraternity would contribute to the aura of exclusivity surrounding fraternities and would prompt the accusation that they were undemocratic institutions.[48]

In at least four cases, according to the 1899 register of Zeta Psi, brotherhood in Zeta Psi seems to have led to additional bonds of brotherhood. The 1894 marriage of Albert Sutton (class of 1889) and Ethel Fidelia Meek made Albert an in-law of William (class of 1888) and Horry Meek (class of 1877). In 1898, Caius Tacitus Ryland (class of 1891) married Agnes Duhring, the sister of Frederick Thomas Duhring (class of 1889). Neither of these young ladies appear in the student rolls at Cal and so must have met their future husbands through their brothers. The bride of Arthur Cross (1887), Elsie Chalip Pheby, whom he married in 1893, was sister to his fraternity brothers Frederick Pheby (1893) and I. B. Pheby (1895). Frederick Willis (1890) married Annie Mabel Rideout, who, given her distinctive last name, must have been related to his Zete brother Norman Rideout (1882). No doubt there were more intermarriages. Through time, then, the fictive family tree of fraternity genealogy came to intersect at points with biological genealogy.[49]

Even though the 1899 register of Zeta Psi provides only four instances of intermarriage between fraternity men's families during the 1870–1903 period (and note that many men from the classes of the mid-1890s onward were not yet married when this register was compiled), it is still reasonable to think that one of the advantages of membership in the fraternity was the opportunity to meet appropriate marriage partners. Co-eds were not necessarily seen as appropriate matches for the fraternity men. There is little evidence of intermarriage between Zetes and university women during the occupation of the first house.

To illustrate my point, I have evidence of three fraternity brothers marrying co-eds. A comparison of wives' names listed in the Zeta Psi register with the 1905 *Alumni Association Register* from the University of California identified two coed wives. J. E. Frick, who himself failed to graduate from the university, married his classmate Nannie Northrup Ridge, graduate of the class of 1883. Some Zetes may have met their brides at the university and married them before graduation. If this were the case, I'd be able to identify the couples only through other means. This is the case for John Elliot Budd (1874), who married Mary Haste (1878). The couple wed in 1876, well before Mary would have completed her course of education. I know of this marriage only because of a cartoon in the 1882 *Blue and Gold* captioned, "The Advantages of Co-education," which shows a bridal couple along with a list of names and class years. The final marriage I've identified between a Zete and a Cal alumna falls outside the expected pattern. J. N. LeConte, Zete class of 1891, who later became a professor of mechanical engineering at the university, married Helen Marion Gumpertz, class of 1884. In this case, the difference in years between their degrees suggests they did not meet as students at Cal. LeConte's father served as president of the university, and it is tempting to wonder whether the couple met through that connection. For the most part, whatever qualities Zete men were looking for in a marriage partner, these did not include "college graduate."[50]

Even though the fraternity brothers' ranks may have included kin, the object of fraternity was to create a new family that had both lateral and vertical dimensions. Items from the *University Echo* refer to Zete alumni returning to the house to visit, and to dinner parties attended by active and alumni members, which were held at various restaurants. Photographs from a Zete scrapbook from the early 1890s demonstrate that on occasion mixed-age groups of men dined and toasted together in the first fraternity house. In *The Blue and Gold* yearbooks published during the occupation of the first house, it was common for many of the fraternities to list their "Fraters in Urbanes," which indicated those brothers who were still locally situated and involved in the fraternity house's life.

Zete alumni were well represented in the early faculty of the university. Leander L. Hawkins (1873) was hired to teach civil engineering, and George C. Edwards was hired as an instructor in mathematics, eventually rising to the level of associate professor. The latter remained active on the campus until his death in 1930. Joseph Rowell was hired in 1875 to serve as the university librarian. These were men of high visibility who were resources for the fraternity brothers not only as alumni but also as insiders in the university hierarchy. Over time, the "Fraters in Urbanes" list also became a way of demonstrating prestige. When John Budd became governor of California, he was listed in the yearbook as "Frater in Gubernatoris."[51]

The presence of alumni in the house at regular intervals would have done much to create a sense of vertical, or generational, genealogies in the house. Mandatory attendance at meals, too, may have contributed a sense of continuity. Joining together over food and drink provided an opportunity for storytelling. The exploits of past brothers could be shared for the benefit of all present and would create camaraderie and a sense of shared experience. In the 1912 edition of *The Blue and Gold*, George Edwards was invited to contribute reminiscences about the early days of the university.

Notably, he included includes in his piece an extended story about L. L. Hawkins's travels to the university—a story that involves breaking in a wild horse to arrive in time for entrance exams. He tells the story as if he had been there, and one has to wonder how many times he had heard it over a companionable stein of beer.[52]

PLANKS

The brothers of Zeta Psi recorded their genealogy in a physical way, too, on the very flesh of their house: the redwood planks bearing initiates' names. After comparing the dates on the planks with *Blue and Gold* yearbooks and the Zeta Psi registers, I concluded that the dates on the planks represent the years that the brothers were to graduate based on when they entered the university. In a number of cases, these years did not correspond to the actual year the student graduated—that is, if he did graduate. This means that, at any time, names could be added to at least four planks in any given year.

When I first identified these planks, I wondered when the brothers began posting them—was this a tradition that started in the second house, where the planks were found, or had the tradition begun earlier? Alumni from the 1920s, 1930s, and 1940s remembered that the planks had been added to each year, so I knew that the tradition was in place during the life of the second house. A few of the older alumni seemed to remember hearing that these planks had been taken from the first house and moved to the second. However, it was possible that the planks had been made for the second house—that previous brothers' names had been engraved on them by year, and that the brothers simply added names yearly after that.[53] But evidence suggests that these planks predate the 1910 house. Consider the drawing of a number of the planks we found (figure 8).

The first panel we have dates to 1873, which predates the first house by three years. Each year that corresponds to the occupation of the first house is on its own plank. At some point, all the planks were apparently inscribed with a pledge year. Years corresponding to the occupation of the second house appear inscribed lower on the planks below the set of earlier dates and names. Imagine a plank-walled room, where each year a new set of names is added to a new plank—until lists of names completely circle the room—and then a new set of names is added below the earlier set. If all the planks had been made for the second house, and previous brothers' names had been engraved on them by year, a more reasonable approach would have been to fill planks with consecutive years and then leave blank planks to be added to in the future. Further, as mentioned before, the planks do not completely correspond to official Zeta Psi national registers of members. If the planks

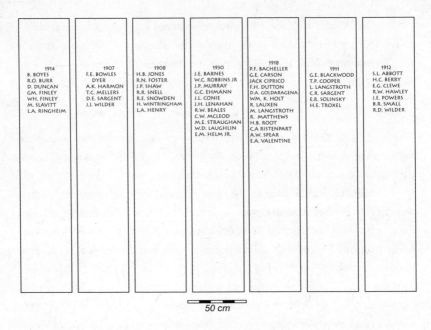

1914	1907	1908	1930	1918	1911	1912
B. BOYES	F.E. BOWLES	H.B. JONES	J.E. BARNES	P.F. BACHELLER	G.E. BLACKWOOD	S.L. ABBOTT
R.O. BURR	DYER	R.N. FOSTER	W.C. ROBBINS JR	G.E. CARSON	T.P. COOPER	H.C. BERRY
D. DUNCAN	A.K. HARMON	J.P. SHAW	J.P. MURRAY	JACK CIPRICO	L. LANGSTROTH	E.G. CLEWE
GM. FINLEY	T.C. MELLERS	R.R. SNELL	G.C. EHMANN	F.H. DUTTON	C.R. SARGENT	R.W. HAWLEY
WH. FINLEY	D.E. SARGENT	R.E. SNOWDEN	J.L. CONIE	D.A. GOLDARAGENA	E.R. SOLINSKY	J.E. POWERS
M. SLAVITT	J.J. WILDER	H. WINTRINGHAM	J.H. LENAHAN	WM. K. HOLT	H.E. TROXEL	B.R. SMALL
L.A. RINGHEIM		L.A. HENRY	R.W. BEALES	R. LAUXEN		R.D. WILDER
			C.W. MCLEOD	M. LANGSTROTH		
			M.E. STRAUGHAN	H.B. ROOT		
			W.D. LAUGHLIN	C.A RISTENPART		
			E.M. HELM JR.	A.W. SPEAR		
				E.A. VALENTINE		

50 cm

FIGURE 8

Zeta Psi pledge panels, as recovered from the basement of
the second Zeta Psi house.

were created after the move, I would expect the early years to more closely correspond to the national's lists of members. Moreover, moving the planks from the
first house to the second would have created a powerful link between the two fraternal spaces.

The planks were recovered not from the chapter room but from the party room.
This location would have been used more frequently than the chapter room, and
more casually. The planks would have provided a visual reinforcement of one's
place within the brotherhood of Zeta Psi. The current incarnation of the fraternity
still engraves pledges' names in wood—but no longer in house panels. Today, I am
told, they use wooden paddles that hang on the walls of the chapter room. One of
the mysteries that remains is why the panels were not removed from the second
house when it was abandoned. Other insignia were. Several alums expressed disgust with the way the university took over 2251 College Avenue, and suggested that
the fraternity did not leave the panels willingly. Others note that the panels were no
longer used after 1947, so perhaps they were no longer valuable to the brothers.

While ritual events like pledging and initiation were important parts of creating a fraternal identity, day-to-day ritualized activities were essential to creating a sense of brotherhood. As in any middle-class or elite household of the time, meals were ritualized events where social identities were performed and created. The dinner table was a place where civility was enacted through one's behavior and compliance with etiquette.[54]

The importance of the dining room in fraternity life is illustrated in *The Blue and Gold*, where the brothers of Zeta Psi contributed selections that referred to their shared meals. The following passage from the 1886 yearbook is a particularly fine example. It helps to read it aloud to fully understand it. Its humor is accentuated when one knows that a number of Zetes through the years had trouble with their German language requirement. | 🛈 |

"Zeta Psi Linguistische Geseffschaft." Organized by Zetes hungering and thirsting after both victuals and de beauties of de Sherman Lideradore. Meetings held in dining room at meal times. Sample of work done.

M-K-.	"Eine outside prere gefalligst."
GENERAL CHORUS.	"Outside piece gefalligst."
K-T.	"Mein lieber, monsieur Crox, reichen sie mir die, -das –le, oh hang it. Cross, hand me the spuds."
H-D.	"Iche habe Houte Fraulein Kuszmich—quick gemashed; Sie ist ein disy."
S-TT-N.	"Oh, mon ami! Sin joken, sie hat on mich gesmiled."
R-S-.	"Oh Shutzaen sie auf, and geben sie mir die gravy."
V-L-.	"Mein lieber shanks, please passez moi le vinegre."
G-N-JA.	"Monsieur, Ich danke."
M-K-.	(waking up) "Who said I was a donkey?"
C-S.	"Please pass the pep-"
R-S.	"Sprechen sie Deutsch, or you won't get anything."
D-G.	(to the cook, in stentorian tones) "Garcon, here. Oh, ich beg your pardon Madamoiselle! Oh shucks, she's Mrs.— Bringen sie some s-il vous plait, thé."
COOK.	(blank with astonishment) We haint got no silver plated tea, Mr. D-g." (withdraws in disgust)[55]

Archaeologists have extensively studied the material culture of nineteenth-century dining—in the houses of urban and rural populations, in institutions, and in households of every socioeconomic and ethnic status. What we have learned is that certain norms shaped, to varying degrees, the kinds of tableware seen as appropriate for particular occasions. During the last third of the nineteenth century, white-bodied, minimally decorated ceramics were especially popular.

There are several reasons these wares were commonly used. That they were relatively inexpensive compared to decorated vessels certainly was a factor for some families. Some historians of diet suggest that the shift from family-style dining to service à la russe may have played a part—after all, if your food is brought to you already on the plate, there is little need for a fancy decoration covering the center of the plate. Ceramics decorated with gold bands, transfer prints, or decalcomanias (at the very end of the century) most often feature white centers and decorated rims. Still others suggest that the plain white ceramics nicely presented the values of simplicity, purity, and cleanliness, which became so important in the domestic sphere—first with the flowering of the cult of true womanhood, and then as domestic science promised to make mothers into managers. I also wonder if the simplicity of these ceramics fit into the populist movements of the late nineteenth century and the nation's accompanying obsession with maintaining democratic values.[56]

The properly set table also had meaning for our civilized man. It represented order, rather than chaos, and the influence of civilizing forces. Any archaeologist who has worked on British colonial sites can tell you that, even in sites in the middle of "darkest Africa" or some other location that could have threatened an Englishman's innate character as a civilized being, you will find British ceramics. When disorder threatened, a civilized table setting could hold off barbarism. In *Peter Pan*'s fourth act, as the Indians stand guard above Peter's house, Wendy and the Lost Boys are seated at the table, having dinner.[57]

There is some evidence that the comforts of a civilized table were appreciated by our men. Zete Joseph N. LeConte ('91) kept a diary of his 1889 geological expedition with his father, Joseph LeConte, geologist and beloved Cal professor, to Yosemite. During their trip, they were invited to dine with a Judge Garber at Stoneman House, a fine hotel. This invitation pleased but also horrified them—they had no appropriate dress.

We were indeed a desperate looking set as we mounted the steps of the Stone-man House, and made our way through the staring tourists. Each was dressed in a loose flannel shirt with a handkerchief around the neck, a decayed hat and a ferocious looking knife at the belt. We went into the parlor and cautiously sat down on some magnificent chairs and sofas. Soon Judge Garber came in and greeted us heartily and then Mrs. Garber and Miss Garber came and were introduced. . . . It was an agreeable thing to get once more amongst nice refined people after knocking about so long in the mountains.[58]

Keeping in mind that this civilized discourse took place at the dinner table, we can extrapolate that civilized manhood willingly cooperated with and co-opted women's practice of organizing the table.

A woman who set her table with white ceramics was demonstrating her role as keeper of her family's moral and physical well-being (and of course, the two were intrinsically entwined, with cleanliness brushing against Godliness). The use of matched sets demonstrated the unity of the family. Families may have differed in how or whether they chose to participate in replicating these societal values and ideals, but archaeological efforts throughout the country have demonstrated that it was a rare household that did not include these ceramics. In well-to-do households, the plain wares were often just one of several sets of ceramics used by the family. Porcelain tea sets and dining services reserved for special occasions or entertaining would be found in the china cabinet next to plain wares.

Plain or *simple* does not necessarily mean inexpensive. Fine English semivitrified wares were the choice of many middle-income families, while white German, English, or French porcelains graced the tables of wealthier families. American wares, fired at lower temperatures, and therefore more susceptible to crazing and staining, were, by economic necessity, the choice of less well-to-do families. The Sears catalogs of the late nineteenth century reified these distinctions, urging consumers to splurge on the finer imported wares.[59] Perhaps the use of similar-looking ceramics across socioeconomic boundaries created a comfortable illusion of equality at a time when the disparity in wealth between the richest and the poorest was growing. Whatever the reason, any woman setting up house would be sure to have a set of plain ceramics.

The table of the first Zeta Psi house was no different than what one would expect from any other middle-class home. Only a small number of ceramics were recovered from this occupation—a measure of the small area that was preserved archaeologically. Several hundred sherds representing a minimum of twenty-nine ceramic vessels were recovered from 8 square meters of excavation. Among the excavated ceramics was a wide range of vessels, most of them tablewares (table 4). The most common tablewares were plain white semivitrified vessels. While all

TABLE 4　Ceramics recovered from the first Zeta Psi house

Vessel form	Ware type	Decoration	Number
Bowl	Porcelain	Hand-painted	1
Bowl	Ironstone	Plain	1
Bowl	Ironstone	Plain	1
Bowl	Ironstone	Decalcomania	1
Bowl	Whiteware	Plain	1
Plate	Ironstone	Plain	2
Plate	Ironstone	Gray transfer-print	1
Plate	Ironstone	Green transfer print	1
Plate	Whiteware	Undecorated	1
Platter	Ironstone	Plain	1
Teacup	Porcelain	Plain	1
Teacup	Ironstone	Plain	2
Saucer	Ironstone	Embossed	1
Saucer	Whiteware	Pink luster	1
Mug	Ironstone	Plain	1
Butter pat	Ironstone	Plain	1
Beer stein	Gray stoneware	Undecorated	1
Teapot	Yellowware	Rockingham	1
Bowl	Pressed glass	Unidentified	4
Mixing bowl	Yellowware	Plain	1
Chamber pot	Ironstone	Plain	1
Flowerpot	Terra cotta	Plain	1
Figurine	Bisque porcelain	Plain	1
Vase	Whiteware	Art pottery	1
Gin bottle	Brown stoneware	Slip decorated	1
Stout bottle	Gray stoneware	Bristol glazed	1

were plain, at least two, possibly three, different sets were represented among the ceramics.

As I noted earlier, no more than twenty men lived in the first chapter house at a time, and during the last days of the house, the average was about ten. Since brothers dined together, we might expect that the house had, at a bare minimum, twenty place settings, but more likely a minimum of twenty-four to thirty place settings, which would accommodate visitors. Depending on breakage rates in the house, a set of china could last for some time, with broken pieces replaced, or the set supplemented, as needed. The men were using a range of vessel forms that situated them within genteel culture. In addition to plates, bowls, teacups, saucers, and mugs, we recovered sherds from a service bowl, a platter, and a butter pat.

I would also expect that some number of ceramics would have come to the fraternity through individual brothers' small contributions. It is easy to imagine generations of brothers abandoning odd ceramic pieces or cutlery to the household kitchen rather than taking them away after graduation.[60]

In another context, the miscellaneous and mismatched ceramics could be interpreted as evidence of a household that could not afford a more fashionable, matched set. Instead, I think we have a small sample of a ceramic assemblage that would be characterized by a single dining set (supplemented when necessary) and an eclectic bunch of additional vessels. As we will see from photographic evidence, the fraternity did have a matched set of plain white tableware, at least in the early 1900s.

Now, let us turn to a photograph taken in the first fraternity house. We see a number of the men surrounding a table (figure 9). By the glazed looks on a few faces, it has been either a late night or a festive one or both. The mixed ages of the diners suggest that several alumni have returned, though I cannot identify them. Note the tableware: white ceramics, underscoring the purity and sanctity of the hearth, graced the fraternal table. In addition, you can see that, despite the beautiful German tankards encircling the railing of the dining room, most of the men are drinking out of plain, matching, stoneware mugs. A few of the older men seem to have tankards in their hands. We can also see a number of saltshakers and a metal (probably silver or silver plate) covered butter dish. Stemware sits on the table, as do plates and bowls of cheese and bread. It is tempting to identify the two men at the head of the table with the pipes in their mouths as senior members of the fraternity—since pipe smoking was a privilege of senior men on campus.

A reading of the photograph, I would suggest, indicates that the men holding the plain mugs are the active members of the fraternity. Use of identical white ceramics would reinforce the bonds of brotherhood between men who occupied the house together. They may later return to the home as brothers once they are alumni, but the relationship will never be the same—it cannot be the same—between them and the actives as it was with their own family of brothers. Fraternities and other secret societies were constantly plagued with the label *undemocratic*. Yet using plain,

FIGURE 9
Dining room of the first Zeta Psi house, circa 1892. Photograph
courtesy of the Bancroft Library.

simple wares drew attention away from individualism and instead focused on values
of community. (The fraternal crest of Zeta Psi apparently embodies this as well. I am
told that the four parts of the crest represent one's movement through life as a Zeta
member, with one's obligations as an alumnus being incorporated into the symbols of
the crest.)

Ceramics in the fraternity were used the same way that they were in other middle-
class households—to reinforce the sanctity of home and family through the symbol
of purity as embodied in the white ceramics. The brothers of Zeta Psi created their
sense of brotherhood at the table, the same way their mothers would have created a
sense of family for them in their homes. Although a small sample, the archaeological
materials recovered from the first house show there were other ceramics available. So
I reiterate: it is my opinion that the ceramics were used to express a sense of family
and communion at the fraternity dining table, and in doing so, they reinforced bonds
of brotherhood between the men.

A final note on ceramics, for now: while the fraternity may have been using
ceramics to express a sense of family, they do not seem to have been using their

ceramics to express the wealth or prestige of their fraternity. We have a range of documentary evidence to suggest that the Zetes were seen as one of the wealthier or more ostentatious fraternities on campus. If this had extended to the dinner table, I would have expected to see more evidence of this, even in our relatively small sample. While the semivitrified plain ceramics found at the site were more expensive than American or even British white earthenwares, they do not make much of a socioeconomic statement. In fact, since the semivitrified wares were fired at a higher temperature, they were stronger than comparable white earthenwares and more likely to survive the rigors of fraternity life.

THE FAMILIAL CONSUMPTION OF BEER

Fraternities may have the greatest reputation among college students for alcohol consumption, but in reality all of Cal's first students were notorious for their drinking. An 1877 letter from Berkeley resident John Chart to the regents of the University of California complained about the use of intoxicating beverages by Cal students. He accused the students of purchasing alcoholic beverages in San Francisco, Oakland, and Temescal.

> We may safely attribute to the immoderate use of strong drink as the main
> cause of the numerous complaints against them. This is the fostering parent of
> all mischiefs and injury to private property around Berkeley. . . . They order
> beer by the keg and whiskey also brought here, and their greatest revelries have
> taken place on University grounds. Have I not seen them, with the kegs around
> a bon fire, in various degrees of intoxication (except dead drunk) and each try-
> ing to make more noise than the other according to the strength of his lungs.[61]

Alcohol played a role in fraternity life. "Beer busts" were an integral part of the social life of the fraternity and, apparently, the rush experience. If we look again at the early-1900s table scene (figure 9), it is clear that the beverage in the brothers' mugs was beer, probably stout or porter, based on the color. Many students today perceive beer as an appropriate route to intoxication, but for nineteenth-century European families beer was a healthful beverage, often prepared in the home, served with meals to all family members. In a world that still failed to recognize the causes of water contamination, beer was a healthful alternative to public water sources. Even the early temperance movement saw beer as an innocuous beverage. A temperance movement propaganda piece from the mid-nineteenth century illustrates a "thermometer of intemperance." At the top of the thermometer were healthful and temperate beverages like water, lemonade, and weak tea, while at the bottom were the worst of the intoxicating beverages, such as peppered rum. The range of beverages that fell between were appropriately ranked on the thermometer. In the illustration, both weak and strong beers are above the threat of intemperance.[62]

The Blue and Gold often featured advertisements for saloons or restaurants, including the Pabst Café in Oakland, which described itself as a "Restaurant and Family Resort" featuring Pabst Milwaukee and imported beer on tap. The advertising section of the 1894 *Blue and Gold* featured an ad by Schlitz Milwaukee proclaiming, "The State Analyst of New Jersey tested a score of beers and pronounced Schlitz Beer more nutritious than milk." While not as catchy as "Drink Guinness, it's good for you," it does illustrate that beer's image differed from that of other alcoholic beverages.[63]

Only at the close of the nineteenth century, when the consumption of beer was increasingly associated with German-run saloons, did beer drinking become associated with drunkenness and poor behavior among some of the upper-class families of the East. Therefore, the consumption of beer likely had a familial as well as social connotation for our brothers.[64] Archaeological evidence from the first house included a range of artifacts related to beer consumption. Even though the assemblage was limited, it included quite a few beer-related objects. A minimum of twenty glass beer bottles and one ceramic stout or ale bottle was recovered.

The brothers apparently did not drink straight from the bottle but used steins or, as was popular with German brews, large-footed goblets. A minimum of six glass beer mugs, all variations on the German-style thumbprint mug, and a grey stoneware Stein, were recovered, as were a minimum of five goblets (figure 10). While drinking out of a mug or stein may seem genteel, in the world of unfiltered bottled beers, controlled pouring from a bottle into a drinking vessel would have saved the drinker from muddying his beer with sediment. Moreover, at that time, as now, kegs were popular containers for beer and would have necessitated drinking vessels.

It may have struck the reader as remarkable that, out of a minimum of twenty-three ceramic and glass tableware vessels for food consumption recovered, a minimum of twelve vessels related to beer consumption were found. When one considers that an additional seven tumblers were found at the house, it would seem that the brothers were drinking many of their daily calories (table 5). In instances like this, archaeologists like to talk about site formation processes—or how things get to be where they are found. Remember where these artifacts were recovered—from

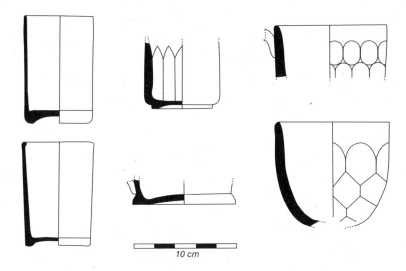

10 cm

FIGURE 10
Examples of drinking vessels recovered during excavations of
the first Zeta Psi house.

the area surrounding the front porch. Photographs of the 1876 house show that it
had a roomy porch with a very large set of front steps—steps that are featured in
many photographs with the brothers assembled on them. The front porch would
have been a pleasant place to convene and share a brotherly beverage, and an unlikely place to bring one's dinnerware. So, while the materials recovered do tell
us about life in the house, they tell us even more about some of the ways the porch
was used.

Beer was not the only beverage consumed by the brothers. A lone soda bottle
was recovered, as were two jugs for milk. A minimum of twelve wine bottles, seven
liquor bottles, four whiskey flasks, and one stoneware bottle that once contained
Amsterdam gin were found. Even if we exclude the beer bottles as examples of intoxicating beverage consumption, it is clear that our brothers spent some time at the
bottom of the temperance thermometer.

I should point out that nineteenth-century alcohol consumption occurred at a
different scale than in the twenty-first century. Estimates for pre-Prohibition America place average consumption of hard liquor at 2.6 gallons per capita per annum in
the years from 1906 to 1910, as compared with around 2.24 gallons per capita per
annum today. These numbers do not include the large number of alcohol-based
nostrums that were still popularly used despite increased regulation. When you

TABLE 5   Glassware recovered from the first Zeta Psi house

Vessel form	Material	Decoration	Number
Beer stein	Pressed glass	Thumbprint	4
Goblet	Pressed glass	Sunburst	1
Goblet	Pressed glass	Thumbprint	1
Goblet	Pressed glass	Grapevine	1
Goblet	Pressed glass	Bull's-eye	1
Goblet	Pressed glass	Unidentified	1
Tumbler	Pressed glass	Commercial	7
Soda bottle	Glass	None	1
Beer bottle	Glass	None	20
Wine bottle	Glass	None	12
Liquor (brandy, bitters type)	Glass	None	7
Whisky flask	Glass	None	4
Milk bottle	Glass	None	2
Vase	Pressed glass	"Cut"	2
Lamp chimney	Blown glass		5
Medicine bottle	Blown glass		16
Toiletry	Blown glass		6
Mason jar	Blown glass		6
Jars	Blown glass		8
Food container	Blown glass		4

consider that we recovered evidence of barely enough alcohol to supply a household of twenty men of moderate consumption for a fifteen-week semester, it would be difficult to argue that the evidence demonstrates that the fraternity was a den of vice. Instead, I can assert only that they were clearly not teetotalers.[65]

OTHER SIGNS OF CIVILIZATION

Certain aspects of the fraternity's home life were explicitly engaged in the creation of a sense of brotherhood, but other parts of daily routines and furnishings address the kind of manhood privileged in the fraternity setting. In other words, they are marks of civilization. The household assemblage contained several highly decorative lamp chimneys, at least two made of deep green glass, one rose-colored one, and several made of milk glass. These likely sat on refined-looking oil lamps or electrical candles. Two glass vases and one ceramic pottery vase were also found. A parian, or bisque porcelain, figurine, popular in Victorian homes of the times, was among the brothers' discarded belongings.[66]

As was fitting of men of their time, the brothers paid attention to their appearance, as evidenced by the recovery of gold-plated brass buttons and porcelain cuff links. The Waterbury button company made one particularly ornate example found. Toiletry bottles, fragments of a bone toothbrush, and ointment jars of the type that often contained deodorant attest to a certain concern about one's appearance.

Germ theory was the dominant medical paradigm of the time , and as a result the sanitation movement dominated discussions of public and personal health and hygiene. Differing standards of hygiene were not just a matter of personal choice but were potentially dangerous to others. A Mrs. Hickox of Berkeley attempted to divorce her husband for his lack of personal hygiene. Her husband apparently went for weeks without washing his face and for months without bathing. Her request for a divorce was denied. While her husband was a former Cal student, he was not a Zete.[67]

Medicines believed to defeat all germs were particularly popular. While I can say little about specific products used in the first fraternity house, the artifactual remains suggest that the brothers tended their health with a range of nationally marketed drugs and pharmaceuticals from local druggists. At least one homeopathic medicine vial was recovered, demonstrating that the men were open to alternative medical ideas. Given that fraternities were accused of instilling members with the inability to think for themselves, this evidence of diverse subject positions relative to health care is refreshing. The one brand-name medicinal product identified was Bromo-Seltzer, a headache cure manufactured in Baltimore and packaged in a distinctive cobalt blue bottle. In the second Zete house, where this product was very popular, its use may have been related more to relieving hangovers than to the stresses of studying. You may have noted that I have not described the recovery of any artifacts related to studying or student life. As I explain in the next chapter, evidence suggests that classes of Zetes went for years without studying.

AS THE ACT ENDS . . .

So what can we say about the men of Zeta Psi at this point? They lived together in a house on the edge of Never Land, but the taint of civilization still marked them as recently escaped from the nursery, rather than as true Lost Boys. They experienced their fraternal life through practices shaped by the households of their mothers: They dined together on respectable, if not expensive, tableware. They brushed their teeth, buttoned their jackets, and sat outside on the porch to drink their beer. Even as they begin to shrug off the trappings of civilization in the 1890s, the material world of their civilized forebears of the 1870s and 1880s shaped their day-to-day lives as they continued to host the older brothers in the same ways, in the same spaces, as previous generations of brothers had. Still, as we will see, outside the house, and in some cases inside it, they presented a public face to Never Land that spoke of their increasingly uncivilized ways.

PROGRAM FOR ACT II

The stage emerges from blackness with a view of the island of Never Land, complete with vistas of an Indian village, pirate ship, and mermaid lagoon. Peter's underground house sits at the center of this island, and it is here the audience's attention is drawn. Seven great hollow trees form entrances to the house—one entrance for each boy. The six Lost Boys, Curly, Tootles, Slightly, Nibs, First Twin, and Second Twin, wearing clothing made of skins and plants, emerge from the house, awaiting Peter's return. They gossip and wrestle as boys do, until they hear the pirates and scurry onto the limbs of a tree. Captain Hook and his men catch sight of Slightly but decide not to pursue him. Hook, as it transpires, sees Peter as his great nemesis: it was Peter who caused him to have a hook instead of a hand. A crocodile swallowed Hook's hand, as well as a clock, and the monster's approach is signaled by the sound of ticking. Peter also instilled in the crocodile a taste for pirate captain. Hook recognizes the house's chimney and plots the merry band's demise. The pirates leave; the boys fret.

Soon their attention is drawn by a strange "bird" in the sky, a large white creature that flaps its arms wearily and says over and over, "Poor Wendy, poor Wendy." Tinkerbell decides to use the Lost Boys' ignorance to her advantage against her presumed rival and tells them that Peter wants the "bird" shot. Tootles obliges, but when they examine the body they realize that they have killed a young lady. Peter arrives and finds Wendy with an arrow apparently through her heart. As he prepares to kill Tootles for his crime, he discovers that Wendy, though unconscious, lives— an acorn Peter gave her has blocked the arrow's blow. Peter sends Tinkerbell away in anger and organizes the Lost Boys to build a house around Wendy. Wendy eventually emerges from the house, recovered, and is declared the Lost Boys' "mother." The act ends with Wendy welcoming the children into her house for a washing and a bedtime story.

ACT II · The Never Land

The Fraternity and the University to 1910

> This is Never Land come true. It is an open air scene, a
> forest, with a beautiful lagoon beyond, but not really far
> away, for the Never Land is very compact, not large and
> sprawly with tedious distances between one adventure
> and another, but nicely crammed.
>
> *Peter Pan*

> Daddy wouldn't give me the dough-dough, dough-dough,
> Daddy wouldn't give me the dough-dough,
> I want to be a Zete
> and stay out very late,
> But Daddy wouldn't give me the dough-dough.
>
> A taunting lyric about Zeta Psi's exclusiveness,
> in *The Blue and Gold*, 1894

Within the confines of their hideout, the men of Zeta Psi created a sense of brotherhood and community, but a broader world and community lay beyond their
house. The house was a space where they would begin to slay the feminizing influences on their domesticity, just as the Lost Boys shot Wendy. Never Land is both a
time and place. Never Land represents that space where one can escape, for a time,
the responsibilities of adulthood, where the inhabitants occupy a liminal social position. In the Never Land that was the University of California, students avoided
growing up and created a cultural world and social geography unique to the campus. Yet, just as Peter traveled to London to hear new stories, the Never Land of the
University of California was always connected, always influenced, by the greater
world beyond it. Peter's Never Land was populated by pirates, Indians, fairies, and
mermaids. The pirates were always the adversaries of his tribe, the Indians' loyalty
could swing in either direction, and the fairies and mermaids were exotic and potentially dangerous creatures. Each group had its counterpart in the university
world. The administrators were pirates who routinely sought to interfere with the
Lost Boys. The uncivilized, uninitiated masses of the non-Greek student body
could, like the Indian tribe in its relationship with Peter, alternately emulate or

revile the fraternity men. The coeds were a diverse group whose members included mermaids, fairies, Indian princesses, and Wendys. The men of Zeta Psi saw themselves situated in the middle of this Never Land—like Peter himself—always central to the life of the place.

The college student, or more correctly, the college man, was a recognized prototype in the late nineteenth century, and still is today. While his peers may enter the workforce and take on responsibilities, the college man consciously postpones adulthood by four (and sometimes more) years. Society allows this because of the perceived benefits the educated man brings to the economic, social, and political spheres of society upon completion of his studies. Particularly for men entering the university in the nineteenth century, attending college was a privilege, not a right. The creation of an almost free public university made education accessible to a wider swath of the population than before, but it was still a very small segment that gained college degrees.[1]

In Never Land, only Peter was immortal. By associating with him, the Lost Boys were able to postpone growing up, but once beyond his protection, back in the real world, they completed the task of becoming adults. At universities the student body never ages—an endless procession of eighteen-year-olds step forward to take the places of exiting twenty-two-year-olds. Each succeeding class enacts the rituals and routines of those who came before, creating a sense of timelessness and tradition—and in Never Land, the timelessness is merely an illusion. Change is constant and ongoing.

At Cal, any number of routines and rituals marked the academic year of the late nineteenth century—the freshman rush, the intercampus debate, midterm examinations, the Junior Day (or Exhibition), university field days, the Bourdon Burial, the annual arrival of *The Blue and Gold* yearbook, and of course, commencement and the presentation of the University Medal to the highest achieving student.

The brothers of Zeta Psi sought to place themselves in the annual routines and traditions of the university, and thereby naturalize their position in the university hierarchy, to make it seem inevitable that, if something of interest was happening, a Zete was at the center of it. A powerful desire to matter, to be meaningful, drove the men of the fraternity in productive and unproductive ways.

The men presented not one single image but one that shifted through the years, just as the broader world around the university did. During the time they occupied the first chapter house, the world changed significantly. Thomas Edison patented the first lightbulb in 1883; telephone service became widely available; the great labor strikes of the late nineteenth and early twentieth centuries unfolded; the horseless carriage—seen by many as a novelty—began to torment the roadways; the frontier was closed; and the United States conducted a brief war against Spain in the New World. For a community of young men at the threshold of adulthood, some of the most striking changes were in the nation's attitudes about what constituted manhood and masculinity. Many scholars suggest that shifts in the idea of what constituted masculinity began in the aftermath of the Civil War, but I believe that the greatest changes in white masculine performance and embodiment on the University of California campus occurred during the period from the 1880s to the beginning of World War I.[2]

MANHOOD, MASCULINITY, AND THE UNIVERSITY OF CALIFORNIA

In a brilliant book, *Houdini, Tarzan, and the Perfect Man,* John Kasson demonstrates how perceptions of white male bodies changed dramatically during this period, with the magician Houdini, the bodybuilder Eugen Sandow, and the fictional ape man Tarzan serving as archetypes of the new male prototype. White men's bodies had to embody the power and control that they exercised over other realms of social, economic, and political life. Men's intellectual superiority had to be matched with their clear physical superiority. Such shifts in ideas were compatible with the social Darwinism that increasingly infected social discourses. "Survival of the fittest" meant that white men needed to defeat other men in all realms.[3]

White manhood was under threat, of course. In the United States, emancipated African American men were not willing, despite the earnest efforts of Southern bulldozers, and despite Northern indifference, to sink quietly back into enslavement. Jack Johnson, the African American fighter, waged a one-man war against white masculinity when he won the heavyweight boxing title in 1908. Throughout the 1880s and until 1893, Native Americans actively and violently challenged the continued expansion of the United State's borders. Globally, the British saw their empire slowly chipped away through the efforts of indigenous peoples.[4]

Women were also increasingly fighting the status quo, and their quest for education, the vote, and careers outside the home drove the eugenics movement's fear that the white race would be wiped out by a combination of neglectful white Protestant women and overly reproductive Catholic and colored women. It is no surprise that Teddy Roosevelt, seen by many as the embodiment of this new hypervirile white masculinity, often played the "race suicide" card in public speeches. Yes, white men had to be visibly strong to discourage those who would seek to upend their power.[5]

Beginning with the appointment of Benjamin Ide Wheeler as university president in 1899, the masculinity movement on campus had a well-connected advocate. Wheeler was a close friend of Roosevelt, and the two traveled between Berkeley and Washington, D.C., at different times to visit. Roosevelt served as the Charter Day speaker at the 1911 annual celebration of the university's founding. A local humor magazine reported that the two regularly had boxing matches when they met, providing a cartoon showing the two (well-muscled) middle-aged men stripped to their shorts, slugging it out. In one university historian's words, Wheeler was like a "dean of men" for the male students of the university, and he actively worked to isolate the growing number of women on campus in a few small academic programs.[6]

The 1880s and 1890s were not easy times for the young University of California. As early as the mid-1870s, the Grangers (members of the National Grange of the Patrons of Husbandry) challenged the university's curriculum. The Morrill Act had explicitly mandated that the public schools it funded would train students in agriculture and mechanical arts. In the Grangers' opinion, the university's curriculum was weighted too heavily toward the arts and humanities, and so the land grant funds were clearly being diverted from their intended use—the university was better suited to turning out gentlemen than farmers, they claimed.[7] The university successfully defended itself during a second state constitutional convention, but attacks against the university were still leveled by the Grangers, by church groups who described the faculty as ungodly, and by temperance groups who accused the students of being drunken and unserious. The administrative pirates, apart from a few well-placed sympathetic alums, were an ongoing threat to the Zetes. The uninitiated "savages"—the student body—alternated between adoring and hating the fraternity men, and then there was the threat offered up by the troublesome feminine element of Never Land.

The fraternities became natural scapegoats for some of the accusations against the university, and antifraternity sentiment was particularly high in the late 1870s and early 1880s. How then, did the brothers of Zeta Psi navigate these waters of change? As we saw, their private life in the first house shows that many of their day-to-day activities depended on a material vocabulary drawn from the domestic sphere of their mothers. But a look at the fraternity's public facade shows that the new masculinity shaped the members' lives outside, and eventually, inside, the chapter house.

IMAGES OF THE FRATERNITY

Anyone wandering by the Zete house had a fair chance of seeing the brothers congregated in large or small groups together on their porch. Descriptions of the fraternity houses at Cal as late as the 1930s discuss the visibility of fraternity men outside their houses, "patrolling their grounds," as one former student put it.[8] As the first house on their road, the brothers of Zeta Psi were likely unable to anticipate that fraternity row would develop in a direction away from them.

The earliest detailed map of structures built in the area is a 1903 Sanborn Fire Insurance map. By this time, Zeta Psi was surrounded by a growing residential neighborhood and an expanding University of California campus.[9] Neighborhood homes housed faculty members, university employees, local business men, and their young families, and how these families interacted with the Zetes can only be imagined. During excavations we found several toy marbles and a toy porcelain teacup from a doll-sized set. Did the outdoor games and activities at the fraternity house draw the attention of neighborhood children? Based on the number of siblings who joined the fraternity, the brothers of Zeta Psi were drawn from families with many children. While marbles are not limited to child's play, the toy teacup suggests child-sized actors. Did neighborhood children remind them of siblings still living at home? Did neighborhood children join the fraternity men's baseball games? Regardless of whatever other sense of community they constructed for themselves in their house, the Zetes were not isolated from other kinds of family life. If nothing else, the mixed neighborhood of faculty, university staff, families, and other fraternities that developed in the neighborhood indicates that college students were not seen at this time as natural sources of noise and blight—or at least, no more so than anyone else. Nor were they viewed as a negative force that families should be protected from.

At this time another neighbor was enlarging its presence in the vicinity. The university had begun expanding its borders through a slow, insidious creep. Hearst Hall, the University Bathhouse, and the women's basketball court had been built on the university's side of College Avenue by 1903. The university football stadium was also conveniently located for the Zete men (figure 11). While none of these buildings were directly across from the Zete house, the open views of the Golden Gate that the Zetes once enjoyed from their porch would have been filtered through campus buildings. Their house was now being drawn into the campus itself and would have become a more visible landmark to those using any of the university facilities in the area. Its proximity to gathering places like the football grounds also made the house a convenient location for hosting social events for the broader university community.[10]

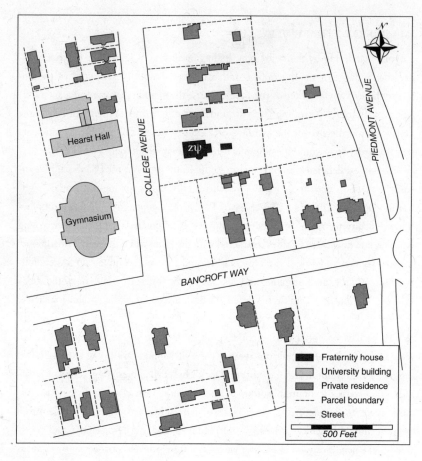

FIGURE 11
Zeta Psi's neighborhood, circa 1903. Based on Sanborn Fire
Insurance maps.

THE UNIVERSITY COMMUNITY

The performance of public identity by most Zetes would have taken place within
the university community, for it was the student body and, initially, the faculty
whom they cared to impress.[11] Perhaps our exploration of Zeta Psi's public face
should begin with a consideration of how the brothers integrated themselves into
the university population. After examining available records—mainly self-reports
recorded in *The Blue and Gold*—to find out which school activities the fraternity's
members engaged in, I divided the result into seven main categories: athletics, jour-

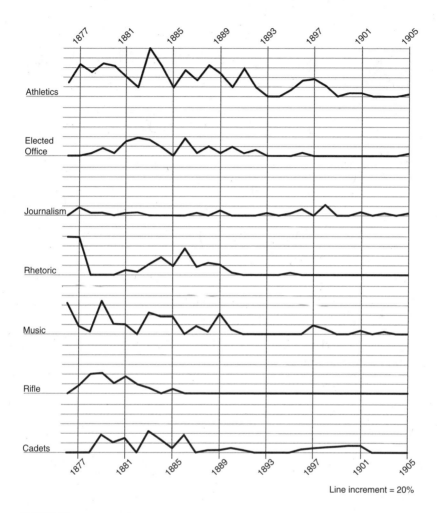

FIGURE 12

Graph of Zeta Psi brothers' participation in campus activities.

nalism, elected office, debate, music and drama, military training (as cadets), and rifle club.³ I calculated the percentage of Zeta Psi men involved in each of the activities on a year-by-year basis. More Zetes participated in athletics than in any other extracurricular activity, and we will look at this particular arena separately.

While the choice of extracurricular activities forms an arena in which to create a public face for the fraternity, it also represents the interests and pursuits of the individuals of the house, so it is important to look at the evidence from both of these angles. The best way to approach this data is graphically (figure 12). Plotting the

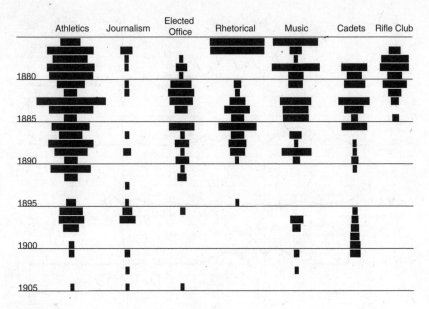

FIGURE 13
Battleship curve representation of Zeta Psi brothers' participation
in campus activities.

activities against one another in a line graph reveals that the data is distributed in a
series of sharp peaks and drops. In fact, the graph looks a bit like a child's representation of a mountain range. If we look at the data another way, drawing on the tools
of archaeology (explicitly, frequency seriation) to construct battleship curves to indicate the rise and fall of particular activities relative to one another, the pattern of
the men's movement from one social activity to another becomes clear (figure 13).
Remember, each brother could engage in multiple school activities, so shifts in
popularity of one particular activity relative to others is not just a representation of
the men deciding against one activity or another.

   The intervals between peaks tell us that the cycles lasted about three to four
years—about the length of the average college career. It is not quite this simple. In
any given year, a new class of recruits is brought in, so there should be a muting effect, in theory, leading to less dramatic graphs. Instead, the data shows us the influence of a few people who were passionate about a particular activity. They introduced their brothers to it, resulting in a peak in participation, and when the
instigating brother·or brothers left or graduated, this produced a corresponding
decline in the popularity of that activity.

This data communicates two very important details about fraternity life. First, as modern critics and researchers of fraternity problems have suspected, there is evidence of a group mentality that shaped the brothers' behavior in the selection of extracurricular activities. At the same time, it is also clear that the brothers did not actively recruit men who replicated themselves in fraternity life. Had that been the case, the data would show a flat line indicating consistent participation levels in particular activities through time.

On a related note, because the popularity of particular activities waxes and wanes through time, there seems to be no attempt by the brothers to define themselves in the long term by their affiliation with particular activities. The brothers seem to have put into practice what they claimed to have been doing when they started the fraternity—looking for congenial men to spend time with. The brothers' decisions to participate in activities together outside the house suggest that the men of Zeta Psi did enjoy one another's company.

From the perspective of others in the university community, this behavior could be (and was) perceived another way. The flocking of the fraternity brothers to a particular activity or organization—be it running for class office or participating en mass in the rhetorical society—represented to some students the efforts of the fraternity (and later, fraternities) to control college life in a way that was decidedly undemocratic.

A CLOSER LOOK AT THE ACTIVITIES OF ZETA PSI

If we consider the activities of the Zetes collectively, we can see the marks of civilization on them. The locus of many of the activities would have been the parlor— a stage comfortable to those men still clinging to the nurturing influences of the nursery.

Music was a consistently popular activity, with Zeta Psi brothers participating in university glee clubs and quartets and arranging their own in-house quartets and orchestras. The popularity of song and music is not surprising when one considers the time period. Before phonographs and radios, playing an instrument was an important entertainment. Accomplished musicianship was also a signifier of class position.[12] While anyone might learn to play a harmonica or even rudimentary piano, to play the violin or cello, as some of the brothers did, represented another order of achievement and refinement. Photographs of the interior of the first house show the brothers gathered around a piano, enjoying drinking and singing together (figure 14).

FIGURE 14

Interior of the parlor of the first Zeta Psi house, circa 1892. Photograph courtesy of the Bancroft Library.

The university yearbooks and literary magazines include numerous songs' lyrics, and the national chapter of Zeta Psi has published its own collection of fraternity music.[13] Joining in song was a way that students came together in any number of university settings.

The rhetorical societies represent another artifact of the period. The literary societies of Harvard and Yale were said to have been the birthplace of the modern fraternities. These societies gave students the opportunity to engage one another in well-reasoned debates on pressing issues of the day.[14] In the hands of a skilled orator, words served as a sword. Articulate expression was a manly, civilized virtue, and it is no surprise that the early Zetes were drawn to it, as well as accomplished in it. Two Zetes represented the Durant Rhetorical Society in the 1877 Inter Society Debate. Their topic, which they argued in the negative, was: "Resolved that the Turkish government should be driven from Europe." They won.[15] The following year, the Durants were led to victory over the Neolean Rhetorical Society by another Zete brother. After a brief hiatus from the rhetorical society in the early 1880s, Zeta Psi continued to participate in it to some degree until 1895, by which time debating societies were less compelling to all students.[16] Not all Zetes aligned themselves with the Durant Rhetorical Society, a small number of brothers debated with the opposition. Of course, we can be cynical and suggest that brothers only joined the opposing society to plant a spy there. College life in the last quarter of the nineteenth century was characterized by much intrigue and espionage, so the possibility is certainly worth considering.

The Zetes' participation in journalism was tied directly to their involvement in the Durant Rhetorical Society, which published the monthly newspaper the *University Echo* and, later, copublished the *Berkeleyan* in conjunction with the competing Neolean Rhetorical Society.[17] The newspapers furnished an important outlet for disseminating information to the public about the fraternity's goals, achievements, and social doings. As antifraternity sentiment on campus grew, participating in publishing, whether as part of *The Blue and Gold* staff or a newspaper staff, was also a strategy for survival.

The *University Echo*, edited, as previously noted, by two of the Zete brothers (from 1871 to 1873), published some announcements related to the fraternity. These illuminate how the brothers liked to be imagined by the broader community. The brothers used the forum of the paper to explain and justify their secret society as well as report its happenings. In most cases, the small news items seem intended to incite curiosity or jealously or to cultivate an image of civility.

In January of 1873, it was announced, "the Zeta Psi fraternity gave a dinner at Temescal, November 23rd. It was a grand success in all appointments." A June 1873 announcement assured readers, "Commencement week promises to introduce a new feature in our University Life. There will be literary exercises by the Zeta Psi fraternity, and by the commencement class proper, besides the exercises of the alumni." Other news items reported a sailing trip: "Quite a number of the students, members of the Zeta Psi, together with some gentlemen from the city, took a sail lately in the fast yacht 'Minnie' at the invitation of a friend. From reports received they must have had a splendid time boating, fishing, swimming, singing, lunching, together with the necessary concomitant." Still others items mentioned banquets, poetry readings, and trips to the grand chapter meeting.[18] Collectively, these entries seem to cultivate the image of a set of glamorous, sophisticated, trend-setting bachelors living the good life.

"The Zeta Psi" as the group called itself, was clearly creating a certain image for public consumption and influencing the media in order to do so. Several motivations may have shaped their actions. First, in reporting the formation of their society, the men had lamented, "Of course, it will be impossible for many of the students to become members of this one society, but there are many others which may be started."[19] Another piece justifying secret societies in 1873 repeated a call for others to create another fraternity. Perhaps the Zeta Psis realized, even at this early date, that there was safety in numbers, that the more men involved in fraternities, the greater the difficulty their opponents would have rousting them from campus. Even Peter recruited new Lost Boys to his cause. By making fraternity life exciting, exclusive, and glamorous, the Zetes were also making it highly desirable to outsiders. This circumstance would have allowed them to continue to recruit members, but it may have also inspired the formation of other fraternities.

Ultimately, other fraternities did follow Zeta Psi on campus: Chi Phi in 1875, quickly followed by Delta Kappa Epsilon in 1876, and Beta Theta Pi in 1879.[20] With the addition of more fraternities on campus, a new dynamic entered fraternity life—competition. Each fraternity sought to distinguish itself as the most prestigious and elite. Zeta Psi was ahead of the others not only in founding but also in securing for itself a house. While the other fraternities were meeting in hotel rooms and rented housing, the Zetes enjoyed their commodious chapter house.

It is not clear what other campus members thought of the fraternities in their earliest days, and for good reason. The Zetes controlled the *University Echo* and were unlikely to publish anything negative about themselves. Zeta Psi men's heavy involvement in the Durant Rhetorical Society assured their participation in the publication of the *Berkeleyan* as well. Finally, the Zetes also helped publish *The Blue and Gold* yearbook. This allowed them to put in pieces that drew attention to both the camaraderie between the brothers and the fraternity's exclusiveness. Consider the following humorous item in the class of 1880's *Blue and Gold* about the Zeta Psi Bicycle Club:

A. L. WHITNEY. "I guess I'll get off," which he does, with more rapidity than grace.

H. A. PEARSONS. 1st small boy: "Who is that?" 2nd small boy: "Why don't you know? That's Hiram Archibald Pearsons, late of San Francisco."

P. E. BOWLES. "Say you fellows, let me go first; I can keep up better when I'm ahead."[21]

As long as they held positions on the major journalistic and literary publications of the campus, the Zetes effectively controlled media representations of themselves.

Editorship also gave the fraternity a forum for disseminating their other views. For example, the Zetes were against the temperance movement from its earliest days. The April 1871 issue of the *University Echo* ran an item on the movement's "testimonials": "Testimonials: The Public are constantly deluged with statistics in regard to the alarming amount of distress produced by indulgence in strong drink; but have the disastrous effects produced by indulgence in testimonials even been investigated?"[22] In March of 1873, the paper noted, "Some of the students have signed a temperance petition. We have been unable to find out the names of the misguided youths."[23]

Control of the media also provided a more nefarious opportunity for the fraternities. The authority of the written word has always been hard to dismiss. In November of 1872, an editorial signed by G. C. Edwards, J. Budd, and E. Parker laments "hoodlumism" on campus and condemns those involved in a recent theft of the clappers on campus. The theft had apparently made it impossible to signal the change of classes.[24] The editorial points out that this is "not a joke but a crime." Unlike in much of the writing in the paper, there is no apparent irony in the piece. Yet note these remembrances of G. C. Edwards (then an esteemed elder faculty person at Cal) in the 1912 *Blue and Gold:*

Of pranks of the small college type there were plenty. The college bell weighing some three hundred pounds was gotten down out of the belfry and hidden away to be brought out a month later and be made the motif (is that the word?) for a camp fire orgie *[sic]* on the campus. Dr. Durant's good old bossy cow, with proper persuasion, one night took up her quarters on the second floor of college hall. . . . I shall always think that the young man who first registered in the University had something to do with those affairs.[25]

The first young man to register at the university was one Clarence J. Wetmore, of Oakland, a Zeta Psi brother.[26] It is hard to believe that Clarence was able to move that bell all by himself, and most cows need persuasion from behind while one pulls at the lead. It may be hard not to laugh at these pranks, but it is also possible to see in the story how a group who controlled the media on campus could manipulate any number of circumstances to their advantage or, at the very least, raise suspicions among nonmembers.

Journalism was not the only activity that allowed the fraternity to exert a high degree of control over campus activities. From 1878 through 1883, Zetes were particularly skilled at getting themselves elected as class officers. Once the student government, the Associated Students of the University of California, was founded, Zetes continued to be represented in student affairs, although to a lesser degree than in their early days.[27]

The Zetes' steady involvement in the Battalion of University Cadets Corps in the early days of the fraternity was another means by which they controlled other campus members. All male students were required to take military courses and participate in drills and other exercises, and some of the students were commissioned.[28] Only officers were included in the corps lists printed in *The Blue and Gold*, and the inclusion of Zetes in these lists indicates they held officer positions. Commandant of the Cadet Corps for 1874 was none other than Colonel George C. Edwards, Zete class of 1873. Edwards assumed this role when hired in 1874 as a math instructor at the university.[29]

As early as 1875, Edwards was accused of exercising favoritism in the selection of officers, in an article in the *Berkeleyan*. The charges were brought before the Academic Senate, which voted to call on the editors of the *Berkeleyan* to prove their accusations. The faculty resolved, "In the opinion of the faculty, none of the charges preferred against Lt. Colonel Edwards of favoritism in his position as Commandant of the Battalion have been sustained by the evidence." The senate discussion ended with a vote of confidence in Edwards. The faculty at that time was quick to defend its ranks from opposition or insult by students. Senate records indicate that they monitored the contents of the student newspapers and demanded apologies for anything they perceived as untoward.[30]

Still, it appears that Zetes were favored in gaining officer positions. For instance, in 1877, Zetes were the highest ranking officers in four of the six companies. Another seven held other officer positions. At a time when there were only eighteen Zetes active on campus, eleven of them held officer positions in the cadets. There were, incidentally, only thirty-six of these positions.[31] In 1880, Zetes held six officer positions out of thirty-five, but four of these were the highest-ranking positions. Even members of Zeta Psi recognized that there was cause to be suspicious of the cadet selection process. In 1880, Zeta Psi members served as the editors for the *Blue and Gold*. This issue announced the University Rifle Team, which was also supervised by Colonel Edwards and, like the cadet corps, contained no small number of Zetes: seven of the fifteen members were Zetes. One could argue that Edwards exhibited a consistent favoritism toward Zetes in selecting students to participate in activities he supervised. The editors explained, "The present rifle team is selected from the best shots in the University. . . . Great care was taken to choose the best marksmen. . . . The names below were chosen in this manner: After each student had made one score, the third with highest scores again shot. From those who made the highest scores this time, ten were chosen to constitute the team, and a few others for substitutes."[32] Notably, the substitutes are not indicated, and one has to wonder how many Zetes were tacked onto the list.

Edwards left the post of commandant in 1884 and focused his attentions on building physical culture (the term was used to describe nonteam athletics, like bodybuilding and physical fitness). His departure was seen by some as an opportunity for change. The *Occident* reported in 1884, "Zeta Psi fraternity until now controlled the military department, membership was [the] only criteria." Although the head of the military department had announced there would be exams for fitness, the editors worried that the new commandant might also be "infected by Zeta Psi." Zeta Psi's profile in both the rifle club and the officers' ranks of the cadets dropped noticeably after 1885.[33]

The amount of control over campus organizations enjoyed by the Zetes, and increasingly by other competing fraternities as well, did not go unnoticed. Beginning in 1878, a new student newspaper was launched, and its critiques of the fraternity system nearly led to the dissolution of secret societies at the University of California. Zeta Psi's role in saving the fraternity system on Cal's campus became an important part of the fraternity's mythology—a great battle discussed and elaborated on through time—but I am afraid we must wait until the next act to discuss this great conflict. Please be patient, it is worth the wait.

Still, despite the growing antifraternity sentiment among some sectors on campus, the fraternities still played a major acknowledged role in many campus events. And even when they were not editing *The Blue and Gold*, the brothers of Zeta Psi were often featured in jokes and other diversions in the yearbook. In the 1893 *Blue and Gold*, for instance, a page labeled "Epitaphs" provides caricatures of different graduating students. Featured at the top of the page are three Zetes, whose close association to one another was apparently recognized in the broader campus community, as reflected in their linked epitaphs: "Edwin Mays: 'The World'; G. B. Foulks: 'The Flesh'; Fred S. Pheby: '——————.' "[34] Apparently the main interests of these three students were well known to the campus community.

Even the antifraternity forces on campus had to recognize the Zetes. This description from the *Occident*, an antifraternity paper, details the funeral procession of the 1882 Bourdon Burial:

> After saluting the President with cheers and roman candles, the procession moved on, making the night bright with their fireworks and transparencies, and hideous with the screech of their toot horns. At each of the fraternity houses, they halted and saluted with a discharge of rockets and a round of ringing cheers. The DKE house was well illuminated, the Chi Phi house had a large bonfire and much fireworks, but the display at the Zeta Psi house was a feature of the evening. Every window in the house, and the entire front, blazed with light and fire. It was an exceedingly pretty sight.[35]

Zeta Psi members apparently preferred to write about themselves in the third person in the media, but one exception to this is the 1880 volume of *The Blue and Gold*, which the fraternity published on behalf of the class of 1881. The latter had managed as a class to get themselves expelled for trying to distribute a bogus program of events for the Junior Exhibition the previous year. Zeta Psi stepped forward superficially to help the university, but mainly as a way do some public relations work following an early 1880 attempt by the regents to outlaw secret societies. The Zetes used *The Blue and Gold* as a forum to present a history of Zeta Psi that featured their version of recent events and valorized their contributions to university life.[36] It is worth citing one of the services to the university that the fraternity claimed: "That generous spirit always characteristic of the Iota, led the members to keep open house on Junior, Class and Commencement days of the year, and though the custom has drawn somewhat heavily on the purse, it has been continued ever since. On such occasions Berkeley is full of friends of the University, and although the authorities provide for their intellectual entertainment, yet other not less important hospitalities are neglected, and the efforts made by private individuals and societies to meet this want cannot be too highly commended."[37]

Part of the Zetes' mystique was clearly their wealth and hedonistic lifestyle. Their access to wealth was, as evidenced by the poem at the beginning of this chapter, noted by the rest of campus. It was viewed with a combination of jealousy and admiration. Note the bogus quote attributed to F. L. Carpenter in the following passage from the 1894 *Blue and Gold:* "F. L. Carpenter is a member of the Zeta Psi fraternity. It is well-known that the members of this Fraternity are the elite of Oakland. [Carpenter:] 'The whole bloody gang is terribly society. Gosh! They go out every night!' "[38] Not all Zetes could keep up with the pace of spending, however; Brother Henry Sabin requested an indefinite leave of absence from the university in 1884 "for financial reasons."[39]

The Zetes, by exercising some control over the media, and by recruiting individuals involved in a range of campus activities, or willing to get involved, managed to infiltrate many spaces of campus life. They cultivated an image that suggested they were central to student social life and governance. In short, the men learned how to manipulate power structures to their advantage.

MASCULINE PURSUITS

The Zetes played political games and exerted their influence through gentlemanly pursuits like debating and governance; a number of other activities they engaged in were closely tied to new ideas about masculinity. I have been discussing mainly the public face of the Zetes, but let us take a quick detour into one of the bedrooms of the fraternity house (figure 15). This photograph dates from the 1890s and is included in a scrapbook.[40] To the modern viewer, the homoerotic overtones of the photograph are probably most striking. This picture shows up in another, doctored version in the scrapbook, where the scrapbook's author makes similar observations about the pose. Remember, at the time the photograph was taken, homosexuality was not seen as a separate category of sexual identity. Homosexuality as an identity was gaining public attention only as a result of the Oscar Wilde case in England. There was no proscription against male physical affection as would become the case in the early twentieth century.[41]

As John Kasson notes in his description of reactions to the barely clothed form of the world famous and publicly idolized bodybuilder Eugen Sandow, "He [Sandow] enlarged the boundaries of the display of the male nude in live exhibitions and in

FIGURE 15

Interior of a bedroom in the first Zeta Psi house, circa 1892. Iota scrapbook, courtesy of the Bancroft Library.

photographs that elicited intense interest from women and especially from men at a time when the categories of heterosexuality and homosexuality did not squeeze so tightly as to inhibit a man's frank admiration of another man's body."[42] San Francisco had become one of the urban centers that were home to a growing gay population, and its bathhouses and public gyms were popular places for setting up liaisons. As Sanday and others have discussed, many fraternity rituals, particularly hazing associated with initiations, and phenomena like the "circle dance," have clearly homoerotic dimensions.[43] But recall that the social world of the time was homosocial—you spent your leisure (and work) time almost exclusively in the company of the same sex. Homosocial relationships could be physically intimate in ways that would be extremely uncomfortable just a few decades later.

So, if you don't focus too much on the homosocial or homoerotic friendliness of the two lads, you will observe some interesting material markers in the room. First, on the bed with the men is a southwestern-style blanket that, if not made by Native Americans, is certainly attempting to look like a Navajo rug. For many U.S. citizens, the massacre at Wounded Knee of that same year represented the official closure of the frontier.[44] By that time, the appropriation of Native American objects and images was already a popular and sentimental way to acknowledge the success of white supremacy over savagery. The perceived eradication of the "Indian threat" was intrinsically tied to the new masculinity.[45] With his traveling Wild West shows, Buffalo Bill Cody glamorized the murder of Indians and, for many, represented a powerful image of masculinity. The choice of an Indian blanket, particularly at this juncture in time, must be seen as a statement about the owner's race, gender, and nationality.

You'll note the pelt of a small animal on the brother's bookcase. Recreational hunting was a popular pastime of the new masculinity. Only a few years hence, Teddy Roosevelt would craft a public image of himself as adventurer and huntsman with carefully posed pictures of himself on hunting trips—including his (in)famous African safari adventures. Hunting became a way of testing one's primal abilities against the cunning and savagery of wild beasts—thus Teddy's refusal in 1902 to shoot a tied up bear cub. To do so would have been to emasculate himself.[46]

While our brothers did not need to hunt to feed themselves, they still hunted. From both the first and second houses, I have evidence of shotgun casings and pellets and the remains of deer, wild fowl, and raccoons. Later oral histories discuss the brothers hunting quail together in the hills behind campus. Was the pelt on the bookcase a souvenir of a kill? For the early brothers of Zeta Psi, gun toting was a normal part of life. Many of the men who came to the university in the 1870s had been raised in mining towns, on farms, or on cattle ranches, but their families had come to those areas from well-to-do East Coast families. Hunting was an established leisurely activity for the well-to-do, who did not need to eat their kills.

As California became more urbanized, shooting was transformed into a sport. In this light, the participation of several of the brothers in the rifle club takes on an additional dimension. Demonstrating one's prowess at sharpshooting would have been evidence of one's inherent masculinity, rather than an accomplished skill. Hunting, as exhibited by Roosevelt's exploits, turned toward acquiring trophies and bigger animals. Fishing as a recreational sport also became established as part of the new masculinity.[47]

There is yet another dimension to this aspect of masculinity, one peculiar to California. In California the preservation and conservation of wilderness took on a grand scale, with John Muir spearheading the movement and, ultimately, gaining the support of Roosevelt, which led to the National Park System. The men of California were part of the well-to-do class who, early on, traveled to natural wonders like Yosemite.[48] Recall the LeContes' 1889 expedition to Yosemite. On this trip young LeConte traveled with two childhood friends from Oakland, rather than with Zete brothers, but he encountered fraternity brothers while there. Before ascending Mount Dana, they encountered a party of five young men from the university who were likewise out adventuring—they had just returned from climbing Mount Lyell. Among their number was Hubert Dyer ('90), one of LeConte's Zete brothers.[49]

On reaching the ten-thousand-foot summit of Cloud's Rest, they encountered other Zeta Psi men. "On the top was the inevitable pile of rocks. Upon a stick amongst the crevices we found the names of Thompson, Demarest, and Terry, of the 'Zeta Psi excursion party.' Also that of Dr. Senger of our University." Since these three men were actives living at the Zete house with LeConte, their ascent must have been a relatively recent event. Given that at least five Zetes had been to Yosemite over a short period, it seems that mountain climbing and adventuring were part of a new proving ground for the elite young men of California.[50]

Returning to the photograph of the Zete bedroom, consider one other notable object in the room. In case you think our lads had eyes only for one another, note the scandalous 1890s porn hanging on the wall. It is a little difficult to see, but the poster is some sort of boudoir shot, perhaps a poster distributed by a beer company or other business. The lady is shown in profile to best display her barely clad form. Ideologies of the new masculinity were making their way into the fraternity house, so let us consider how they influenced the public life of the fraternity.

ATHLETICS ON CAMPUS

Nestled in the middle of an oak-lined pathway on the University of California campus is a bronze statue depicting two young men. They are perfect in their youthfulness, with finely formed limbs and ruggedly handsome faces. The face of each is a study in concentration and focus, signaling their intention to settle for nothing less than glory. One is injured; he stands with his weight against his kneeling comrade, who is wrapping his teammate's wounded leg. Looking at the pair, one would think that they have just stumbled off of a battlefield. Indeed, they have—a battlefield that was still new in their time, but one that remains familiar to us today: the battlefield of the American gridiron. The two combatants are memorialized to honor the great victories of the University of California in 1898 and 1899 over their dreaded archenemy to the south, Stanford University. The annual contest between the two schools is a tradition still known today as the "Big Game."[51]

Today passersby rarely stop to look at this sculpture. In 2006, during the weekend of the Big Game with Stanford, the kneeling player was dressed in a Stanford jersey, the standing figure clothed in a Cal jersey, giving the statue more attention from the campus than it had received for some time. In the late nineteenth and early twentieth centuries, however, this grove of oaks with the statue as its focal point was an extremely popular postcard subject. On a campus that was quickly becoming renowned for its cutting-edge scholarship and research, this image of youthful virility seems to have symbolized the young university (figure 16).

Unlike the nearly professional college athletic programs of today, the late-nineteenth-century Cal teams would have featured young men who came first to attend the university, and who joined the teams only after tryouts. In addition to a varsity and junior varsity team, each college class—freshman, sophomore, junior, and senior—had its own additional team. As the number of fraternities on campus increased, an interfraternity league also developed.[52]

In *For the Blue and Gold*, the fictionalized account of a typical freshman's experiences of the University of California during the 1890s, author Joy Lichtenstein demonstrates that representing the university in athletics was a sacred responsibility of masculinity for those who could assume it. The hero, James Rawson, a strapping lad born to citrus farmers in Riverside, has entered the University of California, where he must navigate the maze of freshman hazing, find housing and work, deal with coeds, and achieve good grades.[53]

Rawson's great conflict comes, however, when he demonstrates potential as a backup kicker and fullback. Football practice interferes with his study time and his

FIGURE 16
The Football Players, by Douglas Tilden. Photograph by
the author.

work serving meals in a boardinghouse, and he decides to step down from the team,
just as the varsity kicker and fullback has to quit the team for health reasons. Rawson sticks to his decision to leave the gridiron, despite suffering the rebukes of his
friends and peers. Ultimately, they come to respect his decision. As the Big Game
against Stanford nears, however, it becomes known that Stanford has been inten-

tionally misleading outsiders as to their level of prowess, and that Cal's kicking could lose them the upcoming game.

> This thought gave James pause. . . . He asked himself if he had done quite the right thing after all. If the college really needed him (dear old college that was putting such fine things in his way—that was opening up an entirely new life to him), ought he not to have cast about for some means, made some sacrifice, in order to help out? This thought took firmer and firmer hold. "I guess I could have found a way, all right, if I hadn't been so much taken up with myself. Yes, I see, a fellow has to make some sacrifices, no matter what you say. It would be pretty bad if we should lose through me.[54]

James finds someone to take over his less-than-masculine job serving meals in a boardinghouse and supports himself working for a professor in an agricultural lab (doing science) while he attends practice and rejoins the team. As one might predict, his masculine sacrifice leads him to ultimately become the hero of Cal's dramatic victory over Stanford in the last minutes of the game. He is successful in his studies, too, is courted by the elite men of the campus fraternities, and gains the adoration of the quiet senior coed (and university medalist) he has admired from afar. He has proven himself to be the perfect embodiment of late-nineteenth-century masculinity—irresistible to men and women alike. Even educated women cannot resist his essential masculine appeal.

James Rawson is a product of his time. A hundred years earlier, such a character would not have been the inevitable hero that Rawson was . On the University of California campus, he would not have been a hero even twenty years earlier, when sport and organized athletics were limited to informal games of baseball.

Athletics provided another arena for the fraternities, too, to distinguish themselves from one another. As competition among them became more marked, regular sporting events between fraternity teams became more common. These were events announced in the school newspapers and open for all to see.

If you look again at the activities represented, you'll see, in figure 12, that athletics was consistently one of the best-represented categories of participation. Zeta Psi brothers participated in athletics at every level—club, junior varsity, and varsity. The popularity of individual sports shifted through time. When the university was founded, baseball drew the best athletes of the university. Zetes were wild about baseball in the 1870s and 1880s, contributing men to varsity, class, and club teams.

Zeta Psi had its own "nine," which practiced in front of the chapter house. In 1876, four of the nine men on the senior class baseball team were Zetes; the following year, two Zetes were on the university team, and ten others represented their respective classes on the class teams.[55]

By the middle of the 1880s, other sports were drawing greater attention on campus. Tennis, biking, and boating all drew new devotees. Football—still very much a close kin of rugby—began to draw the most enthusiastic following, particularly after the founding of Stanford, which proved a worthy competitor in athletic events. As early as 1877, Zetes contributed three players, J. Mailliard, W. Van Dyke, and C. Warren, to the university football team. In 1879, ten Zetes played football as part of one university team or another. The early 1880s saw Zeta Psi's greatest overall interest in athletics, with 100 percent of the men participating in organized sports of one kind or another in 1884.[56]

Zete brother J. D. McGillivray helped to develop the popularity of track on campus as the recognized founder of Field Day, a May event that featured a range of track and field events. McGillivray was a more accomplished athlete than student, and long after his sad academic record had faded from memory, he was still lauded as a great contributor to the traditions of Cal.[57]

Athletics may have led to a brief revitalization of the fraternity's campus popularity in the early 1890s. The Zetes of 1893 featured a number of track athletes of national and international caliber.[58] Not all of the Zetes' athletic contributions to campus that year were made on the track, however. In addition to holding the one-mile walk record for the school, G. H. Foulks was a popular left tackle on the university's varsity football team, where fellow Zete W. H. Henry played right end. After the graduation of these men, Zetes' participation in organized athletics dropped noticeably.[59] This does not mean the Zetes no longer participated in other kinds of physical fitness. The men's gym provided another public space for the refinement of the masculine form.

In the class of 1878's volume of *The Blue and Gold,* the editors lamented that "the long-talked of gymnasium has not yet made its appearance, but doubtless the year 2000 AD will see it."[60] The gym was eventually built a decade later with funding from A. K. P. Harmon of Oakland, at the urging of George C. Edwards. Edwards is one of the men credited with building athletics and physical culture on campus. He developed a keen interest in college athletics and physical culture, and it is in that capacity that he is now remembered on campus—the track field and stadium erected in 1930 bears his name. The 1886 *Blue and Gold Handbook of the University of California* carries a section on athletics written by Edwards. According to him, "Everybody feels the need of physical exercise. None need it so much as the young man at college. By exercise is not meant hard and exhausting labor (either regularly or spasmodically taken), but the stimulation of the nerve, and the charging with blood of each muscle in the body, as can be done in one hour in a well-appointed gymnasium."[61]

Edward's quote is informative—he sees exercise as a necessary leisure—not manual labor. The fitness of body he has in mind is specifically for the educated, and therefore, middle- or upper-class white man. Nonwhite men and the working classes might toil for a living, but theirs was not a manhood to be emulated. Edwards was involved in researching the university's developing need for a gymnasium and, on February 24, 1887, wrote a letter to the university's president (apparently at the latter's request) detailing the equipment needed and estimated costs. The machines listed were exclusively for the development of musculature and body form.[62] Kasson has convincingly argued that the increased focus on the appearance of the nude white male body "reasserted that gender and racial divisions were fundamentally based on innate and natural differences" while also appealing to "the dream of masculine metamorphosis, the possibilities for bodily transformation and, by implication, for a transformation of self and of social standing."[63]

Edwards's list of equipment needed demonstrates that the focus of physical culture was on bodybuilding and gymnastics. Eugen Sandow was just one visible example of the larger culture's increased focus on bodybuilding as part of constructing a masculine identity.[64] However, the decreased presence of Zetes in college athletics at a time when such pursuits were tied more strongly than ever before to definitions of masculinity should also be considered a potential warning sign that the metaphysical fraternal body was not as healthy as it had been in years past. This interpretation is supported by other changes then taking place in the fraternity—particularly in the realm of scholarship.

SCHOLARSHIP

Now that we have considered some of the extracurricular activities engaged in by the Zetes, perhaps it is worth considering how they succeeded in their academic work. Recall that our archaeological assemblage included no definitive artifacts related to studying and writing—no pen nibs or pencil points, no mechanical pencils, ink wells, writing slates, or slate pencils. With the possible exception of the headache cure, there is no evidence of material culture associated with heavy studying, or "grinding," as it was called. Granted, the assemblage was not big, yet, we do have ample evidence of social activities. Success in scholastics would have been a noteworthy achievement on campus.

I was drawn to a consideration of the Zetes' academic work upon finding a rather scathing review of their scholarly achievements that was printed in the *Occident*, a rabidly antifraternity paper. The paper conducted an in-depth review of the sins of each of the university's fraternity chapters. As the first fraternity founded on campus, Zeta Psi was covered first. The review generalized the fraternity's history as one of degeneration—using classic Darwinian terms—with the class of 1876 representing the clear turning point after which the fraternity went sour. Half the men of 1876 had failed to graduate, it stated, and there had been several recorded instances of cheating and suspension. The paper also claimed that from 1876 to 1882, of the fifty-two members, twenty-five, or 48.07 percent, had failed to graduate. Most of the latter had been remanded because of failure in scholarship, expelled, dismissed, or suspended for conduct unbecoming a gentleman; five or six had left for unknown reasons. The paper also made damning accusations against individual members of the fraternity, reporting, for example, that "one member of this fraternity from '79 openly boasted that he had bribed an instructor in one of his courses, and had thus passed an examination. An editorial in an anti-fraternity paper threatened to expose him, but didn't because his parents are of high social position."[65]

I have to admit, I was surprised by the brush with which the Zetes were painted in this article. I had not thought of the Zetes as living embodiments of evil. The Zetes themselves seem to have responded to the article with amusement, a circumstance that only provoked the paper further.

It is rumored that the Zeta Psi fraternity has been buying up the copies of the *Occident* containing their history to send to their friends. . . . At present, so far is known, the members of the chapter number nine. They, in connection with another fraternity, form the backbone of the drinking element in our University. There is not one of them that doesn't drink intoxicating liquors, moderately at least. They are the men that are ready to enter into any student prank, from stoning the president's house to throwing a cat into the literary society, on the shortest notice. If their general wildness was balanced on the other side by something that was worthy of students it might be passed over as a pardonable display of boyish spirit. But it is not, there is not one that has any marked literary standing among the students. Only one of two are ever seen on the platforms of the literary societies, or are prominent among the editors of the local papers. As a class, the members do not, in spite of two or three exceptions, rank up to the average of merit in study on the university reports.[66]

The Zetes did not directly respond to the accusations at the time, though it was reported in papers that the fraternities' party line was that the *Occident* staff was composed of "sore-heads" who had not been accepted by any of the fraternities. I decided to find out if it was possible to check the statistics provided by the newspaper, in order to see how much smoke I could separate from fire.[67]

First, I considered the graduation statistics provided by the paper. I checked these numbers against the Zeta Psi and UC alumni registers. For the class of 1876, the class responsible for the "degeneration" of the fraternity, the Zeta Psi register names four members of the class of 1876—75 percent of whom graduated from the university, not the 50 percent reported in the *Occident*. While the paper reported that fifty-two men were members of the house from 1876 to the fall of 1882, I identified only fifty men (including active senior members). The class of '83, who had to be included in the *Occident*'s count, numbered nine men and could not have been expected to have graduated. There is reason to suspect that the *Occident* editors may not have been completely honest in their statistics. I identified eighteen men who had failed to graduate during this period—one had died, another had left due to health reasons and received a certificate of proficiency. This leaves a significant number of men who had not graduated, but in a 1911 yearbook editorial, Professor (and former Zete) George C. Edwards noted that the university's graduation rates from 1877 to 1907 had averaged around 40 percent. Zeta Psi's graduation rate of 64 percent at this time was not disreputable.[68]

The Zetes had among their ranks two University Medalists. The University Medal is the highest honor granted to a student upon graduation. In selecting a medalist, the Academic Senate considered his or her overall academic record. Based on this information, it might appear that the *Occident* was in fact motivated by soreheadedness; however, once I reviewed the Academic Senate records for 1871 to 1885, it became clear that Zetes had not necessarily been the most dedicated of students. While the *Occident* may have exaggerated and played with some of the statistics, if anything the article underestimated the academic lows that the Zetes would achieve in the following decade.

The Academic Senate records from 1871 to 1885 include descriptions of issues related to student performance and behavior issues. Absenteeism seems to have infected any number of Zetes. Some brothers, like Joseph Mailliard, who eventually left the university for health reasons, were legitimately ill. Others, the majority, seem to have suffered from shorter-term illnesses like spring fever. On several occasions, the brothers skipped classes together. In January 1873, it was noted that "Bolton, Budd and Woodward—absenting selves from exercises in College of Agriculture."

In February of 1875, "brothers Fairbanks, Meeks, Solinsky and Stillman, absented themselves Tuesday February 16th without leave." The faculty voted to have the president privately reprimand them. In January of 1876, J. J. Hutchinson was "absent a great deal from French and Chemistry." In February of that same year, George Reed stopped attending French. The faculty investigated and found that he had taken it upon himself to drop French and take up Spanish. Mailliard was reprimanded that same month for dropping French without permission. Dropping was perhaps the right decision for these two, though, since in June of that year their brothers Dargie and Hutchinson were found deficient in French. Unfortunately for Reed, his Spanish skills were apparently no better than his French skills—he was found deficient in Spanish.[69]

Too many deficiencies could prevent a student from moving on to the next class level with his cohort. Students who had too many deficiencies in the coursework required for their degree programs could be cast out of the university or could petition to become students at large until they had righted themselves. J. D. McGillivray (class of 1878), who was fondly remembered as the student athlete who started the tradition of Field Day, was a constant entry in Academic Senate Records. His academic record serves as an example of the Zetes' lowest academic achievers.

In August 24, 1877, McGillivray petitioned to be a student at large, which was granted, with the stipulation that he address his deficiencies. In September, on the wishes of his parents, he asked the Academic Senate to allow him to take Spanish instead of German. In November, when he petitioned to join the junior class, the faculty approved , with the condition that he pass his Greek exam. However, in December, it was noted that he was absent from his Greek and algebra exams. He was remanded to the sophomore class and asked to appear before the president to explain why he should not be put in next year's freshman class. In January 1878, he again became a student at large with his mother's permission. In December of 1880, McGillivray again petitioned the faculty. He stated that he had completed thirteen hours in prescribed studies and eight hours in studies outside his course of study, and requested that these eight hours count as equivalent to three hours in prescribed courses. The faculty (probably desperate to be rid of him) agreed. Interestingly enough, he's listed in alumni records as having graduated in 1879.[70]

The *Occident* article had suggested that the Zetes used their family connections to bypass university punishments. I did find some interesting circumstances that I'm unable to clarify further by means of existing records. For instance, in November 1874, J. Wilkins ('76) was deficient in too many classes and was dismissed by the faculty. Yet alumni records indicate that he graduated in 1876. In 1877, W. Sherwood was granted an honorable dismissal from the university at the request of his father. This indicated that he was leaving the university in good standing—yet Academic Senate records list him as having graduated in 1877.[71]

Not all of the Zetes' troubles were strictly academic. More serious charges of academic dishonesty, violence, and ungentlemanly behavior were raised against them. In March of 1873, Professor Soule accused Woodward of the university's first matriculating class as being guilty of insubordination and insult to a faculty person (himself). The nature of the insult is not described. The Academic Senate voted to suspend Woodward from the university, but the matter was tabled. At the next faculty meeting, Soule reported that Woodward had made a ready apology and that he had accepted it, and moved that Woodward be reinstated. He was, and he graduated as one of the "twelve apostles."

In 1875, Wilkins, who was dismissed from the university in 1874 and then apparently reinstated, was accused of cheating along with his Zete brother Hook. Wilkins was accused of turning in a drawing not his own. He claimed that he had begun the work, been called away, and that Hook had merely finished it for him. The faculty apparently compared the two men's work and decided that it was all done by Hook. Wilkins was suspended until August 1876, and Hook was reprimanded.[72]

The story does not actually end here. That January, it was reported that the senior class had submitted a petition in support of Wilkins. They made an honor pledge that none of them would cheat, in exchange for Wilkins's reinstatement. The faculty granted the petition. These honor petitions were a fairly common occurrence in the senate records, and are a wonderful example of the notions of gentlemanly honor and behavior that exemplified male ideals of the time. This incident also illustrates that the Zetes were able to garner support among their peers on campus.[73]

Zetes were related to another disciplinary incident in August of 1879, one serious in the eyes of the faculty. Zete brothers R. G. Hooker and W. W. Nelson were among a group of at least six sophomores who admitted to participating in a hazing incident. The sophomores apparently broke into a freshman's room, wrapped him in a blanket, and shaved his whiskers. This was done to four freshmen in all. The faculty saw hazing as particularly vile and dismissed all of the men responsible from the university. As in the Wilkins case, the other students of the university rallied around the dismissed men. The classes of '82 and '83 each pledged not to engage in hazing if the men were reinstated. Again, the petition was approved by the faculty. Hooker graduated with his class in 1882; he was one of a rapidly shrinking number of Zetes to do so.[74]

TABLE 6   Zeta Psi graduation rates during occupation
of the first house, 1870–1900*

| | | Graduated | | Not graduated |
| | | | | |
Decade	Early	On time	Late	
1870–1879		44	2	12
		(75.8%)	(3.4%)	(20.6%)
1880–1889	1	21	3	39
	(1.6%)	(32.8%)	(4.7%)	(60.9%)
1890–1899		27	5	37
		(39.1%)	(7.24%)	(53.6%)

* Overall: 53.9% graduation rate; 46.1% did not graduate.

A very public indication of the fraternity's scholarship was performed on an annual basis—at commencement. As we have already seen, the fraternity's graduation rates at the time of the derogatory *Occident* article were not out of line with the statistics of the university in general. This would quickly change, however (see table 6). While nearly 80 percent of Zeta Psi brothers graduated during the years 1870 to 1879, this proportion dropped to less than 40 percent during the years 1880 to 1889, with nearly 5 percent of those who graduated doing so late. From *1890* to 1899, there was a slight recovery, with nearly 40 percent of the brothers graduating on time and another 7 percent graduating late. If calculated over the thirty-year period, the graduation rate was nearly 54 percent.

The rate was this high, however, only because the number of men recruited to Zeta Psi was falling. While the house had maintained a steady population of nineteen or twenty men per year during its early years, by the 1880s membership was fluctuating wildly, with the house attracting as many twenty-two men and as few as nine (figure 17). Considering the dynamics of fraternity life, maintaining a healthy household from one year to the next requires continuity in 75 percent of the membership—the house's seniors will leave, and the freshmen will be new members. If the house recruits as many men as it loses, then in successive years three-quarters of the men should have lived in the house the previous year. If the house has failed to recruit successfully, then the percentage of men remaining in the house from the previous year will be higher. If a chapter is building by recruiting larger numbers of men, or if it has failed to keep its senior members or is coming off a period of poor recruitment, the percentage of men who lived in it the previous year

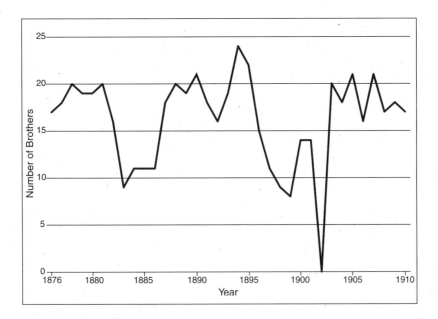

FIGURE 17

Graph of Zeta Psi membership size during occupation of
the first house.

will be smaller. Given this, let us consider the figures for Zeta Psi table 7). Until
about 1888, the population is fairly consistent, with 50–60 percent continuity in
membership. After that date, however, just as the overall population fluctuates, so
does continuity. Remember that house traditions and organizational structure de-
pend on the orderly flow of knowledge and practices from one class of men to another. Zeta Psi's health as an institution was in jeopardy.

The fraternity's problems, in part, were likely the result of growing competition for men on campus. From 1871 to 1890, the number of fraternities on campus
grew slowly but steadily from one to five (figure 18). However, after 1890, new
fraternities were established at a faster pace. Fourteen were on campus in 1900, a
number that grew to twenty-four by 1910. The newer fraternities had the advantage of novelty. They also had the advantage of new houses that had been designed explicitly as fraternity houses. Despite the carefully cultivated aura of so-
phistication and wealth built by previous generations of Zetes, by the 1890s the
Zetes were looking like washed-up has-beens. Their house became emblematic of
the fraternity's decay.

TABLE 7 Continuity in population of the first house, year by year*

Year	Number of brothers living in house	% of house members who lived in house previous school year
1876	17	n/a
1877	18	30
1878	20	55
1879	19	58
1880	19	58
1881	20	65
1882	16	50
1883	9	78
1884	11	55
1885	11	55
1886	11	54.5
1887	18	66.6
1888	20	30
1889	19	79
1890	21	48
1891	18	56
1892	16	38
1893	19	68.4
1894	24	50
1895	22	50
1896	15	73
1897	11	64
1898	9	44
1899	8	50
1900	14	54.5
1901	14	71.4
1902	n/a	n/a
1903	20	n/a
1904	18	55.5
1905	21	38
1906	16	50

TABLE 7 (continued)

Year	Number of brothers living in house	% of house members who lived in house previous school year
1907	21	52.3
1908	17	58.8
1909	18	16.6
1910	17	29.4

* Membership information derived from volumes of *The Blue and Gold*.

REPRESENTATIONS OF THE HOUSE

For the brothers of Zeta Psi, their house was a living embodiment of their status on campus. As the first fraternity to build a house, the size and quality of the structure was a direct statement to others of their success and status on campus. At the time it was built, the structure was fashionably designed and well equipped. There was piped water at the house, illustrated by our recovery of the iron water line and drainage pipes during excavation. Early descriptions of the house suggest it was built with piped-in water. A letter from Eugene Hilgard, professor of agriculture and a resident of a neighboring house on Bancroft Avenue, confirms that the house had plumbing in 1880. On October 7, 1880, he wrote to the regents, "I forgot to tell you today that a regular stream of water has been running today, and at intervals for several days past, from the 'Zete' house down Bancroft. It had better be looked after."[75]

Aside from plumbing, the house featured other luxurious appointments as well. In the 1890s, according to interior photographs (and recovered pieces of light-bulbs), the house had electricity. The mansard roof was a stylistic attribute of the period. But in the progressive period, the emphasis in all arenas was on progress. The neighborhood around the fraternity was filling in during the late 1880s and early 1900s.[76] Modest brown-shingle homes with simple lines and a minimum of ornamentation were being built throughout the city (figure 19). The Zete house stood out as ostentatious, yes, but ostentatious in an out-of-date way. The other fraternities on campus were building their own houses—houses designed in the modern architectural styles and with all the modern updates. Combined with their declining house population—which was only emphasized by the large size of the chapter house—the Zetes began to bear the brunt of campus ridicule, particularly in the pages of *The Blue and Gold*.

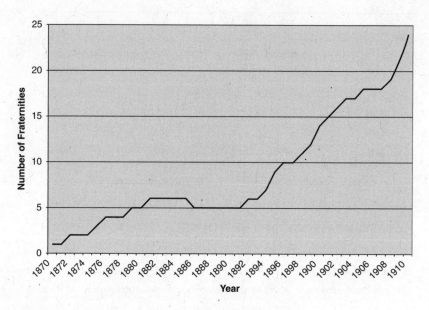

FIGURE 18

Graph of the number of fraternities extant on the University
of California campus, 1870–1910.

By 1900, there were sixteen fraternities on campus. In the 1900 *Blue and
Gold,* the growing competition between chapters for members and the difficulties the older frats were having recruiting brothers was fodder for satire. In
one blurb captioned "Overheard in a grazing ground for Fraternity goats," a
DEKE goat says conversationally to a Beta goat, "They're about played out.
Poor Sigma Chi looks like a resurrected skeleton." The Beta goat replies, "And
that dottering old Zete over there is nothing but skin and bones." To himself, a
nearby Fiji goat says, "If they die,—wonder if I'll get a chance to feed—grass is
mighty scarce."

Another piece in the same yearbook edition claims to include each fraternity's
annual announcement to prospective members. Zeta Psi's reads, "Governor Budd
belongs to our frat. So does Harry Budd, who was his uncles' nephew. Our house is
proud, though unpainted, and so large in comparison with our membership, that
Freshmen can have separate rooms. Don't join any of the 'cheap sport' frats, but
come to us."[77] The nature of the criticism is hard to miss.

FIGURE 19
Example of the type of house surrounding the first Zeta Psi chapter
house. This one, home of May and Warren Cheney, stood at 2241
College Avenue and was built in 1885. Photograph by the author.

The 1903 *Blue and Gold* strikes at the house again. This time, the yearbook includes a column purporting to include the letters of each fraternity to their national.
Here is the one written for Zeta Psi:

 Dear Brother:
 Iota of Zeta Psi sends greeting, rejoicing that she can truthfully bring news of
 Zeta Psi's steadfast prosperity by the Golden Gate.

Ever since we commenced "Rushing" in Brother White's "Auto," a bigger one than Early Anthony's, the laurels have been ours.

Witness—Bro. Solinsky and Bro. Cavalier, both prep school celebrities of the first rank. . . .

In closing, Iota again wishes to remind the custodian of the Strong-box of the decrepit condition of our ancient Chapter Hall, and asks for a remittance of our share, that it may be fittingly repaired.

Fraternally, Herbert Hairy Minor, '04.[78]

The 1904 *Blue and Gold* offers the cruelest characterization of the Zete house, in a fictional narrative of how each fraternity came to get its house. This is a long extract, but I think that you'll find it worthy of inclusion:

In response to your request for an account of how we built our house, I regret to say that our home was built so long ago as to be beyond the memory of our oldest member. However, after diligent search through the records of our chapter, I have discovered enough to enable me to write the account you desire.

Shortly after the close of the Civil War, and while this College was yet in its infancy, a group of choice spirits gathered together for the purpose of distinguishing themselves from the rest of the college. At first their meetings were held in the primeval forest which adorned the east end of what is now the University Grounds. Here, 'neath the starry dome of heaven, they met in solemn conclave to weld the links of that chain which was in future to bind them and their posterity so closely together.

For a time these Druidical Festivities sufficed to render content the soul of each devotee to the mystical shrine. But with the growing western civilization began to be felt need for a less primitive mode of existence. Then was conceived in the brain of one of our predecessor a wondrous thought. They must have a house.

We need not worry you with a detailed account of the hardships undergone by these hardy pioneers in their pursuit of a home. Suffice it to say that the end of sixteen years found them comfortably installed in the palatial residence we now occupy.

At times our numbers have been so seriously depleted as to render difficult the payment of taxes on our home. Of late, however, by making ourselves less exclusive, we have succeeded in increasing our numbers to such an extent that we are free from this haunting dread.

Happy Hooligan Minor, Pro Zψ[79]

While the satires were designed to hit at sensitive parts of the different fraternity's sense of self and history, it was in subsequent volumes of *The Blue and Gold* where the Zetes were hit with the hardest blow: in the later satires on fraternities, Zetes were not mentioned at all. They had lost their social relevance on campus. There was only one solution—the Zetes needed a new chapter house. It could not be just any chapter house, it had to be a structure that spoke to the great history and future of the Iota chapter. In rebuilding the fraternal space, perhaps the brothers could also rebuild the failing fraternal body. Fund-raising letters sent to alumni at the end of the first decade of the 1900s emphasized the necessity of Zeta Psi to rise again from the ashes. To do so successfully would require the brothers to resituate themselves in the rapidly changing social landscape of the University of California's Never Land.

PROGRAM FOR ACT III

Peter and the Lost Boys take Wendy and her brothers to the lagoon to see the mermaids, and they attempt to capture one. A table-sized rock sits in the center of the lagoon, Marooner's Rock, where pirates leave sailors tied to a post to drown in the rising tide. Suddenly, Peter senses the arrival of the pirates, and the group disperses to various hiding places. The pirates arrive in a dinghy with a rope-bound Tiger Lily, who, on the order of Captain Hook, is to be left to drown. From his hiding place, Peter imitates Hook's voice and demands that Tiger Lily be set free. The confused pirates follow his orders, and Tiger Lily escapes. When the real Captain Hook appears, he is first distracted by the news brought to him by his spies that Peter Pan and the Lost Boys have a mother to protect them. He wonders about kidnapping her to keep as a mother for himself and his crew. Once he remembers that Tiger Lily is gone, he becomes angry—and confused that his sailors claim to have been following his orders. They all become convinced that the lagoon is haunted. Peter, again imitating Hook's voice from his hiding place, addresses them, and he nearly convinces Hook and his sailors that Hook is a codfish, not a pirate.

Ultimately, Peter wants his cleverness recognized and reveals himself to Hook. A battle between the pirates and the Lost Boys, the Darlings, and Peter ensues. The crocodile inserts itself into the melee and chases Hook back to his boat. The Lost Boys and the Darling brothers capture the pirates' dinghy and leave, thinking that Peter and Wendy have gone before them. Peter and Wendy awake on Marooner's Rock, where the water is rising. Pan claims to be wounded too badly to fly, and Wendy cannot fly without him. It seems hopeless until a kite they had made earlier floats by. Peter sends Wendy back to his house on the kite, proclaiming that he will stay to meet death face on. He is ultimately saved by a bird who gives him her nest to use as a boat, and, as the act ends, Peter makes his escape.

ACT III · The Mermaids' Lagoon

Coeds and Pirates Threaten Peter's Tribe

HOOK (*griping the stave for support*). Who are
  you, stranger, speak.
PETER (*who is only too ready to speak*). I am Jas
  Hook, Captain of the *Jolly Rodger*.
HOOK (*now white to the gills*). No, no, you are
  not.
PETER. Brimstone and gall, say that again and
  I'll cast anchor in you.
HOOK. If you are Hook, come tell me, who
  am I?
PETER. A codfish, only a codfish.
HOOK (*aghast*). A Codfish?
SMEE (*drawing back from him*). Have we been
  captained all this time by a codfish?
STARKEY. It's lowering to our pride.

For James Barrie, Never Land was specifically a place where true fraternity could exist between boys. Never Land held many threats to that camaraderie—pirates, Indians, and a variety of women. Similarly, the University of California campus held threats to fraternity life. Some were visible, including the attacks mounted by known enemies. Defined battles fought with these foes were recounted by generations of brothers over a shared keg of beer. Other threats were more insidious, slowly building strength and remaining unrecognized until it was nearly too late. The weakening fraternal bonds among Zeta Psi's brothers, and the general degeneration of their achievements and status, should be seen against the backdrop of the university's changing social landscape.

The University of California was not the only battleground where these struggles took place. As the founding of new fraternities accelerated at the end of the nineteenth and the beginning of the twentieth centuries, universities became increasingly concerned about the role of fraternities in student life and the impact of fraternity membership on scholarly achievement. Fraternities were not the only perceived threat to student education. The introduction of female students was seen as potentially destabilizing. The University of California was one of the first public universities to allow coeducation, and others soon followed. The presence of coeds on campus was a visible reminder of the gender wars being waged outside the gates of Never Land.[1] As women increased their numbers and achievements at the university, the subversive nature of their very presence was more commonly recognized. The fraternities found themselves surrounded by pirates on one side and coeds on the other. Each offered particular threats to the stability of fraternity life. To survive the changing social currents, the fraternities would need to meet their critics head on and address their concerns.

PIRATES ATTACK! THE LOST BOYS ARE TRAPPED BETWEEN THE *SCYLLA* AND THE *OESTRUS*

The pirates on campus were the antifraternity men. Had he been there, Peter Pan might have called them "cod fish," but to the men of Zeta Psi, they were "soreheads," men so jealous of the brotherhood shared by fraternity members that they would stop at nothing to destroy the secret societies.[2] Two primary student newspapers taking an antifraternity stance were founded, the *Oestrus*, which was published from 1878 to 1880, and the *Occident*, an expressly antifraternity paper published from 1881 to 1884. While its editors expressed antifraternity views sporadically until the 1890s, the *Occident* became best known during its run as an antieverything paper. By means of the editorial pages of these papers, the editors shot cannon balls at the ship of Zeta Psi.[3]

The *Oestrus* started innocuously enough in early February 1878. The editors introduced it as a weekly college paper whose "columns are open to all, without regard to sex or sect." The paper sailed under an antifraternity banner, but nothing among the columns indicated much of an antifraternity sentiment. In fact, the editors seemed mainly concerned with accusations published in the *Christian Advocate* stating that Berkeley was a godless campus.

The closest thing to a fraternity critique that appeared in the *Oestrus* during the first semester is subtle: the editors informed their readers that "quite a deal of excitement and much rash and extreme language was caused by the appearance last Thursday of a small sheet purporting to come from respectable persons. Some have expressed the opinion that we had a hand in the publication. This we individuals and as a stock company completely deny, and would address some persons to be more careful of their language, and to be sure of their mark before they shoot. In our opinion the paper was written by those who think to gain a point by casting the publication upon their opponents. They will have to be very vigilant to escape detection."[4]

The May 1878 minutes for the Academic Senate meeting refer briefly to a sheet called *Scylla*, which appeared on the day of the Junior Exhibition. The exhibition was an annual ritual that allowed junior class the opportunity to host the community and entertain it with dramas, music, and recitations. Sophomores, by tradition, attempted to co-opt the exhibition by publishing bogus programs that replaced names, lyrics, and so on with bawdy or satirical substitutes. While these were mainly harmless pranks, the faculty was particularly hostile to them and regularly threatened to dismiss students involved in producing them. By releasing the *Scylla* on the day of the Junior Exhibition, its producers guaranteed it would draw attention. The only other note on that matter was that the faculty voted to leave this situation to the university president.[5]

What, then, was the *Scylla?* Its first issue appeared in April 1878, with the following address by the unnamed editors: "This is a new undertaking, and as such requires a statement of its aims and objects. Being published in the interest of the SECRET SOCIETIES, everything pertaining to them will be considered of paramount importance, for we consider them the bulwark of sociality and good order, and by means of this sheet we mean to show the students and the world in general that by upholding them they will prevent deadly class feuds, such as have disgraced the halls of learning in many colleges of our land where these institutions have been abolished."[6] The paper was small, measuring only about six by eight inches, and short, merely four pages. The remainder of the paper includes an announcement of the Bourdon Burial, which was to be followed by a tribute to the god "Bhere Buste," and some bogus advertisements mocking presumed members of the antifraternity movement.

It was the second issue of *Scylla*, released May 3, 1878, that raised a fuss on campus and drew faculty attention. The sheet was still only four pages but, unlike its predecessor, was published on double-sized sheets. While the first issue had a satirical edge, this one was outright cruel. The masthead features an editorial staff including "Hybrid Mohawk Savage," "Fag-end wart on the face of the Earth Henshaw" (presumably meant to be Fred W. Henshaw of Zeta Psi), "Harry Idiot Coon" (Henry Irving Coon), "Wilkinson Humbled Chapman" (William H. Chapman), and Horrible Ranting Havens (Henry R. Havens), and it claims to be an organ of the class of '79. The paper features a series of insulting poems and articles caricaturing students. Robert Poppe, presented as "Rum Guzzling Busted Poppe" was the focus of a bogus article that reported: "From Sonoma, [he is] noted for kleptomaniacal propensities, known as a drinker, joined the Berkeley Temperance Society and fell in love with blushing damsel Fitzgerald." He supposedly bored the young maid for two months, until he was kicked out by the father. He then turned to drink and was expelled from the Berkeley Temperance Society, and "it was only a few nights ago he was found in the gutter tenderly embracing and addressing in soft accents an empty beer keg, fondly imagining it to be the form of his lost love." "Wilkinson Humbled Chapman" hailed from Sacramento and was reported to have been beaten regularly by his wicked stepfather before coming to the university, where he still held a grudge.[7]

The strongest words were saved for certain women. Several women clearly had Tiger Lily tendencies that intimidated the paper's authors. Mary McHead, portrayed as Marry McHead, was described as born to be a lawyer and quoted as saying, "I know I am a woman, but what is that to me? A woman may have children and still a lawyer be!" The "Marvelous Writer Shinn," Millicent Shinn was described as follows: "In '75 to Berkeley came a maiden thin and pale, that looked just like a Petticoat pasted to a rail . . . till she fell in with a Prof, then she beguiled the Silly Prof, He surely was roped in, for a man of sense could never endure this moping maiden Shinn."[8] Shinn, incidentally, became the first woman granted a PhD at Berkeley, and she later served as editor of the *Overland Monthly*. A formidable coed indeed.[9]

This verse and similar ones intimated a love triangle between Millicent Shinn, Anna Head, and Edward Sill, professor of English language and literature. These probably drew the attention of the faculty, since insults to the dignity of the faculty were not tolerated. Combined with the ungentlemanly representations of coeds, the *Scylla* seemed designed to draw attention to itself in unfavorable ways. Only one additional issue was published, in September of 1878. The sheet, published in the same small format as its first issue, was only two pages in length. Its most notable aspect is an editorial (as in the first issue, no editorial staff is named) stating,

> The attribution of the *Scylla* to the *Oestrus* men through a misconception of our intention has been the most stunning blow of which we have received. It is the "unkindest cut of all" to have our labors which the Societies pride so much, pass as honors to our enemies, and for the benefit of the skeptical we now state distinctly that the *Scylla* is, heart and soul, the organ of the Secret Fraternities. . . . Since our last appearance, the DKE have united with us, and now hand in hand we will march to victory.[10]

What did all this mean? The *Scylla* appeared no more, but, beginning in August of 1878, the *Oestrus* started a systematic campaign of editorials against the fraternities, calling for their abolishment on campus. The editorials focused on several repeating themes, which can be summarized as follows:

1. Fraternity men work together to aid their brothers, leading to them acquire fraudulently high standing in classes to the detriment of hardworking individuals.

2. Fraternities create a false sense of exclusiveness with their claims of being the upper 10 percent of the campus community. Their belief that they constitute a campus aristocracy makes them undemocratic institutions.

3. Fraternities train their members to think alike, so that members are deprived of character and the ability to form independent opinion necessary to intelligent citizens.

4. Fraternities destroy university feeling by fostering disharmony within and between classes.

5. Fraternities destroy morality, for brothers sink to the moral behavior of their worst brother.[11]

These critiques sound much like the views of anthropologist Peggy Reeves Sanday, whose work I discussed in the prologue of this book. Little has changed in the essential arguments made against fraternities in the last 150 years. The editors of the *Oestrus* argued that fraternities were responsible for all the social ills on campus—cheating, drunkenness, and other disciplinary problems. The paper inspired some students to write in support of the antifraternity stance, escalating campus tensions. On March 31, 1879, the *Oestrus* published a letter to the editor written by "a Freshman" excoriating the fraternities.[12] According to the writer, at the class meeting where the president was to be elected the fraternities "stole" the election through deceitful tactics.[13]

Why did this matter to anyone? Did it really matter if a fraternity man was class president? In this particular historical circumstance, it most certainly did. The freshman class president for the spring term was responsible for organizing and ensuring the success of the Bourdon Burial. This particular class ('82) was trying to run a dry Bourdon; the fraternities were accused of selling subscriptions to support a beer bust following the Bourdon and, therefore, undermining the majority vote of the class. When a small number of people are living in close proximity without the distractions of computers, videogames, cell phones, radios, or, due to their dry leanings, saloons, such topics apparently take on incredible importance.

So much, in fact, that the men named in the article took offense and demanded a retraction, bullying an editor in the process and starting a sequence of events gleefully reported in the *Oestrus*.

According to the April 7 issue, "On Friday the author of the communication in our last *[sic]* (a small man) was cowardly assaulted from behind by the same man [that he described in his letter] and an attempt was made to horsewhip him. Of course, again, the assailant was strongly backed by members of his fraternity and has since received the hearty congratulations of the members of the other fraternities for his brave and manly conduct."[14] Note the implication that fraternity behavior was not manly. The suspension of the student responsible did not ease campus tensions. In May, as reported in the Academic Senate minutes, the president of the university called the attention of the faculty to the distribution of "an obscene bogus program" on the occasion of the Junior Exhibition and appointed a committee to investigate.[15] The sophomore class apparently had a great deal of class spirit, and refused to identify those responsible. In a dramatic move, the faculty expelled every member of the class of 1881 from the university. While terms were eventually negotiated for the return of some of these students, the action was seriously bad publicity for the university, particularly at a time when the university was taking criticism from a variety of outside groups.[16]

Whether or not the fraternities were involved in the production of the bogus programs, the combination of those programs, the *Scylla* (which had been ascribed to the fraternities), and the assault (definitely committed by a fraternity member) had to weigh on the minds of the regents. Regent Stebbins moved at a May 7 meeting to authorize the faculty of the College of Science and Letters to take such measures to regulate and abolish "college secret societies" as they deemed proper. The resolution was passed. The faculty developed a pledge—presented at the August 22, 1879, Academic Senate meeting—for all freshmen to sign, in which they promised they would not join any secret society while at the University of California.[17]

There were the fraternities, the life bleeding out of them as their membership dwindled away. I cannot help but think of Peter Pan. After he has freed Tiger Lily from the clutches of the pirates, he is captured by Captain Hook and left to die on Marooner's Rock, unable to fly away. The water is slowly rising and soon will engulf him. He declares bravely that "to die will be an awfully big adventure." Hook has left him behind, ever pleased with himself. The *Oestrus* likewise fled the university scene: in October 1879, the paper announced its last issue, chortling and taking credit for the regents' decree banning students from joining secret societies. "Therefore our job is done," it proclaimed proudly.[18]

Are you not just a bit worried about the Zetes as they sit on that rock, watching the things they have worked to build threaten to wash away? And who published the *Scylla*? The fraternity men blamed the *Oestrus*, and the *Oestrus* blamed the fraternity men.

In 1880, in their only public response to the *Scylla* question, Zeta Psi declared that they had not been involved, and that to prove it they had hired a private investigator to uncover the true culprits. Of course, we have reason to question their truthfulness. After all, they did pen a false editorial in the *University Echo* to protect the brother who was bell-clapper thief.[19] Still, to attribute the *Scylla* to the fraternity men requires us to accept that their pride was so great (or that they were so stupid) that they could not recognize the possible consequences of publishing such a rag that insulted a professor and portrayed coeds in an ungentlemanly way. No, the Zetes may have skipped classes and been involved in some less-than-noble behavior, but they do seem to have been politically savvy.[20]

There is certainly reason to suspect the editors of the *Oestrus*. They did not begin their antifraternity editorials until after the *Scylla*'s publication. They structured their critiques using certain phrases found in the *Scylla*, like "the top tenth of the university." In none of the publications known to have been published by Zetes about fraternity life do they ever use this language. How better to set up critiques of the fraternities by first setting up the fraternities?[21]

If the *Scylla* had been an organ of the fraternities and intended, in part, to mock the antifraternity men, shouldn't C. M. Davis, chief editor of the *Oestrus*, have been the recipient of greater venom? He is mentioned only briefly and escapes any extreme cruelties at the hands of the *Scylla*'s writers.

Finally, the *Oestrus*'s own pages include potential evidence of their part in the *Scylla*. Almost a year after the *Scylla* appeared, the *Oestrus* noted, "Rumor has it that the three fraternities have united to publish a third college paper. Good opportunity, they think, as the *Berkeleyan* is about on its last legs. It must be hard work for the fraternities to make common issue on anything after the opinions they have expressed of each other. But 'politics makes strange bed-fellows' and changes the bitterest enemies into the warmest friends." In any other instance where the *Oestrus* editors could throw past behavior in the collective face of the fraternities, they did. Why in this instance, when they could have pointed out that the last time the fraternities had colluded it had resulted in the notorious *Scylla* publication, did they omit mentioning it? Perhaps they knew that the fraternities had not been involved in the *Scylla*?[22]

Peter Pan tricked Hook's pirates into releasing Tiger Lily by perfectly imitating Hook's voice. Even Barrie admitted in his notations for the play that Peter could imitate Hook so well that sometimes even he, the author, was confused as to who was really speaking. Did the *Oestrus* write as the fraternities, or did the fraternities write to blame the *Oestrus?* This author is confused as well.[23]

The fact remains, though, that the situation did not look good for Zeta Psi and the other fraternities. A grand chapter meeting of the fraternity was held that year in San Francisco, and men rallied around the fraternities at the University of California. In December 1879, a letter was printed for distribution to the faculty members of the College of the Letters and Science of the University of California. It was signed by eighty-eight men, including district judges, state senators, former governors and U.S. senators, educators, and district attorneys from throughout the state. One notable signer was A. K. Harmon, who later donated the funds necessary to build the men's gymnasium at the university at the urging of Zete alumni Colonel George Edwards. An eight-member Committee on Behalf of Zeta Psi, as well as five other prominent Zete alumni, was among the signers. Two men of the Kappa Epsilon fraternity were also represented. Noticeably missing among the signers were members of Delta Kappa Epsilon, the recognized "bad fraternity." The letter was a petition asking the faculty to rescind their order against the secret societies. It explained in detail that eliminating them would ultimately injure the administration and injure the university throughout the state, that it was unjust, and that, ultimately, it was illegal.[24]

Several of the petition's statements clearly relate specifically to Zeta Psi, the only landholders among the secret societies. The petition states, "Such a regulation is unjust because 1. It operates indiscriminately upon the acknowledged good as well as the bad fraternities, 2. It will result in the confiscation of at least $12,000.00 worth of property already acquired by one society as well as destroy other property rights; and 3. It will prevent material assistance to worthy students and thus drive them from the university."[25]

The members of the Academic Senate discussed the petition but concluded that the regents had left them no other choice but to develop a means to outlaw the secret societies, and they kicked the matter back up to the regents. Letters to the regents demonstrate that Zeta Psi alumni Arthur Rodgers and Thomas Carneal each wrote letters on their law office letterhead asking for information on the state of the resolution. The senate apparently disposed of the matter on January 1, 1880, when someone wrote on a torn scrap of paper: " 'D' resolved that all resolutions, orders and suggestion heretofore passed or made by the Board in regards to the suppression of college secret societies be and the same are hereby rescinded and abrogated."[26]

Against all odds, the Zetes, like Peter, had escaped a watery death. The fraternities would continue on campus. For Zeta Psi, this victory would become an important part of the way they told their history. As mentioned earlier, in 1880 the fraternity stepped in for the suspended class of 1881, who should have been the publishers of *The Blue and Gold* that year, and published that year's volume. They took advantage of their editorial role, as they had so many other times in other publications, to set forth their version of the events.

> It is well to note in this connection that individual members of the Faculty, openly testified that no charges were preferred against the Zeta Psi fraternity, but that the Faculty's action was made mandatory by the Regents. Shortly after[,] a general council of all the Zeta Psis on the coast was held at San Francisco, at which it was resolved to contest the action of the authorities in every honorable way. Previously it has been agreed, however, that as the Chapter had always pursued an honorable, upright line of conduct, it would be our magnanimous duty to terminate the career of the society, (should the decision of the Regents and Faculty be legal and irrevocable). Subsequently the University Alumni Association met in Oakland, and condemned the action of the authorities as being inimical to the best interests of the University. Several leading newspapers of the State took a similar view of the case. A petition requesting the Regents to reconsider their decision was signed by many prominent citizens.
>
> Finally the matter was brought before the Board on February 10, 1880, when they rescinded their resolution of August 1879, only two members voting the contrary. The faculty likewise abrogated their decree. The "*Oestrus*" stopped publication.[27]

Note that the Iota historian conveniently includes mention of the halt of the *Oestrus* as if it had been defeated by Zetes, when in actuality it had prematurely declared victory. The history went on to state, "If there be any manliness in the other secret societies at Berkeley, on their part some feelings of gratitude are due the Iota Chapter for having, almost unaided, fought their fights and pulled them out of the mire; and it is hoped that in the future only a generous rivalry will animate them in their dealings with our fraternity."[28]

Although it would rear its head again in later decades, the antifraternity movement at the University of California never regained the momentum it had under the pressures of the *Oestrus*. The *Occident* was founded as an antifraternity paper, and, while it made many accusations against Zeta Psi and the other fraternities, the rest

TABLE 8   Zeta Psi alumni and sympathetics on the
University of California Board of Regents

Regent name	Year graduated from Cal	Years of service on board
George Ainsworth	1873	1883–1895
Arthur Rodgers	1872	1883–1902
James Herbert Budd	1873	1895–1899
John Elliot Budd	1874	1896–1913
Phoebe A. Hearst	n/a	1897–1919*
Phillip Ernest Bowles	1882	1911–1922
Jean C. Witter	1916	1945–1946
Gerald Hagan	n/a	1951–1964+

* Hearst, in what may be seen as an enlightened move, was appointed to the position of regent by Governor James Budd, an Zeta Psi Iota brother. This move may have been motivated in part by Hearst's status as a Zeta Psi mother—William Randolph Hearst was a Zeta Psi Rho at Harvard, class of 1886.

+ Hagar, an Oakland lawyer, had a son in the Iota chapter, class of 1954.

of campus seemed little interested in driving them away. As at other universities, there was little incentive for the administration to remove the secret societies. As more society houses were built, providing more housing for more students, the pressure on the universities to build dormitories or provide decent housing was reduced. Instead, the organizations became more popular, and the university did what it could to facilitate the formation of house clubs and Greek societies.[29]

Zeta Psi alumni did their part as well to secure the safety of fraternities on the campus. Beginning in 1883, Iota alumni were regularly appointed to the board of regents. George Ainsworth was appointed in 1883, followed by Arthur Rodgers later that year.[30] The *Occident* published a tirade against this situation in 1883, noting, "It is quite evident, even to a careless observer, that a campaign against the Board of Regents has been carried on in the interest of the Zeta Psi fraternity[, with] . . . a second regent appointed from the Zetes within two months of the first and within five months of the incoming new administration." The paper claimed that the state's lieutenant governor was the partner of a well-known Zete with considerable influence. What really seemed to bother the newspaper editors was that the Zetes on campus bragged about this turn of events.[31] The Zetes of the Iota chapter were continuously represented on the board of regents through 1922. As late as the 1950s, the Iota Zetes had representation on the board of regents (table 8).[32]

With the support of the regents, the fraternities were safe. By the end of the nineteenth century, the tide was turning and the campus community now favored the fraternities. In President Benjamin Ide Wheeler, hired in 1899, the university had a leader who actively supported the fraternities. For instance, in his welcoming remarks to the freshman class of 1904, he urged students to take care in selecting a fraternity:

> When you choose a club or fraternity, proceed cautiously. You are practically certain to be very greatly influenced in your whole life career by the fraternity you join. It is a serious matter. The opportunities of association and friendship offered in a good fraternity are invaluable. . . . On the whole I think the associated life represented in the life of the fraternity house constitutes a sufficiently important part of the educational opportunity of a college life to warrant me in advising a student as a general thing to look toward becoming a member in some organization.[33]

While the pirates of the antifraternity movement and the administration were temporarily tamed, dangers still lurked in Never Land. Little did the members of Zeta Psi know, but their brotherhood faced another rivalry, one that was slowly surrounding them, a menace they had failed to adequately judge—coeds.

THE WOMEN OF NEVER LAND

Females take several forms in Peter's Never Land. There are the fairies, a bunch of jealous and gossiping, possessive females. Tinkerbell primps and preens, adjusting her shirt and skirt, showing her figure to advantage, but she also possesses a cruel streak—on more than one occasion she insults people by calling them "silly asses."[34] Tinkerbell's type of female is found not so much on the campus Never Land as in the lower parts of Oakland, in Emeryville, and in the red-light district of Kearney Street in San Francisco.[35] Then there are the treacherous mermaids, who, while flirtatious with Peter, would as soon drown any competitors for his attentions, and nearly do drown Wendy. There is the Indian princess Tiger Lily, a member of a prominent family, who sees the brave Peter as a match potentially acceptable to her powerful father. And of course, there is Wendy, the vain yet clever girl-woman who sees Peter as her heart's desire—as the father to their household of Lost Boys.

Other scholars have suggested that Barrie had intimacy problems with women,[36] and while I hesitate to disparage a man's virility, it is hard to deny that the women of Never Land are a potentially emasculating bunch. Fortunately, they are almost all sexually unavailable as well. The fairies, while beautiful and fine of form, are too small to be sexual partners; the mermaids lack human genitalia and, ultimately, are nothing more than teases. These women are easy for the men of Zeta Psi to recognize, and easy for them to dismiss.

More dangerous to the free-spirited primal masculinity of brotherhood are Tiger Lily and Wendy. Tiger Lily is a formidable woman. She holds a high rank in her community, but it is not a rank that shelters or protects her. She fights pirates and leads her men in battle. She meets men as their equal. As such, she is the most threatening of Never Land's women to the masculinity of the men of Never Land—her womanhood transcends traditional gender boundaries. At the same time, this very quality makes her less likely to entrap Peter or the Lost Boys, for she deals with them as an equal. The most dangerous woman in Never Land is Wendy.

As Stacy Wolf observes, "Wendy plays out the lesson of the cult-of-true-womanhood femininity: she is dependable and a caretaker; she tells stories, makes a home for the Lost Boys, falls in love with Peter Pan."[37] She is a potential wife and mother, seemingly with no ambition for other than that role. She is ultimately what the brothers of Zeta Psi want in a marriage partner. There is only one problem for the Zetes: in the university setting, it can be difficult to separate the Tiger Lilies from the Wendys. A seemingly demure coed can hide the heart of a feminist. Few Zetes who lived in the first chapter house married coeds. Because the number of women students in the university came to almost equal that of male students, such a pattern can only be seen as a deliberate choice—and one that provides insights into how Zete men imagined their adult lives would be (table 9).

The coeds threatened men on campus in other ways too. With their suffrage agitations, women proposed to upset white male power; women's dedication to their studies threatened the men's right to academic honors; women's commitment to temperance threatened the social life of the fraternity house; and finally, women's increasing presence on campus threatened the very university traditions that reified manhood. From the perspective of the secret-society brother, any of the threats to fraternity life that arose in the late nineteenth and early twentieth centuries could, in ungenerous terms, be laid at the daintily shod feet of the coed. With that in mind, let us consider more fully the women of the University of California.

There has been surprisingly little research done on the experiences of women on the University of California campus. My focus here is on women's lives as they were likely to intersect with and shape the Zetes' experiences of the campus and campus life. Lynn Gordon's work is of particular value here, since she focuses on the experiences of Cal women during the Progressive Era.[38]

TABLE 9   Graduates of the University of California,
1870–1900

Year	Number of women	Number of men	Total
1870	0	4	4
1871	0	11	11
1872	0	8	8
1873	0	5	5
1874	1	24	25
1875	0	28	28
1876	3	31	34
1877	1	29	30
1878	3	27	30
1879	8	54	62
1880	9	32	41
1881	4	26	30
1882	5	38	43
1883	10	22	32
1884	9	17	26
1885	8	25	33
1886	5	16	21
1887	7	37	44
1888	3	33	36
1889	5	34	39
1890	8	39	47
1891	6	50	56
1892	20	44	64
1893	19	57	76
1894	33	71	104
1895	38	78	116
1896	53	101	154
1897	70	94	164
1898	100	142	242
1899	100	129	229
1900	90	146	236

Perhaps because her study focuses on the period of 1890 to 1920, Gordon paints a more dismal view of women's campus life during the period of 1870–1890 than I gained from my readings of archival materials. Gordon and I agree that the structure of university life and class events marginalized women students. The violent aspects of freshman rush, the athletics programs, and even the distinctive dress traditions of male classmates were not available to women, who had to cheer from the sidelines and communicate a separate set of values through their clothing—that of propriety and gentility. Housing for female students was limited, and many lived at home. As noted before, there may be some truth to Ferrier's suggestion that the difficulty of travel from Oakland to the new university campus led to significant withdrawal rates by female students.[39] I have to disagree, however, with Gordon's assertion that "female students sparked no interest in the faculty or community, had no access to the main currents of student life, and did not, during the first generation, create a strong campus presence."[40] The numbers of women graduating from the University of California were small during the 1870s and 1880s. The first degree awarded to a woman at the university was granted in 1874. Only seventeen other women graduated from the university during the 1870s. By the 1880s, however, small but consistent numbers of women were graduating every year; sixty-five graduated that decade.[41] And although small in number, these successful women insinuated themselves into many facets of campus life. Ultimately, their successes attracted the support of generous benefactors, most notably Phoebe A. Hearst in the 1890s. I am not suggesting that women's lives on campus were easy or that women were welcomed. Still, the quiet progress they made during these early decades is worthy of our attention.

When the University of California was founded, women were not explicitly blocked from entrance; they were not actively recruited, either. California suffered from a shortage of teachers, and the university provided greater educational opportunities than the small private normal schools and colleges found throughout the state. The attitudes of male students toward the coeds seem at first to have been welcoming—at least, welcoming in a patronizing way, but not openly hostile.[42]

One of the first women students gives us a rare opportunity to hear about the female experience on campus. Josephine Lindley, daughter of a prominent Berkeley family, was, remarkably, one of three original editors of the *University Echo;* her name appears on the masthead for March 1871. It was surely she who penned the article in favor of coeducation at the University of California. It is worth quoting a sample from the piece here, where the editorial acknowledges that the original reaction of many male students to women entering the university was negative and then goes on to explain why men should favor coeducation.

> Feminine delicacy is certainly a necessity requisite to true womanhood, but it does not suffice in itself. Every young lady should be fitted to *do* something in life. Too many of this period are raised in extravagance, and care only for the superficial glitter of an easy, exciting social life. Men cry out against woman's extravagances and trifling, yet they are the first to condemn the opening of nobler paths to her. Her education will not necessarily prevent her from properly filling her sphere in domestic life.[43] [Emphasis in original.]

Note that Lindley is using a tactic commonly used to support women's participation in higher education—arguing that education will not conflict with women's traditional roles. Note also that Lindley has avoided making the argument that education will enhance woman's role as a housekeeper—she clearly did not believe such a thing.[44]

Lindley is interesting to us for another reason—the other editors for the *Echo* at this time were none other than Zeta Psi brothers E. B. Pomeroy and F. H. Whitworth. Three other Zetes—Ed Parker, George Reed, and T. Carneal—were business editors for the newspaper. One might wonder how Zetes came to be editors, even if only for a short time, alongside a coed, particularly given the anticoeducation attitude later attributed to them. There is a simple answer to this question—brotherly and gentlemanly behavior would dictate that they treat Lindley, the sister of Zete David Lindley, with respect. This, combined with any support Lindley may have provided for his sister's appointment, may have led to this extraordinary arrangement. Examples of Zeta Psi men collaborating with campus women as equals are not common in the history that followed.[45]

A less complementary portrait of coeds appeared in the *University Echo* in 1873, after Josephine Lindley had left the university. The essay was written under the name "the chaplain." The piece is somewhat confusing. Letters to the paper indicate that several readers took the essay as a serious call to action against coeds, because the writer urged men to treat coeds with contempt and to bitterly oppose coeducation. Yet there are aspects of the essay that suggest "the chaplain" is a straw man for ignorance, that the essay is intended to galvanize support for coeducation. Consider this passage: "When women are settling themselves up for astronomers, naturalists and the like, and moreover gaining countenance and standing among those powerful but ungodly men—the scientists, and when the girls at our schools are doing so abominably well, it behooves us to take a firm stand. But fear not dear brethren, women are not our equals. St. Paul is greater with statistics. Instinct is higher than reason. Institution is higher than demonstration. There is a God-given instinct in man that tells him woman is his inferior—never mind the facts."[46] Whatever the writer's intent, he or she accurately describes the conflicts that were to arise on campus—man's instinctual sense of superiority was going to be challenged on every front, intellectual, physical, social, and political.

The second volume of *The Blue and Gold* features a description of women's arrival on campus. "In the year 1872, on one of September's sunniest days, fifty-seven young hopeful hearts assembled on the old university campus. . . . Eight of these were of California's fair daughters, who came for the first time to battle for educational honors, and well they have sustained their part, gaining at once the esteem of professors and students."[47] I have reread this passage, and the larger text it comes from, several times, and I can find in it no evidence that we are to take these comments as satirical or ironic. As time went on, however, increasingly open hostility was expressed toward coeds.[48]

SENIOR SURVEYS

The senior surveys in *The Blue and Gold* provide some interesting insights into attitudes toward women on campus. During the 1880s, many editions of *The Blue and Gold* included senior surveys, which presented the vital statistics of the senior class, as well as their plans for the future, preferences, and attitudes on debates of the day. Height, weight, desired future occupation versus probable future occupation, political affiliation, and favorite drink were all categories included in the survey at different times. These surveys provided students with an opportunity to make humorous remarks or obliquely refer to particular events of note in their college careers. One of the most interesting categories was "Position on Coeducation." This was not a consistent feature of the survey but was included often enough to be worthy of some discussion, particularly the Zetes' answers.

The senior class of 1880, composed of sixty-four persons, included eight women. Only twenty-eight of the class members spoke in favor of coeducation. Notably, four of the women were among those against it. Among those for it was Anna Head, who later distinguished herself as a Berkeley educator. Five Zetes were listed as graduating that year: Henry R. Havens, John D. McGillivray, Frederick W. Henshaw, Joseph Mailliard, and Walter H. Nicholson. All indicated they were against coeducation.[49]

Forty-two of forty-three graduating seniors of the class of 1881 decided to answer the coeducation question. This class was overwhelmingly in support of coeducation—twenty-seven responded in the affirmative, while only fifteen were negative. Only one of the nine women indicated that she did not favor coeducation. Such was the harmony between the sexes in this particular class that even two of the four Zete brothers—Arthur Leslie Whitney and Edward Henry Shepard—voted in support of coeducation.[50]

The harmony of the class of 1881 was not shared by that of 1882. This was the class that had been decimated by the "Bogus" in 1879. Perhaps residual tensions from that event shaped the class dynamic. Still, the women had been active in campus life, with a woman serving as senior class essayist and poet. There were twenty-three graduates, nineteen of whom voted "no" on the question of coeducation. The only affirmative answers came from the women. As in 1879, all the graduating Zetes expressed their displeasure with coeducation. At least one of the women in this graduating class demonstrated a sharp sense of humor. In response to the question What is your favorite beverage, Kate Ophelia Sessions responded, "Vinegar." She listed her future occupation as "women's rights."[51]

Sessions's answers may reflect some of the experiences of her female classmates with the men. Tensions within the academic year that extended beyond the graduating class are hinted at in the yearbook, which defines *coed* as a "nondescript, a snob." The freshmen seemed to have suffered dissention within their ranks as well. The "Freshman Notes" section of the yearbook remarks, "The young ladies bravely took the Glee Club in hand, but because of the want of cooperation upon the part of the young men, it has not yet proved a decided success, so far as the development of our voices is concerned." J. Frick, a Zete, was the only male member of the Freshman Glee Club. Frick was also the only Zete not pursuing a degree in the science related fields, opting rather for the literary course, where the women of the university were concentrated. Perhaps his participation in the Glee Club represents an open mind on his part about supporting his coed classmates. Perhaps a lovely coed convinced him they absolutely needed his tenor. Frick was one of the few Zetes from this period to marry a coed classmate.[52]

The Zetes may not have supported coeducation, but they certainly enjoyed female company under the proper circumstances. An 1883 article in the *Occident* complains about the behavior of some couples at the Charter Day celebrations. The article observes, "It is a somewhat remarkable fact as indicative of their standards of manhood and womanhood, that they are almost without exception opposed to coeducation, and it is more remarkable that they receive attentions exclusively from a faction among the young men who have been, and are now, open and avowed opponents of coeducation of the sexes."[53] The remarks about the implicated men seem directed at the fraternity men, who were as a group anticoeducation in their opinions.

The question of coeducation was not asked of the class of 1883, but there is a curious aspect to the senior survey for that year: none of the eight senior women filled in the blank next to the question about future occupation. In previous surveys, women had responded, "At home," or "None" when they planned to marry and become homemakers. One is tempted to wonder whether the lines left blank represent censoring of the women by the editors of *The Blue and Gold*.[54]

For the class of 1885, the question of coeducation returned, and the some of the twenty-seven respondents displayed creativity in of their answers. Ten members supported coeducation; twelve, including four women, did not. In addition, one responded, "Forgot," another responded "Was," and another responded in a way that could possibly be viewed as affirmative: "Yum! Yum!" Zete brother Frank H. Powers supported coeducation. His brother Harry Badger contributed an emphatic "No!" to this question, but also offered that "girls" were his hobby.[55]

In *The Blue and Gold* for the class of 1886, it is apparent that any kind of sociological insights the survey might have provided are lost, as the survey had degenerated into a competition to see who could create the cleverest response. Thirty-eight graduates, of whom eight were women, responded. Six responded with "yes," thirteen responded with "no," and two responded with "indifferent." The responses "depends on the coed," "certainly," "slightly," "yes with some doubt," "sometimes," "perhaps," "never," "violently," "not decided," "oh-no," "oh yes," "of course," "only in the public schools," "no ∞," "vacillating," "no sir!" and the emphatic "no!" were recorded once each. Zete brothers were among the less colorful respondents, with brothers Sutton, Stone, and McAllister all responding "no." Perhaps the range of responses represents what students already knew—as contested as coeducation at the University of California was, it was not going to end and, therefore, was no longer an issue for serious debate.[56]

THE QUEST FOR ACADEMIC HONOR AND RESPECT

In 1880, the faculty awarded a woman student, Mary A. Hawley, the University Medal. There was apparently little fuss over this, for there is little notation of it in the Academic Senate's records.[57]

The following year, the faculty was faced with a dilemma: two students had extremely close records, and deciding between them proved difficult. The academic record of Zeta Psi brother Douglas Lindley showed he had earned 21 course-hours of first honors, 13 course-hours of second honors, and 5 course-hours of third honors, and had 2 course-hours that he simply passed. Alice E. Pratt had earned 24 course-hours of first honors, 22 course-hours of second honors, and 4 course-hours of third honors. In the 1883 Academic Senate records, an entry explains how grade points were determined. Every hour of first honors was worth 95 points, each hour of second honors was worth 85, an hour of third honors was worth 70, and a pass was worth 50. A student needed a 60-point average to earn a degree. Using these calculations, Pratt had an 88.6 average, qualifying her to graduate magna cum laude. Lindley had earned an 86.58. The medal should have gone to Pratt, who had carried a heavier course load and achieved a higher grade rank.[58]

While the notes of the Academic Senate meeting do not explain what the problem in the matter was, they clearly *thought* they had a problem. Professor Martin Kellogg suggested that the faculty recommend to the regents that the medal be divided between the two students.[59] The matter was referred to the regents, who in turn had referred the issue of the medal back to the faculty. The medal, it would appear, was not divisible.[60]

Lindley's record magically changed between meetings of the Academic Senate. He had now earned 24 hours of first honors, 19 hours of second honors, and 5 hours of third honors. His "passed" grades had disappeared. But with 48 hours instead of 41, and his grades miraculously raised, his 88.4 average was still a fraction of a point lower than Pratt's. It would be wrong, perhaps, to suggest that the presence of multiple Zete alum on the faculty (Stillman, Hawkins, Edwards) may have helped his cause, yet one cannot help but wonder about academic integrity when such things happen. Unable to decide who had earned the medal, the faculty did not award it that year. Each of the outstanding scholars was to receive a certificate of commendation.[61]

The following year, the senate was faced with a three-way tie for the medal. This time, the medal was divided among students David Bancroft, John Joseph Dwyer, and Catherine Hittell, the second University of California woman to receive the University Medal, or at least part of it. Six more women were awarded the medal between 1882 and 1910.[62]

Although small in number, the early women students of the university did insinuate themselves into student groups. May Sheperd served as literary editor for the

Berkeleyan (which was still heavily affiliated with the fraternities) and the *Oestrus*. She was frequently mentioned in the papers for her affiliation with the Neolean Rhetorical Society and the Glee Club. Millicent Shinn, too, served in a number of literary positions, including that of class poet. Other women, too, regularly participated in glee clubs and rhetorical societies. Perhaps because their numbers were too small for them to effectively organize and effect broad-scale changes in student culture, they were ribbed but did not face the open hostility that came to typify gender relations on campus in the early 1900s.[63] The image of the serious, always studying, coed was entrenched, and was embodied in the slang term *pelican*, but we should not necessarily see this as an intended cruelty.

The caustically humorous portrayal of a university instructor in *The Blue and Gold* produced by the class of 1896 caused a campus uproar. The butt of the joke physically threatened the yearbook's editor with a cane for insulting his fiancée's honor. Students asked to remark on the case thought it all very absurd, noting that it was an honor to be important enough to rate mention, even if it meant a laugh at one's expense. One student recalled a coed who had done several crazy stunts during the year, enough to warrant mention in the yearbook, but who had been figured out by the editor and was, therefore, not mentioned.[64] While some limericks and bogus stories might be dismissed as good-natured poking by classmates, as time went on there was less humor and more malice; fewer jabs and more stabs.

Despite the achievements of women as scholars, not all faculty members respected their presence. The appointment of Benjamin Ide Wheeler, a man who held nineteenth-century views of women, as president seems to have emboldened bad behavior toward the women by faculty and students alike. Although appointed in 1899, Wheeler neglected to address the female students until 1904. When he did, it was to remind them that their duty was to become housewives and mothers, not spinsters and schoolteachers.[65] The full extent of his comments were published on the front page of the student newspaper the *Daily Cal*, and one can only wonder about the psychological impact of these statements on the university community. Whereas the presidencies of Davis and Kellogg had seen quiet progress for women on campus, the Wheeler administration represents a period of extreme gender unrest on campus. Wheeler, as most clearly evidenced by his friendship with Teddy Roosevelt, not only was in favor of keeping women in the home but also was an advocate for the new masculinity that had come to be favored.

Debates about coeducation at the college level were being waged nationally. The experiment of coeducation had been going on in some places for several decades, and administrators weighed in on the merits and weaknesses of the project. Some of the critiques are not surprising—coeducation was blamed for an increase in coarse behavior among women. Edward Parsons of Colorado College complained about the behavior of coeds he witnessed following a football game between two coeducational institutions: "On the side lines were a host of shrieking young women, and after the game was over the young women of the victorious college marched with the young men in procession down the street . . . screaming and waving their banners. If this is what coeducation means, I said to myself, I want none of it." Parsons wasn't completely negative about coeducation; he did concede that at least coeducation had cut down on "extravagant affections of young women for one another," or "crushes," as they were called, that were the "curse" of all women's colleges![66]

Parsons and others were concerned that women were driving men from coursework in the humanities and letters. In an address to the Modern Language Association of America in 1909, A. G. Canfield lamented, "Visit any class where a course in literature is being given and there will be found such a one-sided predominance of skirts over trousers that one fancies there must be some deeper connection between petticoats and poetry than that of accidental alliteration."[67] Ellen Hinsdale, of Mount Holyoke College, countered this observation, suggesting that men were leaving the humanities for the sciences due to market forces. "So long as undeveloped resources of this country afford large opportunities for making money, so long will commercialism prevail, so long will the pursuit culture be largely in the hands of the women."[68] Still, male faculty took advantage of the separation of the sexes along curricular lines to create all-male spaces within the university. Such conflicts became visible at Berkeley at the same time they were being debated nationally.[69]

In 1903 and 1904, the actions of two faculty members who barred women from their classrooms drew attention from the broader California community. A January 3, 1903, article in the *Daily Cal* appears under the headline "No Coeds Need Apply: Professor Gayley Saves His Class for Men Students through Heroic Efforts." Gayley's course on great books was being held in the newly built lecture hall in the students' observatory and was overenrolled, forcing some students to stand to hear the lecture. The *Daily Cal* reported that "gallantry prompted the men to give up their seats to the young ladies, who constituted the major part of the audience." Gayley had apparently designed the course for the men of the engineering college and ordered the women to leave so that the 'those for whom the course had been specially designed might enjoy it under the most auspicious circumstance.' The request was rather startling, but was complied with in apparent good grace. Roll call hereafter will probably show a large number of women students absent."[70]

The event triggered angry letters, published elsewhere and reprinted in the *Daily Cal*. A letter originally printed in the *Sacramento Bee* declared that it was time for newspapers to interfere in college affairs:

Professor Charles Mills Gayley is attracting attention because he has set his face against the scheme of co-education in a college guaranteed by its charter to be co-educational. Martin Flaherty, instructor in English, declares that his classes are open to the properly prepared, but women do not feel that they are wanted by Martin Flaherty.

There are undoubtedly too many professors in the University of California not in sympathy with the liberal-minded policy of the pioneers who founded it. The professorial spirit of exclusion of women, expressed openly, though merely by segregation, as in the "Great Book" affair, is much cruder in the cry of the fellows. And this is the cry: "The co-eds should not crowd us out" as if they were first and women as after-thought.[71]

Following up on this letter was a letter from an alumna published in the *Daily Cal*:

Co-education is an integral part of the policy of the University. Whatever may be a man's individual opinions on the subject of its advisability, he cannot deny its popular ratification into the State Constitution. Any blow at its legitimacy and propriety is a direct blow at the existing structure of the University. We look to our University president and faculty for the most affectionate, loyal and consistent support to our University, and when men from these ranks are guilty of denunciation of co-education, public or private, direct or implied, we must regard it as a flagrant breach of their oath of service. Moreover, such sentiments from a faculty man, uttered in a caustic and undignified manner, occasion a newspaper furor that breeds infinite gossip against the University's best interests, and many loyal hearts are heavy with apprehension of the ultimate results of such a movement.[72]

Despite the uproar, less than two weeks later, the *Daily Cal* announced yet another faculty person excluding women—this time from a French club that met in the home of Professor M. J. Spinello, who asserted, "Men and women are no longer to associate in a University French Club. It has been found that the presence of the gentler sex leads the men to emphasize the social rather than the educational value of such a society."[73]

The move to isolate women on campus spread from faculty to students. In 1904 a new drama group, the "In the Meantime Club," intended for men only, was founded. Class rallies and glee club performances before the Big Game were declared men-only events, since the presence of females was believed to inhibit the enthusiasm and natural expression of the male fans.[74]

While the women of the university may have found themselves powerless against professors who blocked them from classes, they refused to take similar abuse from other students. As the male students of the university followed the professors' leads and increasingly began to exclude female students from university spaces and activities, the women pushed back.

SPACES OF THEIR OWN

The men of the University of California became accustomed to creating the spaces of the campus in their image. They had superior numbers and, as a result, were able to claim many spaces as their exclusive realms. They populated open spaces with their athletic games and rushes, they colonized the outdoor benches on the basis of their class standing, and they lounged on stairways in groups. They built houses and rented others for living quarters. At first, the university women worked around their male colleagues. They attempted to fill in little spaces left behind. When lounging men blocked one flight of stairs at North Hall, the women dutifully walked to the stairs on the other side of the building. Eventually, as their numbers swelled, so did their confidence. It occurred to the women that they deserved spaces of their own, and conflicts ensued.[75]

In 1879, the *Oestrus* demonstrated that fraternity men were not the only members of the campus community who annoyed the paper's editors. An editorial complained about the "girls" in the area of the ladies' room at North Hall: "It is a great pity that classes should be interrupted and the quiet necessary for study should be disturbed by six or seven, and that all, who go near the Ladies' Room, should get credit for being among the disorderly ones." The editorialist went on to lecture that the women responsible were "big children, who have not yet learned the difference between the play ground and the school room or parlor."[76]

Well, Wendy wasn't all that interested in growing up either, was she? Why should the Lost Boys have all the fun? There is a subtext here: the university men had staked out the stairs of North Hall as their territory and could be found lounging there in the sun; they also had a senior men's room in North Hall. The creation of a ladies' room in a building that had been claimed as masculine space was likely the source of the irritation expressed. Nor were the ladies content with just a room. As early as 1893, they agitated, in a polite and ladylike way, for the means to practice physical culture:

> A frail body won't support the kind of work men want to do here, and, were it not for the careful and systematic work done in the Department of Physical Culture, many a man would be unable to go very far in his University career. But why should such advantages be open only to the young men of the University? With the present accommodation there are only two hours a week (drill hours) when the young women can use the gymnasium. We need a Department of Physical Culture for Women. The extent to which they avail themselves of the meager opportunities which are now offered promises well the success of such a department should it be established.[77]

Until they had a gym, the women would find other ways to develop their bodies as well as their minds. They engaged in boating and archery, and in 1891 organized a tennis club. By 1896, they also had a basketball team that competed with Stanford.[78] They gym they desired would have to wait nearly a decade, however, until Phoebe Hearst, philanthropist and patron saint of the California coed, donated her home, Hearst Hall, to the university for use, in part, as a women's gymnasium. The magnificent structure was relocated to a site on College Avenue and dedicated in early 1901. Next to it was built a set of tennis courts and a ladies' basketball court. The building was more than a gymnasium; it became a center of women's student life, complete with lounges and meeting areas. The beautiful structure and well-equipped facility drew appreciative (and jealous) comments from the men.[79]

It is worth noting that Hearst Hall was located almost directly across from Zeta Psi's chapter house (figure 20).[80] The formerly isolated fraternity had, by this time, come to be surrounded by families, including those of their professors. This circumstance, while not ideal, was not out of keeping with the image of the Victorian fraternity as an alternative household. As masculinity displaced Victorian manliness, however, the community of men would have felt more out of place. The new intrusion of women—so many women—into their corner of campus must have raised conflicting emotions in the men. Instead of the bay, the men would have now have bustling coeds in their view. Depending on their frame of mind, this could be a great improvement or a source of irritation.

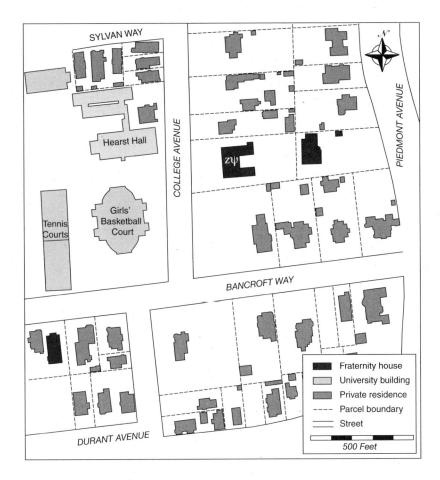

FIGURE 20
Zeta Psi's neighborhood, circa 1911, based on Sanborn Fire
Insurance maps.

The men of the university sometimes mocked outright the efforts of women to
create their own university landscape. A 1916 *Daily Cal* article titled "Feminist
Movement Gains Great Victory" told of the installation of a food counter in the
room used by the Associated Women Students (the women's branch of student
governance). "The Coed Joint will be located in the center of the AWS room,
where lunch counters and high swinging chairs will be installed. Sam the Booth-
black *[sic]* will lose his entire trade in maple nut cornucopias, for the menu includes
ice cream cones, together with milk, coffee, chocolate and sandwiches."[81]

The women's increased access to spaces of their own did not keep them from invading the territory of the men. During the summer of 1906, women caused a near riot on campus when several coeds decided to blatantly ignore the time-honored tradition that had designated the North Hall steps as a men-only spot and used those stairs to get to class—repeatedly. The outraged *Daily Cal* reported:

> Some of the most enterprising of the students of the "Summer Session" who would have the "steps tradition" kept up have put up a sign which is intended as a warning to all women from violating the privilege which has been in the past particularly for the men students. A prominent senior at the University who is attending the Summer Session said when spoken to about the subject:
>
> > "I cannot understand why it is that these women refuse to keep off North Hall steps. It is not through ignorance, because I have seen women stop, read this sign, and then deliberately make use of the steps. If they persist in refusing to conform to the tradition, the fellows should form a guard to sit around more and whenever a woman turns up, blow so much tobacco smoke on her that she will be glad to make her departure."[82]

The men apparently retaliated by pouring buckets of water on two of the women, leading to an editorial protest in an Oakland paper. The *Daily Cal* countered that the tradition of reserving those steps for men was upheld by the female university students without problem, and that this was an instance of two troublemaking women from San Francisco coming over to raise a fuss. The paper suggested that, instead of calling the men who threw the water brutes, readers should question the unladylike behavior of the two women.[83] Note that the men were no longer concerned with maintaining gentlemanly behavior.

It is questionable whether the university women respected the tradition or merely feared retaliation that might follow any attempt to challenge that tradition. The writer of a 1904 letter to the *Daily Cal* remarked, "I have many a day had to go the double length of North Hall and make the third floor in about three minutes, and I am one of hundreds with the same experience. Opposed to this the men advance these two arguments, also containing some good horse sense, whatever else it may show: 'North Hall Steps for Men Only' is the only tradition in which all men students share. 2. If the men students are driven from the Steps what single attractive spot on the entire campus is reserved for men only? We submit the opposing propositions for consideration."[84]

The North Hall steps issue was resolved in a simple enough way. North Hall was torn down in 1917, an event that inspired speechmaking and reminisces from male alumni remembering the good old days on the steps. Strangely enough, the women did not contribute to these discussions.[85]

While the North Hall Steps drew much debate, women contested other male spaces as well. In 1907, women strolled into the men's gymnasium. "After gazing at the frolics of the freshmen for some time they slowly sauntered out seemingly unconscious of the shocked gaze of the freshies, who modestly hid themselves behind barbells."[86] Through their actions, the women let the men know that they were in an expansionistic mood. This mood extended to campus governance.

FEMALE GOVERNANCE: AWS AND ASUC

Men had organized the Associated Students of the University of California (ASUC) as a student government body in 1887. This was a patriarchal organization that allowed women to be voting members but did not let them hold leadership positions. Women organized their own group, the Associated Women Students (AWS), in 1894; it existed both separately and as a subdivision of the ASUC. This ambiguous status became problematic later. The latter became the institution through which women students organized activities, set up athletic clubs, ran an annual Women's Day, and introduced new women to the university. The AWS raised money to build a senior women's hall and, in 1901, organized a women's honor society, the Prytaneans.[87]

The apathy that the ASUC engendered in women students was demonstrated in 1900, when it was reported in the *Daily Cal* that they were less likely than male students to have paid their annual one-dollar dues to the ASUC. The male treasurer of ASUC exhorted them to pay these dues, laying out the financial problems for student activities that would arise if they did not pay. Ironically, the same article complained that women did not take advantage of the opportunities on campus.[88]

In 1902, the *Daily Cal* advocated the separation of the AWS from the ASUC, following up on notification from someone in the AWS that the organization was considering withdrawal from the ASUC. The newspaper's editors argued that, in close elections, the female vote often had a negative impact on outcomes, and that it would therefore be desirable for women to withdraw from the ASUC. The issue was raised again in 1906. Again, the editors of the student newspaper said it was unfair that the women belonged to both the ASUC and the AWS while paying only the one-dollar dues for membership in both organizations. Underlying the *Daily Cal*'s effort to drive women out of the ASUC was the editors' conviction that women were interfering with the election of male officers.[89]

An account of the 1906 student elections blasted women students. "One special source of gratification is that all of the successful office-seekers were elected by the intelligent and thinking vote of the students—that of the men. The women as usual voted the way they were told or coaxed to vote regardless of 'race, color, or previous condition of servitude.' Fortunately the female ballots had no evil effects on the election." Two days later, the editors defended their position, stating that the women had based their votes only candidates' appearance.[90]

The editors noted that the women ran all their own activities and therefore did not need the ASUC. They also complained that the AWS took away three-quarters of the dues that the women paid to the ASUC, and again argued that the organizations should divide. The editors failed to recognize that, if the women were organizing all their own activities, it was absurd for the ASUC to take *any* of the women's dues. In 1907, it was reported that the AWS had proposed to the ASUC to become a separate organization. The women recognized that it was to their advantage to retain 100 percent of their dues rather than 75 percent. Their proposal included the following conditions: (1) the ASUC would be renamed the Men's ASUC; (2) 100 percent of the women's dues would go to the women; and (3) the officers of the two organizations would meet and collectively decide on matters of mutual interest. However, the amendment that went before the ASUC did not include the structural changes requested by the women, and it would only further disenfranchise them from governance of the university. They urged the men of the ASUC to vote against the measure—which to their credit they did, in January 1908.[91] It is likely that squabbles about women's voting rights on the campus level were fueled by the growing national suffrage movement, a movement that would soon have a high profile on campus.

SUFFRAGE

No other political issue shaped relations between the sexes on the University of California campus more than that of female suffrage. California women in general gained the vote in 1911, well before they could vote in national elections. While there were women students at Cal who identified themselves as part of the Women's Rights political party in the 1880s, there is no evidence of sustained political action on the part of campus women in regard to suffrage or other women's rights issues beyond campus boundaries until 1908, when Mrs. Charles Parks, a suffrage advocate, addressed campus women. The *Daily Cal* notes that it was the first time women's suffrage "was permitted to be introduced" at the university. President Wheeler gave her a tepid introduction, but the crowd response to Mrs. Parks was said to be wildly enthusiastic.[92]

A mere three weeks later, perhaps on the wave of enthusiasm generated by the visiting lecturer, it was announced that campus women were organizing a suffrage club. The club declared itself to be pro-suffrage and invited all university women to attend its meetings. Notably, a Zeta Psi neighbor, May Sheperd Cheney, now the university's appointment secretary (the head of the career center), was quoted as a supporter of the club, saying that it was an issue of which "no educated women of the present day can afford to be ignorant." In 1910, the club received a donation of a library collection. The club hosted many visiting lecturers throughout the years of 1910 and 1911 and, to a lesser degree, following the passage of the California state law allowing women the vote.[93]

Most of the club's meetings were held at private homes off the university property, and at least one ad for the group reassured readers that both sides of the issue would be considered. Such caution was necessary. President Wheeler did not support suffrage, and in 1911 his wife hosted a lecture by an antisuffragist from Massachusetts who addressed female students.[94] Male students were not supportive either. The *Pelican*, a campus humor magazine, had the following to say:

> Pelly was always for co-education until it produced suffragettes. Too bad, too bad! Pause a moment, dear ladies, and consider it well before it is too late. Remember that these bad habits we form in our impressionable youth sometime ruin what little chance of future happiness we have. A Co-ed and a Suffragette—heavens! What a reputation to live down in the eyes of us unreasonably exacting men. Pelly is laying two to one without any takers that good judgment will prevail and none of you will show up next meeting.[95]

The women students had answers for these critiques, but got to voice them in print only in the women's issues of the *Pelican* and other campus journals. The 1904 women's issue of the *Pelican* carried a pithy comeback: "Men say that when a girl enters college she renounces all hope of marriage. Looking at the college man, can you blame her?"[96]

In 1909, the University of California debate team, whose membership was restricted to men, competed against Stanford's team on the question of female suffrage. Cal's team argued against suffrage and won the debate. When Stanford's team asked,

"Why should women be excluded on the grounds of sex?," the Cal team responded that debates were not contingent on such questions. Instead, they argued, because voting was a privilege, there had to be a practical benefit to extending the vote to women. They recognized two types of women as populating the world, the economically dependent and the economically independent. They argued that there would be no societal benefit to extending the vote to either, because "the first class would vote as their husbands did; the second, a transitory class, would divide practically as the men, while the vicious element would be a class working naturally for evil." Apparently these arguments were convincing to the male judges, who awarded the debate to the Cal team.[97]

While the suffrage organization on campus was able to bring in men sympathetic to suffrage from outside the campus community, within the university this issue was one that, at least in public discourses, divided the students along gender lines.

THE SORORITIES

After the fraternities successfully fended off the attacks of the antisociety pirates in 1880, an extraordinary organization was formed on campus, a women's fraternity, Kappa Kappa Gamma. Very little is actually known about this organization. It first appears in *The Blue and Gold* yearbook in 1882, with a list of thirteen members, all women. The Kappa Kappa Gamma masthead proclaims that the fraternity was founded in 1880. Kappa Kappa Gamma, as a national fraternity, was founded in 1870. This is an interesting group of women. Of the thirteen listed in 1882, nine went on to graduate, a 69 percent graduation rate at the time when the graduation rate for male fraternities was 53 percent, and for the overall university was 39 percent. Of the nine women who graduated, only three had married by the time the 1905 *University of California Alumni Directory* was published. This is in contrast to the 83 percent of women overall who ultimately married after graduating in the 1880s. Among the members was Fannie McLean, who became a Berkeley High School teacher and a noted local suffragist.[98]

Kappa Kappa Gamma disappears from the yearbook in 1885. The purpose of the group and the reasons for its dismantling are at this time unknown, but the group was the earliest women's secret society on the university campus. Another would not follow until 1890, when Kappa Alpha Theta was founded; included among its members was Julia Morgan, the well-known architect. In 1891, that sorority had nineteen members, a number that grew to twenty-three by 1893. The short-lived Tau Delta, established in 1893, had eleven members. The University of California

Sorosi was founded in 1894 and had an initial membership of thirteen. Throughout the 1890s, these groups continued to grow in both number of organizations and number of women involved.[99]

The founding of sororities and women's clubhouses was encouraged by Dr. Mary Ritter, who was hired as a physician and hygiene instructor for the women's physical culture program, and by Phoebe Hearst, who funded the first two nonsorority clubhouse residences for women. Ritter had found in her dealings with female students that the expense of living on campus forced them into unsanitary housing conditions and often malnourishment. The clubhouses allowed for communal living in a healthy environment where women were surrounded by other students and could share expenses in a way that would improve their standard of living.[100] While clubhouses filled a dire need for women from less elite backgrounds, the sororities seem to have drawn no small number of their members from the same families that provided fraternity brothers. There are surnames on sorority rolls that match those of Zeta Psi and other fraternities. While the presence of sororities threatened the exclusive male nature of secret societies, they also offered the possibility of a class of coeds who would potentially be appropriate marriage partners.

IN PERSPECTIVE

The Progressive Era brought many changes to campus life. As men and women debated where the social, political, and economic boundaries between them should be placed, a populist movement attempted to chip away at the elitism of the secret societies. Zeta Psi, as envisioned by its earlier members, had become an anachronism. To compete in the brave new world, the fraternity would have to redefine itself, to rebuild itself and create new ways for its members to express their brotherhood to one another. This would have to be done in ways not indebted to the domesticity of their mothers and the civilized manhood of their fathers. They would have to re-create fraternity as a complete expression of their newfound masculinity. The brothers of Zeta Psi would do this by recrafting the space in which they lived out their bonds of fraternal life, and by recrafting the daily rituals through which they embodied those bonds.

PROGRAM FOR ACT IV

The act opens with the Indians protecting the Lost Boys' hideout—Tiger Lily is providing protection in return for Peter having saved her life. In Peter's underground house, Wendy is beginning to find her role as mother exhausting—especially since Peter has made it clear that he doesn't relish the role of father, even if it is only pretend. Peter expresses his confusion over exactly what it is the women in his life want from him— leading to a rare display of unity by Tink and Wendy, who agree that Peter is a "silly ass."

The bedtime story that Wendy tells this evening is about Mr. and Mrs. Darling and how they miss their escaped children, who have flown to Never Land. The distraught parents keep the window of the nursery open in the hope that their children will return. Wendy is so moved by her own story that she convinces her brothers, who are already forgetting home, that they must return home immediately. She convinces all the Lost Boys to join them, certain they will be welcomed into the Darling's domestic realm. Peter refuses to join in, sending Tink instead, who darts ahead.

As the children prepare to go, the pirates attack the Indians, and the battle is heard below. The Lost Boys, the Darling brothers, and Wendy take their leave after Peter assures them that the beating of the tom-tom means the Indians have won. Wendy pleads one last time for Peter to join them, then urges him to at least take care of himself and to continue to take his medicine. The group leaves. Unfortunately, the pirates have imitated the sound of the drums to trick the youngsters, and as they exit, the pirates grab them. Unaware, Peter has fallen asleep, and Hook sneaks into the house and poisons the medicine Wendy left for

Peter. Tink returns to tell Peter just as he is about to take the medicine. He doesn't believe her, so she drinks it herself to save him. As her light slowly fades, Peter urges the audience to believe in fairies so that her life can be saved. Tink is saved, and as the act closes, the pair exit to fight the pirates and rescue their comrades.

ACT IV · The House Underground

Zeta Psi's New House

PETER (*with a drum beating in his breast as if he
were a real boy at last*).   To die will be an
awfully big adventure.

Peter Pan

ZETES.   Let us eat, drink and be merry for tomorrow
we die.

The Blue and Gold, 1893

PETER.   Why, Tink, you have drunk my
medicine! (*She flutters strangely about the
room, answering him now in a very thin tinkle.*)
It was poisoned and you drank it to save my
life! Tink, dear Tink, are you dying? (*He has
never called her dear Tink before, and for a
moment she is gay; she alights on his shoulder,
gives his chin a loving bite, whispers "You silly
ass," and falls on her tiny bed. The boudoir,
which is lit by her, flickers ominously. He is on
his knees by the opening.*)
    Her light is growing faint, and if it goes out,
that means she is dead! Her voice is so low I can
scarcely tell what she is saying. She says—she
says she thinks she could get well again if
children believed in fairies! (*He rises and throws
out his arms he knows not to whom, perhaps to the
boys and girls of whom he is not one.*) Do you
believe in fairies? Say quick that you believe!

Peter Pan

When Wendy was brought to Never Land, the Lost Boys built her a little house under
Peter Pan's direction. It was to be a little cottage that she could set up as a domestic
space all her own. While Peter wanted the Lost Boys to experience some of the benefits of a domestic presence, such as storytelling and being fussed over, he clearly was
not interested in having that domesticity infiltrate the underground home where he

and the Lost Boys resided. Whereas the Darling brothers would be housed with the Lost Boys, Wendy was to be alone in her little house. She could enter Peter's home under prescribed circumstances; with its earthen floor, pumpkin seats, dangling tree roots, and basket beds, the home underground was a decidedly masculine space.

The new masculinity that emerged was ultimately about re-sorting gender categories—about clearly demarcating again what made men into men and, as men saw it, relegating women to womanhood. Women sometimes found it to their advantage to segregate their activities and spaces from the men, yet at other times they found themselves unwillingly isolated and neutralized. While the Victorian period had embraced, at least in theory, the idea of home separated from work, at the turn of the century it became clear that two different spheres had replaced them: the women's world and the men's world. The complementary relationship that had marked the domestic and public spheres of the Victorians no longer existed; in the twentieth century, the male sphere was clearly constructed as socially, politically, and economically superior. Women might venture out into the worlds of college education and employment, but they were to do so within social, economic, and political spaces allowed them by men. Contradictorily, these separations and segregations were taking place at a time when men and women were spending more time socializing with one another than ever before.[1]

One part of the segregated social cultural life was a continued commitment to maintaining male-only spaces: the football field, rallies, and the North Hall steps, as already noted, were spaces on campus claimed by men. In Greek life, men claimed the right to fraternal societies; women were free to create sororities. Even the governance of these two sets of letter societies would be separated, their practices distinct and apart. The fraternities would dictate when and how the organizations could interact.

The fraternity house, more than ever, was a house underground—both metaphorically and physically. Fraternity architecture in the early 1900s became more ritualized and elaborated, with houses being designed to accommodate the ritual and practical needs of specific chapters. Basements housing chapter rooms and other ceremonial spaces became the norm.[2] The men literally disappeared underground to reaffirm their masculine bonds to one another. It was in this context that the men of Iota built their new chapter house on the University of California campus.

THE TEMPLE OF IOTA

In the winter of 1910, the brothers of Zeta Psi, past and present, gathered to watch the placement of a granite stone at the southwestern edge of what would become the new Zete Psi chapter house. This stone contained ritual paraphernalia of the fraternity (which closely guarded the stone to protect it from theft by other fraternities) and would serve as the house's cornerstone. After enduring years of taunting about the state of their magnificent old chapter house, Zeta Psi's active members had rallied their alumni troops and raised the funds necessary to build a new one. To celebrate the start of construction, all the available alumni came together to watch the laying of the ritual cornerstone. This was followed by a banquet in Hearst Hall, and finally by entertainment in the old chapter house, consisting of "a vaudeville show prepared by the active members of the fraternity now in college and ending with boxing matches and other prepared stunts."[3]

The *Oakland Tribune* gave the event front-page coverage—a testament to the stature of many of the men attending the ceremony. Prominent alumni mentioned in the paper included the former regent Arthur Rodgers, former governor James H. Budd, E. B. Pomeroy, Colonel D. B. Fairbanks, and Horry W. Meek. Lawyers Frank Powers, Frank Solinsky, George C. Edwards, Judge Thomas Denny, and Frank Duhring were mentioned as notable speakers at the event.[4]

The new house was designed by Sutton and Weeks, a well-known San Francisco architecture firm. Albert Sutton was a Zete alum (class of 1889) whose designs were much in demand. He clearly incorporated nods to Zeta Psi in his architecture. The *Oakland Tribune* featured an artist's conception of how the new house would appear (figure 21). It was a grand structure, reportedly costing thirty thousand dollars to build. Designed in the Georgian, or Greek revival, style, it would be a brick house with a tiled roof, symmetrical arched doorways across the front of the building, and medallions bearing the fraternal letters on the front of the house and the chimneys. The brick would contrast with the cheaper, wood-shingled houses of competing fraternities.[5]

It is worth considering whether the Zetes really needed a new house. Their membership had grown slightly in the years leading up to this point. Perhaps plans for the new chapter house enabled the brothers to attract more men to their ranks. The new house did not provide any great increase in sleeping space; when the fraternity's size did increase in the 1920s, surplus brothers had to live in other quarters. The original house was equipped with plumbing and electricity, features not shared by many Berkeley homes at the time the house was built. Despite the jokes about the great age of the house, the reality is that the house was only a little more than twenty years old when the mocking began. True, the house was as old as the men who lived in it, but by no stretch of the imagination is a twenty-year-old

FIGURE 21
The new Zeta Psi house as it appeared in 1936.
Photograph courtesy of H. Forkner.

house old. During the cornerstone-laying ceremony, Frank Solinsky (class of '77) offered his thoughts on the new and old houses:

> The Spirit of Zeta Psi meant an ideal to us, a something that nothing will ever be able to obliterate from our memories. And we have faith that that idea of fraternalism will live and survive in the hearts of these younger men of the new generation. But I, living here in Berkeley, as I do, realize more potently than many of the older members, I believe, that the old building is out of date. The times have changed. I realize deeply the need of the new building to meet the needs of today. There is a friendly rivalry among fraternities of the University, and ours, the first and greatest, must not be behind in anything. The new building must rise as a temple to the spirit of Zeta Psi, the spirit that is to make this fraternity the greatest and truest fraternity on this coast, perhaps the finest in America.[6]

The purpose of the new house, then, was to present a new face to the campus, one that would make it clear that Zeta Psi was a fresh and competitive fraternity, that Iota was relevant and still a powerful presence. Architecture spoke forcefully to both viewers and users.

Zeta Psi was not the only group on campus concerned with the messages that its architecture was sending. Members of the faculty sometimes found their notions of modernity in conflict with the spaces they inhabited. On the opposite end of the campus from the Zetes was the University Conservatory, a building that had been constructed as part of a retention offer for Professor Eugene Hilgard. Hilgard, a Zete neighbor, was part of the older faculty who had been reared in the educational traditions of old Europe and the Victorian era. The conservatory, built to his specifications, was a series of glass houses intended for the cultivation of particular plants involved with his soil science experiments. The finished structure had a huge domed palm house that was to store the university's tropical plants. The structure featured ornamental ironwork and had a feminine feel to its curved ceilings. For Hilgard, such a structure was necessary for the campus—all the great European campuses featured similar plant houses, he had argued to the university administration.[7]

Hilgard's younger colleagues did not agree. In 1916, when the building was renovated to serve as classroom space and laboratory space for a younger generation of the agricultural program, faculty members made it clear that they saw no future for the building on the campus. In 1929, Hilgard's glass elephant was dismantled and the space it occupied paved over. There was no functional reason to erase the building from the landscape; symbolically, however, the obviously dated building style had no place on a campus striving to construct itself as an exemplar of scientific (white masculine) progress and modernity.[8] The new masculinity, embedded as it was in discourses on whiteness, had an explicit commitment to modernity and scientific product. Male students flocked to the sciences at Cal, while women were discouraged from these courses of studies and steered instead to studies in the letters or, if it was absolutely necessary, the appropriately feminine domestic sciences.[9] Zeta Psi's need for a new, modern house was part of its embrace of the new masculinity. But the new chapter house was more than just an appropriately styled domestic space. It was also a material manifestation of the rituals and ideological values of the fraternity.

Solinsky's comparison of the house to a temple was not accidental. Temples were components of Masonic societies, places where ritual was enacted and embodied by its members; some fraternity chapters kept rooms or separate buildings they called temples, sometimes building altars in those rooms.[10] The new Zeta Psi house was designed by an Iota alumnus who knew the values, traditions, and rituals of the house. He was also, apparently, familiar with trends in the architecture of fraternal structures, be they Greek letter societies or Masonic societies. These were architectural spaces designed to communicate explicit meanings and ideas to those who used them. The new Zeta Psi house incorporated design elements that spoke both to the general values of Zeta Psi and to the specific history of the Iota chapter. To better understand how the house spoke to the ritual needs of the chapter, we must consider more broadly the role of ritual in fraternity life.

RITUAL LIFE OF FRATERNITIES

In the remains of the first house, we found little evidence of the ritual life that surely must have been part of the fraternity experience. We know that ritual—both as a means of initiation and as an expression of membership—played some role in the fraternity. There is mention of the pledge pin, an outward symbol of one's affiliation (figure 22). The Zetes themselves referred to the importance of ritual to affirming the bond between brothers. Zeta Psi, as a fraternity founded by Masons, borrowed heavily from that source in its rituals. Zeta Psi was described in 1899 as "impressing upon its members, rather more than some like organizations, the importance of profound secrecy regarding the society and its affairs."[11]

An examination of the available evidence leaves the nature of the rituals largely invisible to us, but it is possible to make some generalizations. P. F. Piper, a late-nineteenth-century essayist, provides a general overview of fraternity ritual at that time. He observes that, in general, there was much overlap in the specific rituals of the various organizations—largely because the different organizations had taken to stealing from one another. The use of initials that represented a motto and which gave the fraternity its name, and the system of signs, grips, passwords, sets of colors, flower, and crest, characterized all the organizations.[12] Piper also describes a typical hazing ritual: "There is usually a preliminary ordeal, during which the neophyte is obliged to submit to many ridiculous indignities. During this time he is required to obey all orders given by any member of the chapter to which he is pledged. Thus it happens that often a candidate may be seen rolling a peanut along a street, using a toothpick as a lever, others sell newspapers, black boots, or wheel baby carriages."[13]

Piper acknowledges that more dangerous feats were not unknown, and refers to the death of a man at Cornell and one at Yale, which had occurred just a few years earlier. At Cornell, a young man who was blindfolded and led to the edge of a gorge disobeyed the order of his brothers and stepped forward, causing all three to fall to the bottom of one of Ithaca's infamous gorges. The young man died of his injuries, but not before exonerating his companions. In the Yale case, a blindfolded man was led to an alley, where in the dark he collided with a wagon and died from his injuries. The author seemed to think that these two incidents had done much to curtail more dangerous initiation rituals among students.[14]

FIGURE 22

The design shown on Zeta Psi's pledge pin, as illustrated in the
1880 *Blue and Gold*; Joseph Mailliard wearing his pin. Photograph
courtesy of the *Condor*.

A comparison of descriptions of late-nineteenth-century Masonic initiations and
late-twentieth-century accounts of fraternal initiations show remarkable similarities
in form, given the hundred years that separate them.[15] It seems safe to suggest that
Zeta Psi's ritual was a variation on the Masonic model. In each instance, the initiate
is separated from the rest of the fraternal community—usually through the obscur-
ing of his vision—and often in some state of undress. The vulnerability of the initiate is emphasized by his lack of sight and clothing. He must trust his future brothers
that he will make it through the initiation ritual. This test puts his loyalty to the fraternity against his concern for bodily safety. The test usually results in a symbolic
death, which the initiate overcomes through courage and loyalty to the ideals of fraternity. Elaborate rituals could include a mock burial in a coffin or grave or kneeling
at a gravestone. Or an initiate might believe that he is to lose an appendage or suffer
a great wound, only to find that he is saved at the last minute. The following description provided to Peggy Sanday is probably representative of such rituals, past and
present: "He was taken blindfolded down a cold, damp passageway and into a warm
space filled with incense. He was pressed to his knees, and when his blindfold was
removed, he was kneeling in front of the president and secretary, who sat at a table.

On the table lay an iron dagger and a contract. The president pointed to the contract with the dagger. By signing the contract, Sean swore never to reveal any of the fraternity secrets."[16]

Whatever form it took, the point of the ritual was to create a sense of death and rebirth into a new state—the state of brotherhood. Particular symbols related to this are the recurring motifs in fraternity crests and pins. Axes, knives, and swords are all common, as are representations of skulls. Photographs from inside the first Zeta Psi house show that representations of—or possibly real—human skulls adorned mantels in several rooms of the house (see figures 9 and 14). The skull would have represented both the victory of brothers over their symbolic deaths and the immortality of fraternal brotherhood.

While rituals were supposed to be secret, they were poorly kept secrets. *The Blue and Gold* featured illustrations introducing each section of the yearbook, and in many editions the pictures introducing the section on fraternities depicted robed figures threatening bound men. The women's issues of the *Pelican* provided an opportunity for sorority women, often the target of the magazine's sharp humor, to mock the fraternity's rituals and hazing. A cartoon in 1908 depicted men being "tubbed." Likewise, a doctored photograph from the 1936 *Blue and Gold* shows tubbing. Tubbing was a popular punishment for freshman at Zeta Psi.[17] In literature on fraternity hazing, tubbing and paddling are most often mentioned. A 1893 photograph from the front of the first Zeta Psi house shows two men holding paddles (figure 23).[18] Based on alumni accounts, branding was, at least by the late 1940s, practiced by Zeta Psi as part of the initiation. Many alumni today are willing to roll up their shirt sleeves and show their faded brands, located on the upper right forearm. How far back the tradition goes is uncertain. I have found photographs from other Berkeley fraternities showing branding only as early as the 1930s.[19]

What role the initiation played in creating bonds of brotherhood is open to speculation. Sanday has argued that initiation serves to strip the pledge of his unique identity so that he is rebuilt in the image of the fraternity. She sees the ritual of initiation as responsible for the callous corporate attitudes toward women and sex that she identified in late-twentieth-century fraternities. Paula Fass, in her study of student college life in the 1920s, focuses some attention on initiation as a means of fostering a group identity. She also believes that widespread practices like razzing—the sustained teasing of those who acted or dressed in ways outside of what was considered normative student behavior—led to conformity in student populations, both within and beyond fraternities on college campuses.[20]

FIGURE 23
Members sitting on the front stoop of the first Zeta Psi house,
circa 1892. A comparison of photographs suggests that G. H.
Foulks and Fred Stratton were among the alumni in attendance.
Photograph courtesy of the Bancroft Library.

While the nature of ritual life in the first Zete house remains poorly outlined for us, the ritual life of the second house is more clearly displayed, in both the standing architecture of the house and the artifactual remains excavated from it.

THE RITUAL SPACES OF THE ZETA PSI CHAPTER HOUSE

One of the challenges for the architect of the new house was to honor both the memory of the original house and the traditions that its spaces had engendered. When a representative of the Zeta Psi national chapter visited the second house in 1995, he commented to me that the house was clearly designed as a Zete chapter house, and that it had many embedded meanings. I took his observation as a challenge to try to "read" as much of the architecture as I could. In visiting other houses on campus, I found that many chapters still residing in houses built for them

FIGURE 24

Hallway of the second Zeta Psi house, circa 1923. Photograph
courtesy of the Zeta Psi Iota chapter archive.

have stories about what different architectural elements meant. Some are obscure.
One sorority house has an oak tree planted outside the door that represents some
particular value of sisterhood; another sorority has a circular staircase that the sisters say represents one of their letters. I realized that I could not hope to identify
any but the most obvious of design elements that represented Zeta Psi. In some of
my interpretations I may be overreaching, but based on my experiences in other
houses, I suspect that, if anything, I have missed much.

Sutton, the architect for the second house, had lived in the first house, and we can
assume that, in no small way, his senses of fellowship and fraternity were situated in
the spaces of that house. The new house retained many aspects of the layout of the
first. Recall that, according to the 1880 description of the first house, upon entering
the main hallway one would turn to the right to enter the parlor. The room had
pocket doors that allowed it to be opened up or partitioned as necessary to create a
larger or smaller space. To the left of the main hallway, one would enter the dining
room; the kitchen lay behind it. The bedrooms were situated upstairs.[21]

This plan served the new house too, but on a grander scale. When you enter
the extant 1910 Zete house, you find yourself in a large foyer with ornate arched
ceilings painted with Greek key edging and illuminated with a large hanging
chandelier (figure 24). You can easily imagine this space serving as a reception

FIGURE 25
Ceiling detail from the second house's parlor. Photograph by the
author.

area when the fraternity opened its door to visitors during sporting and other
campus events.

If you turn to the right, you pass through a massive pair of oak-and-glass
pocket doors into the spacious "lounge," as it was called on plans. The walls are
covered by oak paneling and ornate oak-and-plaster ceiling wainscoting. To
honor the chapter's place within the University of California, details in the ceiling
are gold leaf and blue—the campus colors (figure 25). A large fireplace and oak
mantel dominate the southern wall of the room, and it is possible to see the out-
line where a Zeta Psi crest was once mounted. Arched doorways with glass doors
surround the room, communicating with the brick patio along the front of the
house and allowing ventilation. The room's eastern wall features a pair of mir-
rored oak pocket doors, which, when open, allow the parlor to merge with the
library behind it.

If you turn left upon entering the house, you encounter the dining room
through a pair of oak pocket doors matching those of the lounge. A large fireplace and mantel grace this room, a mirror image of those found in the lounge. A
pair of holes in the mantel indicate where a crest was once mounted. According to
photographs, this room featured a large mission-style table that could seat all the
brothers at once. The kitchen can be entered from the east side of the room. Its
pantry cabinets remained intact until 2001, when a blundering contractor removed them during the building's retrofit. This continuity in ground-floor layout

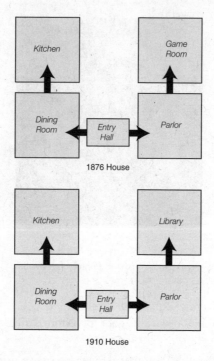

FIGURE 26
Schematic of layout of the first and second houses.

ensured that visiting alumni who had lived in the old house would recognize the social spaces of the home as familiar (figure 26).

As in the old house, study rooms and bedrooms were located upstairs. Although of varying sizes, the rooms were designed to house two brothers each. Corner rooms were larger than the others and were reserved for the use of the fraternity officers. Oral histories demonstrate that men changed rooms from year to year. Also on the second floor, in the eastern rear of the building, were the living quarters for the house servants—it is unclear whether servants had lived in the previous house or merely came as day workers. The servants' quarters featured a separate bathroom. Their quarters were connected by a separate staircase to the rear entrance of the kitchen, had a separate exit from the house, and had access to the root cellar. The layout of this portion of the house ensured that the servants did not traverse the same social spaces as the brothers, and that their presence would be a muted one within the family of brothers (figure 27).

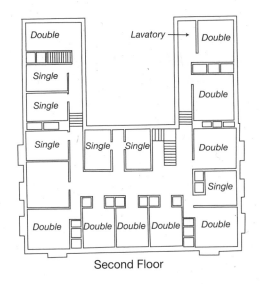

Second Floor

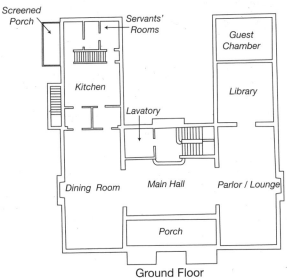

Ground Floor

FIGURE 27
Plans of the first and second floors of the second Zeta Psi house.

Unlike the previous house, the second house is laid out in a *C* shape, with a large central courtyard that can be viewed from any number of interior windows on the second floor (figure 27). Today, the archaeologists housed in the structure use these windows to yell (in a gentile way, of course) to one another, to converse without having to run through the building to find one another. It is easy to imagine the Zeta Psi brothers using the design in a similar way. I have several notions about why the house was given the courtyard arrangement it has. The house can be clearly seen as a *C*. The University of California has a number of associations with the letter *C*. On the hill above Zeta Psi's house is the "Big C," for example, a concrete *C* visible throughout the area. The letter began as a tradition dictated by President Wheeler when he banned the freshman rush in 1904 as a barbarian tradition not worthy of college. Instead, in the spirit of university cooperation, each year before the big game a concrete *C* would be laid out and painted. Eventually, the *C* became permanent and the repainting became the annual event. The Zete house could be seen as the little *C* under the big *C*. A number of other fraternity houses took this shape at the same time.[22]

Another possibility is that the *C* shape is really part of a Psi shape. If we were to look down on the structure and imagine the pathway leading up to the house and through the courtyard, we could see that it makes the shape of a Psi (figure 28). We could also see the courtyard layout merely as the influence of Spanish architecture on California design notions. After all, the enclosed plaza design has strong Spanish colonial associations in California. The *C* shape created a private exterior space for the men to use.[23]

My favorite interpretation for the courtyard design, however, involves the placement of the first house. The first house was set back from where the cornerstone was laid for the second. Excavations demonstrated to us what maps could not be relied upon to illustrate—that the front door of the first house is aligned with the front door of the second house. The footprint of the front portion of the first house's foundation is preserved within the courtyard (figure 29). Literally, the second house surrounds the ghost of the first, rather than obliterating it. The second house was not replacing the first so much as growing from it—a logical evolutionary progression. You may not be convinced that the architect would have been thinking in such terms, but as you are introduced to some of the other symbolic design elements of the house, you may not find my interpretation far-fetched.

The most notable new feature of the new house was the addition of a basement— the underground part of the house. The basement had a practical function—the coal bin and root cellar were located directly under the kitchen and the servants' quarters.

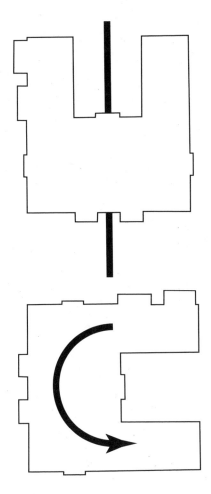

FIGURE 28
Possible symbolic interpretations of the Zeta Psi house layout.

The other spaces, however, were for specific fraternal uses (figure 30). The chapter room (or "tong," as it was called in the 1950s), a party room, and the "tub room" were located in the basement. These were distinct spaces the brothers would descend into as part of the ritual life of their chapter. There are several reasons for these spaces to be in the basement. First, the descent into them is similar to the mythical journey to the land of the dead in classical mythologies. Remember that much of fraternal ritual revolves around the triumph of brothers over forms of death. As a highly important ritual space, the basement was not a space likely to be visited by

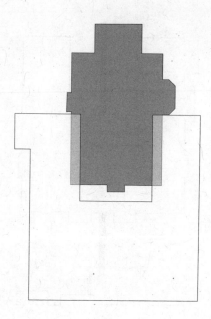

FIGURE 29

Layout of the first house relative to the second, based on excavation
findings and extrapolation from Sanborn fire maps.

outsiders. Second, the basement lacked windows and had controlled access, which
added to the privacy and secrecy of the spaces.

The chapter room was where formal chapter meetings and initiations took place.
Several alumni from the fraternity noted that pledges did not even know of the existence of the chapter room until initiation took place. The room was originally
protected by a steel door. Unfortunately, this room was severely modified by the
university after it assumed ownership of the house, so the original appearance of
this room is largely unknown. Zete alumni recalled entering the room during initiation and finding it to be dark except for a single light on the far side (western edge)
of the room that illuminated the chapter officers in their ceremonial garb. During
the retrofit of the building, a recessed alcove that was wired to contain a single
lightbulb was discovered under a more recent drywall on the western side, con-
forming to alumni memories.

The chapter room is located on the northern side of the basement. It can be ac-
cessed either through a staircase that leads from the basement to the outside, or via
the central staircase of the house. If one enters the room directly from the outside,
then it is necessary to first wind through a zigzag passageway that is Z shaped. This

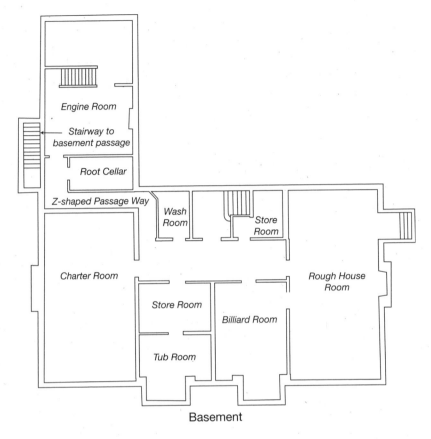

Engine Room

Stairway to
basement passage

Root Cellar

Z-shaped Passage Way

Wash
Room

Store
Room

Charter Room

Store Room

Billiard Room

Rough House
Room

Tub Room

Basement

FIGURE 30
Detail of the layout of the basement in the second Zeta Psi house.

was the entrance that initiates would use. If you think of the initiation rituals described for other fraternal settings, it becomes easy to imagine how the architectural
spaces shaped some of Zeta Psi's initiation ritual.

Imagine, if you will, the blindfolded Zeta Psi pledges being led down the staircase from the outside. According to some alumni, the pledges would have been
blindfolded for as long as twenty-four hours at this point. All they know is that they
are moving from the outdoors to a damp and confined space. Perhaps they are told
to make their way unassisted through the passageway. There are no lights in this
passageway, so even had they had not been blindfolded, they still would squint,
looking for signs of light. As they fumble in the dark, they put out their hands and
feel the wall. They walk, hands tracing the wall as it winds. As they move, their

bodies trace the letter Z, one of the Greek letters by which they will soon be known. If they are holding out their right hands, they will find the doorway of the chapter room. Perhaps they are met at the door by some of their future brothers, who lead them from the passageway to the officers of the fraternity. There they are commanded to remove their blindfolds. Even though the room is barely lit, they blink and try to understand what they are seeing. They are in a room they have never seen before, surrounded by shrouded figures.[24] It is easy to feel the butterflies that swirled in the initiates' bellies, the constriction of their throats, and the momentary sense of disorientation and fear.

What else does the initiate see? A dagger or sword? A representation of the fraternal charter? A leering skull? Unfortunately, the spaces remain mute as to what other spectacles faced a pledge. It is clear that he would be made to feel that his life or body was in jeopardy, and at the last moment he would be saved by his fraternity brothers, and be so grateful to them that he would profess his eternal devotion to them (Yes, I do believe in fraternity! I do believe!). His faith would be rewarded with rebirth and new life as a brother. If he stood strong and resolute (and based on ethnographies of fraternal societies, even if he did not), he would be welcomed as a brother at the end of his ordeal. In future years he would play other roles in this performance, perhaps even being one of the officers who had the solemn duty of leading the ritual.

When I give tours of the former Zeta Psi house, I joke that the Z-shaped passageway is the birth canal of the house. There is earnestness in this description. On emerging from this passageway, in which the men literally embody the shape of the Zeta through their movements, they are born into a community of men. They have ended their life as sons of women and emerged as sons and brothers of men. In case you think I belabor this point, this passageway is not the only "Zeta"-shaped feature of the second house's architecture. In the upstairs living space, the rooms in the east-west arm of the C are both designed as split levels. As a brother ran back and forth between rooms on these wings, he would be enacting the "Zeta." More Zs can be found throughout the brickwork of the house, in its walls and exterior pathways.

While the chapter room lies beneath the dining room, the party room underlies the lounge. It was in the party room where the fraternal planks were hung. Despite our late-twentieth- and early-twenty-first-century notions of fraternity parties, in the case of Zeta Psi the alumni have indicated that parties were limited to brothers—alumni and actives—from Iota and sometimes from Mu (the Zeta Psi chapter at Stanford, founded in 1892) and, on rare occasions, female dates. Socials were generally held outside the house, in Oakland or San Francisco hotels. The party room has a doorway leading out to a very small patio, so outsiders would have been able to access the party room without entering any of the other fraternal spaces. To celebrate the end of Prohibition, the Zetes built a bar in this room. Wives of alumni remembered being invited to the party room and remarked on the bar. One remembered a fountain once being in the room.[25]

The other basement space that held a strong place in communal memory was the "tub room." Tubbing was a well-known means of fraternal hazing. Several alumni remembered their tubbing very clearly, but noted that it was generally something that one endured only once. A fraternal diary from the 1933–1934 school year supports this assertion—only on one day does the word "TUBBED!" appear in the diary collectively kept by that year's pledges. This occurred shortly before their spring initiation. The tub itself was an unremarkable thing, a cast-iron bathtub kept in a small room in the basement. A description of "tubbing" told to me by a Zete alumni from the 1940s is probably representative of the experience in general. When I have repeated this telling to other alumni, they have nodded in agreement, laughed, and generally said something like: "Yes, that's about right."

Tubbing, I am told, was used as a punishment for some perceived offense committed by a pledge. While an individual might be singled out as responsible for the offense (through admission or being identified by a brother—usually a sophomore), all members of the pledge class (brothers who had been invited but not yet initiated) would be punished together. Clearly, the shared tubbing experience was an important component of cohort formation among initiates. The pledges would learn of their upcoming ordeal at breakfast. One of the seniors would, in his capacity as a stern but caring father of the fraternity, relay the nature of the offense to the house and order that the tub be filled by the sophomores. The offense could be as simple as a failure to obey an order or a failure to adequately clean the bathroom. Upon getting their orders, the sophomores would go get ice to fill the tub. The pledges were ordered to return at lunchtime. The ice was left to melt into water during the morning.

After agonizing about what exactly they would be facing for the entire morning, the pledges returned to the house and were told to strip down to their neckties (versions vary as to whether one kept one's knickers on or not; variations may reflect the hesitancy of alums to mention nudity to the female students who conducted some of the interviews). The men were lined up in the Z-shaped passageway, pulled out at random, and led to the tub room. The pledge was forced to stand in the tub. One brother would hold him by the necktie, another would punch him in the stomach. As he exhaled, the pledge was yanked underwater by his necktie and held there for some amount of time. One can imagine that the pledge's lack of breath held in the diaphragm, combined with the freezing water and his inability to judge how long he might be held underwater. would be uncomfortable and frightening. Some alumni from the 1950s also indicated that "more than water" could be in the tub when this happened. I will refrain from speculating, but one's imagination can conjure some pretty horrific and gross possibilities. The sight of one's fellow initiate emerging from the tub room sputtering (perhaps vomiting), gasping for breath, blue and shivering, would have increased the anxiety of the group awaiting their turns. Tubbing falls into the category of what some would, at the time, have called "roughhousing."

Clark's 1915 discussion of the pros and cons of roughhousing are worth considering. He notes that most of the activities fall into the category of harmless pranks. For example, fraternities were inclined to send prospective brothers out "on a quiet stroll to the cemetery clad in empty flour barrels, to set them to wheeling doll baby carriages about the campus, to make them fish all day, with a pin hook in the dry 'boneyard,' or to force them to beg for a hand out at the President's back door." He observed that most of these stunts only served to make fraternities look foolish and to reinforce some of the public's negative views of them. He also admitted that he had heard of more brutal activities.

> There were other sorts of goings-on of which I have been told, some of them devised with the keenest insight into the methods of human torture, mental and physical. There were personal insults and physical abuse, such as painting the body of the victim, torturing him with electrical horrors, feeding him with nauseating messes, and beating him up to see how much pain he could stand without flinching or crying out. The fake violation of the oath was a form of mental torture which when worked skillfully made the initiate writhe. I have known boys who broke down and sobbed and who were upset for days by the memory of the disgrace which they thought they were going to suffer.[26]

Clark interviewed members of fraternities, past and present, to get their perspectives on the role of roughhousing within the fraternity structure. One man's answer is particularly revealing.

> In my own experience in watching freshmen "put through" in the manner with which I am familiar, I give my unqualified approbation to "horse play." The average freshman is young, untried, and usually fresh from high school triumphs; his ego is largely developed, he does not consider that the fraternity is conferring a favor on him, but that his presence is largely a condescension. This last attitude is partly due to rushing methods and largely due to imperfect rearing by parents. He is distinctly not a man, and the fraternity must take up the task of character

shaping where the parents left off or never began. His exaggeration of his own omnipotence must be dissipated, and as one of our own freshman puts it, he usually cannot reason it out, so other methods must be used. If he could fully comprehend the significance of fraternity ties, "horse play" would be unnecessary, but he cannot do this, and more material means are necessary.[27]

Note that the man quoted is quick to blame poor parenting for the character flaws of the freshman. While he does not explicitly state it, since most child rearing was seen as the realm of women's work, this is a criticism of the female influence in a young man's life. The abusive side of fraternity initiation was, therefore, necessary because the female influence on a pledge had to be removed before he could properly commit to the bonds of brotherhood. While the opinions of the men surveyed by Clark were split on whether roughhousing (physical trials during initiation) and horseplay (public stunts in the period leading up to initiation) served any real purpose, they shared the notion that fraternity brothers should demonstrate the courage and strength of character of "true men."

Alumni were, understandably, reluctant to discuss the ritual life of the fraternity. A member of the class of 1958 did show the student interviewing him a faded brand under the crease of his elbow that was a "ZΨ." This brother emphasized that the Zetes kept their initiations within the confines of the house and did not involve humiliating practices . He did recall that Monday night was "joke night" for the pledges, who had to get up and tell a joke. "If they didn't like the joke, you had to wash someone's car. Big deal. And I washed a lot of cars, because I was a terrible joke teller!"[28]

While the rituals and practices that led up to initiation were an important part of the fraternal annual calendar, brotherhood was constructed every day, through any number of mundane shared routines. In the new chapter house, brothers continued to use aspects of domestic life to reinforce their connection to one another. Unlike in the first house, however, where the materiality of domesticity and family life was couched in the language of the female sphere, in the new chapter house some of the materials demonstrated the same attention to ritual and symbolism found in the architecture of the house. This ritualization of ordinary practice served to mark the house as an explicitly male space.

Historical circumstance also brought new challenges to some of the old traditions of the chapter. The passage of the Eighteenth Amendment posed particular difficulties for the brothers' beer-drinking traditions. Likewise, the world wars drew the chapter's elder brothers away from the house, threatening the orderly transmission of house traditions from one generation to another. Still other traditions remained unchanged, although, because of the passage of time, more pronounced within the house's population. Finally, despite the efforts of the household to maintain a sense of tradition and connection to older generations of Zetes, activities in the house were shaped by the new expectations of masculinity that shaped the broader world in which the brothers lived.

MEMBERSHIP IN THE SECOND HOUSE

During the Zetes' occupation of their first chapter house, the University of California had a smaller student body. The school was a community in which members of the same class would know one another well. In 1876, when the first chapter house was built, there were not even 200 students in the entire university; in contrast, in 1910 the Registrar's Office reported that 3,301 students had enrolled. This population steadily grew, reaching more than 10,000 in the 1934–1935 academic year, and more than 20,000 immediately following the end of World War II, in the academic year 1946–1947. As the population grew, student publications and campus life changed, and students became less likely to know, or even know of, one another.[29]

While earlier editors of *The Blue and Gold* knew the members of the senior class and ensured that all were represented in the yearbook, later editors depended on participants' self-reporting. No longer was there room to name every student in every organization, and the pages of jokes that had clarified the nature of social relations and provided insight into life within the fraternity disappeared. The faculty and staff of the university had also grown, and the Academic Senate was composed of multiple committees. The faculty no longer discussed all the students as a group. Newspapers covered organizations and activities, not individuals, and the number of activities had grown to such a point that not even all groups could be covered in the pages of the student papers. The historical record for this period is less personal, and the kind of evidence available about the students of Zeta Psi is different. In speaking about the second chapter house, I present demographic data here in the same way that I did for the first house when possible, but in some cases, much less evidence is available.

Legacies remained an important part of the fraternal family tree during the occupation of the second house. Fictive kinship was often combined with consanguineal kinship. Due to the differences in the available documentary record, to identify potential relatives I used a comparison of surnames. I compiled the names of men who were listed as Zeta Psi seniors in *The Blue and Gold* yearbooks from 1910 to1957. There were 309 men who fell into this category.[30]

TABLE 10   Identified legacies in the Zeta Psi Iota chapter:
families represented by three or more members, 1870–1957*

Surname	Member	Graduation Year
Baldwin	Harry C.	1891
	W. Isaac	1944
	Page	1946
Brown	Brainard C.	1870
	Sanford	1936
	Malcolm	1944
Budd	James	1873
	John E.	1874
	Henry B.	1898
Ciprico	John O'Neil	1918
	Edmond	1922
	Frances	1931
Davis	George T.	1903
	George C.	1903
	Charles Henry	1915
	George C.	1934
	Gilbert	1957
Duhring	Frederick T.	1888
	Frederick S.	1916
	John Herman	1920
	Stephen R.	1922
	Frederick	1944
Dunlap	David	1932
	Gordon S.	1934
	Frank L.	1936
	John	1944
Dyer	Hubert	1890
	Ernest	1894
	Ephraim	1907
	Ephraim	1938
	Peter	1940
Finley	George	1914
	William	1914
	Theodore	1917
Foster	W. A S.	1900
	Arthur W.	1903

TABLE 10 (continued)

Surname	Member	Graduation Year
	Robert N.	1908
	Paul S.	1910
	Paul S.	1934
	Robert N.	1942
Hall	Hiram T.	1905
	Winslow	1933
	Houghton	1935
	Samuel	1937
Holt	William	1918
	Thomas	1921
	Ted	1950
	Donald	1954
	Douglas	1954
Hoogs	Albert	1928
	Richard	1929
	William	1940
	John	1949
Hyde, Hyde-Chick	Ralph	1894
	Henry	1894
	Orra C., II	1919
	C. Burrel	1931
	Orra III	1952
Jackson	Edwin	1896
	Andrew	1898
	Harry Andrew	1921
King	Thomas	1909
	William Norris	1913
	Alexander	1915
Knight	Robert S.	1888
	Remi	1914
	Robert	1956
Martin	Richard	1882
	Edward	1931
	George	1934
	William	1936
	John	1937
	Carmel	1942

TABLE 10 (continued)

Surname	Member	Graduation Year
Mays	Edwin	1893
	Robert	1895
	Grant	1897
	George	1922
	Roderick	1932
	Laurence	1951
	Harry	1956
McGillivray	John	1878
	James	1881
	G.	1885
McMurray	Valentine C.	1882
	Orrin K.	1890
	John P.	1930
Meek	Harry W.	1877
	William E.	1888
	William H.	1909
Miller	Roswell	1915
	Charles	1937
	Royal	1945
Minor	Henry	1904
	Herbert	1904
	Paul	1937
Nelson	William	1882
	Theodore	1943
	Hack	1946
	Edward	1952
	John	1953
O'Brien	George	1919
	Edgar	1921
	Lloyd	1928
	Robert	1949
	Peter	1953
Powers	Frank	1884
	Aaron	1889
	Jay E.	1912
Procter	John W.	1898
	John W.	1927
	Thomas	1928

TABLE 10 (continued)

Surname	Member	Graduation Year
Reis	Gustav	1913
	John	1917
	John	1943
Robbins	Ruel	1894
	Lloyd	1897
	William C.	1902
	William C.	1930
Rowell	Joseph	1874
	Edward	1884
	John	1931
Sherwood	William	1877
	Harry Hamilton	1881
	Lionel C.	1898
Solinsky	Frank	1877
	Frank Jr.	1906
	Albert C.	1910
	Edward R	1911
	Frank J.	1931
	Edward H.	1937
	Jack D.	1942
	E. Dean	1943
	Robert	1946
Stephens	Franklin	1909
	William	1940
	Thomas	1942
Stillman	John	1874
	Howard	1877
	Stanley	1882
	Edmund	1916
Sutton	John G.	1885
	Albert	1889
	Charles Zook	1915
	John G.	1922
Taylor	Thomas C.	1897
	Reese H.	1922
	Lawrence	1942
	Edward	1952
	Thomas	1954

TABLE 10 (continued)

Surname	Member	Graduation Year
White	Josiah	1902
	William	1905
	Edwin D.	1905
	Alden	1906
	Edwin D.	1931
	Bertram	1954
	David Jr.	1959
Witter	Dean	1909
	Jean C.	1916
	Willis G.	1917
	Edwin D.	1922
	Guy Phelps	1922
	Charles	1924
	John	1924
	Wendell	1931
	Jean C.	1942
	William	1945
	Edwin	1950
	George	1951

* Graduation dates are based on volumes of *The Blue and Gold*. In the cases of common last names, it is possible that the brothers shared names but not ancestry.

I first looked for duplication of surnames within this population, then compared all names on this list with membership rolls from the first house. I found that just over 43 percent of the men had one of fifty-two repeated surnames. In thirty-five cases, the surnames were shared by only two men. In nine instances, surnames were shared by three men. The remaining eight names were shared by at least four men each. Forty men who lived in the second house shared one of these eight surnames, representing nearly 13 percent of the house's total population (table 10). These eight families were a significant presence in the second chapter house; seven of the families had contributed brothers from the earliest days of the fraternity. The Fosters and Solinskys were represented by three generations of men. The Witters, however, whose family entered the fraternity beginning with the graduating class of 1910, became almost synonymous with Zeta Psi's second chapter house, contributing fifteen brothers between 1910 and 1957. A number of the Witters quickly established themselves on campus as "big men" and were strongly associated with the prestige of Zeta Psi's second house.

RITUALIZED DINING

Dining with the Lost Boys was an important part of community building for Peter Pan. He presided over the table like an imaginary father. It was the act of dining together that was important, not necessarily the food or the utensils Wendy found it disturbing that many of the meals did not even feature real food; instead, all members of the community were expected to eat imaginary food with great gusto. Peter, although he had willingly abandoned his own family, recognized the symbolic power of sharing a meal. In the second chapter house, the Zetes continued to share at least two meals a day. Unlike Peter, they did care about the utensils they used and the quality of the food they consumed.

With the transition to the new house, we see an interesting shift in the ceramics. Beginning in 1918, the fraternity purchased ceramics from the Dohrmann Commercial Company in San Francisco, specially manufactured for the fraternity by the Onondaga Pottery Company of Syracuse, New York. The chapter continued to order ceramics from the Onondaga Pottery Company through 1963, after the brothers had moved to the new house on Bancroft Avenue. These thick, white porcelain wares are decorated with a green annular band and the fraternity crest (figure 31). We recovered a wide range of vessels ; the greatest number of vessels were found in the Prohibition-period trash pit. Vessels included berry bowls, dinner plates, chop plates, demitasse cups and teacups, pitchers, and tureens (table 11).[31]

The introduction of decalcomania decorations facilitated the production of personalized tea sets, and I have found that at least three local fraternities had similar house china sets (figure 32). Use of fraternity-specific china seems to have been a nationwide phenomenon during the first half of the century. Today the practice is seen at Cal only among some of the sororities. Times have changed, of course, and associations between gentility and fine tableware have faded in many parts of the country. A 1940 issue of *Fraternity House Management*, a magazine directed at house managers, included an article titled "Chinaware: Its Selection and Maintenance." The author, Edward Schramm, recommended that fraternity houses select vitrified, medium-weight ceramics with rolled edges, which were more chip resistant. Wares such as these were designed for the hotel, restaurant, and cafeteria industries and were manufactured by any number of companies, including Buffalo China, Hall, Syracuse, Shenango, and, locally in the Bay Area, TEPCO in El Cerrito,

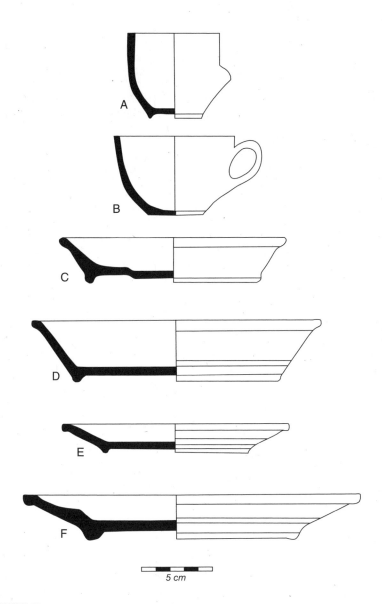

FIGURE 31
"Fraternity ware" recovered from excavations at the second
house: A. demitasse cup, B. teacup, C. tea saucer, D. berry bowl,
E. small plate, F. dinner plate.

TABLE II   Ceramic and glass tablewares recovered from the
second Zeta Psi house

Context	Ceramic type	Vessel form	Minimum number of vessels
Yard midden (1911–1956)	Yellowware	Mixing bowl	1
		"Rockingham" bowl	1
	Whiteware	Embossed saucer	1
		Black transfer-printed saucer	1
		Embossed saucer (12-cm diameter)	1
		Black transfer-printed wash basin (faux marble)	1
		Blue stenciled saucer (14-cm diameter)	1
		Plain plate	1
		Plain saucer (12-cm diameter)	1
		Green art pottery plate (Fiesta style)	1
		Art pottery vase	1
	Ironstone	Plain teacup	2
		Plain bowl (14-cm diameter)	1
		Scalloped saucer with gold rim (16-cm diameter)	1
		Plain mug (6-cm base)	1
		Gray transfer-printed plate (24-cm diameter)	1
		Blue-tinted bowl	1
		Plain teacup	1
		Blue-tinted teacup	1
	Hotel ware	"Fratware" plate	1
		"Fratware" saucer	1
		"Fratware" pitcher	1
		"Fratware" chop dish	1
		"Fratware" bowl	1
		"Fratware" plate (18-cm diameter)	1
	Porcelain	Toy saucer	1
		Japanese porcelain teacup	1

TABLE II (continued)

Context	Ceramic type	Vessel form	Minimum number of vessels
	Stoneware	Bristol glazed bottle	1
	Stoneware	German gray stein	1
	Stoneware	Bristol glazed crock	1
	Stoneware	Crock	1
	Stoneware	Crock	1
	Stoneware	Bauer-type green glazed bowl	1
	Terra-cotta	Flowerpot (12-cm rim, 10-cm base)	1
Trash pit (circa 1923–1925)	Hotel ware	Fraternity plate (18-cm diameter)	1
		Fraternity fruit saucer (14-cm diameter)	2
		Fraternity soup plate (22-cm diameter)	4
		Fraternity coffee saucer (10-cm diameter)	3
		Fraternity coffee cup	4
		Fraternity oval baker	1
		Fraternity teacup	5
		Fraternity plate (14-cm rim)	1
		Fraternity tea saucer	1
		Fraternity plate (16-cm diameter)	1
		Fraternity chop plate	1
		Fraternity plate, unidentified size	1
	Ironstone (semivitreous earthenware)	Plain platter	1
		Plain plate	1
		Plain teacup	2
		Plain saucer	2
		Plain plate (10-cm diameter)	1
		Plain bowl	4
		Embossed teacup	1
		Transfer-printed plate (24-cm diameter; Maddock and Sons, England)	1
		Decalcomania floral-decorated plate	1

TABLE 11   (continued)

Context	Ceramic type	Vessel form	Minimum number of vessels
	Whiteware	Plain coffee mug	2
		Plain teacup	1
		Plain plate	3
		Embossed plate	2
	Porcelain	Gold-rimmed egg cup	1
		Embossed porcelain saucer	1
		Plain saucer	1
		Plain sugar box lid	1
		Hand-painted plate	2
		Match holder with strike surface	1
	Stoneware	Cooking crock	2

who began producing these wares in 1922 and, judging by manufacturer-marked examples found at local flea markets, made ceramics for several fraternities. Schramm advised students that decorations could include simple line bands, prints in one or two colors added by engraved plates, decalcomania (decal) patterns in many colors, and hand-painted treatments, and he recommended for durability's sake that underglazed wares be selected.[32]

The tablewares were not inexpensive. The Onondaga Pottery Company (now Syracuse China) archive includes a receipt for the Iota chapter's Zeta Psi wares. The cost of these wares was equivalent to the prices of the most expensive porcelain available to domestic households. In 1909, Sears Roebuck and Company advertised Haviland's "Rose Wreath" porcelain, one of the most expensive of the popular tablewares of the time, for $27.50. This set included one hundred different vessels, including service vessels, which tend to be more expensive individually. In 1927, Sears sold this same Haviland pattern in a ninety-piece set for $50.75. The purchase of the Syracuse china represented a significant financial investment for the fraternity. The Zeta Psi ceramics consisted of twelve place-settings of sixteen different vessels—at a cost of $146.90. Additional sets were ordered in 1925, 1931, 1937, 1942, and 1963.[33]

Under what circumstances were these tablewares were used? Were they intended for daily use, or for special use only? On the face of it, there were not enough in the

*artifacts not to relative scale

FIGURE 32
Examples of ceramics used in the early twentieth century by other
fraternities. Author's collection.

initial order of twelve place-settings to serve all the brothers at once on the same
vessel pattern. However, the original shipment was purchased during the Great
War, when many of the brothers were listed as "absent on leave" or "in the service." In 1925, the fraternity had purchased enough place settings to serve twenty-
four of the thirty-two men who lived in the fraternity, assuming minimal breakage
in the original set. Perhaps use of the china was restricted to upper classmen. Or
perhaps the plate size one used depended on one's rank. If the three dinner plate
sizes—7.5-, 8-, and 9-inch diameters—were used at the same time, there were
enough to serve all members of the house. Perhaps upper classmen enjoyed eating
from plates larger than those of their younger brothers. By the 1950s, the fraternity
ceramics were used at all mealtimes.[34]

We recovered other ceramics recovered from the house as well, so apparently no
brother would have had to eat with his hands. Plain ironstone and white earthen-
ware vessels matching those recovered from the first house were recovered archaeologically from the second house as well. In particular, marked examples made by

John Maddock and Sons, Johnson Brothers, and Homer Laughlin each had manufacturing date ranges that spanned the occupations of the two houses. Also recovered were transfer-printed and embossed wares and some examples of matched vessels found in the earlier house's assemblage.[35] Overall, we recovered a minimum of seventy-five ceramic vessels from the 1923 pit and a minimum of thirty-five more from the yard midden (table 11). The abundance of materials recovered from the second occupation, after the institution of public trash collection, suggests that at one time there were probably trash pits associated with the first Zeta Psi house occupation that have been destroyed by subsequent campus development.

Aside from the prestige of having ceramics bearing one's fraternal crest, the ceramics held symbolic meanings as well. To brothers dining together, the image of the fraternity crest reinforced a sense of community and brotherhood, providing a visual reinforcement of their ties. The crest is not merely a decorative device but has important meanings for initiated members of the fraternity. The imagery in the crest specifically represents the stages of initiation and fraternal life that the pledges and initiates experience, culminating in their obligations to the brotherhood after college. In other words, the crest represents the transition from fraternity boyhood to adulthood—it is the material representation of the journey each makes from initiate to alumnus. For those outside of the fraternity, the crest would have reminded visitors whose hospitality they were enjoying and underscored their position as outsiders.

It is worth noting depositional pattern discernable with the fraternity ceramics. The only instances of crests found archaeologically were buried in the 1923 pit. All other fragments of the fraternity ceramics, which were clearly recognizable as examples of the Onondaga Pottery Company's "Syracuse china" line, found at the site were rim or body sherds that featured only portions of the band or no decoration. In addition, several functional but damaged vessels were recovered from the trash pit. One was an intact teacup that had a crack running through the crest; the other was a demitasse cup missing a handle (figure 33). Each of these vessels was fully functional for any range of uses but had been thrown away. Is it possible that the fraternity had special disposal practices for representation of the crest? With the exception of the planks, the fraternity removed all removable crests and symbols from the house before vacating it—in effect, ritually killing the house.[36]

In addition to the fraternity ceramics recovered from the site, 1920s photographs also show beer steins marked with the Zeta Psi letters, something not seen in earlier photographs. The ritualization of fraternity paraphernalia served as a way to clearly delineate the fraternity from other kinds of households and, in doing so, cleanly sev-

FIGURE 33
Demitasse cup with missing handle, found in the 1920s trash pit.

ered the men of the fraternity from their mothers' kind of domesticity. The use of the
crest and other symbols, like Zeta Psi's "TKO" motto, as well as the distinctive architectural features of the building, marked the house as a special kind of male space.

The representation of a wide range of vessel forms in the second house assemblage suggests that, like their forebears, the brothers of Zeta Psi were expected to
eat politely. Writers who supported fraternity living focused on their role in shaping a man's social manner. Clark described this:

> In this regard as in others the fraternity may well emulate the home. Table
> talk, and table dress, and table behavior will usually follow the standards set
> by the older men. A good old lady I knew in my boyhood always said that her
> boys always behaved themselves better when they were dressed up, and I have
> frequently noticed that as fraternity men have held themselves to careful
> dressing and careful talk at table their general manners were improved. The
> more carelessly dressed a fraternity permits its men to come to the breakfast
> or the dinner table, the more slovenly and crude will their talk and their
> general behavior at table be.[37]

Alumni of the Zeta Psi fraternity remembered the importance of attending dinners with their brothers. Dinner in the second house was an occasion for which one
dressed appropriately. Alumni recalled dinner as a time when the familial aspect of

TABLE 12   Food and condiment containers found at the second Zeta Psi house

Context	Type of container and contents	Minimum number found
Yard midden	Glass jar	9
	Food bottle stopper	1
	Catsup bottle	2
	Mason jar	2
	Food bottle	2
	Food lid	1
	Stoneware soy sauce bottle	1
Trash pit	Del Monte catsup bottle	56
	Heinz catsup bottle	1
	Curtice Brothers catsup bottle	1
	Heinz Worcestershire sauce bottle	1
	Eddy's brand sauce bottle	1
	Milk jug	2
	Tournades Kitchen Bouquet bottle	6
	Unidentified food jar	1
	Cherry jar	1
	Mustard barrel	1
	Relish jar	1
	Pickle jar	1
	Milk-glass Mason jar lid liner	2
	Sauce bottle stopper	2
	Milk-glass cheese jar	1

life was created, with elder brothers taking the role of house elders and serving themselves first from the platters, passing the food on to the others by class rank.

While the brothers ate from fine china, there is some debate over the quality of the food they enjoyed. A 1933 fraternity diary entry disparaged the fraternity food: "There was a rushing dinner which was only represented by one rushee. It is too bad that the brothers in the house do not rate the good food that the poor rushees do (and don't enjoy it half as much as we do)."[38] Most college students complain about the quality of institutional food, but the archaeological evidence does suggest that the cuisine of the time was less than inspired. Faunal remains from the site include

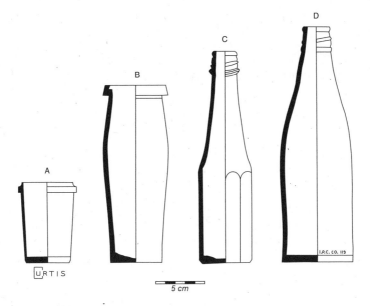

FIGURE 34
Examples of condiment bottles excavated from the second house
deposits: A. jam jar, B. pickle or chutney jar; C. Heinz ketchup
bottle; D. Del Monte ketchup bottle.

cow ribs and lower leg bones, or shanks, and sheep legs. These tend to be inexpensive cuts of meat that require long cooking times. Less frequent in abundance were
lamb ribs (lamb chops), cow vertebrae (T-bone steaks), turkey, deer legs, and egg
shells. Based on the recovery of at least two ceramic egg cups, some of the men enjoyed their eggs soft-boiled. The faunal assemblage suggests that the quality of
meat consumed by the fraternity men could be either very good quality or average
quality. Cooking vessels recovered archaeologically included large crocks, which
would have been perfect for simmering soups and stews.

The large number of condiments associated with the second house suggests that, at
the very least, the food required additional flavoring at the table (table 12). The most
abundant food containers were Del Monte catsup bottles. At least forty-six whole and
partial bottles were recovered from the pit, and at least four more were found during
excavations of the courtyard. The bottles were manufactured by the Illinois Pacific
Glass Company of San Francisco sometime between 1902 and 1930 (figure 34). The
pit also contained a single Curtice Brother's catsup bottle and a Heinz catsup bottle.
Catsup was, and is, generally used to flavor already cooked food. Other commonly

recovered condiment bottles were those for several different brands of Worcestershire sauce (represented by three bottles), and Tournades Kitchen Bouquet (represented by six bottles), products used to flavor foods during preparation.

Preparing menus and meals for large numbers of men within a set budget is a challenging task. The house manager, a senior classman, was responsible for controlling the grocery budget for the fraternity. The journal *Fraternity Household Management* featured a regular section on menu preparation and numerous recipes. Rather than a house servant and cook, by the 1950s the fraternity had only a full-time cook and students (including some Zetes) who worked as "hashers" in the kitchen, doing food preparation, serving, and cleaning. One of my students, Carolyn Luong, interviewed Zeta Psi's cook in 1995 to learn about food challenges at the fraternity. The cook employed at that time had been with the fraternity since 1980. He prepared two meals a day for forty men. He rotated the menu every three weeks to ensure the men did not eat the same meal too often. The fraternity's food was purchased in industrial-sized containers from a local wholesaler. The fraternity men rotated the responsibility for cooking breakfast and cleaning up. Clark in 1915 pointed that the household-management responsibilities conferred on members of the fraternity were among the major advantages of fraternity life.[39]

In talking to alumni, we found that the quality of the food as indicated by the archaeological assemblage was a sensitive topic, and they were quick to defend the fraternity's food. An alumnus who had been house manager in the late 1920s said that, when he was manager, the food was good quality. He also said that he had had to fire the previous grocers for the house because the quality had been poor. This alumnus attributed the high incidence of catsup to his brothers' love of corned beef hash. "Who ever heard of eating corned beef hash without ketchup?" he asked.

There are other possibilities: ketchup can be an ingredient, not just a condiment. Archaeological evidence shows that the men cooked on open fires in the courtyard from time to time. Ketchup, Worcestershire sauce, and Kitchen Bouquet all appear as ingredients in 1950s barbeque sauce recipes, as well as in 1940s meatloaf recipes.[40]

Another alumnus, from the class of 1940, had a different interpretation of the archaeological evidence. He thought that the cheap cuts of meat were evidence of prudent household management. He noted that the brothers who had lived in the house earlier had worked hard to pay down the mortgage on the house, and that when they had succeeded in paying off the note in 1938, they had had a mortgage-burning party and celebrated with thick steaks. He assured me that, after the note had been paid, the brothers ate very well indeed.

Based on these alumni responses, the substance and quality of meals was perceived as a means of defining the status of the fraternity. One alumnus chose to contest the archaeological data that contrasted with his memory, while the other chose to find an explanation for the data that fit with his own perceptions of the fraternity's past and ideals. The excerpts from the 1933–1934 diary, however, suggest that the low quality of food in the fraternity was not only a subject for humor but also a shared group experience that increased the sense of community identity in the brothers.

PROHIBITION AND ALCOHOL CONSUMPTION

I have suggested that beer drinking was more than a social activity enjoyed by students, and that its consumption, both socially and as part of ritual toasting, was a means of reaffirming bonds of fictive kinship. My assertion that beer was itself a symbolically charged beverage choice is supported by evidence of beer consumption in the second house. I focus here only on the bottles recovered from the bottle dump discovered in 1995. Because this dump contains materials deposited during Prohibition, it provides the opportunity to see how Prohibition affected not only alcohol consumption but also beer consumption specifically.

A minimum of 139 alcohol bottles was recovered from that dump. A number of them were liquor and wine bottles, but the majority of the bottles—114 of them— were beer bottles. Well-known beer bottle manufacturers like Illinois-Pacific Glass Company, W. Frazen and Son, and Root were represented, as were specific brew houses like Pabst, Anheuser Busch, Balboa, Stroh's, and Schlitz. We used label remnants to identify John Weiland's brand beer (table 13). We know, from a photograph, that the pit was not dug until the early 1920s. Based on the materials found in it, we can say that it was not used as a dump for more than a few years—we found no artifacts manufactured after 1925. So, while we know that all the beer bottles were thrown out at about the same time, an analysis of them shows that they were not necessarily manufactured close to the time they were thrown out. The manufacturing dates of the beer bottles represent a range of twenty years.

The reason for this likely relates to the dump's use during Prohibition. The Volstead Act, which became the Eighteenth Amendment, prohibited the production and sale of alcoholic beverages. It was legal, however, to consume alcohol that had been produced and purchased before the amendment became law. Huge amounts of liquor were smuggled from Canada, Mexico, and the Caribbean during Prohibition, and

TABLE 13 Glass artifacts found at the second Zeta Psi house
(excluding food containers)

Context	Artifact type	Minimum number found
Yard midden	Beer bottle	17
	Wine bottle	4
	Soda bottle	14
	Whiskey bottle	4
	Brandy bottle	1
	Bitters bottle	1
	Case gin bottle	1
	Milk jug	2
	Tumbler	16
	Goblet	5
	Stemware	1
	Teacup	1
	Bowl	1
	Plate	3
	Vase	1
	Stein	3
	Jug	4
	Lamp body	2
	Lamp chimney	4
	Lightbulb	4
	Lampshade	1
	Inkwell	1
Trash pit	Beer bottle	114
	Wine bottle	11
	Hard liquor bottle	14
	Soda	27
	Lightbulb	4
	Lampshade	2
	Inkwell	

there was a thriving internal trade in counterfeit product labels with pre-Prohibition dates. Large beer brewers like Busch stayed in business by producing near beers, beer with the alcohol removed. The removed alcohol was sold, with no small amount of aid from the brewers, on the black market as "hooch."[41]

Historical works about Prohibition often indicate that beer consumption greatly decreased during this time. Arguments have been made that, given the difficulty of transporting beer in barrels, Americans switched to drinking hard alcohol, which was cheaper and more easily hidden and provided more kick. At the Zeta Psi site, while the 114 beer bottles greatly outnumbered the 11 wine bottles and 14 hard liquor bottles, the beer bottles do represent smaller per-container servings and lower alcoholic content. A similarly large proportion of beer bottles was recovered from the Crags Country Club, a hunting lodge and Prohibition-period elite drinking club located in the Malibu Hills of Southern California. The archaeological records at both Zeta Psi and Crags Country Club suggest that beer consumption remained important. Like the fraternity, Crags Country Club was a uniquely masculine space. In fraternity halls, hunting lodges, sporting events, and military garrisons, beer was a beverage that came to possess masculine associations in the twentieth century.[42] Today, beer remains the alcoholic beverage of choice in sporting venues.

Historical documents provide some evidence of alcohol-related activities on the California campus. Up until 1915, *The Blue and Gold* yearbook ran advertisements for alcohol, including some for a store called the Widow, which delivered alcohol to several fraternities, including Zeta Psi. Delivery services were necessary because of the strong antisaloon movement in the city of Berkeley. The city passed laws prohibiting the sale of malts and other liquors within a two-, one-, and one-half-mile radius of the campus in 1873, 1876, and 1909, respectively. Despite these early restrictions on alcohol, it is apparent from documentary and archaeological evidence that alcohol consumption was part of the students' social experience.[43]

Alcohol continued to be available to students during Prohibition, which began in 1920. Photographs from a 1923 beer bust show Zeta Psi brothers toasting one another with steins over a keg of beer in the Berkeley Hills. A freshman house diary from 1933–1934 describes the house sponsoring beer busts and attending similar events at the chapter house at Stanford University. *The Blue and Gold* yearbooks of the time demonstrate that maintaining a consistent level of beer consumption was important to fraternity men. The yearbooks published during Prohibition include many photographs of men from other fraternities smuggling kegs of beer, drinking beer, and surrounded by empty beer bottles. While we may have found archaeological evidence of Zetes' beer consumption, they were at least wise enough to keep photographs of themselves drinking from being published in the yearbooks.[44]

Prohibition was repealed on November 8, 1933. The Zeta Psi diary from that year does suggest that some of the brothers drank near beers. For instance, an October 1933 entry reads, "Everyone feels fine this morning, as President Roosevelt's 3.2 beer does not give hangovers." This passage refers to a near beer of the later Prohibition period, which had a 3.2 percent alcoholic content, rather than the 2 percent of earlier Prohibition brews.

Alumni indicated to us that some fraternity brothers were involved in producing home brew off-site. A pledge diary entry dated September 10, 1933, may refer to home-brew: "John Jones came home with twelve bottles of beer. The beer proved to be very good and everyone who drank it enjoyed it immensely." The small number of bottles mentioned, and the writer's note that everyone enjoyed the beer, may indicate that it was not a usual commodity.

Based on manufacturers' marks, at least ten of the bottles recovered from the site were manufactured prior to Prohibition. Twenty-three bottles could have been manufactured either before or after Prohibition, and while only six of the bottles from the pit have manufacturers' marks that occur only after Prohibition, these bottles had to contain near beer. The bottles with earlier dates may represent stocks of beer that had been collected and stockpiled in anticipation of Prohibition, or may represent bottles that had been reused to contain home brew. In interviews, alumni emphasized that, while they may have enjoyed the fruits of illegal alcohol production, this production did not take place in the chapter house. Whether this represents sanitation of the historic past or is true is not clear. In support of the alumni's contentions, no wort cans were identified at the site. Wort was a malt extract used to make a rather nasty home brew.

It is possible that, by banning production of alcoholic beverages at the chapter house, the fraternity was protecting itself. Photographs and oral histories demonstrate that much of the illegal drinking took place away from the chapter house. Based on the documentary evidence available for Zeta Psi's pre-Prohibition days, the consumption of beer, not other kinds of alcohol, was central in interactions between brothers.

The archaeological presence of near beers is evidence that not all beer consumed by the fraternity had alcoholic content. Also, at least one of the brothers went to a doctor (a Zete alumni perhaps?) to receive a prescription for "medicinal brandy wine" found at the site (figure 35). And as was the case in the first Zeta Psi house, there was ample evidence that beer was being consumed from ceramic tankards and glass goblets and mugs.

*artifacts not to relative scale

FIGURE 35
Examples of beverage containers excavated from the second house deposits.

The archaeology of this period demonstrates that beer consumption, whether the beer had alcoholic content or not, was an important part of fraternity social and ritual life, and was a social activity distinct from other forms of alcoholic beverage consumption. For fraternity men, there was a significant difference between "having a beer" and "going for drinks," a difference that is made clear in the Prohibition dump.

MASCULINITY AND APPEARANCES

Photographs from Zeta Psi's second house demonstrate that the brothers, particularly compared to college students today, were a well-dressed lot, wearing trousers, jackets, and often ties at the table and around the house. Clothing-related artifacts recovered from the second house included forty-six buttons (table 14), four cufflinks, shoe buckles and eyelets, suspender buckles, and a brass ROTC hat crest. ROTC was required for all male students, and the ornament found would have been from the hat of an upper classmen.[45]

Maintaining appearances would have entailed good hygiene practices. Hygiene had class and gender implications. Good personal hygiene was a measure of good

TABLE 14 Personal adornment artifacts found at the second Zeta Psi house

Context	Item	Number
Yard midden	Prossier cufflink	2
	Bone button	1
	Shell button	3
	4-hole Prossier button	2
	Vegetable-ivory button	1
	Bakelite 4-hole button	1
	White metal star	1
Trash pit	Shell button	34
	Iron button	1
	Iron button cover	1
	Prossier cufflink	1
	Copper alloy shoe eyelets	5
	Copper alloy shoe buckle	1
	Gold-plated hat pin	1
	Glass bead	2
	ROTC brass hat ornament	1
	Zinc snap	1

background, and the men of Zeta Psi were concerned with appearances—and bodily odors. Vessels that had contained Vaseline, a popular hair pomade of the time, were found—a minimum of five vessels: four from the dump and one from the midden. Vaseline could have also been used as a skin softener and burn relief. Photographs from volumes of *The Blue and Gold* published during the second and third decades of the twentieth century show that slicked-back hair was a popular style among college men, the Zetes included.

Other toiletry items were represented by bottles that once held Colgate and Company products and Ed Pinaud's cologne. Colgate made soaps, toilet waters, and tooth powders. Listerine was represented in the dump by a minimum of four bottles; it served as both an antiseptic and a mouthwash. One could suggest that, after drinking as much alcohol as they did, the men of Zeta Psi might desire to hide the evidence from their breath. A minimum of three ceramic toothpaste jars, including a

TABLE 15   Pharmaceutical and health-related products recovered from the
second Zeta Psi house

Context	Artifact	Minimum Number represented
Yard midden (1910–1956)	Generic medicine bottle	13
	Homeopathic vial	3
	Ointment jar	1
	Bromo-Seltzer bottle	1
Trash pit (1923–1925)	Generic medicine bottle	31
	Generic antiseptic bottle	2
	Graduated medicine bottle	5
	Fratelli Branca bitters bottle	1
	"Blue Ribbon Quality Purity" graduated medicine bottle	1
	Up John Phenolax Wafers, laxative bottle	1
	Phenique Chemical Company antiseptic bottle	1
	Owl drug pharmacy bottle	4
	"McK & R" bottle	1
	Bowman's Drug, Berkeley, citrate of magnesium bottle	1
	Bowerman's Pharmacy, SF, bottle	1
	Ayer's Sarsaparilla bottle	1
	Homeopathic vial	2
	Pill bottle	1
	"Medicinal Brandy from Pure Wine" bottle	1
	Piso Cure bottle	1
	Bromo-Seltzer headache cure bottle	2
	Listerine bottle	11
	Mentholatum jar	1
	Mum deodorant jar	1
	Vaseline jar	3
	Tooth powder jar	1
	Bone toothbrush	2
	Colgate and Company toiletry jar	4
	Ed Pinaud perfume bottle	1

marked example of John Gosnell's cherry toothpaste, were also found, along with a minimum of three bone toothbrushes that would have applied the paste to shine the brother's pearly whites. Ayer's Sarsaparilla, found at the site, was, among other things, a tonic for the skin and a treatment for acne. A minimum of four unmarked milk-glass ointment jars may have held cold cream or deodorant. By the 1920s, there was a growing prescriptive literature that focused on the proper presentation of the masculine physique and facade. One could be primal in his masculinity; one simply didn't want to look or smell that way.[46]

Brothers relied on a range of medicines to treat illnesses and keep themselves healthy. Medicines recovered from the site included mass-marketed drugs and some products from local companies. Among the nationally known brands were Up John's /sic/ Phenolax Wafers, used for indigestion; Fernet-Branca Bitters, which could be consumed as either an alcoholic beverage or a tonic for indigestion; the Phenique Chemical Company's antiseptic; Bromo-Seltzer, the headache remedy; and the Piso Company's cure all. Local drugstore chains, like Owl Drug, Bowman Drug, and Bowerman's Drugs, were also represented among the bottles (table 15). While it is often difficult to identify the contents of pharmacy bottles, the Bowman's bottle contained citrate of magnesia, a common stomach cure. Given the earlier discussion of the food at the fraternity, it is notable that so many of the identified cures are related to stomach upset.[47]

MOTHER'S CLUBS, RACE, AND MASCULINITY

Zeta Psi alumni were emphatic that women were not allowed to violate the space of Zeta Psi—except, as in the case of Wendy entering Peter's house—in certain prescribed circumstances. The chapter house contained a guest room, which opened out onto the courtyard but had no doorways to the interior spaces of the rest of the fraternity house. A person attempting to enter or leave the guest room would be on display to anyone overlooking the courtyard. Several brothers noted that, if a lady had been too late at a social (one of the prescribed times women could enter the house), she would be allowed to stay overnight in the guest room.

The other occasion when women could enter the house was during the monthly meetings of Zeta Psi's "Mother's Club" /sic/. It is not known when the Mother's Club for Zeta Psi was founded, and there are no references to it in the early historical documentation. But alumni from the 1920s and beyond remember the Mother's Clubs. The club consisted of brother's mothers and, sometimes, alumni's wives, who had a vested interest in the housekeeping and maintenance issues of the house. The club would determine if chairs needed to be reupholstered, curtains replaced, or rugs cleaned. One alumnus remembered the mothers raising money to purchase a vacuum for the house. They would meet on an afternoon, be served tea, and be entertained by the pledges. Just as the pledges were responsible for doing a great deal of cleaning and polishing in the house, it was also their responsibility to serve as hosts for the mothers.

Considering the roles that the younger classmen, particularly pledges, played in the house, it would be tempting to suggest that the junior classmen of Zeta Psi served as the symbolic women of the fraternity family. I argue forcibly against this. The health of the fraternity always depended on its lower classmen successfully making the transition to leadership positions in only a few short years. To construct these young members as anything less than men would be to risk the future of the fraternity. Instead, these young men were the younger brothers of the fraternity, and a number of practices underscored the shared masculinity of the brothers at all times. If junior classmen were seen as less than full men, it was in their context as pledges rather than initiates. As discussed earlier, at least some fraternity men saw initiation into the fraternity as erasing any feminine influence in the men. All the pledges possessed the innate ability to become grown men in the chapter members' view. This was not the case for all men who lived in Zeta Psi's house, however. House servants were denied full masculinity, not just by virtue of their status as fraternity outsiders but also by virtue of their skin color.

All documented house servants at Zeta Psi were Chinese, Japanese, or Filipino men. From 1910 until at least the early 1930s, but not later than the end of World War II, Zeta Psi had live-in servants. California was a highly racist society, which in many ways modeled its racial hierarchy after that of the Spanish. Unlike the northeastern and midwestern states, where Jews, Irish, Italians, and eastern Europeans were constructed in the late nineteenth century as less than white, in California all Europeans seemed to be recognized as potentially white, with Latinos, Asians, Africans, and Native Americans falling into lower social categories. The rolls of the fraternity include names such as McGillivray, Solinsky, Soule, and Zook, all names that suggest ethnicities that would not be represented in the eastern chapters of the fraternity at the same time. In the West, the Irish, Italians, and eastern Europeans of a particular economic class were as white as any white Anglo-Saxon Protestants— wealth and social status were synonymous with whiteness for any European, thus the large number of Irish surnames and, by the early twentieth century, Italian surnames on Iota's register.[48]

Such opportunities did not exist for Asian men. Scholars of Asian American history have noted the feminized role that Asian men were forced to occupy in California society. Filling positions as laundry workers, cooks, and domestics, and forcibly denied their own family life through a series of immigration laws known as the Exclusionary Acts, Chinese men, and later Japanese and Filipino men, were less than men in the eyes of whites. Racist depictions of Asian men emphasized dresslike garments and long ponytails (queues) as evidence of Chinese men's female qualities.[49]

Zeta Psi was not the only fraternity to employ Asian men; it was standard practice, according to the 1900, 1910, and 1920 census records. The 1890s yearbook entry about Zeta Psi's German dining club referred to a "cook" who was clearly female, but she was portrayed as having an accent that marked her as a member of an unspecified ethnicity. As noted before, it is not clear that there were servants' quarters in the first house. It may have been seen as inappropriate for the fraternity to have women servants working and living in the chapter house. Still, the employment of Asian house servants demarcated the shared whiteness of the brothers and the otherness of their employees.[50]

A 1901 newspaper article gives some extraordinary insight into how relations between the fraternity brothers and their Asian employees were gendered. This *San Francisco Call* article was intended to provide an overview of the fraternity experience at the University of California. The following is its description of Zeta Psi:

> The Zeta Psi boys have the proud distinction of owning the oldest "frat" house
> in Berkeley. It has stood the bangs and knocks of dozens of lively boys for
> twenty-six years and is still in fine condition. And wonder of wonders, they have
> kept the same Chinaman for fourteen years straight running! No bribes or
> envious matrons have been sufficient to induce him to leave his boys. He knows
> the old members much better than do the boys who live in the house. It is easy
> for them to have a dinner. All they have to do is remember one thing—to let that
> Marvelous Chinaman into their confidence. Then he does the rest. He sees that
> the house is in perfect order, plans the menu and hires the necessary help. If any
> is needed. The boys dress in their best bib and tucker and come downstairs at the
> proper time, without further bothering their heads. Ain't they to be envied?[51]

I suggest that the reader look over this description again, but replace the word *Chinaman* with *wife*. The paragraph reads naturally and very clearly demonstrates the alternate masculinity represented by the Asian servants.

Brothers kept themselves separate from their employees, who lived in quarters behind and above the kitchen. Only limited evidence of Asian influences on foodways was recovered from the site. Sheep and beef remains from the dump site had cleaver marks on them. Cleavers were widely associated with Asian butchering techniques of the time. The only evidence of Asian foodstuffs was recovered from the doorway immediately outside the servants' quarters and consisted of sherds of brown Chinese stoneware that typically contained soy sauce or preserved foods. Soy sauce had not become a common condiment for non-Asian persons at the turn of the century, and interviews with brothers made it clear that Asian foods were viewed with some suspicion, at least in the late 1920s and early 1930s.[52] An alumnus from the class of '29 remembered his disgust when he discovered that their Chinese employees had negotiated grocery contracts for the house in Oakland's Chinatown. As house manager, he cancelled those contracts and renegotiated with, in his words, a proper Italian grocer.

The abuse of Chinese house servants and cooks at the hands of the fraternity men was apparently well known among the student population, and jokes about the subject were made in cartoons, poems, and rhymes in the literary magazines, yearbooks, and newspapers. In particular, references were made to cutting off cooks' queues. A 1904 *Pelican* describes such an occurrence in an entry called "Fraternity Rules." "Cutting off the cook's queue and coiling it in the soup as macaroni will no longer be regarded as a childish amusement. Several sickly sophomores have failed to digest the humor of it."[53] It is worth recalling that early hazing on campus involved kidnapping freshmen men and forcibly shaving their whiskers. The removal of hair had emasculating connotations for the men who both inflicted and endured this form of abuse. Even as these sentiments were expressed, Asian men were increasingly visible as students on the University of California campus. Although they were not included in the fraternities or the house clubs, Asian men with Chinese and Japanese surnames, and sporting the same hairstyles and clothing as other Cal men, are visible in the pages of *The Blue and Gold* as early as 1911. Their presence would increase, and assaults on their masculinity would continue for some time to come.[54]

LEAVING THE HOUSE

The second house of Iota served as a highly structured symbolic space in which the fraternity men constructed adult identities that accommodated shifting notions of white masculinity. Within the house, domesticity was recast in ways that served to neutralize any feminine associations. The space was explicitly male, and women were allowed to enter the house only in prescribed ways. While domestic activities associated with household life retained their importance in reaffirming brotherly ties, new ritualized aspects of dining, like the use of fraternity ceramics, under-scored the masculine nature of the activity.

In its earliest days, the new masculinity was a means for men—explicitly white men—to reassert their social, economic, and political dominance. Soon, global affairs would provide men with new ways to express what they saw as their exclusive claim on citizenship rights. The Great War would permit students to serve their country on the battlefield. And this would provide them with an opportunity to demonstrate their virility in a war whose ferocity would match that of the American Civil War. With World War I would come other changes to university life, including changes in the ways men and women related to one another. Let us leave the underground house and explore how the men of the second Zete house navigated the social landscape of the campus Never Land.

PROGRAM FOR ACT V

The first scene of this act finds us aboard the *Jolly Roger*, Captain Hook's ship.
Even though Hook believes that Peter is dead, and that he, Hook, is at last
triumphant, he feels compelled to make his dying speech (in case there is no
opportunity to make it when the time comes). He complains of the injustices he
has suffered at the hands of Peter and those who admire Peter. The boys are
brought to the deck of the pirate ship, their hands bound. Before they are forced to
walk the plank, Hook asks if any of them would prefer to join the pirates as cabin
boys. All refuse. Wendy is brought to see her children die, and she urges them to
"die like English gentlemen."

Peter flies in and circles the boat, making a ticking noise like the crocodile. A
pirate is sent to investigate, only to be grabbed by Peter and thrown overboard.
Peter's comrades realize he has come and feign fear that a ghost is on the ship. One
pirate, then another, is sent to retrieve a whip from the ship's cabin, only to fall
prey to Peter as well. Now Hook and the other pirates fear that the ship is haunted,
and the fearful pirates threaten mutiny. Hook, who is also afraid, sends the
Darlings and Lost Boys to kill the spirit in the cabin, not realizing that he is
helping Peter, who releases them and arms them. The pirates think the boys, too,
have been killed, and advance upon Hook, who puts the blame on Wendy and
threatens to throw her overboard. Peter stops them and a battle ensues, until there
are only two combatants left able to fight—Hook and Peter. The fight becomes so
hopeless for Hook that he decides to dive into the waiting mouth of the crocodile,
thus ending the scene.

The second scene finds us back in the Darlings' nursery. Mr. and Mrs. Darling
are asleep in chairs. We learn that Mr. Darling has been so devastated by the loss
of the children that he has been traveling to work carried in Nana's doghouse,

where he also usually sleeps. Mrs. Darling has suspected that he enjoys the attention he receives from the neighbors as a result, but she has tried to be generous. Despite Peter's attempt to bar the nursery window, the children return and slip unnoticed into their beds. Their mother awakes but doesn't at first realize they have come back—she has so often dreamt of the sight that she cannot believe it when she first sees it. There is general rejoicing, and then Wendy brings the Lost Boys out from hiding, who are quickly adopted by the Darlings and Eliza the servant. Peter appears, and Mrs. Darling offers to adopt him as well, but he rejects her, declaring that he doesn't want to grow up—"No one is going to catch me, lady, and make me a man." Peter wants Wendy to return to Never Land with him. Peter and Mrs. Darling compromise; agreeing that Wendy can return to Never Land once a year for spring cleaning. We see them a year later in Never Land as Wendy prepares to return home with the aid of a broom. Wendy has grown, Peter has not. He has forgotten the Lost Boys and the pirates, and even Tinkerbell, yet he is eternal. As Wendy leaves, the play ends with Peter center stage, playing his pan pipes as the curtain closes.

The Public Face of Iota

> HOOK (*suddenly*).   So! Now then, you bullies,
> six of you walk the plank to-night, but I have
> room for two cabin-boys. Which of you is it
> to be? (*He returns to his cards*).
> TOOTLES (*hoping to soothe him by putting the
> blame on the only person, vaguely remembered,
> who is always willing to act as a buffer*).   You
> see, sir, I don't think my mother would like
> me to be a pirate. Would your mother like you
> to be a pirate, Slightly?
> SLIGHTLY (implying that otherwise it would be a
> pleasure to him to oblige).   I don't think so.
> Twin, would your mother like—
>
> *Peter Pan*

The Zetes may have settled their second house at the same location as their first, but just as the ways they lived at that address had changed, so had the social world around them forever changed. Never Land had a new social geography. The new masculinity was an entrenched, lived reality for campus men of the second decade of the twentieth century and beyond. To be male was now firmly seen as being the opposite of female. "Sissy men" and gay men were recognized as unacceptable types of masculinity, categories that blurred too easily into the performative realm of "womanhood" and "femininity." Changes in conceptions of masculinity had been shepherded in by changes in attitudes toward physical culture (and the appearance of the white male body), notions of scientific progress, the racial other, and insecurities fed by the feminist movement. It was the Great War, however, that solidified the male notion that masculinity was a naturalized identity beyond the reach of women, no matter what social, economic, political, or fitness advancements women made. After all, it was men who had freed Europe and successfully waged the war to end all wars.[1]

Women also had reason to feel successful. In 1912, California women won the vote, a right that was reaffirmed at the national level in 1920. On Cal's campus, women took advantage of men's low numbers during the war to challenge spaces that had been reserved by tradition for men. They solidified their campus organizations and the autonomy of those institutions, developed new house clubs and sororities, and created traditions like Women's Day and the Prytanean Festival that celebrated the successes of their gender. By the time the men had returned from war, the women were bobbing their hair and exposing dramatic amounts of leg, and they had finally tossed aside the wasp-waist corset. These changes had profound implications for the ways that men and women interacted on campus.[2]

Other important changes, too, transformed campus life at this time. New extracurricular activities came to replace the favored activities of old. While small numbers of students still participated in glee clubs and drama and debating societies, it was the activities associated with expressions of school spirit that garnered the most participation, and many of these revolved around the new star in the galaxy of national student life—college athletics. Fraternities also enjoyed growth in popularity, both locally and nationwide. Increasing numbers of students jockeyed for invitations to pledge, and a growing number of new organizations developed to meet the demand.[3]

The national popularity of these organizations—for men and women—drew the attention of college administrators throughout the United States. Instructors and administrators noticed that students in the 1920s and 1930s were drawn to college for its social life as much as, or in many cases more than, for its intellectual life. Campuses conducted and published studies exploring whether fraternities, among other student organizations, were nurturing anti-intellectual attitudes among students. Administrators and scholars debated both the benefits and disadvantages of fraternity life for their students and their campuses.[4]

We will now again explore the ways that the Zetes were perceived by the other communities of Never Land. The characters remained the same. The coeds were still divided into Tinks (fun to date but not marry), Tiger Lilies (the "Pelicans" of old), and Wendys (potential wives and mothers), but the sexual revolution under way in the 1920s made the lines between them more difficult to distinguish. There was still a community of Lost Boys—made up of not just the members of Zeta Psi but also the many other men on campus who identified as fraternity brothers. They recognized, despite their different chapters and organizations, that they faced a shared threat at both campus and national level from administrative pirates who would, if not eliminate them, at least attempt to interfere in their lives. As yes, of course there were pirates. Unlike the pirates of the earlier decades, who sought to abolish the fraternities outright, these administrators had grown sly. Just as Captain Hook attempted to recruit the Lost Boys to join him rather than to walk the plank, administrators sought ways to "work with" Greek letter societies to reform them. The fraternities responded by creating the Interfraternity Conference, which met nationally and reproduced itself locally on different college campuses.[5]

CHANGING TRADITIONS

The twentieth century saw the end of a number of Cal's original traditions. Some faded away; others were forcibly ended. The Bourdon Burial had been only sporadically observed during the 1890s and was celebrated for the last time in 1903. The curriculum and nature of university experience had changed so much by that time that the idea of a shared intellectual experience within the university based on class year was outdated. The university had grown too large and the course offerings and programs of study too diverse for students to share an identification with any particular class or primer.[6]

In 1905, President Wheeler declared that the annual Charter Day freshman and sophomore rush had been abolished. He challenged students to come up with activities that would foster unity and school spirit rather than factions along class lines. Wheeler was clearly drawing on the imagery of civilization and modernity in describing the old tradition as barbarous and unbecoming to a modern university. There was some tension leading up to Charter Day, as it was unclear whether the president's decree would be respected. When the time came, however, the classes who would have been involved in the rush instead worked together to create a physical symbol of college spirit. The Big C, which I described earlier—a concrete letter that still graces the hillside above campus—was constructed by the classes of 1907 and 1908 in place of the rush. The repainting of the concrete C became an annual event, and a Big C Society, composed of varsity-letter earners, was named in its honor. In 1907, a freshman-sophomore brawl was introduced, and it was overseen by the Big C Society to ensure that no excessive rowdiness or roughness took place. This event was more a competition of athletic prowess, and for a number of years it included a giant ball push between freshmen and sophomores. Yes, you are probably imagining this correctly—teams of men trying to push a ten-foot ball onto their opponent's side. Jousting, tugs of war, and other events were also regular parts of the brawl, which was celebrated annually into the 1960s and even came to incorporate women.[7]

In student publications of the 1900s, writers discussed the shedding of traditions with little sign of remorse, noting that such traditions did not suit a modern university. They went on to observe that, since Cal students abhorred anything smacking of an invented tradition, there was no expectation that other events would rise to replace the dead ones. This prediction proved incorrect, and the twentieth century did see the rise of new campuswide events, as well as the elaboration of a few remaining late-nineteenth-century ones. By the 1920s, when students were particularly concerned with campus social life and activities, the *Daily Cal* ran regular columns explaining the history of university traditions.[8]

Fraternal organizations instituted several campus events. In 1892, students organized Skull and Keys, an honor society for junior and senior fraternity men. Each year the new initiates were introduced in an event known as the "Running of the Skull and Keys." Members dressed in tails and tan pants. They performed skits and sometimes presented floats, and their antics drew large crowds annually. The event was notable on campus through the 1940s. Skull and Keys was highly secretive, and its annual introduction of initiates was the only evidence of its presence on campus. The public introduction could feature mortification dates (where one humiliated a date in various embarrassing ways) and service to sororities, singing, vaudeville programs, and general public humiliation. The Iota scrapbook kept in the early 1890s includes several photographs of the Running of the Skull and Keys, whose founding members included several Zetes.[9]

In 1916, the Channing Way Derby was born. The event grew out of the practices of the Sigma Chi fraternity during the culmination of the annual sorority rush, the day when pledges were announced. The men, whose house was located on the corner of College Avenue and Channing Way (several blocks south of Zeta Psi's house), would sit on their roof and watch women going to each of the sorority houses. They apparently would count and rate the women headed to each house to evaluate the quality of pledges. The misogynistic overtones of the fraternity's behavior should not be overlooked, but the sororities did decide to play to the men, and soon a range of activities and faux sporting events or challenges was laid out for the pledges to compete in. Photographs of the event from the 1920s yearbooks demonstrate that Sigma Chi mounted a large board on the side of their house where they posted scores (figure 36). The sorority women competed in weigh-ins, where they attempted to increase their weight by drinking milk before stepping on the scales. Photographs show women taking part in pie-eating contests, seated on rowing machines, and engaged in tugs of war. The spectacle drew large crowds of Greeks and non-Greeks alike in a block party atmosphere. The event was abolished in 1942 in observance of the war.[10]

The greatest range of new events on campus, however, revolved around college athletics. While the nineteenth-century student was likely to demonstrate school spirit by participating in sports, the twentieth-century student participated mainly as

FIGURE 36
The Channing Way Derby and the scoreboard kept by Sigma Chi,
in the 1930s. Photograph courtesy of the Bancroft Library.

a "rooter," or fan. Already, sports events in the early twentieth century could draw
thousands of spectators. Football, still looking more like rugby than the modern incarnation, was particularly popular, and the West Coast had many powerful teams
established within the first two decades of the twentieth century. Many of the teams
of the modern Pac-10 (Pacific 10) athletic conference were playing one another in
the 1920s—Cal, Stanford, Washington State, University of Washington, and University of Southern California. Fierce rivalries between schools were established, including the ongoing feud between Cal and Stanford that still annually culminates in
the Big Game. Average students, unable to play football at the level required, could
support their universities only through their presence in the stands. Attending spirit
rallies, participating in team yells, wearing school colors, and either commiserating
or celebrating after the game was the extent of their participation.[11]

Still, the athletic programs were seen as physical embodiments of the health and
rigor of the collective student body. Shame on the field was shared by all, as were
great glories. In this context, sportsmanship was less interesting than success and

TABLE 16 Cal football scores from the 1922 season*

Visitor	Visitor score	Cal score
Santa Clara	14	45
Marines	0	80
St. Mary's	0	41
Olympic Club	0	25
University of Southern California	0	12
Washington State	0	61
Washington	7	45
Nevada	13	61
Stanford	0	28

* From the 1923 volume of *The Blue and Gold*.

complete domination. The 1922 football season is an excellent example of this mentality. Cal had an extremely successful team that year, a fact trumpeted endlessly by *The Blue and Gold*. The schedule pitted Cal against nine opponents: Santa Clara, the Marines, St. Mary's, the Olympic Club, University of Southern California, Washington State, University of Washington, University of Nevada, and Stanford. The Cal team was victorious in all of its games (table 16) and had no qualms about running up the score against weaker teams. Editors of *The Blue and Gold* were particularly pleased that Cal had scored a total of 398 points over the season and had allowed opponents to collectively score only 34. The success of the team was clearly, as the editors saw it, a measure of the virility of the larger community.[12]

The link between athleticism and maleness is perhaps no more plainly illustrated than in the decision to build a structure honoring the university's war dead of the Great War. The structure selected to pay "tribute to those who died in the great war for humanity" was a football stadium—Cal's Memorial Stadium.[13] Nationally, sports stadiums in general became worthy places for honoring masculine sacrifice. The association of athleticism and masculinity had implications for female students. In the first decade of the 1900s, student bodies still debated whether it was appropriate for women to come to athletic events, whether they should root, and whether they should be included in rallies and pregame events. Men saw athletics as a masculine realm, regarding even pregame rallies, such as the "Smokers," where men gathered to smoke and talk, as events where women's presence would dampen the fervor and enthusiasm of the true fans, the men.[14]

This gender tension seems to have dissipated as the twentieth century progressed, and women became common in the stands. Certain highly coveted campus "spirit" positions like "yell leader" (known today as "cheerleader") and membership in the Big C Society were reserved for male students. Members of spirit groups commanded a great deal of attention in *The Blue and Gold*, and yell leaders were almost as highly lauded as the players themselves. Women may have had more opportunities to participate in athletics and athletic teams on campus, but their efforts were considered secondary to the accomplishments of men—a scenario familiar in the sporting world today.[15] In this context, let us consider what constituted the "ideal" college student of the time.

BIG MEN ON CAMPUS

From 1910 through the 1930s, college students focused primarily on social rather than academic experiences of university life. School spirit and participation in student groups and activities were measures of one's success as a student. The pinnacle of achievement was to be recognized by one's peers as "a big man on campus." The big man on campus was an archetype established in the popular college-life-themed literature of the first half of the twentieth century. The big man was popular among his peers and was visibly involved in a range of campus events, societies, and organizations. Participation in athletics, spirit events, elected student offices, honor societies, or Greek life was a clear measure of one's community connectedness.[16] *The Blue and Gold* recognized these new priorities: the "Senior Record," which in its early manifestation was a separate section of the yearbook, listed graduating seniors' campus activities and achievements. Later, the "Senior Record" was joined by the "Senior's Photographic," which included individual photographs of the students. There was also, in the 1920s, a section called "Hall of Fame," which included full-body photographs of a small number of students and longer descriptions of their achievements.[17]

A notable expression of these new priorities was the sudden explosion of honor societies on campus. It is not clear what the criteria for membership in these societies were. Among them was the Golden Bear, which was the senior men's honor society; the Winged Helmet, the junior honor society; Tri-une, the sophomore honor society; and the Blade and Scabbard, the military honor society. Honor societies for students enrolled in drama, foreign language, music, prelaw, premed, mining, or business classes, as well as for students engaged in pretty much anything imaginable, were formed. Membership in these societies may not have been associated with any particular intellectual achievements. While Zeta Psi men were involved in any number of "honor societies," I have not identified any men from the second house who made it into Phi Beta Kappa. As in Phi Beta Kappa, however, members in an honor society were awarded a brass badge or pin.

A student recognized as having many affiliations was described in the student literature as "packing brass."[18] It would appear that the proliferation of societies was a way of generating more opportunities for students to earn brass. In the 1928 *Blue and Gold*, the brass phenomenon was explained—sort of:

> It seems that the dreams, the hopes, the ambitions, the very roots of happiness
> of one's junior year depend on BRASS. It matters not whether it is shining brass,
> tarnished brass, dull brass, or even raw brass. Just BRASS! According to our modern
> code of ethics, a junior is judged by the pile of brass he is able to take up in one
> brief year. Brass is acquired by apple polishing, by grabbing gravy and making
> oneself look important—and drunk . . . , by getting onto committees and slinging
> gravy, by lapping up more gravy for any powers that might happen to be. We did
> so want to explain all this, but the professional brass men insisted that we tell it all
> in a muddled way so no one would understand, or not tell it at all.[19]

Fraternity men certainly cultivated an image of being central to campus life. John Kenneth Galbraith, who attended Cal as a graduate student in the early 1930s, presents a particularly evocative memory of fraternities at the time through the eyes of an outsider.

> Coming up Bancroft Way to the International House on an evening, one saw
> the fraternity men policing up the lawns of their houses or sitting contentedly in
> front. Walking along Piedmont at night one heard the shouts of laughter within,
> or occasional bits of song, or what Evelyn Waugh correctly described as the
> most evocative and nostalgic of all sounds of an aristocracy at play, the crash
> of breaking glass. Here were men with a secure position in society and who
> knew it and were content. On a Friday night they would do their duty at the
> pep rally shaming the apathetic; on Saturday they would be at the stadium, and
> on Saturday night, win or lose, they joined with the kindred souls of earlier
> generations, men they did not hesitate to call brother, to whoop it up as a
> college man was meant to do.[20]

Intentionally or not, Galbraith eloquently captures the romance and allure of fraternity life for the outsider. This was exactly the image that the fraternities were cultivating for themselves.

CHANGING LANDSCAPE

Zeta Psi's public life in the second house would have been shaped in part by the neighborhood surrounding the house, which by 1936 had nearly completely evolved from one filled with families to one inhabited by university employees, students, and services (figure 37). University buildings like Cowell Memorial Hospital, the U.S. government's National Park Service lab, and Boalt Hall, the law school, had encroached on the neighborhood by 1911. And Zeta Psi was no longer the only fraternity in the neighborhood: seven other Greek houses could be found in the immediate vicinity. Longtime Zete neighbor Professor Hilgard had long since passed into the celestial agricultural school, but his aging spinster daughter still lived in the family home on the 2700 block of Piedmont. How ironic for her, spending her last years surrounded by so many single young men. Her father, who had warned the Academic Senate against the moral depravities of college group living, would not have been pleased by all the fraternities. Some other old neighbors remained too: the now elderly and widowed May Cheney, who had been the appointment secretary, still lived in her home, as did several other long-term residents. These families must have felt stripped of their privacy and quiet when crowds poured into Memorial Stadium, located just across Piedmont Avenue. These neighbors were not destined to stay long: by 1942, the university had acquired most of the properties in the neighborhood.[21]

How then, did the Zeta Psi fraternity's Lost Boys navigate this new campus world? Did their new house help their cause or not? If part of the goal of building a new chapter house was to revitalize Zeta Psi's presence on campus, it was a success. The 1911 yearbook features in its advertising section a photograph of a palatial parlor satirically labeled, "Inside the woodshed of the Zeta Psi House." Along similar lines, in the 1912 satirical ragging section of *The Blue and Gold,* a fictional freshman is being taken on a campus tour and shown another fraternity house. The freshman asks, "Is it as expensive as the Zete house?" and is bluntly told, "No." In the 1922 yearbook, a satirical tour of the fraternity houses shows a picture of a bank next to the listing for Zeta Psi, which reads, "This is where Looie LeHane lives. He is the literary athlete. Ted Ciprico lives here, too. He is the athletic actor. The Zetes used to have a nice house, but it was getting messy and out-of-date during the last few years." The jab is unmistakable. Unlike in the decade before the construction of the new house, the Zetes were again mentioned with great regularity in the yearbooks.[22]

This is not to say that the fraternity's image was completely positive. The 1912 *Blue and Gold* features a mock-up of the different fraternal crests, and Zeta Psi's

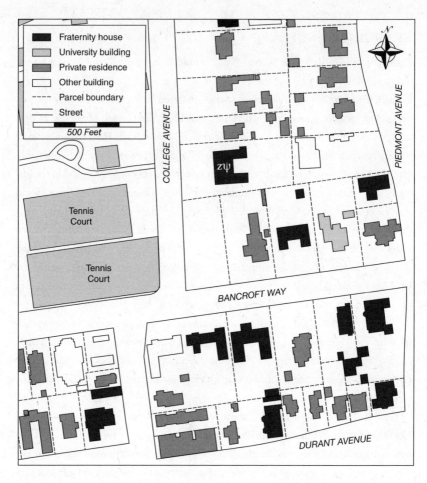

FIGURE 37
Zeta Psi's neighborhood in 1929, based on Sanborn Fire
Insurance maps.

depicts two famous members, beer, cards, the new house, and the motto "Flunk
Out" (figure 38). In 1922, in a fake advertisement for Schilling and Bell's Grape-O,
"the New Temperance Drink for all Campus functions," the company is described
as the "Purveyors Extraordinary to Zeta Psi." The implication, of course, is that it
was anything but a temperate beverage. Of course, in the increasingly social cli-
mate of campus, a reputation for leisure and socializing was not entirely negative.[23]

The revitalization of the fraternity is also apparent from the size of the chapter.
Membership hovered at or below twenty members in the first decade of the twentieth

FIGURE 38
Satire of the Zeta Psi crest, as conceived by an artist for the 1911
Blue and Gold, versus the official crest.

century, but by the end of the next decade the house had a stable membership numbering over thirty men. The only time when the house membership ever dipped to levels as low as those seen at the first house was in 1944, when war took all but fifteen brothers from campus (table 17). The increasing size of the fraternity had implications for space in the house.

By the 1950s, the membership was larger than the house could accommodate, and while earlier generations of Zetes had lived together as a family, this tradition changed. An alumnus from the class of 1958 recalled that many of the brothers did not live in the house until their junior or senior years. This altered the model of family that had been practiced in the fraternity until that time. When freshmen and sophomores were no longer living under the supervision of the senior classmen, the sense of community and brotherhood that had been developed through shared practice in earlier times diminished. In fact, this same alumnus recalled that the only important divisions in the house were between pledges and those who had already been initiated.[24]

TABLE 17   Zeta Psi population during occupation of the second house

Year	Number of Zetes	Year	Number of Zetes
1910	18	1935	32
1911	17	1936	41
1912	21	1937	40
1913	24	1938	40
1914	23	1939	31
1915	26	1940	37
1916	31	1941	32
1917	39	1942	42
1918	37	1943	38
1919	32	1944	16
1920	34	1945	n/a
1921	n/a	1946	33
1922	39	1947	49
1923	39	1948	40
1924	37	1949	38
1925	32	1950	54
1926	34	1951	35
1927	33	1952	38
1928	36	1953	41
1929	36	1954	38
1930	34	1955	41
1931	36	1956	36
1932	41	1957	30
1933	37	1958	36
1934	44		

The Zetes, their house, and their chapter personality and individual personalities were frequently depicted in the pages of *The Blue and Gold* through the 1920s and, to a lesser degree, the 1930s. Still, in the changing social landscape, fraternities were judged on their ability to recruit particular high-profile men. One description from the 1922 *Blue and Gold* demonstrates how particular individuals came to represent particular fraternities for the college campus. A blurb appearing next to the Zete house stated, "Hocking is notable among the numerous major sports of these celebrities. The less prominent brethren still prostate themselves at the feet of the supreme Louie and Ted. The Witter clan is able to escape this forced worship only by their policy of 'there is strength in numbers.' " Just as the humorous depiction of the crest included portrayals of famous Zetes, the entire brotherhood was represented by a few strong presences. Interestingly, nowhere in the blurb is there specific mention of Zeta Psi itself—the house was a landmark recognizable to the campus community. Throughout their occupation of the second house, the Zetes maintained their reputation as aloof, snobby, and exclusive. They also maintained their reputation as drinkers and gamblers.[25]

The Zetes competed for brothers in an increasingly crowded field. There were twenty-six fraternities located at Cal in 1911, and by 1928 this number had grown to sixty-one. In addition, men's and women's house clubs were also founded, with the aid of the university. Mary Ritter, the university's female physician and administrator, recalls the system developed by the university to facilitate student cohabitational groups, or clubhouses. "The plan was that the Board should loan to each club the equivalent, in furniture, of one thousand dollars without interest, the same to be returned in annual installments of one hundred dollars. . . . Forty-two such groups of students have been aided by the establishment of club homes. Of these, twenty-three club houses are for women and nineteen for men. Four or five of them became sororities or fraternities after their indebtedness for furniture had been met."[26]

On campuses throughout the country, a sizeable proportion of men belonged to national and local fraternities during the period of 1911 to 1929 (table 18). Even during the Great War, when there were fewer men on campus and a reduced membership recruitment, 30 percent of university men were members of a fraternal society. In 1927 and 1928, over 40 percent of male students were fraternity brothers. If we were to include members of house clubs as well, the percentage would be even larger. Scholars of student life in the early twentieth century identify the new importance of fraternities and other campus social clubs as a marker of the United States' incipient obsession with youth culture. Popular magazines and novels reported on the styles and culture of college life in ways that glamorized the student experience.[27]

How did the men of Zeta Psi see themselves? During the occupation of the first house, Zetes were common representatives on college publications, and the early alumni who stayed on campus had various opportunities as well to express in print their thoughts and opinions on their fraternity. During the occupation of the second house, , the Zetes made fewer contributions to the documentary record. In interviews,

TABLE 18   Overall membership in fraternities at the
University of California, 1900–1925

Year	Number of men in social fraternities	% of male population
1900–01	113	10.2
1905–06	353	23.4
1910–11	386	18.1
1915–16	927	30.9
1920–21	1452	37.4
1925–26	1761	36.9

alumni of the second house may admit that they kept to themselves, and that the fraternity had many members who were wealthy or well-connected in society, but they also stress the importance of legacies in the fraternity. They talk of the importance of fraternity life in developing responsible manhood, and of the importance of the friendships they developed in the house. Some have stayed active in the national organization, and some visit the third house. Student publications provide little insight into how the fraternity saw itself. Most editions of *The Blue and Gold* featured the fraternity crest and pictures of the active members, and sometimes a photograph of the house and a blurb about the founding of both the national fraternity and the local chapter. In 1948 and 1949, however, the yearbook provided a brief synopsis of each fraternity on its chapter page, presumably written by, or at least in conjunction with, the fraternity. The 1948 blurb is particularly insightful.

"We were here first!" could well be the motto of the Zeta Psi's. They have the distinction of being the oldest fraternity west of the Mississippi, the first on the Pacific Coast, and first living group at the University of California. Here they set up the first tepee in 1870, and they now look back with pride on their many accomplishments and traditions. For a long time the Zetes have been considered aloof as they don't participate in exchange dinners, picnics and sings with the girls' living groups on campus—but they are not really anti-social or woman haters!! Their annual "Post Mortem" dance, given after finals, is definite proof of that! Ted Rademaker and Billy Montagne were outstanding in sports among the Zetes this past year. Besides sun-bathing, last minute dating, and raising the fraternity scholastic rating, the Zetes are best known for keeping out of newspapers!!![28]

It is interesting to ponder what the Zetes meant by keeping out of the papers. I have searched the 1947–1948 papers and found remarkably little mentioned about fraternities. Many of the issues of the day surrounded the Red Scare—in particular, whether or not the YMCA and YWCA were supporting the activities of communists. (As we shall see, the Zetes may have bragged too quickly about their low profile.) The 1949 blurb is much shorter, but it emphasizes many of the same points:

> They call themselves conservative but the Zeta Psi's have lots of uproarious fun. The Cal Zetes were the first fraternity to be established west of the Mississippi, and in Cal's swaddling days had fun helping publish the *Blue and Gold* at various times. The Zetes were proud to have footballer Bill Montagne among them. Other men of athletic distinction are Bob Losey, John Raggio, Jacque Pry and Bob Witter, members of the varsity rugby team. A "lively" time was had at the Post-Mortem dance, annually given after June finals, and the pre-Christmas formal was another bright spot in the social calendar of a gay, happy school year.[29]

The campus community may have had certain perceptions of who the Zetes were, but the Zetes' participation in campus life creates a slightly different portrait.

ZETES' SOCIAL ACTIVITIES

The Zetes' selection of activities while living in the second house reflects the new values of the broader campus community. The divisions of activities I analyzed for this period are somewhat different from those I analyzed in act 2 while examining what the brothers of the first chapter house engaged in. I found that activities of the men living in the second house could be grouped into the following categories: athletics, honor societies, student government, publications, spirit committees, military training, and drama/arts (table 19). I derived my calculations from self-reports of activities by students in the "Senior Record" portion of *The Blue and Gold* and by reading available participant lists for different activities. This information was available only for the senior class in any year, and so is not directly comparable to the information for the first house. It is worth noting that these figures represent the minimum participation in any set of activities.

While the men of the first house had participated in a wide range of sports, the number of men in the second house who could play organized sports was limited. Sports like football and baseball were considered major sports, while track, tennis, rugby, crewing, and basketball were minor sports. Zeta Psi is known to have

TABLE 19   Percentage of Senior Zeta Psi brothers participating in campus activities during occupation of the second house*

Year	Athletics	Honor societies	Student government	Publications	Spirit committees	Military	Drama/arts	Overall
1911	50	50						50
1912	33	100	66.6		66.6			100
1913	25	50					25	75
1914								0
1916	12.5	75	25	12.5	75	12.5	75	75
1917	12.5	37.5	12.5		25			37.5
1919		100			100			100
1920	11.1	33.3	11.1	11.1	22.2		22.2	33.3
1922	33.3	66.6		16.6	33.3		33.3	50
1923	28.4	42.8	14.2	14.2	56.8		14.2	100
1924	22.2	33.3	11.1	11.1	33.3			33.3
1925		50		12.5				62.5
1927	28.4	56.8			14.2			56.8

Year								
1928	28.4		56.8					56.8
1929	50	12.5	37.5		12.5			50.0
1932			75		50		25	75
1933	11.1	11.1	11.1		11.1			22.2
1934	20		20					30
1936	55.5	11.1	66.6			10		77.7
1937	20		70		10		10	70
1938	20		50	10	20			50
1939	50	16.6	66.6					66.6
1940	62.5		75	25				100
1947	25	8.3	58.3		25			58.3
1948	14.2	14.2	14.2					28.4
1949	36	9.0	54.5					63.6

* It was not possible to make these calculations for all years.

participated in interfraternity sports (though rarely with any great success), but I did not include this in the analysis. Instead, athletics is defined here the same way it would have been on campus—I included only sports played by teams representing the university. Zeta Psi believed it was important for college athletics to be represented in the house. The Zetes have a small but consistent group of brothers recognized as university athletes or connected to the athletic teams. Particularly notable Zete athletes included members of the rugby, football, swimming, track, crewing, and tennis teams.[30]

The generations of Witters who became fixtures of the second Zete chapter house were an athletic force of their own. John Witter ('24) brought glory to Zetes as a footballer. In 1922, the year of Cal's most celebrated season, it was noted that "Jack was shifted from fullback to tackle at the beginning of the season and played a strong game in the latter place despite his inexperience. He will probably be back at full for the 1923 season." At least nine other Witters played varsity sports from the 1920s to the 1950s.[31]

Students who could not play on teams could still earn honor as managers, including earning a coveted place in the Big C Society.[32] Zete brothers collected brass as members of honor societies, most typically from Skull and Keys, Golden Bear (senior honor society), Beta Beta (an honorary society), ONE (a sophomore honor society), and Winged Helmet (junior honor society), though some brothers branched out into other arenas, such as theater, engineering, and the military.[33]

Only a few brothers participated in activities like music, drama, or glee club. The student publications they were most likely to be involved with were *The Blue and Gold* and the *California Pictorial*. During the second house's occupation, only two brothers are known to have pursued military student groups beyond the mandatory participation in ROTC. Given the instability of global politics of the time, many would have the opportunity to serve the U.S. military in World War I, II, or the Korean conflict. There was no need to seek out additional military experience at the university.[34]

In activities related to school spirit, however, the Zetes were prolific. Yell leaders, alumni committees, rally planning, Senior Week or Junior Day committees, dance organizers: these were roles that the Zetes filled with great consistency. These positions demonstrated both the fraternity's connectedness and its commitment to university social life. The best of the Zetes, the "Big Men," were involved in athletics, honor societies, and spirit activities. These were the brothers who helped add to the chapter's fame and stature.

The new standards of evaluation by the campus community created some particular challenges for Zetes. As noted earlier, Zeta Psi, as a function of its long history on Cal's campus, came to be characterized by its large proportion of legacies among its membership. Its commitment to take legacies (and the necessity to do so, given its dependence on alumni support) had an effect on recruiting. The Zetes had few available spaces for fraternity newcomers. A review of student activities suggests that, in particular, Zeta Psi targeted and rushed promising athletes to bring notoriety to the fraternity. With the exception of the Witters, who followed as legacies of Dean Witter, almost none of the high-profile athletes were legacies.

ZETES AND COEDS

Debates over coeducation had not subsided in the first decade of the twentieth century; the establishment of women's suffrage led to lines drawn ever more emphatically than before. That large numbers of men had been taken from campus by the war convinced those men left behind that they needed to more rigorously protect men's dominance on campus. Separation of the sexes in student affairs was well established, and although President Wheeler retired from his position in 1919, in the creation of an underfunded and understaffed domestic science department he left a legacy of separate but unequal treatment for women students and faculty alike.[35] Similar treatment occurred at the *Daily Cal:* the women's editor put forward stories about meetings of suffrage events and summarized visiting lecturers who spoke about the equal intelligence and abilities of women, but the paper remained primarily a voice of the male students.[36]

A 1919 article from the *Daily Cal* captures the dismissive and mocking tone typical of articles related to gender relations on campus written by men. The story tells of an incident in a lecture where a female student complained about the lecturer's use of the term *ladies.* The news item appeared under the headline " 'Ladies an Obsolete Term' says Fair One."

> It happened in this way. F. E. Scotford gives a class in advertising. Last Monday he constructed on the blackboard of the lecture room a neat little advertisement designed to sell shoes—ladies' shoes. So the world "Ladies" was used frequently. Every one was satisfied, all but one. From the back of the room a voice was raised in protest. It was a voice silvery sweet in tone, but it had a ring of determination in it that caused the lecturer to pause abruptly, chalk in air.
>
> "I object to the use of 'ladies' in that advertisement. Since we are allowed to vote, we don't want to be called Ladies, we are 'women.' W-O-M-E-N."

Scotford, nonplussed for the moment, automatically erased the 'ladies' while he murmured, "How homelike this seems."[37]

While by in 1920s some students may have still jockeyed over the pros and cons of coeducation, most of them fully expected to be educated with members of the opposite sex. Student cultural life had shifted so profoundly that new dimensions entered into student relations—most significantly, attitudes and expectations about sexual relations underwent tremendous changes.

It would be naive to expect that students prior to the 1920s were not engaged in sexual activity with one another. As early as 1904, Wheeler made references to sexual behavior in his welcoming remarks to incoming freshmen. He advised students to "keep your mind clean. Unclean thoughts invariably taint the mind. Dwelling upon them rots it to putrefaction. One of the commonest causes of insanity is unclean thinking. Sexual uncleanness opens the surest way to bodily decay and moral death."[38] While Wheeler's "thou shalt not" comments reflect his Victorian upbringing, other members of the campus staff and faculty were dealing more realistically with changing norms. In the 1890s, the campus women's physician, Mary Ritter, hastily arranged marriages to cover overly amorous relations. The first dean of women students, Lucy Sprague, recalled that she had to give students lectures on venereal disease. What changed in the 1920s was that young people expected to experiment sexually, and taboos about sexual activity were greatly lessened within college peer groups. In her study of youth culture in the 1920s, Paula Fass suggests that changing attitudes about sex allowed young men and women more social freedom within their peer groups to experiment with "petting" as part of dating, which even extended to acceptance of premarital sex for couples who were engaged or otherwise seen as being in a committed relationship leading to marriage.[39]

Male attitudes about their female peers were also slowly changing. The image of the "pelican," the destined-to-be-spinster female student, was still a recognizable stereotype on campus, but bright, academic women, while still intimidating, were no longer regarded as untouchable. Horace Marden Albright, a Cal alumnus of the class of 1912, recalled meeting a pretty coed at a party.

> In my junior year, a girl invited me, along with two boys from my Club, to a
> dance at her home in Berkeley. I enjoyed the party very much, dancing twice
> with a classmate whom I thought was a lovely, charming girl, a vivacious
> brunette with big brown eyes. Over the weekend I dreamed of taking her to
> various college affairs if she would go with me! On Monday afternoon, walking

up the central path toward North Hall, she passed me with an armful of books and gave no sign of recognition. When I was working in the Recorder's Office, I peeked at her scholastic record. It was so much better than mine that I was further disheartened. I realized she was too pretty, too charming, too smart for me. Eventually, as graduate students, we became acquainted. In 1914, we became engaged.[40]

The memory is insightful as well as sweet. Female students had reached a new parity with men, inviting them to parties, dancing with them, and competing with them in scholastics. Notably, it did not occur to Mr. Albright to offer to carry the young woman's "armful of books" as she crossed the quad. This was no feeble coed who required a doting male presence! In fact, the qualities that intimidated the young Albright seem to have also continued to draw him to her, judging from the outcome. As time passed, female students appeared again on editorial boards with male students, were lauded in yearbooks for their school spirit and participation in activities, and were seen as partners in both sparring and love.

The 1928 *Blue and Gold* provides a clear illustration of how much the relationship between men and women students had changed since the days when coeds were seen as ensuring their own future status as spinsters. The editors of *The Blue and Gold* observed in 1928, "A junior's love is too serious to be just a big joke and too humorous to be really serious—but it all disappears like nothing at all when everyone has to wake up and study for finals in order to become a REAL senior. . . . It is the main object of one's senior year to fall in love seriously and more or less permanently. It has been maliciously said that girls come to college for husbands— we hope so!"[41]

While the available records do not allow me to calculate statistics about marriage patterns of the men of the second house, it is clear from interviews with alumni and alumni records that dating and even marrying coeds was a regular occurrence for the men of Zeta Psi during the first half of the twentieth century. While the early members of the Iota chapter had to be concerned about meeting appropriate women—and many of them dated the sisters of their fraternity brothers—the sorority system that existed during the occupation of the second house provided a pool of women who had undergone the social interrogation of their peers and been deemed suitable. [42]

This is not to say that the sexes were seen as equal—despite all appearances of separate but equal status, they were not. However, gender roles had settled enough that men could appreciate successful women as long as this success lay in the women's spheres of the university. The notion that men were men and women were women, and that there should be no ambiguity between the sexes, is most colorfully illustrated in a phenomenon that became prevalent on Cal's campus in the first half of the twentieth century, particularly among fraternity men—cross-dressing.

BOYS WILL BE BOYS; BOYS WILL BE GIRLS; AND SOMETIMES, GIRLS WILL BE BOYS

Having sat through nearly five acts of the play *Peter Pan* together, it is time that we look more closely at Peter. Of course we know that he is immortal, an impossible boy old enough to be Wendy's size but who inexplicably still has all his baby teeth. Had we sat in the play's first San Francisco audience in 1907, our programs would have told us that none other than the stunning Maude Adams was playing the lead role of Peter. Adams was a diminutive Scottish actress who had won acclaim for her leading role in James Barrie's play *The Minister's Daughter*. Before *Peter Pan*, this Barrie play had held attendance records at the Empire Theater in New York. Publicity photographs show Adams in that role with a mane of untamed hair and large, liquid eyes. The wild, loose hair would have been a shockingly seductive sight, and the photographs were widely reproduced in articles about the actress.[43]

Despite Adams's appeal as a female figure, she appeared in a number of roles that required her to portray male characters. Peter Pan is the most famous of these, and in another play she portrayed Napoleon's son, in full military regalia, and even portrayed a rooster in the play *Chanticleer*. The casting of a woman to play Peter had its precedent in Barrie's original London production, and to this day theater productions almost always cast a woman as Peter. But while it was common for male actors portray women in burlesque and other venues, women cross-dressing in the theater was seen as more transgressive. The everyday wearing of pants by women was still decades away. In New Orleans during Mardi Gras, women used carnival as an excuse to enter male domains like bars; some went as far as dressing as men and smoking cigars—but they did so at a risk, for newspapers were likely to label women who engaged in such activities as prostitutes.[44] This contradiction raises two interesting questions: why was it all right for Peter Pan to be played by a woman, and why was cross-dressing okay for men (including college men)?

Cross-dressing entertainers in the early twentieth century fell into two categories: those who were honestly performing "womanhood" or femininity, and those who satirized women as part of a burlesque. Cross-dressing was a popular entertainment the United States in the 1920s. Great female impersonators wowed audiences with their ability to embody, literally, all the mannerisms and physical endowments of perfect womanhood. A number of female impersonators were said to be better women than the most perfect of women. One of the most famous female impersonators of the twentieth century was Julian Eltinge. Scholars who have studied Eltinge and other female impersonators have suggested that they remained successful only as long as they simultaneously exhibited perfect manliness. Eltinge, for instance, was often featured in boxing demonstrations so that he could illustrate his masculinity.[45] Perhaps Maude Adams transcended the boundary between male and female because she had so clearly established herself as an object of male desire. Other scholars have suggested that women were acceptable in the role of Peter Pan because, like the boy who would never grow to be a man, neither could they.[46] Vaudeville burlesque, the other arena of entertainment where cross-dressing was popular, was a close relative of the English pantomime, from which Captain Hook's effeminate pirate no doubt derived. In this tradition, the intent was not emulation but satire.[47]

How does this relate to Cal? While I found no evidence of cross-dressing on campus during the nineteenth century, there is growing evidence of cross-dressing on campus in the twentieth century—including among the Zetes. While the popular impersonators may have demonstrated that a good man could be a better woman than a woman, this is clearly not the case in these examples. In 1900, Skull and Keys players introduced cross-dressing in one of their skits in a Shakespearian fashion—one of the characters disguised himself as his sister to confuse his aunt and uncle.[48]

Four years later, Skull and Keys expanded on this theme, as reported in a *Daily Cal* article, "College Actors Need No Aid from Actresses." The author writes, "Of the masqueraded actors, Carelton Curtis was the prettiest girl in the show. If all had come up to his aesthetic standard there would have been no need of a relief detachment from the Co-educational dramatic society. Oliver Orrick had the difficult part of a jealous wife, and carried it off with considerable force. Jack Geary impersonated a farcical music teacher to the appropriate amusement of the audience."[49]

In 1905, the main skit of the Running of the Skull and Keys included a melodrama, "A Fair Lily from Head's School."[50] Since the skit was performed by all men, it is assumed that the play featured men dressed as women. Zeta Psi's brothers consistently contributed members to Skull and Keys and, therefore, would have been involved in these antics. Photographs from the fraternity's archive show several brothers posing outside the Zeta Psi chapter house in flapper drag (figure 39). The same photo album, in which several pictures are dated 1923, includes pictures

FIGURE 39

Cross-dressing flappers outside the second Zeta Psi house. These
men were likely to have been part of the Running of Skull and
Keys. Photograph courtesy of the Zeta Psi Iota chapter archive.

of a monkey, who, according to a *Blue and Gold* album of 1924, was named "Stella"
and aided in the Running of the Skull and Keys. It is likely that these Zeta Psi brothers pictured as flappers were Skull and Keys initiates.

The men in the photograph seem as if they're trying not to look too much like
women. We see parody, not emulation. The choice of the flapper to parody may have
had a political edge. Flappers pushed the sexual boundaries of the twenties, chopping
their hair short, strapping their breasts flat, showing leg from the knee down, aggres-
sively drinking, engaging in premarital sex, and insisting on frolicking in mixed-sex
company. Flappers blurred the clear binary of male and female and, in doing so, may
have created tension in the fraternity men.

Skull and Keys was not the only context in which male cross-dressing took place.
In 1908, a *Daily Cal* headline announced: "Pseudo Co-eds to Play Gentlemanly
Game of Football." The article described an upcoming exhibition rugby game.

Clad in co-ed gym suits and sixteen-button long kid gloves, the manly youth of California will, after their arduous toil Saturday morning, give an exhibition of this refined game on California field Saturday afternoon. Prospective spectators are assured there will be no rowdyism or rough play indulged in. . . . Teams have not yet been selected, but it is probable that excellence in class work during the present term will be made the basis of selection. Sayre MacNeil will be the captain of the one team and S. J. Hume of the other. Capt. Hume has announced his intention of wearing a feather boa around his neck to protect his voice. All the players will wear long gloves to keep their hands clean. Cedric S. Cerf will referee the game but none of the other football men will take part as Saturday's contest is designed to bring out new talent.[51]

This is not the only instance in which cross-dressing occurred in the context of athletics. In fall 1907, in anticipation of an upcoming "football carnival," the *Daily Cal* announced that an election fund-raiser would be held to select the "Queen of Carnival." The carnival described seems to be an early version of the "Big C Sirkus," and it was organized and put on by the Big C Society beginning in 1904. The original carnival had been arranged as a fund-raiser to send the track team east to compete. The event, which featured a parade of costumed participants and skits and other performances, was originally held at California Field and then moved to Idora Park in Oakland in 1915. The Sirkus was celebrated as recently as 1936. Apparently the queen was a long-standing feature of the parade, but in 1907 the organizers decided to elect the next one. The 1907 *Daily Cal* reports,

No campaign which has been on the campus of late years nearly rivals the present contest for "Queen of the Football Carnival" which is at present convulsing the University. Never before have so many candidates been in the field for any college honors as are out for this coveted office. Men in all walks of college life are out, men prominent and notorious, popular and friendless, brilliant and stupefied; all are struggling for this prominent office. . . . Although only men are eligible, many petitions have been received from aspiring co-eds asking admittance to the contest. They base their claim to eligibility on the fact that the title "queen" bears with it a feminine significance. But this is an innovation and the significance of the title is not to be forgotten.[52]

In 1936, the queen of the Sirkus was female. I haven't been able to determine when the shift took place. Still, in 1922, cross-dressers could be found at football

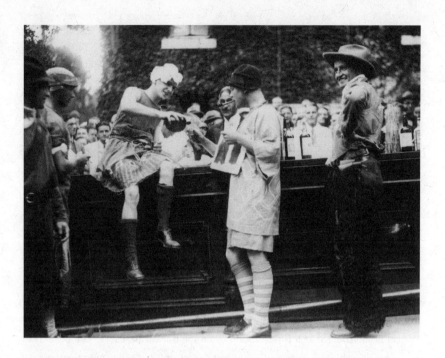

FIGURE 40

Cross-dressing men at the Channing Way Derby, 1930s.
Photograph courtesy of the Bancroft Library.

rallies. The Pajamarino Rally, which occurred before one football game, featured class stunts. According to *The Blue and Gold*, "The Freshman class stunt characterized the friendly rivalry existing between the two under classes, as it was a farcical representation of the Sophomore guarding the Big 'C.' The stunt depicted the 'C' being guarded by a number of 'queeners.' "[53] Whereas the nineteenth-century insult to a junior classman's masculinity was to remove his facial hair, for the early twentieth century man it was to be called a "woman" or "queen."[54] A review of photographs demonstrates that cross-dressing was most commonly photographed at a range of campus events during the 1920s and early 1930s. After that time, it became a less widespread phenomenon, but still one most closely associated with fraternity men. For instance, men dressed as women were commonly photographed at events like the Channing Way Derby, which took place annually until 1942 (figure 40).[55]

The university cross-dressing phenomenon appears to promote the same notion that allowed Eltinge to perform: that only a truly masculine man can be trusted to embody and represent womanhood. Cross-dressing parodies seem to have been common in the 1920s and onward in fraternity life, and seem to be one means that fraternity brothers used to draw an "us versus them" distinction between the sexes. The new masculinity was a heterosexual one, and cross-dressing underlined distinctions between fraternity brothers and any other embodied sexuality, whether that of women or gay men. Photographs from the University Archives demonstrate that men—particularly fraternity men—appearing in drag, was a photographed phenomenon up until the 1960s.[56] In contrast, I have not located any pictures of sorority women—or any women, for that matter—dressed as men. As *Peter Pan* has so clearly indicated, a woman might play a boy, but only as long as she promises to never grow up to be a man.

THE PIRATES ATTEMPT TO RECRUIT THE LOST BOYS

In early 1915, Representative Milton Schmitt of San Francisco introduced an act into the lower house of the California legislature that would ban fraternities. The proposed legislation would amend a 1909 law that had eliminated high school fraternities to include similar organizations in colleges and universities, educational institutions that were exempt from paying taxes. Other lawmakers predicted that the legislation would die over the recess, but promised to fight it if it somehow survived. While the legislation did indeed languish, it represents just one volley in what was the next attack by outsiders to dismantle the college fraternal system. The 1889 ban had been part of a more localized movement, but by the early twentieth century, administrators and educators across the country were debating the pros and cons of fraternal life.[57]

As fraternities became the center of college students' social lives, administrators turned a scientific eye toward them and asked what good and bad could come of the situation, publishing their findings in a range of national outlets. From our perspective, these articles not only shed life on fraternal life nationwide but also demonstrate that science had become the problem-solving discourse of masculine debate. Whereas earlier debates had been won or lost on the strength of arguments for or against fraternities, fraternities were now subjects of investigation. Some findings shaped administrative policies. The University of Illinois, where Thomas Clark was employed as the dean of men, was at the forefront of this scholarship.

In the journal *Science*, C. H. Forsyth raised the question of whether fraternity living encouraged extravagance among groups of young men. He conducted a comparison of total expenses of nearly three hundred fraternity men and an equal number of nonfraternity men at the University of Illinois. A member of each of the twenty-three fraternities at the university was asked to canvass his fraternity's members and to secure from each man a record of his expenditures over a nine-month period. Forsyth found that the average fraternity man spent about $180 more over that period than nonfraternity men.[58]

In 1914, an article by Arthur Warnock in *Science* tackled the question of how participation in fraternity life affected scholarship. For this study, records were kept on each of the fraternities, beginning in 1910. After Warnock began publishing the results semiannually, his reports on led on campus to an increase in grades that was attributed to the natural sense of competitiveness among the fraternities. Overall, Warnock found that "among fraternity men the desire for high grades usually gives way to a feeling of satisfaction with passing grades. Other rewards, not open to non-fraternity men, come to take the place of the delight in high grade work which very often is the most satisfying delight of the non-fraternity man's college life."[59] Warnock suggested that universities publish grades to create an incentive for excellence and require fraternities to delay initiation until men had finished eleven hours of coursework.

Not everyone agreed with Warnock's analysis. L. B. Walton, in a 1915 response in *Science*, blasted Warnock's analysis, pointing out that there must have been a downward trend in the nonfraternity population's scholarship, which could simply imply that bright students were moving into the fraternity pool rather than that the fraternities were spending more time studying.[60]

In 1915, C. H. Benjamin entered into the discourse, presenting a study of fraternity grades and social activities at Purdue University. His analysis was more along the lines of Warnock's. Benjamin argues that "observation of the grades of various individuals and classes has shown that carelessness in pledging is largely responsible for fluctuations in scholarship. A sudden drop in the standing of an organization is usually due to the entrance of an inferior group of freshmen. Sometimes this one class will handicap the whole organization." He continues, "The fraternity or social club suffers from certain tendencies which are more or less unavoidable in this kind of community life. First, there is a disposition to choose pledges hastily and from considerations apart from the real value of the man. On the score of relationship, of social standing or of athletic prowess, many candidates are chosen in haste and repented of at leisure. Second there is the tendency to relax the house rules and to permit more loafing, singing, smoking and card playing than is in the best interests of the organizations. . . . Third, there is the fact that fraternity men as a rule engage in student activities to a greater extent than non-fraternity men."[61]

Scientists were not the only ones considering the influence of fraternities on college campuses. Also writing in 1915 of his experiences at Amherst University, George Harris discussed the ethics of college students in the *Harvard Theological Review*. His take on college social life was considerably more supportive. "Drinking has been diminished in recent years. An intoxicated student is rarely seen. There are few men of dissipated habits. The Dean of Amherst College recently said: 'Some years ago drinking in the fraternity houses, which had not been tolerated by a number of our leading fraternities for years, was banished by all, and that by the action of the fraternities themselves.' He also declared that 'Hazing is no longer practiced in respectable colleges. Physical violence and personal indignities are brutalizing to those that inflict them. To be sure, even when inflicted, it was understood by both parties that insults and injuries are impersonal, that the student suffers and is made to appear ridiculous because he is a freshmen.' "[62]

The University of California was not isolated from these discourses, and it is clear that Berkeley administrators were aware of these debates. As early as 1915, the *Daily Cal* was providing updates on the progress of first-year students at the beginning of the spring semester. The editors reported that, of the 5,299 students who had registered in the fall, 165 of them had been disqualified (had flunked out). Of these, 45 were reported to have been from frats, 14 from house clubs and 120 unattached. Two weeks later, the editors announced that they would published the fraternity grades for 1914 and fall 1915. The grades were published five days later, but as a composite for the fraternities versus house clubs and unaffiliated men. The fraternity men were declared to have had consistently the highest grade-point averages in both semesters of the 1913–1914 school year and in the fall semester of 1914, with the house clubs following and unaffiliated men ranking lowest. Zeta Psi was not listed as one of the fraternities that had achieved one of the top three grade-point averages. Still, that the paper felt this information needed to be published suggests that the role of fraternities in student culture on Cal's campus had not gone unnoticed.[63]

The Cal administration also made it clear that it was aware of fraternity goings-on. In September of 1923, the dean of men announced that he had new expectations for the upcoming rushing season. "All organizations' initiations should be confined to premises, states Prof. J. H. Hildebrand, Dean of Men. Students who are sent forth during the late hours of the night run a considerable danger and they may be a source of alarm to the Citizens of Berkeley."[64]

Fraternities were not unaware of the scrutiny they were receiving. At both the national and the local levels, fraternities attempted to find ways to protect themselves.

Despite the history of competition between them, one way that fraternities attempted to protect themselves was to join in a larger organization. National organizations made several attempts, dating as early as the 1890s, to create an interfraternity organization. Early attempts were made in the 1880s and 1890s to create a larger fraternity-governing organization, but they failed until the creation of the Interfraternity Conference in 1909 in New York. They met annually. To belong to the conference, a fraternity had to be national, to have been established fifteen years, and to have at least ten chapters. The 1928 guide to the conference describes it as "an association of about 65 men's national college fraternities, which provides a forum for the discussion of fraternity problems, a reservoir of informed opinion concerning fraternity matters, a vehicle for joint action in protecting and promoting fraternity interests, and an instrument for developing cooperation among fraternities on the one hand, and, on the other, between fraternities of which they are apart." The conference provided representation for fraternities for negotiating with campus administrations and for discussing issues that affected fraternities at the national level, and it published materials in support of fraternal life as part of public education. It is not surprising that, at a time when collective bargaining and representation was gaining national attention, fraternal groups, which had weathered multiple waves of adverse public sentiment, would decide to organize.[65]

At Cal, attempts to organize the fraternities at the university level were in evidence as early as 1915, when the *Daily Cal* noted that the fraternities were going to meet to discuss creating a permanent interfraternity organization within the university; the meeting was, however, postponed. In 1923, the paper described a meeting of the Western Greek Letter Association, which had formed to bring closer cooperation among the chapters, faculty, and alumni. The association represented thirty different chapters but had no long-lasting future. An Interfraternity Council was finally founded in 1928 on the Cal campus. The formation of this student governance body was both a statement of autonomy and an accommodation. To agree to work as a collective, the Greek letter societies were accommodating the concerns of university administrators. In a very real way, they were joining the pirates they had taunted for so many years.[66]

To educate the public about fraternity governance, in 1928 the first fraternity manual for the University of California was published, by Robert Fouke. The manual was intended to be published semiannually, and was compiled "for the purpose of furnishing information regarding the personnel, location, and purposes of the many campus organizations to the University Public and People of Berkeley." At the time of publication, forty-eight organizations were listed as members of the

Interfraternity Council, and another fifteen were listed as "house clubs and frater-nities" that were not council members.[67]

The Interfraternity Council (IFC) had a president, vice president, and secretary-treasurer, and was scheduled to meet four times during the fall semester. Represen-tatives from each recognized fraternity sat on the council. To belong to the IFC, a fraternity had to have existed on campus a minimum of four years, and had to be approved by two-thirds of the standing members. Notably, Alpha Phi Alpha, his-torically a black Greek letter organization founded at Cal in 1921, had not been ac-cepted as a member of the IFC. Sororities had an equivalent governing body, the Panhellenic Association of the University of California.

The IFC set some guidelines for rushing and initiation. No pledge could be initi-ated until he had successfully completed one semester's work at Berkeley, Los An-geles, or Davis, and no student on academic probation could be admitted to a fra-ternity. It was also stipulated that no fraternity could entertain freshmen, either on its premises or at any other place, during the regularly scheduled meetings of the orientation period.[68]

The Panhellenic Association had many more regulations regarding rush and overall behavior of women, including curfews. The curfews were liberal, however, and demonstrate how much young people's social lives had changed. During the week, women had to be back from campus functions by 8:30 P.M. On weekends, women had to return from dates by 2 A.M. The night of the Big Game and assembly night were exceptions. These curfews were also instituted in all the female board-inghouses. No similar rules were imposed on college men, though anyone dating a university woman would find himself bound by the same curfew rules by default.[69]

A review of the Interfraternity Council's workings shows that every step the council made to improve fraternity life on campus required a concession to the ad-ministration. For instance, in April 5, 1928, the Interfraternity Council declared its autonomy from the student oversight committees of the Associated Students of the University of California. The Associated Students could not assert authority over social fraternities, because the latter were not using the campus for meetings or ac-tivities and maintained that the fraternities had never granted the Associated Stu-dents jurisdiction. Instead, the IFC would oversee disciplinary cases affecting fra-ternity members and fraternities. The organization's ability to negotiate this right was probably derived from an earlier campus concession.[70]

In one of its first acts, the Interfraternity Council negotiated with the dean of men a new way to calculate grade-point standings. The old system, the *Daily Cal* reported, "gave a false impression as to absolute standing. The new method will rate houses on the success or failure of their members to earn grade points. 'Improved standing,' Dean Hyde said, 'will be indicative of improved scholarship, whereas in the past improved standing may have been due to a drop in general averages.'" It seems that Dean Hyde was following the publications in *Science* regarding fraternity grading. The new system used a five-group system, with Group I consisting of those fraternities that had achieved A averages; Group II was composed of organizations maintaining high-B averages; Group III, mid-B averages; Group IV fraternities had mid-high-C averages; Group V was composed of those that had maintained a C average or below. Men had to maintain a C or above to be allowed to pledge. In 1927, Zeta Psi sat firmly within Group IV—able to initiate its pledges, but not particular impressive scholastically. In 1928, Zetes had increased their average enough to join Group III.[71] The competition between fraternities over grades invoked the ideals of the new masculinity: by comparing chapter grade-point averages, administrators were making academics a form of intellectual athletics.

At Zeta Psi, alumni remembered as early as the 1920s an increased concern with enforced study periods. The library of the second house was augmented with donations from alumni and was used for studying. The Bromo-Seltzer headache powders represented at the second house may have been used to treat headaches caused by the eyestrain of studying. Among the archaeological evidence recovered from the second house were artifacts associated, if not with studying, then at least with activities associated with students and schoolwork—writing paraphernalia. A minimum of fourteen glass ink bottles and one brass inkwell was recovered from the 1923 dump. Well-known brands like Higgins, Carter's, Sanford's, and Waterman's inks were represented among the bottles (figure 41). In addition, we recovered pencil stubs and erasers and parts of mechanical pencils from both the dump and the atrium deposits associated with the second house. There was no evidence of similar artifacts from the first house, but we can say that at least in the second house the men appeared to have been involved in their studies, perhaps supporting their 1948 claim that they were bringing up fraternity grade-point averages.

Despite attempts to improve their scholarship, the Zetes' traditions, rituals, and social lives ultimately earned them some unwelcome notoriety on campus. In January 1953, the *Daily Cal* reported that Zeta Psi's "treasure room of 'borrowed' loot" had been found. The incident began over the 1952–1953 winter break, when a Berkeley police officer noticed a broken window in the Zeta Psi house. The officer entered the house through an unlocked back door and found evidence of burglary, including four broken doors, one of them made of steel. Burglaries of fraternity houses were not

FIGURE 41
Examples of ink bottles and wells recovered from the second Zeta
Psi house.

uncommon. In 1947, the *Daily Cal* reported that a rash of burglaries had affected the campus fraternities. In one incident, a fifty-eight-year old woman with $1,250 on her person was found in one of the houses. She fled, was later apprehended and was released. So, it was not necessarily a malicious act for the officer to enter the house. It is at this point, however, that the story becomes interesting.

> In the chapter room, the location of which is kept secret from even the
> pledges, police found quite an array of plaques, trophies, mugs, victory skins,
> a letter to Benjamin Ide Wheeler from Theodore Roosevelt and seven original
> charters—none of which belonged to the Zetas. Also found in the room was a
> metal plaque identified by police as possibly belonging to the original senior
> bench. The inscription is from the class of 1921 to the varsity football team of
> 1920. The only thing missing from the room was the original charter of the
> local Delta Kappa Epsilon fraternity chapter, police said. The charter had
> been in the Zeta house since 1935. The articles, which had apparently been
> accumulating for a period of years, were turned over to Chaffee Hall, Dean of
> Men, for redistribution. Police, Hall and fraternity officials conferred and
> decided there will be no prosecution, it was reported.[72]

There is no word as to whether DEKEs were ever pursued in connection with the case or not, though they are likely suspects, since their charter was the only one missing. Thefts between fraternities was common. Two questions quickly arise from this article: why did the Zetes have these items, and why did they escape with such a light punishment?

To address the first question, the pinching of items from other fraternities was a tradition well-established early in their history and part of the rivalry between them. When the cornerstone of the second house was laid, the *Oakland Tribune* account reported that important fraternity papers were enclosed in the cornerstone, but assured readers that they were safe from those who might attempt to steal them. During the retrofit of the 2251 College Avenue building, I was hopeful that the cornerstone would be affected and need to be opened. No such luck, alas: the important papers of Zeta Psi of 1910—which probably included, if not the original charter, then at least a copy—remain entombed in the cornerstone of the house. It may be that the collection of campus trophies was part of the fraternity's initiation trials, or hell week. Accounts make it clear that nighttime escapades were part of hell week. Although the dean of men advised men not to take their initiation rights outside of the fraternity house, they clearly did. A 1947 letter to the *Daily Cal* complained of some of these escapades. The letter followed a series of epistles regarding a bunch of loud dogs that were disrupting lectures with their riotous barking.

TO THE EDITOR:

"Brothers:" yapping dogs are a trivial distraction compared to other noisy antics around the campus at night last week. There we were, two struggling freshmen beating our brains out for a chemistry exam Friday morning, while right outside under our window, a crowd of loving "brothers" were beating the hell out of their pledges. Their whooping and hollering drove us from the realm of concentration. We think the spirit and enthusiasm of the fraternity initiations and the election campaigns are fine, but "the b-b-boys" might at least have the consideration to carry on their boisterous activities in the Oakland Ball Park.[73]

It would not be unreasonable to assume that the trophies were gathered by young men attempting to prove their worthiness before initiation.[74]

The leniency shown the Zetes in this matter was probably the result of several factors. First, there is some question over the legality of the police officer's entry and search of the premises. There were enough lawyers among Zete alumni to ensure that they would have had access to legal advice. Second, the name Chaffee Hall suggests another extenuating circumstance. Chaffee Hall Sr., class of 1909, and dean of men, had a son, Chaffee Hall Jr., class of 1938, who had been a Zeta Psi brother. Once again, Zeta Psi's campus connections may have helped them. Such was not the case the following year, when they faced the judgment of the Committee on Student Conduct, chaired by Dean Irving Stone.

After Prohibition had ended, campus restrictions on alcoholic consumption had relaxed. Rules put in place in 1949 had banned all alcoholic beverages from the campus, and students were punished when caught illegally drinking. Sigma Chi's chapter at Stanford was seen as an example of administrators' intolerance for intemperance. The fraternity brought liquor to its Wild West party, resulting in a drunken brawl that led to a year's suspension for nine men. The national chapter of Sigma Chi upheld the decision and went a step further, canceling the chapter's charter. The incident was a sobering reminder for the Cal Greek community, who often partied with their brethren to the south.[75]

But there is no reason to suspect that drinking was not rampant on campus during the late 1940s and 1950s. So it came to be that, in November 1954, four fraternities were put on social probation for the remainder of the school year. Social probation prevented the chapter from having formals or other social gatherings. The action came at the hands of Dean Stone, who himself was not necessarily a foe of fraternities. He had once addressed the national Interfraternity Conference, and in that speech he indicated that he saw attempts to remove clauses in fraternity charters that protected their racial composition as evidence of communist interloping.[76] Stone was prone to seeing communists everywhere on campus, and it is somewhat amazing that he failed to see the socialist overtones of groups of men living as brothers. Still, Alpha Delta Phi, Delta Tau Delta, Phi Gamma Delta, and Zeta Psi were all affected by the social probation. Rumors circulated that the university had created a secret gestapo to conduct raids of fraternity houses.[77]

The associate dean of students, Katherine Towle, assured students that no such effort existed, and that the university had received several complaints from Berkeley townspeople, students' parents, and a fraternity alum about "questionable behavior" at some parties.[78] She noted that it would not be surprising if a concerted effort to monitor the fraternities was being made by the university. The following academic year, a new bargain was made between the IFC and the administration of Chancellor Clark Kerr. The original 1949 language that barred all "alcoholic beverages" would be changed: "alcoholic" would replaced with "intoxicating," allowing fraternities (but not living groups who occupied university-owned buildings) to serve beer in their homes. In exchange, a new governing body, the Fraternity Affairs Advisory Board, was created. The board would be made up of three students, three alumni, three faculty members, and William Shepherd, dean of students. The Interfraternity Council agreed, but this arrangement significantly limited its autonomy and power.[79]

The golden days of fraternity life on campus was fading. The GI bill had brought a new group of men to campus. A review of post–World War II yearbooks demonstrates that it was not unusual for men to have wives and children when they returned to, or began, their studies at Cal. Housing soldiers on their monthly allotment became a challenge, and the *Daily Cal*'s letters-to-the-editor columns demonstrate that there were tensions between GIs and other students. The post–World War II generation was less interested in the frivolities of campus life. To survive, fraternities had to demonstrate an increased attention to the serious side of college. Slowly but surely, they had become part of Hook's pirate crew.

The Zetes had been involved in many of the behaviors that resulted in punishment for other fraternities. While the Zetes may have gotten off fairly lightly compared to other fraternities on campus, alumni reported that there was a price to pay. The alumni association decided that the men of the fraternity had gotten out of hand. For a short period, the association imposed a "house mother" on the fraternity. The poor woman was to live in the house and, ironically enough, attempt to domesticate the Lost Boys. This woman was no Wendy; she quit in disgust after a year. Even fifty years later, alumni who remembered this period of history were somewhat ashamed at how the Zetes had harassed the house mother. In particular, one brother recalled that all the men would call her on returning home from a night of gallivanting—just to check in. Unfortunately for her, the brothers usually returned at 2 A.M.

Brushes with the police, their charter room violated by a rival fraternity, their social privileges suspended for most of an academic year, and the imposition of a house mother by their own alumni: by all appearances, it was a less than golden period in Zeta Psi's history. Perhaps it was time to do what Iota did when times were hard—build a new house.

THE ABANDONMENT OF THE SECOND CHAPTER HOUSE

The University of California continued to expand around the Zeta Psi chapter house. To make room for new university construction, bulldozers razed the houses that had once graced the frontage of Bancroft Avenue. The construction of Memorial Stadium necessitated moving several houses from the east side of Piedmont Avenue to the west side, where other residential structures were demolished to make room for them. May Cheney, Zeta Psi's long-term neighbor to the north, had sold her property to the university in 1939, only three years before she passed away. The university acquired the Cheney's two properties and used them as student housing. Further to the north, a health center had taken the place of residences (figure 42).

FIGURE 42
Campus map as of 1965. Stadtman, 1967.

Where Hearst Hall had once stood, the university planned to build Kroeber Hall to house the growing anthropology department and museum. The large community of Greeks had become concentrated in the neighborhood bounded by Warring, Bancroft (on the south side), Channing, and College Avenues.[80]

Zeta Psi may have been first to found a house at Cal, but the Zetes found themselves increasingly isolated from the rest of the Greek letter societies. This circumstance, combined with the increased surveillance that proximity to academic units surely must have brought, may have made the old College Avenue site less appealing to the Zete brothers as the century progressed. The master plan of the university clearly delineated the university's plans to close College Avenue and acquire the properties in that area. While the records are not complete, it appears that, by 1953, the University of California President's Records demonstrate that Zeta Psi was negotiating a land deal with the university.

Eugene Hilgard had willed his home at 2728 Bancroft Avenue to the University of California, though the conditions of the gift required that his spinster daughters be allowed to live there until their deaths. On Miss Hilgard's death in 1952, the Bancroft house and the property on which it sat became the university's land. A March 17, 1952, letter from James Corley, the university's vice president of business affairs, to President Robert Sproul suggests that the university consider using the Zeta Psi house as a dormitory for law students. This is the earliest mention of Zeta Psi's building having been vacated by the fraternity, and even in this letter the Bancroft property and the Zeta Psi structure are seen as linked. A January 5, 1953, letter suggests that Zeta Psi had approached the university about trading their College Avenue property for the Hilgard property, which would have allowed them to build a new chapter house. Records following this demonstrate that the university then undertook negotiations with the fraternity.[81]

Ultimately, the regents approved the transfer of the Hilgard property to Zeta Psi, as well as a ten-thousand-dollar payment. The Zetes were allowed to occupy their old house until their new house was ready, which was expected to be during the winter recess of 1956. The university documents state that the university expected to take possession on January 1, 1957. An entry in the 1957–1958 *Blue and Gold* shows that the Zetes were at their new address when the yearbook was assembled.[82]

For the university community, the Zeta Psi house was a desirable property. An early letter suggests that the university considered knocking down the building.[83] Writing in 1954, James Corley told President Sproul that he had heard there were plans to demolish the house. He reiterated his hope that the building would become a dorm and advised Sproul that "I do not believe it is wise for us to destroy a building of this type. I am sure it would bring considerable criticism not only from our own Regents, but from the public at large."[84]

Letters in the Chancellor Records for 1956 demonstrate that a number of different groups jockeyed to gain the space. H. J. Dauphinee, president of the Theta Chi fraternity, contacted Chancellor Clark Kerr to request that Theta Chi be allowed to rent the old Zeta Psi house during the remodeling of their chapter. The Committee on Campus Planning had other ideas, and assigned the house tentatively to the

Institute of Child Welfare at the request of Howard E. Jones, who wanted to subdivide the dining room into offices. The law school continued to hope that the property might become a dorm, until a March 23, 1956, report noted that, while the law school hoped for a dorm that could house fifty-two to fifty-six persons, the Zeta Psi house could not house more than twenty-four students comfortably.

In a July 27, 1956, letter, the university temporarily assigned the Zeta Psi house to the Department of Psychology to house the department's animal colony and animal research facilities while the ventilation system in their building was fixed. For the first time in its history, the Zeta Psi fraternity house was truly an "animal house."[85]

Some brothers recall that the fraternity had expected the university to move the house, not acquire it. Many feel the new house is not as fine as the second house. Whatever bad feelings the move engendered among Zeta Psi brothers, the fraternity did well to negotiate the exchange when they did. They were able to acquire a property that placed them within the boundaries of the Greek community, and they gained funds from the university to help build a new chapter house. Others who were relocated later seem to have had worse negotiations with the university. Letters between administrators and Clark Kerr in 1959 demonstrate that a ruling by the attorney general of California prohibiting universities from supporting groups that restricted membership on the basis of race, color, religion, or national origin was seen as a way to avoid paying damages to fraternities forced from their homes by the university's master plan. By volunteering to relocate earlier, Zeta Psi had ensured itself a prime campus property.

It is worth considering, then, how the Zetes came to negotiate this transfer. A clue comes from the regent's meeting in which the land transfer was approved. The notes for the August 19, 1954, meeting indicate that "Regent Hagan asks that he be recorded as not voting as his son is a member of Zeta Psi fraternity."[86] While Hagan did not vote, it is unlikely that he abstained from the discussion. Further, one wonders whether having a regent close to hand gave the Zetes' access to information about plans for campus expansion. Once again, apparently, the Zetes had used their connections in high places to ensure the security of their community. If the Zetes had learned anything over the years, it was that it is always good to have a couple of sympathetic pirates in high places. On a final note, before we leave the men of Zeta Psi to build and occupy their third house (without our oversight), I must point out the irony that the neighbors who annoyed Hilgard with their leaking water pipes should now live on the site of his former home.

BACK AT THE NURSERY

Only for Peter Pan, that eternal spirit of youth, does the Never Land of college life endure endlessly. All grow up—as graduates or drop-outs—all eventually move onwards. The Wendys marry and raise families; the Tiger Lily 's fight battles on other war grounds; the Tinkerbells fade into forgetful memory; and the Lost Boys, well, the Lost Boys go out into the world and seek the adventure of secure employment. The student publications of their times record the triumphs and tragedies that seemed so important to the campus community. Perhaps, we could choose to leave our understandings of the Zeta Psi men at that, permanently frozen in youth, forever frolicking with their brothers, challenging pirates and generally raising hell. If we are to understand their experiences more broadly, however, and assess strengths and weaknesses of their journey as fraternity brothers, then we must, leave Never Land ourselves and follow them back into the Nursery.

WENDY.   When you come for me next year,
Peter—you will come, won't you?
PETER.   Yes. (*Gloating*) To hear stories about
me!
WENDY.   It is so queer that the stories you like
best should be the ones about yourself.

Peter Pan

Alas, it is time to leave Never Land, but at least Peter will play his pipes for us as we prepare to go. We have nearly run the course of our play; only a few matters remain to be considered: How did their experiences in the house under the ground shape the Lost Boys of Zeta Psi as they embarked on lives in the adult world? And how do the experiences of the generations of Zeta Psi men speak to us of fraternal organizations in general; and specifically, what do they say about the abuses commonly found in some fraternities today? Finally, has this exercise provided us with insights into why these groups have historically been so popular with college men?

There are two ways to approach the first question. We can consider what the men of Zeta Psi did after graduation, and we can also look at what they had to say about their college experiences after leaving school. It is possible to make broad generalizations about what the Zetes did after graduation based on alumni records published by the University of California and by the Zeta Psi national alumni publications.[1]

The careers that drew most of the Zetes who occupied the first house were law, engineering, mining, and business, and a goodly number of the men ultimately served in education. The importance of law is not surprising—many of the Zeta Psi brothers seem to have had political ambitions. The law was, as now, seen as an appropriate route to politics. A number of the early Zetes went into politics. Everett Benedict Pomeroy ('71) was a U.S. district attorney for the state of Arizona. James Budd ('73), who on more than one occasion cut classes at Cal, became the governor of California. Elliot McAllister ('84) was a California state senator.[2]

No small number of Zetes were political appointees: John Budd ('74) was a UC regent, as was George Ainsworth ('73); John Randolph Farrell ('74) was the chief engineer on the staff of the governor of Arizona, served as a regent to the University of Arizona, and served as an elector for the state of Nevada in the electoral college. Vincent Hook ('76) was a member of the central committee of the Republican party. William Hall Phelps was a supervisor of the Fifth Ward of the city of San Francisco.[3]

Others continued to serve the university. Joseph Cummings Rowell ('74) was head librarian for many years, and was credited with building the university library to a world-class level. John Maxson Stillman ('74) was a chemistry instructor at Cal before becoming a traitor to his alma mater by moving to Stanford for a professorship. He eventually became the vice president of that trade school. Joseph Nisbet Le Conte ('91) became a professor of mechanical engineering at Cal.[4]

Still others served their communities in other ways. William Evelyn Hopkins ('79) was the chief eye surgeon for the Children's and County hospitals in San Francisco. Joseph Mailliard ('79) pursued his passion for ornithology after college and built one of the largest comparative specimen collections on the West Coast. After the California Academy of Sciences lost its collections in the San Francisco earthquake, Mailliard donated his vast collection to the academy. Frank Adams ('81) too was a surgeon, and was a member of Oakland's Board of Health.[5]

Residents of the second house followed many of the same employment trends, with men continuing in high-profile professions. Engineering, mining (with an emphasis now on oil extraction), and the law were still common occupations among Zetes. Banking and finance became of greater importance, and this can be attributed to Dean Witter and the rest of the Witter clan. Dean Witter founded Blythe, Witter and Company in 1914 with Charles Blythe, then later founded Dean Witter and Company in 1924. The latter company was founded with fellow Zete brothers and relatives, Guy, Jean, and Edwin Witter. These two companies also hired other Zetes. The Witters served in high-profile service positions, too, chairing the Red Cross War Fund, becoming regents of the University of California, and serving as presidents of the Alumni Association.[6]

From 1901 to 1910, more alumni reported working in the field of engineering than in any other field. Other well-represented occupations were those of merchant, banker, and farmer. From 1911 to 1920, reported occupations included attorney, banker, and "oil." From 1921 to 1930, the majority of the men reported being in banking, followed by farming, management, and the law.[7]

One striking difference between the first and second houses is the lack of second-house alumni working at the university. This reflects a change in the culture of academia more than anything else—the days of hiring one's undergraduates had largely ended. This is not to say that the Zete alumni of the second house were less committed to the university. Among the Zetes there were still men who served on campus committees, particularly the alumni organizations and university foundations, who gave money to the university, or who served in appointed positions, like that of regent.

Did the ideologies of the new masculinity exhibit themselves in the Zetes' postgraduate lives? To answer this question, let us explore the lives of several alumni more closely.

John Nesbit LeConte grew up on the University of California campus, in a little cottage on the location now occupied by the faculty club. His father, Joseph LeConte ("Professor Joe"), was a beloved geology professor on campus. His uncle John LeConte was also a university professor, whose family home fronted on Bancroft Avenue and whose backyard was kitty-corner to Zeta Psi's chapter house. John enrolled as an undergraduate with the class of 1891. Accompanying his father on geological trips inspired a lifelong love of the outdoors in John, but he went on to become a mechanical engineer of great repute. Following graduation in 1891, he traveled to Cornell, one of the nation's few universities to offer graduate training in engineering. Having earned his master's of science degree, he returned to Berkeley as an assistant professor in mechanical engineering in 1892.[8]

LeConte introduced his new colleague Clarence Cory, an electrical engineer, to hiking and mountain climbing. Together in 1895 they surveyed the watershed of the Kings River in search of suitable sites for hydroelectric dams. LeConte, using a cathode ray tube brought from Germany by his uncle, also developed the first radiograph photograph on the West Coast, perhaps the first in the country, after another professor's three-year-old boy was accidentally shot in the arm. LeConte photographed the injury to aid surgery. Among his other achievements was his design of a harmonic analyzer, which contributed to the development of electrical power transmission line expansions.[9]

LeConte's love of the outdoors never faded, and he remained an avid mountain climber until illness required the amputation of his leg late in life. An article celebrating LeConte's forty-fifth birthday illustrates that his passion for climbing mountains was well known on campus. " 'Give the mind an occasional change and it will think better,' says the Roman fabulist. That's the way Professor Joseph Nisbet LeConte looks at it. So when his university duties begin to pall he takes a jaunt up some unexplored mountain side for diversion's sake. . . . In fact, California is indebted to him for much of the present extant knowledge of the high Sierras," according to the *Daily Cal.*[10]

LeConte's obituary refers to the importance of his early-twentieth-century maps of the Sierras. LeConte and his father were among the Sierra Club's charter members in 1892. The younger LeConte served as president, secretary, treasurer, and director, and was appointed as honorary president from 1931 until his death in 1950. It is worth quoting from a letter cited in his university obituary.

> When I look back over the years of my life, what a wonderful life it has been.
> I had wonderful parents, a most happy boyhood, and a perfect married life. On
> my graduation from college, I got an ideal job, one that I held for my whole life.
> There are not many people who hold down just one job for a lifetime, and
> particularly a job to his liking. All through my career at the University, no one
> ever told me what to do. I built up my own courses, loved the subject I taught,
> and loved my students. Then I always had the three months in summer which
> allowed me to pack through the High Sierra. Oh! the glory of it all. And for
> forty-five summers I camped in the mountains. What more could a man
> want?"[11]

Renowned scientist and accomplished outdoorsman, Le Conte was an early embodiment of the new masculinity.

Many of the Witters too are excellent examples of the new masculinity. While at Cal, a number of them were successful athletes, and the family continued to support Cal athletics after graduation. The rugby-loving Witters built a rugby field for the university and sponsored a crewing trophy. The Dean Witter Foundation supports graduate education in business and conservation in California.[12]

The new masculinity equated a strong male body with success in other realms of society. Perhaps Dean Witter, with his love of big game hunting and safari adventures, is seen as best mimicking the lifestyle advocated by Teddy Roosevelt, one of the Zetes' masculine role models. Witter wrote books about his safari experiences, as well as his less glamorous, but no less masculine, fly-fishing outings.[13]

DEFENDING THE MEMORY OF ZETA PSI

Given that the new masculinity became an entrenched way of being for the men of the second house, how did alumni make their experiences relevant to the younger generations of Zeta Psi brothers? The men of the first house were not raised in the same ideologies of masculinity as their brotherly descendants. For them, savagery was to be conquered not exalted. Yet these men of the first house also recognized that expectations about what it was to be a man had undergone profound shifts, and in the stories they told tell about themselves and their brothers they spun their tales in ways that ensured they would all measure up to modern standards of masculinity.

George Edwards, writing in 1911, shared a story about the journey of his Zete brother L. L. Hawkins from the Sacramento Valley to registration at Cal. He had worked as a cowboy in the mountains and was paid for his labors, in part, with a horse of his choosing:

Hawkins went out among the horses, selected a perfectly built roan four year old that had never had a rope on him except when, as a colt, he had been thrown and branded. In speed he was the leader of the band. After some little racing over the hills he was gotten into the corral, lassoed, worked up to the snubbing post, blind-folded, his ears tied down, and the hackamore and saddle put on in proper style. The reata was released, coiled and tied to the saddle. Hawkins mounted, released the ears, raised the blind, and found that he was stride of the hardest bucking horse that he had ever ridden. The horse was so strong, however, that he kept his feet. After a few minutes of hard bucking around the corral, he shot out through the opening and the ride to Oakland and the University was begun. The ride lasted four days, the first day only a few miles were made, but by night, both man and horse were pretty well done up. The fourth day Hawkins rode from Stockton to Oakland, a distance of 80 miles. The next morning he commenced his entrance exams. What became of the horse, did you say? He had developed a good case of spring halt, but was used by his master for a year or more, on a newspaper route, for it was as a news carrier that Hawkins met his expenses during the early part of his college course.[14]

The story demonstrates to multiple generations of listeners Hawkins's masculine achievements. Edwards's peers would recognize the power of the civilizing force of man's will over the wild horse, while the younger generation would appreciate the romanticized version of the cowboy riding as one with a wild steed over untamed land. To a young generation that was seeing automobiles rendering the horse and carriage obsolete, the story would have additional impact.

An unusual account of a Zete's life appears in the obituary of Joseph Rowell, class of 1874, who served as the university's librarian from 1874 until his death in 1938. The essay is a remarkable piece. It appears in *In Memoriam*, a volume published annually by the University of California and containing obituaries for university faculty who died in the preceding year. Generally, these are short, no more than a page or two. In the case of Rowell, however, the essay goes on for sixty pages and was published as a separate booklet. The piece begins with an extended consideration of Rowell's father, a minister who brought his family from Panama to San Francisco during the gold rush. Clearly, the essayist, who is unnamed, felt it necessary to situate the aged librarian in the appropriate masculinist discourse. At a time when Frank Capra was denigrating librarians as mousy spinsters in *It's a Wonderful Life*, perhaps the defense was seen as necessary. As a child, Rowell, accompanied by a pet monkey, would climb on abandoned wharfs to watch sharks "with their menacing green eyes." In college,

> he was by no means bookish. His tough body, his masculine and even pugnacious mind, his love of social intercourse, and his abounding humor stirred him always to crave the company of manly men. He was now a star on the college baseball team, with which he went to Oakland to defeat the Wideawakes and other local teams. Early in his career he became a member of the Zeta Psi fraternity, winning the confidence and affection of its brothers and, as one of its most prominent members, the respect of the members of the faculty from the President down. . . . He passionately enjoyed outdoor life, including the physical punishment incidental to roughing it. He was an ardent and extraordinarily successful hunter and fisherman, particularly the latter.[15]

Joseph Mailliard ('79) became a noted ornithologist after graduation, and published numerous articles in the *Condor*, an outlet of the Cooper Ornithological Society. In 1924 Mailliard was asked to write an autobiographical essay for the journal. A relatively low-profile Zete on campus, he had played football while at Cal, and his major disciplinary problem had been dropping French without permission.

> In those old Berkeley days things were very different from what they are now, and we often had some rather lively times. But let it suffice to say that my slate was clean for the final examinations of the senior year, when, a few weeks before the date set for them, a second attack of pneumonia gripped me by the heels, as it were, and at graduating time, my earthly career was fast being brought to a close. Tender care from my family and a devoted physician, most unselfishly assisted by my associates of the Zeta Psi Fraternity, to whom I owe a deep debt of gratitude, staved off the evil day. A year of convalescence ensued—nearer two years in fact—during which time I was under strict orders to lead an outdoor life.[16]

A photograph accompanying the article shows Mailliard in his junior year, his Zeta Psi pledge pin visible on his tie. There are several interesting points to this narrative. First, Mailliard mentions his Zeta Psi brothers along with his family and physician. Recall that some of the men who lived with Mailliard were Philip Bowles, Jim McGillivray, Howard Stillman, and Frank Solinsky, men well-known to the academic senate for their absences and, in some cases, repeated demotions. Mailliard's account provides a different insight into these men—as a caring extended family. Also interesting is Mailliard's description of his college career as "lively times." While he doesn't elaborate, he clearly knows that the popular perception of college at the time emphasized the social. He is careful to note that he was social, but also that he had completed the requirements necessary for graduation.

Mailliard's illness prevented him from graduating with his peers; instead, he applied for and received a certificate of proficiency from the Academic Senate in 1880.[17] In noting that the treatment for his illness was his strict orders to lead an outdoor life, not only was Mailliard repeating a common medical prescription of the time, but he was also clearly aligning himself with the modern masculinity. Teddy Roosevelt often touted his commitment to an outdoor life as the cure for the weak constitution of his youth.[18]

For Zetes, the new masculinity was also synonymous with a strong regional identity, that of the Californian. In a state that prided itself on the adventuresome spirit of its pioneers, the new masculinity provided a recognizable structure on which to construct biographies of the elite founding families.

In oral histories gathered from brothers, there is further evidence of the desire to present their experiences in modern terms. In a television interview about the archaeological excavations in 1995, John Beales, class of '29, was comfortable talking about the brothers' visits to speakeasies in Emeryville during Prohibition. Despite photographic evidence to the contrary, however, he could not stomach the suggestion that any of the brothers had ever cross-dressed. "These men were World War I veterans." he growled. "They weren't into any of that business." It did not matter that the men in the photographs were part of Skull and Keys, or that such "queening" was common at the time. Beales, a lifelong resident of the Bay Area, was probably concerned that the burlesque of his fraternity brothers' youth would be judged according to the modern sexual politics of cross-dressing.[19]

When undergraduate Lorinda Miller interviewed a number of Zete brothers for a class paper in 1996, she found that the brothers would call one another, consult, and call back to alter their stories, presenting a united history that presented the brothers in the strongest light. While such active constructions of the past are common in oral history research, they also demonstrate the close-knit nature of the brothers' community, even decades after their school years.[20]

This short look at the postgraduate life of a few Zetes reveals that the connections made during college continued to be utilized across fraternal generations during men's lifetimes. One small example may be the fact that the California Academy of Sciences, rather than the Bancroft Library, has archived materials related to Dean Witter's and John Nesbitt Le Conte's adventures. The Witters had many connections to the University of California, making the Bancroft an appropriate repository for their personal papers. I wondered if these materials came to be curated at that facility because of Joseph Mailliard's long-term association with the museum. There is no doubt that some system of social, economic, and political relations allowed Zetes to maintain representation on the board of regents and other university committees over the years. This aspect of fraternal life deserves book-length attention of its own.

LEAVING THE STAGE: IMPLICATIONS AND CONCLUSIONS

Fraternities have provoked suspicion and distaste in society for nearly two centuries. The reasons for this have changed over time, however. In the past, fraternities were accused of fostering aristocracy within a democratic society. Within universities, fraternities were seen as using their connections to rig elections and control student activities, thereby excluding others. The history of Zeta Psi shows that some of these accusations were true. The brothers moved like a swarm from college activity to activity and, by their sheer numbers, would have dominated them. But there seems to have been no maliciousness in their actions, at least not among members of the first house. Patterns are more difficult to discern for the second house. And there is no evidence that Zeta Psi sought to dominate any particular activity.

This is not to say that Zetes did not use their numbers to their advantage. When chapter houses had robust populations, they also had a large number of supporters, and this facilitated the election of brothers to student government positions. Despite rumors to the contrary, the rivalries between fraternities prevented them from colluding too much. Recall that it took nearly a hundred years for Cal fraternities to join together in an Interfraternity Council. Their lives after the fraternity house indicate that the men of Zeta Psi learned to use social connections and constituencies to their advantage. Connections with alumni saved fraternities from being dismantled on campus. And connections with other alumni led to Zete alumni consistently having seats on the University of California Board of Regents. But in aiding their brothers, what exactly were these alumni protecting?

The men of Zeta Psi's first house were not without their flaws. As women joined the university in increasing numbers, they threatened the Zetes' sense of civilized manhood and blurred the divisions between the domestic and public spheres. After some initial indulgence and support of coeds, the men of Zeta Psi almost uniformly dismissed them, mentally assigning them the status of untouchable spinsters. The fraternity men were not unique in this position. Their fears and concerns about changes in the social order were shared by middle-class and elite men throughout the country. Just as these men were troubled by the threat to whiteness represented by the strong bodies of the ethnic minorities who labored in physically demanding blue-collar jobs, the strengthening voices of women sounded like disorder.

The new masculinity, with its emphasis on strength, rigor, and brutality, was adopted by white men of the managerial classes. The brothers of Zeta Psi sprang from these elite social classes—as did many of the nonfraternity men on Cal's campus. The fraternity house provided an environment in which the brothers could develop and experiment with this new masculinity, but it was not the only such environment where it flourished. The saloon, the barbershop, the gym, the boardinghouse, these were all places where men taught one another how to perform this new incarnation of maleness.

In the first house, this masculinity was still new, still evolving. To create a household of men, the brothers turned to the materiality of their mothers. Plain white ceramics that communicated the sanctity of home life graced their tables. Over time the men learned to differentiate their house from those of their families—by manipulating architecture to create fraternity-specific spaces, and by marking their spaces and things with their crest. Whereas the men of the first generations of Zeta Psi marked their bodies (with pledge pins and perhaps more permanently by branding), the men who lived in the second house marked their mugs, their ceramics, their walls, and their mantles—as well as their bodies—with representations of their crest. They embedded their symbols in the very fabric of the house, in its concrete and bricks, and even within the cornerstone.

Beer, a beverage originally shared by families at the supper table, became a liquid bond between brothers, a fluid that almost came to symbolize the blood of fraternal brotherhood. During Prohibition, the brothers, and not just those of Zeta Psi, smuggled beer into their homes, risking punishment. The archaeological materials demonstrate the importance of beer consumption as both a casual and a ritual activity. Glass steins and pilsner glasses speak to drinking and conversing over a meal, a time when the sense of fraternal family was nurtured and developed. The toasting tankards speak of a more ritualized shared time, when orderly rounds of toasting, songs, and joke telling provided brothers with the opportunity to formally stand and reassert their bonds to one another. While young people flirted with the sophisticated cocktail during the Roaring Twenties, it was beer that spoke to fraternity men. So strong were the connections between beer, family, and brotherhood that, even when the only available beer was near beer, the brothers still convened over their mugs, though perhaps not as merrily.

Zeta Psi shifted with the times. When students embraced the notion of the "big man on campus," Zeta Psi recruited and participated accordingly. Athletes and spirit leaders, as well as legacies, filled the chapter house. Zetes participated in the quest for "brass" along with the other campus communities. And while some brothers may have been recruited because of their ability to draw attention to the house, rather than because of other qualifications, there is no evidence that they were treated as lesser brothers. In fact, many Zete men who seem to have been recruited for their athletic abilities had other members of their family join the fraternity as legacies later on. It is also possible to see that, over time, the men of Iota took the increased emphasis on scholarship seriously enforcing study hours and showing some evidence of improved grades and even archaeological evidence of schoolwork.

Still, while the organization may have fit itself to its time, Zeta Psi was not completely fluid. Old ideals and values remained entrenched. Foremost, it remained an institution dedicated to the value of fraternity as constructed in the mid-nineteenth century. Fraternity was a value independent from and distinct from sorority, not a complement to it. But Zetes were not women haters, as they were accused of being, so much as disinterested in women in relation to their brotherhood. They did not define themselves through relationships with female organizations, but through their relationships to one another—as a chapter house and as a complex genealogy of families who had come together as part of Zeta Psi over a period of eighty years.

Maintaining a sense of shared identity among so many men over such an expanse of time was not an easy feat; it had to be worked at. The architect who designed Iota's second chapter house was aware of the alienating potential of a new house. Sutton intentionally alluded to the first house in his design, encircling the grave of its foundations with the new house's open courtyard, centering the doorways on one another. In many ways this design is a fitting tribute to the lessons of fraternal initiation—the pledge may die, but he is born again as a stronger, truer man, one who is welcomed into the world of true brotherhood. The transfer of furniture and even architectural features from one house to the next further materially reinforced the connections that endured.

What is less clear is how much continuity linked the old houses and the most recent Iota chapter house. University records indicate the Lost Boys of the third house chose to replace all their furniture; we also know they stopped using the formal china of their ancestral Zetes, and left behind the pledge panels with the names of their forebears. In making a fresh start in the new house, they may have wiped the slate too clean. When I first started working on the archaeology of Zeta Psi in the mid-1990s, alumni and representatives of the national organization fretted that Iota had lost its way from the path of brotherhood. Several alumni from the second house expressed a sense of isolation from the new one. If nothing more, this anecdote suggests that fraternal relationships require constant nurturing.

As I mentioned in the prologue to this work, the Zetes were not always a likeable bunch. Some of their attitudes toward coeds and women's rights annoyed this feminist. The more law-abiding reader might be disgusted by pranks in which students disfigured or "borrowed" university property. Those who frown on drinking might be alarmed by the Zetes' blatant refusal to respect university, town, state, and federal laws regarding the consumption of intoxicating beverages. Earlier Zetes' attitudes concerning African Americans and Chinese Americans were appalling—and completely typical of their time and social class. While the Iota scrapbook contained a couple of Sambo-type representations of African Americans, and some of the attitudes about the Asian men who worked in the house were unsettling,[21] I found no evidence that the men of Zeta Psi were any more racist than their university peers. A review of any college publications of the same periods show that these racist stereotypes were prevalent in the student population. I do not apologize for their behavior. Instead, I prefer to keep in mind Dean Thomas Clark's admonition that, just as a few rotten apples can ruin a whole barrel, a few disorderly men can make their entire organization look foolish.[22]

This is not to say that I am unaware of the role of fraternal life in reifying white male power. Through the institutionalized exclusion of certain men from fraternal life—an exclusion made clear in the charters of many fraternities—fraternities created safe spaces for privileged white masculinity. Those of different colors or races who actually made it through the process were branded (literally as well as figuratively) to demonstrate that they had achieved whiteness. This is a consistent and nefarious undertone of Greek letter societies. As a 1956 editorial in the *Daily Cal* notes, despite the fact that only a few fraternities on campus had charters that explicitly dictated segregation by color and class, "fraternities at the University have succeeded in remaining almost completely segregated throughout their entire history here." Women responded to the sex segregation of fraternities by creating female fraternities, and people of color created their own organizations.[23]

Still, perhaps I am guilty of reinforcing the stereotypical attitude that "boys will be boys" and of allowing the men of Iota chapter a pass for bad behavior. I must admit that, if my intention was to escape the romantic trope of historical archaeological writing, I failed miserably. Despite my greatest efforts to remain distant from, and perhaps outraged by, the Zetes, I found them to be likeable, though flawed, human beings. I have sniggered at their outrageous cockiness, rolled my eyes at their bad jokes, and shaken my head at their crazier antics. Yes, despite myself, a self-avowed feminist (which is not synonymous with *man hater*, as often misrepresented), I am fond of the men of Zeta Psi in all their dimensions. Perhaps it is not possible to dig through people's trash without recognizing their shared humanity; just possibly, there lies the strength of historical archaeological approaches to the past. Perhaps I am such a romantic that I still believe in fairies and still recognize the brighter side of humanity while appraising individual shortcomings.

Yet, we cannot ignore certain questions about fraternities raised by modern scholarship. Does a historical perspective suggest that, ultimately, fraternities like Zeta Psi are destined to become places where the kinds of sexual abuse and violence explored by Peggy Sanday and others take place? While Sanday took certain acts of extreme violence and extrapolated them to the entire fraternity system, justifying its abolition,[24] I cannot come to the same conclusion. Yes, times have changed, and rape is discussed more openly than in the past; but apart from a single racy picture in a man's bedroom and cartoons suggesting that Zetes may have visited an African American brothel or gin joint in Emeryville, there is nothing to suggest that Zeta Psi, or any of the other fraternities up to the 1950s were engaged in systematic violence against women, as modern fraternities have been accused of doing. If anything, my work suggests that fraternities are microcosms of the societies in which they live, and if we are to deal with sexual violence and abuses found within Greek letter societies, then we must deal with these in our society, not only in the fraternity house.

As I conducted this research, I was troubled by the apparent disconnect between my research and the scholarship focused on contemporary fraternities. In the 1980s, the public's rape awareness grew and became a focus of research inquiry among scholars. Notable cases like those studied by Sanday brought attention to date rape and gang rape in fraternity houses. It is not clear whether the incidents in the 1980s drew attention because of this new awareness, or whether the new awareness arose from the emergence of a new and terrifying fraternal practice.[25] In other words, when did rape become part of fraternal life? What would misogyny look like in the archaeological and archival record available? I turned from my consideration of Zeta Psi to the broader context of the campus. During the time when Zeta Psi was moving from its second to its third house, I found the first evidence that fraternity attitudes and actions toward women were changing in profound ways—and once again, these shifts reflected the broader society.

Let us turn our attention back to our guide, Peter Pan. The first half of the 1950s was a busy time for him. In 1953, Disney released its animated version of the tale; and in 1955 and 1956, Mary Martin received a Tony and then an Emmy for her portrayals of Peter on stage and television.[26] In the year that Martin graced television screens in Peter's pants, the women of the University of California lost their panties. In the notorious panty raid of 1956 at the University of California, I caught my first glimpse of systematic physical male aggression toward coeds on a mass scale.

On May 17, 1956, papers around the San Francisco Bay Area covered what was initially referred to as a riot on campus the previous night.[27] The weather was extremely hot on May 16, and by midafternoon large numbers of students had gathered on the edges of campus to participate in "water-bagging" (water balloon fights) to cool off. Word went out that a large-scale water fight would take place at 6:30 P.M. Thousands of students converged for what began as so much good-spirited hilarity. Most of the action was concentrated in two areas, the north side of campus and Greek row on the south side of campus, in the area bounded by Piedmont, College, Channing, and Bancroft Avenues. According to witnesses, the water fight died down around 9:30, and the Channing group, as news reports called them, had started to disperse. Meanwhile, on the north side, the group split into two, and one group began a "lingerie raid" on the women's dorm, Stebbins Hall. The other part of the mob moved to Greek row, where they revitalized the crowd of onlookers, and, in the words of the *Daily Cal*, "the reinforced mob led by a lingerie standard-bearer stormed sorority after sorority. Hundreds of men poured into the houses as policemen stood helpless and watched."[28] Only fifteen officers were on duty, and some witnesses reported that they were laughing and not attempting to help.

"Panty raids" had begun in the early 1950s and were seen as a spreading campus fad. The raid at Cal had begun in good spirits, with the women adopting a grin-and-bear-it attitude and inviting men into their houses. That women did not begin the evening scared of the crowds seems to communicate that they were not accustomed to seeing their male classmates as potentially dangerous. The tone quickly degenerated. "Girls attempted to defend their property by brandishing hot irons and any other articles they could obtain."[29] An editorial written by a woman who lived in the area stated that "the few girls who dared to face the mob with hot irons, paddles or table lamps were knocked around, assaulted, carried outside in pajamas or nude. Housemothers fared no better, several being shoved aside and even knocked down by the mob."[30]

This editorial, with its sensational details, quickly garnered unwanted international attention for the university. The official report of the incident compiled by Chancellor Clark Kerr discredits this account and assured the public there was no nudity and that this was an irresponsible piece of journalism. This same editorial indicated that the fraternity men of the campus were responsible for originating the riot. Certainly, the sorority women's initial welcome of the rioters also suggests a fraternity connection.

When the mob finally dispersed, an estimated twelve thousand dollars worth of property damage had been incurred, and over twenty-five hundred articles of lingerie, valued at ten thousand dollars, had been turned into police. Twenty-five sorority houses had been entered and vandalized. University women had the unpleasant task of sorting through the piles at the Berkeley Police Station to attempt to locate their garments, a sight photographed by a number of papers.

Let us evaluate Clark Kerr's assertion that media coverage of the raid was sensationalized.[31] Kerr's report suggests that the local papers' coverage was largely made up of responsible reporting; he indicates that out-of-area papers sensationalized the event. Interestingly, the university report fails to mention eyewitness testimony that contradicts the university's contention that the women were in no danger. A reporter from the *Oakland Tribune* spoke to one girl barricaded in a sorority house during the attack. "At one house a frightened girl told a reporter by phone, 'We're OK here, but they have taken over the houses on both sides. There's no trouble here. Oh no, here they come.' The line went dead." *The Berkeley Gazette* reported that "a girl at the Alpha Gamma Delta house, 2424 Warring Street, was carried upstairs and displayed to the crowd from a balcony." The following day, that same paper noted, "Mrs. Eileen Ready, member of the Berkeley School Board and house mother at Alpha Phi sorority at 2830 Bancroft Steps reported she received a bruised shin in the invasion of the house by 200 males. She also reported a drunken student tried to get in bed with a coed on the third floor. He got a hard slap for his efforts."[32] Despite the university report's claim that "no women were stripped or carried from a house, no one was injured and drinking was not a factor," there is evidence from named sources that women were injured and threatened as part of the raid and, at the very least, terrorized.[33]

What then of the accusation that the fraternities were responsible? The Interfraternity Council started its own inquiry into the matter and quickly established a fund that each fraternity would contribute to in hopes of underwriting the costs of damages to the sororities. Witnesses, and later university interrogations, established that high school students and older men, as well as college students from the full cross-section of men's campus groups, were represented in the mob. Six fraternities—Alpha Gamma Delta, Alpha Omicron Pi, Chi Omega, Phi Mu, Alpha Epsilon Pi, and DSE—were cleared of any participation. Apparently, at least some members of each of the other more than fifty fraternity and men's groups on campus participated in the riot. Note that Zeta Psi was not one of the exempt organizations. In the weeks following the riot, it was also reported that several sororities received threatening phone calls urging them not to reveal the names of men involved. Given that estimates placed the mob at two thousand to three thousand men, the seventy-six men punished by the university for participating seems small. The police's record was even worse—only one arrest was made, and that was for public drunkenness.[34]

What was the trigger for this event? The chancellor's report suggests that the heat, combined with changes in the academic calendar that had eliminated any vacation time for students between December and May, was to blame. In other words: boys will be boys. I must contradict the university's opinion. The panty raid coincided with the decision by the university's executive committee to eliminate the male-only rooting section in the stadium. The vote was close, eight-to-six with two abstentions. In supporting the abolition, Dean Irving Stone had compared the men's section to a "mob"—an ironic or prophetic choice of words given what would transpire that evening. The introduction of coeds to the rooting section was supposed to have a civilizing influence.[35]

My theory that the two events are linked is supported by events that happened two weeks after the riot: four of the sorority houses were further vandalized with graffiti, including messages that read, "Hey girls, try and sit with us," and "Give the girls back their panties," which the *Daily Cal* writer recognized as a reference to the abolition of the men's section.[36] The university report makes no mention of the desegregation of the cheering section or the subsequent vandalism. I see the panty raid as a transitional event—one that was reproduced on many other campuses during the 1950s—a public display of new attitudes toward women. For the first time in my research, I could see the historical trajectory between the fraternal communities

I had studied and those depicted by scholars studying rape and sexual abuse in some contemporary fraternities; I could imagine how attitudes found at one time could manifest themselves in more violent ways in another. To further explore the issue, let's turn an archaeological eye toward sorority life.

While fraternity men—including, apparently, some from Zeta Psi—were involved in the raid, they were not alone in expressing a deep-seated animosity toward the women of campus (predominantly those of sororities). The panty raid was participated in by all men of the local community, university and nonuniversity alike, participated in the raid. In reading the papers leading up to and following this event, I was struck by the oppressiveness of the world in which the young women lived. The YWCA, an organization that had once promoted women's rights and advocated for the abolition of racial segregation, was sponsoring a series of lectures for college women on the importance of their role in family life. Family life was not, however, all it was cracked up to be. During the months of April and May alone, the *San Francisco Chronicle* had reported two separate cases of local women killing their children, then themselves. In one case, the article explicitly noted that the woman had been unsuccessful in her attempt to divorce her husband, before killing their two sons and herself.[37]

Page after page of advertising in the *Chronicle* featured scantily clad, unrealistically thin, female figures. The female figure lounging in lingerie was a staple of every newspaper page, drawing the male gaze. Perhaps in such a context, stealing a woman's undergarments makes sense—they existed for men's use anyway. Other advertisements and articles in the women's section of the paper featured advice on weight loss and dieting. Women had been forced back into the home, not, like their nineteenth-century counterparts, as its keepers and protectors, but as its captives. The panty raid underscored an important lesson for women of the time—they were not safe at home. Even so, like Wendy, they were supposed to recognize their twin destinies as mother and housekeeper and accept those roles on male terms. Again, fraternal and university attitudes followed those of broader society—not, apparently, the opposite.

CURTAIN CALL AND FINAL BOW

When we view Zeta Psi through a historical lens, we can see an organization that, like any other community, went through periods of success and periods of failure. The Iota chapter had a glorious origin story—it was the first fraternity on campus, the first fraternity in the West. This origin story became an important part of the fraternity's mythology about itself. There were several other important stories that the fraternity also liked to tell about itself: that they were the best, that they saved the other fraternities on campus, and how many campus buildings are named after famous Zetes, among others. The stories not only linked multiple generations of men to one another in brotherhood but also underscored their shared maleness—even if the ways that maleness is expressed has changed over the years.

Many of the men of Zeta Psi left university life with a strong desire to do public service. Men who skipped classes, who were demoted in class year, or who stole bells (and many other things) still managed to grow up to be productive citizens. The University of California would not be the institution it is today without the contributions of Zetes as faculty, elected representatives, regents, and benefactors. My point is, we cannot lump a set of societal institutions as long-lived and as complex and variable as men's Greek letter societies into categories defined by late-twentieth- and early-twenty-first-century experiences. This is why metaphors suggested by James Barrie's Never Land are useful in understanding fraternity life.

Barrie's work has been an important vehicle for explaining the gender conflicts that characterized the experiences of the white middle class at the nexus of the nineteenth and twentieth centuries. The hapless characters of Mr. Darling and Captain Hook embodied the fears and insecurities of Victorian men who found themselves oppressed by the very trappings of civilization they had created. Worse yet, their social and moral positions of privilege were being questioned by women and ethnic and minority groups. The caricatures represented in *Peter Pan*—the indulgent (but ultimately unmindful) wife, the frazzled and disrespected husband, the girl attempting to entrap a boy in domesticity, the dominating female, the jealous flirt, the free-spirited boy, and the mangy band of Lost Boys—may have been created out of the social debates of the early twentieth century, but they remain familiar and poignant to us still.

In times when gender tensions increase, Peter Pan returns to us from Never Land—in revitalizations of the play, in movies, and in new books. During the postwar 1950s, a time when whiteness and masculinity were again under siege, *Peter Pan* was revitalized. Today, in the early twenty-first century, in the guise of celebrating his hundredth birthday, publishers and studios have brought Peter out again in new books and films. Is it a coincidence that he has returned at a time when normative notions of the family are being challenged and women's reproductive rights are again under assault? Perhaps we should not be quick to embrace this immortal boy when he comes to call from Never Land. I remain more convinced than ever that the cast of *Peter Pan* is made up of characters who allow us to recognize and understand the social prototypes who peopled the social categorization processes of campus life. *Peter Pan* is a creation myth for twentieth-century gender roles.

There is an additional dimension to *Peter Pan*, and that is its location, Never Land. Just as I began this work with a discussion of Never Land, so I will end it. For it is in understanding the allure of Never Land that we can understand why Zete alumni sought to protect the fraternity. When I first embarked on this project, I was worried that the connection between fraternities, *Peter Pan*, and changing notions of masculinity was too contrived. After all, there were women in Never Land, women who, despite their obvious satirical edge, were still among the heroes of the plot. But imagery of men's initiations strongly influences the story *Peter Pan*.

Just as pledges had to face death to be reborn into their community, each of the major characters in *Peter Pan* faces death in order to be judged worthy of inclusion in Never Land. When it appears that Tootles has killed Wendy in Act II, he faces death at Peter's hand. In Act III, all the Lost Boys face Hook and his pirates, and Peter is left to die on Marooner's Rock. In Act IV, Peter faces death by poisoning, and in Act V, all the Lost Boys and Peter again face and defeat death. And it is not only the males who undergo this rite of passage. Tiger Lily bravely faces death by drowning in Act III, and Tinkerbell takes Peter's poison to save him in Act IV. Wendy, perhaps to counteract the heavy cloak of domesticity that envelops her, faces death thrice, when she is shot down by Tootles, left to drown with Peter on Marooner's Rock, and finally, is about to be thrown off the pirate boat in Act V. All who enter Never Land undergo an initiation not unlike those of fraternity pledges. The Lost Boys and their companions truly are members of a fraternity.[38]

Peter, as the embodiment of eternal boyhood, may rule Never Land, but it is not his alone. Never Land is a place where the inevitable trek to adulthood is magically stopped in midhike. Time passes at a different pace in Never Land. We never get a sense of how long any of the Lost Boys spend in Never Land, just as we cannot be sure how much time passes for Wendy and the Darling boys. College campuses remain such spaces today. They are places where odd traditions take hold, whether a Bourdon Burial or a Smoker rally. The calendar of the university Never Land fails to conform to the January-to-December calendar of other people, beginning in August and ending in May as it does. Progress is measured in credit hours, not age, and while Never Land is connected to "real worlds" like London, Berkeley, San Francisco, and Oakland, it is easy for an inhabitant to become so entrenched in campus affairs that the outside realities recede.

Pan's Never Land is a place of constant adventure. Chasing mermaids, attending fairies' weddings, sword fighting with pirates, powwowing with Indians, and dining together on imaginary meals, these are the activities that fill the days of the Lost Boys. The Lost Boys of Zeta Psi had their own pranks and rituals that engaged their attentions, although these were fewer and further between than those of Peter's chapter. The documentary evidence suggests that much of the time spent in Zetes' Never Land was spent eating, playing games (particularly card games), drinking, singing, talking, and general loafing around. There were manly, and later, masculine, adventures that involved camping, mountain climbing, and hunting, and there were trips to follow the football team. Sometimes there were parties and dates with women, but generally, there was a quiet routine of sociability with one's brothers.

There was something so compelling in this simple, lazy routine that grown men, men who had left the fraternity and Never Land, defended it through politicking and financial support. And here we are left with this final question: why? Of course, they could: the alumni of Zeta Psi included prominent lawyers, doctors, politicians, bankers, and professors. They had the connections and economic ability to support their fraternity. They had the finances to ensure that the chapter house was the finest on campus, and they had the political connections to ensure that the active members of their brotherhood were sheltered from pirates and others who would do them harm. So perhaps the basic question to be asked is, *what* was so important that they were protecting? It is possible to argue about the economic benefits of fraternal bonds—for young men, the opportunity to make connections in the adult world, perhaps leading to better employment opportunities. For older men, fraternities created not only an established network of older peers and age-mates but also a yearly crop of new graduates to pick among. And it is possible to argue that fraternities reified white privilege, creating further economic benefits and advantages for members. But these answers seem stale, and they fail to explain why a fraternity only eight years old was so powerfully defended by so many prominent California men in 1879 and 1880.

In studying men's fraternal orders, Mark Carnes ultimately decided that the appeal of these organizations was visceral.[39] There was a need in men for belief in something larger than themselves, a need left unmet in their female-dominated, officially sanctioned church life. The need was so strong that they turned to the fraternal temple for solace and fulfillment. I think the college fraternity served a similar yet distinct purpose.

The San Francisco journalist who described *Peter Pan*'s first presentation in San Francisco, in 1908, writes, "Every man who sees 'Peter Pan' recognizes in him the romantic restlessness of youth—the desire to 'try one's wings' on the flight of this or that mad fancy."[40] Peter makes a similar claim for himself. In the final act of the play, while their sword blades clash, a frustrated Hook turns to Peter and says, " 'Tis some fiend fighting me! Pan, who and what art thou?" Peter gleefully responds, "I'm youth, I'm joy, I'm a little bird that has broken out of the egg." Peter's youth and glee prove too much for the pirate, who chooses to dive into the waiting jaws of the crocodile.[41]

Here then, is our answer. Never Land is a place of fancy, a time in one's life when the future is a series of wispy dreams and anticipations and so far away from the present. Truly, in Never Land the future does not come. Perhaps it is the curse of Western society that children spend a lifetime thinking that adulthood can never happen to them, only to find that it does, and that when it arrives, time speeds up. As long as there is an active chapter of one's fraternity, there will always be eternal youth: young men, from eighteen to twenty-two years of age, living the same adventures, year after year, for eternity. In Never Land, the Lost Boys and Peter Pan always win; the Indians always serve Peter Pan; the pirates are always defeated; and even the women have to face the trials of brotherly initiation. Through one's connection to the house, an alumnus can hold on to that fading pixie dust—just enough to remind themselves what it felt like to fly for the first time. For alas, as all fraternity men know, all boys grow up, all save one.

Membership of Zeta Psi Iota as Compiled from Alumni Registers, Wall Panels, and Yearbooks

1870	Brown, Brainard C.	1874	Parker, Edward A.
1871	Learned, Charles	1874	Perkins, James Coffin
1871	Pomeroy, Everett B.	1874	Price, John R.
1871	Whitworth, Fred H.	1874	Rowell, Joseph C.
1872	Reed, George W.	1874	Stillman, John M.
1872	Rodgers, Arthur	1874	Stuart, Charles D.
1872	Whitworth, John N.	1874	Turkinginton, William
1873	Ainsworth, George J.	1875	Alexander, John F.
1873	Bolton, John M.	1875	Deering, Frank P.
1873	Budd, James	1875	Eastman, Clem
1873	Edwards, George C.	1875	Hinton, I. T., Jr.
1873	Hawkins, Lester	1875	Holman, Frederick V.
1873	Whitmore, Clarence	1875	Low, Arthur F.
1873	Woodward, Thomas P.	1875	McLean, F. R.
1874	Budd, John E.	1875	Rhodes, Sameul R.
1874	Carneal, Thomas D.	1875	Webb, Harry H.
1874	Farrell, John	1876	Hook, Vincent
1874	Griffiths, David D.	1876	Overacker, Charles B.
1874	Lynch, Leo	1876	Wilkins, James H.

1876	Wright, George T.	1881	Russell, Harry A.
1877	Fairbanks, P. B.	1881	Sherwood, Harry Hamilton
1877	Meek, Harry W.	1881	Storey, William B.
1877	Phelps, W. H.	1881	Stratton, Frederick S.
1877	Sherwood, William R.	1882	Berry, Rufus
1877	Solinsky, Frank	1882	Bowles, Philip E.
1877	Stillman, Howard	1882	Hooker, Robert G.
1878	Chapin, Samuel A.	1882	Martin, Richard
1878	Dwinelle, Herman	1882	McMurray, Valentine C.
1878	Finnie, Walter F.	1882	Nelson, William W.
1878	McGillivray, John D.	1882	Pollock, Alexander F.
1878	Van Dyke, W. M.	1882	Rideout, Norman A.
1878	Warren, Clarence H.	1882	Stillman, Stanley
1879	Dargie, William E.	1883	Frick, Edward C.
1879	Fairbanks, Joseph F.	1883	Mailliard, John W.
1879	Henshaw, Frederick W.	1884	Badger, Henry S.
1879	Hopkins, William E.	1884	Barton, William F.
1879	Mailliard, Joseph	1884	Blinn, Frank L.
1879	McNeil, Godwin	1884	Frick, Jesse E.
1879	Nicholson, Walter H.	1884	McManus, Francis
1879	Tompkins, John W.	1884	McNear, John A.
1880	Bryne, James W.	1884	Powers, Frank
1880	Havens, Henry R.	1884	Rowell, Edward F.
1880	Shepard, Edward H.	1885	Brittain, William G.
1880	Stow, Vanderlyn	1885	Leet, W. McNeil
1880	Whitney, Arthur L.	1885	McAllister, Elliott
1881	Adames, F. L.	1885	McGillivray, G.
1881	Alexander, Charles O.	1885	Stone, Andres L.
1881	Jaynes, Louis L.	1885	Sutton, John G.
1881	Lindley, Douglas A.	1886	Whipple, Albert B.
1881	McGillivray, James J.	1887	Babcock, Allen H.
1881	McMicken, Maurice	1887	Cross, Arthur D.
1881	Pearsons, Hiram A.	1887	Makinney, Fred W.
1881	Rhodes, Edward L.	1887	Sabin, Henry W.

1887	Variel, William J.	1891	Hittell, Franklin T.
1887	Wines, Melvin L.	1891	Le Conte, Joseph Nisbit
1888	Cyrus, James W.	1891	Ryland, Caius T.
1888	Duhring, Frederick T.	1891	Tay, Charles F.
1888	Gilson, Livingston, Jr.	1892	Denson, Harry B.
1888	Knight, Robert S.	1892	Hanna, Walter R.
1888	Meek, William E.	1893	Clark, L. Linwood
1888	Rowlands, William E.	1893	Foulks, George H.
1889	Dow, William A.	1893	Henry, Walter Hugh
1889	Jordan, Leslie A.	1893	Mays, Edwin
1889	Powers, Assron H.	1893	Pheby, Frederick S.
1889	Ralston, William C.	1893	Thorne, Walter M.
1889	Sands, John A.	1894	Carpenter, Frank L.
1889	Steffens, Lincoln	1894	Clary, Edward De W.
1889	Stone, George Frederick	1894	Dyer, Ernest I,
1889	Sutton, Albert	1894	Fine, William A.
1889	Thompson, Charles R.	1894	Griffith, Rupert T.
1889	Weighel, William McM.	1894	Hyde, Henry C.
1890	Calhoun, Walton H.	1894	Hyde-Chick, Ralph
1890	Demarest, David C.	1894	Patterson, William E.
1890	Dyer, Hubert P.	1894	Robbins, Ruel D.
1890	Hill, Edward C.	1894	Weed, Benjamin
1890	Lakenan, C. B.	1894	Whittier, William R.
1890	McCord, Harry H.	1895	Anthony, Marc
1890	McMurray, Orrin K.	1895	Bunnell, George W.
1890	Richardson, Frank R.	1895	Denny, Thomas C.
1890	Terry, Wallace Irving	1895	Gray, De Witt H.
1890	Willis, Frederick M.	1895	Mays, Robert
1891	Allen, Walter C.	1895	Pheby, Thomas B.
1891	Baldwin, Harry C.	1896	Dean, Charles D.
1891	Bouse, John	1896	Jackson, Edwin R.
1891	Cook, John P.	1896	Kelley, Rollin M.
1891	Costigan, George D.	1897	Catlin, H. C.
1891	Hillborn, Edward P.	1897	Gregory, Julius

1897	Marston, Frederick C.	1905	Edwards, Harmon
1897	Mays, Grant	1905	Hall, Hiram T.
1897	Robbins, Lloyd M.	1905	Houghton, Shirley
1897	Smith, Felix	1905	Schilling, Rudolph
1897	Steele, Edward L. G., Jr.	1905	White, Edwin D.
1897	Taylor, Thomas C., Jr.	1905	White, Wiliam T.
1898	Budd, Henry B.	1906	Cavalier, William
1898	Faulkner, Louis G.	1906	McKevitt, F. B., Jr.
1898	Jackson, Andrew R.	1906	Solinsky, Frank, Jr.
1898	Morgan, Walter H.	1906	White, Alden
1898	Procter, John W.	1906	Whiteny, Arthur St. John
1898	Sherwood, Lionel C.	1906	Woodward, Robert S.
1898	Soule, Beach C.	1907	Bowles, Philip F.
1899	Bonestell, Horatio S.	1907	Dyer, Ephraim
1899	Brizard, Henry, F.	1907	Harman, A. K. P.
1899	Dutton, Henry F.	1907	Mellersh, T. C.
1899	Jessen, George H.	1907	Sargent, Bradley
1899	Mott, Geroge M., Jr.	1907	Wilder, Theodore
1899	Rutherford, Walter S. K.	1908	Foster, Robert N.
1900	Foster, W. A. S.	1908	Henry, Leslie Albert
1901	Bruntsch, Ernest A.	1908	Jones, Hugh B.
1902	Pearce, Edward H.	1908	Shaw, James P.
1902	Robbins, William C.	1908	Snell, Richard A.
1902	White, Josiah H.	1908	Snowden, Raymond F.
1902	Wilcomb, Norris L.	1908	Wintringham, H. B.
1902	Zook, Edgar T.	1909	Boswell, F. King
1903	Davis, George C.	1909	King, Thomas S.
1903	Davis, George T.	1909	Meek, William H.
1903	Foster, Arthur W., Jr.	1909	Snell, Henry F.
1903	Glass, Frank F.	1909	Stephens, Franklin
1904	Minor, Henry Samuel	1909	Witter, Dean
1904	Minor, Herbet H.	1910	Andrew, John F.
1904	Mitchell, R. B., Jr.	1910	Brownlie, Arthur C.
1904	Robbins, Irving W.	1910	Brush, Edmund S.

1910	Foster, Paul S.		1916	Baker, George Washington
1910	Hayden, Curtiss		1916	Beauman, Louis Charles
1910	Mick, Clark J.		1916	Duhring, Frederick Sterns
1910	Solinsky, Albert C.		1916	Forbes, Edwin Floyd
1910	Whiting, L. D.		1916	Maze, Charles George
1910	Witcher, William V., Jr.		1916	Short, John Douglas
1911	Blackwood, Gordon, F.		1916	Stevens, Leslie
1911	Cooper, Thomas P.		1916	Stillman, Edmund Hathaway
1911	Langstroth, L. A.		1916	Witter, Jean Carter
1911	Sargent, Charles		1917	Earl, Arthur
1911	Solinsky, Edward R.		1917	Finley, Theodore
1911	Troxel, Harry E.		1917	Reis, John
1912	Abbott, S. L., Jr.		1917	Ruffo, Henry
1912	Berry, Irwin C.		1917	Tietzen, James
1912	Clewe, Ernest,		1917	Witter, Willis G.
1912	Powers, Jay E.		1918	Bacheller, Paul Fuller
1912	Small, Barrett R.		1918	Carson, George Earl
1912	Wilder, Roswell D.		1918	Ciprico, John O'Neil
1913	Baker, Verne Allen		1918	Goldaracena, Orel Andrew
1913	Brownlie, John W.		1918	Holt, William Knos
1913	Hawley, Raymond William		1918	Langstroth, Malin Thomas
1913	King, William Norris		1918	Lauxen, Richard
1913	McPeak, Daniel		1918	Matthews, Randsdell
1913	Reis, Gustav Crittenden		1918	Ristenpart, Clayton Arthur
1914	Finley, George Mearns		1918	Root, Homer Dolce
1914	Finley, William Howard, Jr.		1918	Spear, Albion Whitney
1914	Knight, Remi C.		1918	Valentine, Edward Autrey
1915	Bretherton, Sidney Elliot		1919	Adams, Josiah K.
1915	Conklin, Alva Putnam		1919	Connor, William D.
1915	Davis, Charles Henry		1919	Guthrie, Robert A.
1915	Gilmour, Lloyd Straube		1919	Hanna, Donald J.
1915	King, Alexander Mann		1919	Harvey, H.
1915	Miller, Roswell		1919	Holbrook, James E.
1915	Sutton, Charles Zook		1919	Hyde, Orra C., II

1919	Jolly, Edwin J.	1922	Hines, Fulmer
1919	Nickerson, Randolph	1922	LeHane, Louis
1919	O'Brien, George	1922	Lyen, Louis
1919	Rennie, Willam	1922	Mays, George A.
1920	Alverson, William Brinkley	1922	St. Sure, Paul
1920	Duhring, John Herman	1922	Sutton, John G.
1920	Gifford, John Sweeny	1922	Taylor, Reese H.
1920	Metcalfe, George Brownlow	1922	Witter, Edwin D.
1920	Owsley, John Guy	1922	Witter, Guy Phelps
1920	Sharon, Hufford Clarence	1923	Loskamp, Charles
1920	Spear, Lewis Emerson	1924	Chapman, Philip
1920	Walrond, Henry Ernest	1924	Grier, Lisgar
1921	Alverson, Wallace Brinkley	1924	Hammond, Floyd
1921	Ashurst, Griffin	1924	Harris, Warren
1921	Brock, McKinley Parker	1924	Maupin, William
1921	Finnell, Simpson	1924	McHenry, Merl T.
1921	Grier, Thomas Johnson	1924	Monahan, William W.
1921	Holt, Thomas Johnson	1924	Toll, Gerald S.
1921	Hull, Roswell Lee	1924	Walker, Bethel
1921	Jackson, Harry Andrew	1924	Whitney, Merril
1921	Maupin, Janes Lawrence	1924	Witter, Charles
1921	Metcalfe, Stephen Brownlow	1924	Witter, Guy Phelps
1921	O'Brien, Edgar	1924	Witter, John
1921	Raggio, John	1924	Woods, William
1921	Sanson, Thomas Alexander	1925	Allen, George
1921	Schafer, Ward Conneau	1925	Bush, James R.
1922	Armstrong, Ward Dwight	1925	Cass, William
1922	Brier, Lisgar	1925	Dorst, Warrington
1922	Ciprico, Edmond	1925	Fanning, James
1922	Clowes, Roscoe	1925	Hannan, James
1922	Duhring, Stephen R.	1925	Soule, Everett
1922	Dunne, Raymond	1925	Soule, Beach C., Jr.
1922	Graff, Edwin	1925	Terry, Wallace
1922	Hammond, Hollander	1925	Tibbens, Floyd

1925	Tucker, Shepard	1929	Elliot, William
1926	Boles, Wilbur	1929	Hartwell, Jordan
1926	Carr, Homer	1929	Hoogs, Richard
1926	Gross, Frances	1929	Johnson, Llewlyn
1926	Holmes, Benton	1929	Knowland, William
1926	Lawton, Payne	1929	Mabee, William
1926	Mott, Dick	1929	Seawell, Emmet
1926	Nichols, Norwood	1930	Barnes, James W.
1926	Thompson, Edward	1930	Beales, Ross W.
1927	Brumbaugh, Nathan	1930	Crim, William R.
1927	Chapman, John	1930	Ehman, George C.
1927	Hutchinson, Hardy	1930	LeConte, Joseph, Jr.
1927	McNoble, Hubert	1930	Lenahan, John
1927	Mead, John	1930	McMurray, John P.
1927	Procter, John W.	1930	Robbins, William C.
1927	Rounthwaite, Sterling	1931	Ciprico, Frances
1927	Sproul, Harold	1931	Clarke, Ted
1927	Walrond, Frank	1931	Cornwall, Sherman
1928	Barry, Max	1931	Hyde, C. Burrel
1928	Crowell, Paul	1931	Martin, Edward W.
1928	Gilmore, Harry	1931	McCoy, William
1928	Hamilton, Craig	1931	Reyland, Frederick
1928	Hoags, Albert	1931	Rowell, John
1928	Holmes, Perrine	1931	Solinsky, Frank J.
1928	Janes, Howell	1931	White, Edwin D.
1928	Larson, Eduan	1932	Dunlap, David
1928	O'Brien, Lloyd	1932	Mays, Roderick
1928	Plehn, Branerd	1932	Snowden, Wayne
1928	Procter, Thomas	1932	Whites, David
1928	Rhoades, Roger	1932	Witter, Wendell
1929	Barnes, Frank	1933	Bagg, Charles
1929	Beales, John	1933	Barry, Ronald
1929	Burg, John	1933	Christenson, Edwin
1929	Draper, Lawrence	1933	Hall, Winslow

1933	Hand, Edgar	1936	Wegge, William A., Jr.
1933	Hunt, Preston	1937	Atthowe, Charles H.
1933	Moore, John	1937	Barber, Harry S.
1933	Reinhardt, Frederick	1937	Hall, Samuel
1934	Foster, John B.	1937	Lee, Warner W.
1934	Beedy, J. Crosby	1937	Martin, John
1934	Chamberlain, Selah	1937	Masie, A. Harper
1934	Davis, George C.	1937	Miller, Charles H.
1934	Dunlap, Gordon S.	1937	Minor, Paul D.
1934	Foster, Paul S.	1937	Panton, Edward B.
1934	Hein, Charles H.	1937	Solinsky, Edward H.
1934	Martin, George E.	1938	Carter, Willam F.
1934	McKay, David L.	1938	Carter, William F.
1934	Rector, E. William	1938	Clinch, Downey C.
1934	Whitney, Robert L.	1938	Cushing, John E., Jr.
1935	Clewe, William F.	1938	Cykler, John F.
1935	Hall, Houghton	1938	Dyer, Ephraim
1935	Harmon, Albion K. P.	1938	Hall, Chaffee E., Jr.
1935	Hogle, James E.	1938	Hincks, William P.
1935	Hoover, Holman	1938	Lincoln, Theodore
1935	Jones, John E.	1938	Milligan, Royal S., Jr.
1935	Richards, Gilbert C.	1938	Weaver, Kent M.
1935	Sifford, Benton	1938	Wegge, J. Robert
1936	Blackenburg, William	1939	Abbot, Samuel L.
1936	Brown, Sanford	1939	Barber, Stephen T.
1936	Dunlap, Frank L.	1939	Beesemeyer, Jay C.
1936	Endress, John Z.	1939	Hays, Alan W.
1936	Johnson, Harry D.	1939	Leonard, Hobart S.
1936	Martin, William P.	1939	Lincoln, Charles S.
1936	Massie, J. Standish	1939	Merritt, John B.
1936	McKevitt, Frank B., III	1939	Ohm, William H.
1936	Newhall, Scott	1939	Shine, E. Earll
1936	Ristenpart, Chester H.	1939	Zook, Edgar T., Jr.
1936	Watkins, Harold F.	1940	Bundschu, Towle

1940	Caswell, George B.	1943	Nelson, Theodore R.
1940	Dyer, Peter R.	1943	Paxton, Clyde E.
1940	Forkner, Hamden L.	1943	Peek, Presley E.
1940	Grieg, Robert W.	1943	Reis, John F.
1940	Hayden, Curtiss	1943	Shaw, William L.
1940	Hoogs, William H., III	1943	Solinsky, E. Dean
1940	McEachen, Francis X.	1943	Stock, Lester H.
1940	Milligan, Richard H.	1944	Baldwin, W. Isaac
1940	Pryor, Gaillard	1944	Brown, Malcolm
1940	Slattery, Bradley	1944	Burrill, Gerald
1940	Stephens, William G. H., Jr.	1944	Cook, Sheldon
1941	Balliet, Samuel	1944	Duhring, Frederick
1941	Hendrick, James W.	1944	Dunlap, John
1941	Lamoreaux, William E.	1944	Eschen, James
1941	Landon, Morris F.	1944	Henle, John
1941	Merritt, A. Leland	1944	Landon, Eliot
1941	Pelletreau, Robert W.	1944	Meullerschoen, George
1941	Snowden, Robert F.	1944	Sinclair, Neil
1941	Youdall, Peter G.	1944	Wheeler, Rollo
1942	Donoghue, John R.	1945	Ruffo, Henry
1942	Foster, Robert N.	1945	Doerr, Donn
1942	Martin, Carmel C.	1945	Fleharty, William
1942	Muller, Fred A., Jr.	1945	McKee, George
1942	Solinski, Jack D.	1945	McKee, Van
1942	Stephens, Thomas M.	1945	Miller, Royal
1942	Taylor, Lawrence	1945	Pollard, Frank
1942	Witter, Jean C.	1945	Wilson, Joseph
1942	Wood, Charles G.	1945	Witter, William
1943	Brush, Frank E.	1946	Baldwin, Page
1943	Demarest, James F.	1946	Cavalier, William
1943	Dinmore, John J.	1946	Fleharty, George
1943	James, Robert A.	1946	Hibbitt, William
1943	Lucas, Fred V.	1946	Lucas, James
1943	MacBride, G. Hall	1946	Merriam, Robert

1946	Morris, John	1950	Theiss, Ted
1946	Nelson, Jack	1950	Witter, Edwin
1946	Otto, Alfred	1951	Badger, George
1946	Sharon, William	1951	Brinck, William, Jr.
1946	Solinsky, Robert	1951	Gallinatti, Alan
1946	Somers, Lawrence	1951	Mays, Laurence
1947	Burril, Gerald	1951	McCulloch, John
1947	Randsdall, James T.	1951	Robertson, Charles
1948	Sellier, William	1951	Ruxton, Walter
1948	Solinsky, Robert	1951	Shaffer, James
1948	Sommers, Lawrence	1951	Witter, George
1948	Vincent, Robert	1952	Forgy, Fred, Jr.
1949	Giffen, Price	1952	Hutchinson, James
1949	Healy, John	1952	Hyde, Orra, III
1949	Hoogs, John	1952	Nelson, Edward
1949	Losey, Robert	1952	Scott, Alan
1949	Mattei, Peter	1952	Taylor, Edward
1949	Montagne, William	1952	Warren, James
1949	Morris, Austin	1952	Witter, Ronald
1949	O'Brien, Robert	1952	Wyatt, Edwin
1949	Petray, Clay	1953	Breck, Samuel
1949	Pry, Jacque	1953	Doulon, Dave
1949	Raggio, Thayer	1953	Fink, William
1949	Randall, Denny	1953	Gallagher, John
1949	Tourtellotte, James	1953	Horrall, Kenneth
1950	Ball, George	1953	Nelson, John
1950	Burroughs, Joe	1953	Newell, Pete
1950	Ford, Ed	1953	O'Brien, Peter
1950	Giffen, Mike	1953	Schade, Hugh
1950	Holt, Ted	1953	Wills, Le Baron
1950	Keresey, Jim	1954	Buwaldda, Robert
1950	Price, Jim	1954	Grant, Robert
1950	Rademaker, Ted	1954	Hagar, George
1950	Smith, Russell	1954	Hamilton, William

1954	Holt, Donald	1957	Davis, Gilbert
1954	Holt, Douglas	1957	Fits, Larry
1954	Howden, Douglas	1957	Gaspardone, Leo
1954	Rhoades, Donald	1957	Grant, Jack
1954	Roemer, Thomas	1957	Green, Charles
1954	Rosson, Perry	1957	Griffin, Andrew
1954	Schurnmacher, Gerald	1957	Hobson, Douglas
1954	Swenson, Burton	1957	Jaeger, Joseph
1954	Taylor, Thomas	1957	McCubbin, William
1954	White, Bertram	1957	Schultz, Dave
1955	Bancroft, Daniel	1957	Shannon, Robgert
1955	Buwalda, Robert	1957	Wallis, Robert
1955	Rhoades, Donald	1958	McGuire, Donald
1955	Wallis, Robert	1958	Peterson, Edward
1955	Wiegman, Marvin	1959	Benedetti, John De
1956	Barker, Dwight	1959	Berryhill, James
1956	Beckman, Lemoin	1959	Doolittle, Alfred
1956	Floyd, William	1959	Haines, William
1956	Green, Alanson	1959	Jordan, Frank
1956	Horrall, Kenneth	1959	Osborne, David
1956	Hutchins, Robert	1959	Perkins, Charles
1956	Knight, Robert	1959	Torintino, John
1956	Mays, Harry	1959	White, David, Jr.
1957	Bridges, David	1959	Willocks, Jack
1957	Brigham, Charles	1959	Wofenden, William

NOTES

PROLOGUE

1. James Crawford, "Sane Adults Unblushingly Tell Peter Pan They Believe in Fairies," *San Francisco Call,* June 11, 1907.

2. Ferrier 1930; Nerad 1999.

3. Zeta Psi 1899; Associated Students of the University of California (ASUC) 1960.

4. Carnes and Griffen 1990; Carnes 1989; Kimmel 2005, 2006.

5. Historical archaeology developed its disciplinary identity as the archaeology of the disenfranchised and underrepresented peoples of the historic period. The conceit is that these groups are misrepresented in the documentary record. The fraternity site is an interesting set of contrasts—the men were certainly from the elite strata of society, but they participated in a group identity that has been long vilified. As such, the documentary record related to fraternity life is as problematic as any other text-based study of a disenfranchised group. For further discussion of the role of historical archaeology in studying the roles of disenfranchised peoples, see DeCunzo and Jameson 2005; Orser 2001; Hicks and Beaudry 2006; Beaudry et al. 2001; Buchli and Lucas 2001; Deetz 1994; Little 1992. Although it has been unpopular in historical archaeology of late to focus much attention on the lives of the elite, the reality is that any understanding of social inequality must consider those who resided in the upper echelons of society.

6. Nevius 2007.

7. Sanday 1990: 192. While Sanday focuses upon the attitudes of fraternity men, the notion that it was rape to engage with women who were not capable of giving consent was a new idea for men of all walks of life. See also Moffatt 1989 for discussions of college

student sexual behaviors and attitudes in the 1980s, and Stombler 1994; Kalof and Cargill 1991; Martin and Hummer 1989 for other considerations of sexual misconduct in fraternity settings.

8. Black et al. 2005, Brown et al. 2005.

9. Sanua 2000; Black et al. 2005: 388; Sanday 1990.

10. Whaley 2005: 417.

11. For instance, Carnes 1989; Clawson 1989; Dunmenil 1984. These authors share a concern for understanding how ritual creates a sense of unity among participants.

12. Carnes 1989: 173.

13. Brown et al. 2005; Kimbrough 2003; Sanua 2003. For examples of self-published Greek histories, see Zeta Psi 1899, 1926; Interfraternity Conference (IFC) 1928.

14. Dunmenil 1984.

15. IFC 1928.

16. A wide range of documents was made available to me by members of the Iota chapter of Zeta Psi, who at different times provided me with access to some of their archival records. In addition, many alumni generously wrote me with their reminiscences and walked through the standing structure with me. Because floods and boiler room disasters at different times damaged the Iota chapter's archives, I suspect that little documentary evidence has been preserved beyond what I saw. It is unclear that my outsider status affected my access to any but the Iota chapter's most "sacred" information related to ritual activities.

17. Carnes 1989; Sanday 1990.

18. For instance, see Wilkie 2000a, 2003; Wilkie and Farnsworth 2005.

19. White 1975.

20. For further discussion of modes of archaeological writing, see Joyce 2002, 2006.

21. In good feminist self-reflective tradition, I think it is worth discussing some of my other personal encounters with fraternity life. I am not oblivious to the threat to women's safety that can exist in some college fraternity houses. In my freshman year, I found myself targeted by a fraternity brother in a computer class who constantly asked to work on labs with me and who invited me to several frat parties at his house, even though I also knew he had a "serious" girlfriend. Our class was in session during the semester he was pledging. He was a handsome, well-built man of some obvious wealth, and I wondered why he continued to pursue me when I clearly was not interested in him (and, based on pictures of the girlfriend, was not his type). He told me about his hell week. Among other ordeals, he and his pledge brothers had been stripped naked, tied up, thrown in a trunk, driven to an unknown location, dumped off, and told to find their way back. He seemed to think this was hysterically funny.

I never attended any of the parties at his house, which had a reputation as one to stay away from if you were non-Greek (in other words, you had a high risk of being drugged and date-raped). My failure to attend irritated him no end and would lead to a barrage of questions about why I hadn't come. I never saw this man after the semester we had a class together. Based on my reading of Sanday's book, which focuses on fraternity life in the mid-1980s, it is possible that I was being set up for more of a "party" than I was interested in. Sanday, in *Fraternity Gang Rape* (1990), describes non-Greek women being brought to parties as potential victims for group sex. The multiattacker sexual assault at the center of her analysis involved a woman who had been drugged or intoxicated to the point of being unable to consent. She was a student, but not from the same university. Her status as an outsider to the Greek community made it easier, in Sanday's opinion, for her attackers to victimize her. I was concerned that I was being pursued by this particular man as a potential trophy. It was common knowledge among non-Greek women at the university that one should never attend a fraternity party alone, never accept a drink from anyone unless one poured it from the keg oneself, and never, ever, go upstairs in a fraternity house. I went to perhaps two, maybe three, fraternity parties but never stayed long. It was fairly clear that, unless you partook of alcohol or intended to sleep with a brother, these were not very interesting events. Several acquaintances rushed to be "little sisters" for several fraternities, and their stories made it clear that acceptance required a high degree of sexual permissiveness.

I did have a positive undergraduate fraternity experience, at a formal event, as the date of a friend. While not an unpleasant experience, it was somewhat surreal, leaving me with the sense that we were trapped in some sort of 1950s prom night. While there was a token attempt at integrating the fraternities on Syracuse's campus, there was also at least one African American fraternity active on campus. This group was notable for their processions around campus. None of my African American friends were involved in this part of the fraternity system, so my contact was very limited. Overall, I left the university with an ambivalent view of the Greek system. Greeks attended different bars, had different majors, and in general, kept to themselves, and I did little to seek them out.

22. See Robbins 2004 for graphic descriptions of sorority hazing.

23. Wilkie 2001.

24. Wilkie 1998b.

25. For examples of the kinds of work historical archaeologists are doing on gender and sexuality, I recommend Galle and Young 2006; Schmidt and Voss 2000; Voss 2000a, 2000b; Beaudry 2006; Barile and Brandon 2004. In Wilkie and Howlett Hayes 2006, we provide a broad overview of gender and sexuality research in historical archaeology.

26. While masculinity studies in the social sciences have blossomed of late, gender studies in archaeology are primarily focused on the experiences of women. There are

a small number of scholars who have explicitly discussed masculinity and manhood, some more theorized than others, e.g. Hardesty 1994; Knapp 1998a, 1998b; Knapp and Meskell 1997; Joyce 2001; Harrison 2002; Alberti 2006. Others have looked at men and women as social beings interacting with one another, e.g. Gilchrist 1999; Meskell and Joyce 2003; Meskell 2002; Joyce 2000; Wilkie and Howlett Hayes 2006.

27. Zeta Psi 1880, 1899, 1926; Classes of 1875–1880, 1882–1928, 1874–1879, 1881–1927; ASUC 1928–1958.

28. Sharer and Ashmore 2000; Thomas 1991 provide excellent overviews of how archaeologists in prehistoric and historic settings deal with the notions of time and chronology. Examples of finely dated sites include Ludlow Collective 2001; and Praetzellis and Praetzellis 2004.

29. Zeta Psi 1899, 1926.

30. Clark and Wilkie 2006.

31. Personhood approaches encourage archaeologists to consider the multiple subject positions that any actor occupied during his or her lifetime. By focusing on the embodied experiences of our subjects, archaeologists are uniquely positioned, through our interpretations, to rehumanize in the present those whose humanity is otherwise muted or distorted in the historical record, and to pursue interpretations that recognize the complexities of social relations between members of a community. A personhood approach allows us to recognize the diversity of subject positions within the fraternity house at anytime. For instance, see Clark and Wilkie 2006; Meskell and Joyce 2003; Fowler 2004; Gilchrist 2000.

32. Hall 2000: 16. Hall dismisses the notion that the archival and archaeological records are distinct and instead employs the concept of "transcripts" in his interpretive work that recognizes that each are the products of the same cultural context.

33. Moreland 2001: 110–111.

34. Brooks 1997. Alasdair Brooks's studies of literary themes portrayed on transfer-printed ceramics are a notable exception. Brooks looked at how the popularity of particular writings was related to designs used on some ceramic tablewares produced in Britain.

35. E.g. Beaudry 1988; Claney 2004; Scott 1997; Tarlow and West 1999.

36. Wilkie 2000b, 2003.

37. Heneghan 2003. Recently, Bridget Heneghan has provided a brilliant analysis of how tea wares and ceramics are used in Harriet Jacob's ex-slave narrative, *Incidents in the Life of a Slave Girl,* to demonstrate to white readers the gentility and propriety of Jacobs. Heneghan convincingly argues that Jacobs was aware of the symbolic role of ceramics in communicating domesticity and motherhood to white audiences and actively manipulated those meanings to generate greater sympathy for her plight.

38. Barrie 1916; Birkin 1979; Crawford, "Sane Adults Unblushingly Tell Peter Pan They Believe in Fairies."

39. For more on Barrie's personal life and Peter Pan, see Birkin 1979; Jack 1991; Dunbar 1970; Rose 1984.

40. Bederman 1995.

41. Bederman is not the only one to think along these lines. The notion that Victorian manhood shifted to a model focused on physicality and athletics by the early twentieth century is shared by many historians. Bederman provides a vocabulary and delineation of these shifts that is particularly relevant for the Zeta Psi material remains. For other examples of works that play on this theme, see also essays in Carnes and Griffen 1990; Kimmel 2005, 2006; McLaren 1997; Pendergast 2000. For considerations of broader chronological considerations of multiple masculinities, see Beynon 2002; Benwell 2003; Murphy 2004; Clatterbaugh 1997. All these works, of course, accept a constructivist view of gender—that masculinity is one form of preformed maleness, and that in any given historical time, there are multiple and conflicting ideologies of maleness at play. Connell's 1995 and 2000 works and bell hooks's 2004 book are examples of works that consider in depth the theorizing of maleness within an explicitly feminist framework.

42. Bederman 1995; Starr 1981, 1985; Green 1986; Mechling 2001.

43. Stevenson 1967.

44. London 1988, 2001; Amory 1969: 245; Stevenson 1948, 1967, 1999; Burroughs 2003; Kasson 2000, 2001.

45. Summers 2001; Gordon 1990.

46. Hollindale 2005.

47. According to Birkin 1979, Barrie's marriage was widely known to have been a chaste one nearly from its beginning. The author was plagued by rumors of pedophilia throughout his lifetime and after.

48. Barrie 1916, 1928, 1957.

49. Barrie 1916. Authors who have spent significant analytical effort in understanding Peter Pan include White and Tarr 2006; Hollindale 2005; Schott 1974; Wolf 2003.

50. Jenkins 2000.

51. Hogg et al. 1995.

52. Clark 2006; Fox 2006; Garber 1992; Roth 2006; Routh 2001.

53. Wolf 1997, 2003; Fried and Vandereychken 1989.

STAGE DIRECTIONS

1. The following authors provide interesting insights into the reformulation of women's roles that took place during the second half of the nineteenth century and provide general background: Ryan 2006; Faust 1996; Melosh 1993; Ullman 1997; Smart 1992; Smith-Rosenburg 1985.

2. Wall 1994, in particular; Kimmel 2005, 2006.

3. Ryan 2006; Kimmel 2005.

4. Kimmel 2005: 31.

5. Bederman 1995: 12.

6. Kimmel 2006: 40.

7. Armstrong and Armstrong 1991.

8. Riddle 1997; Oakley 1984; Ryan 2006.

9. Faust 1996.

10. Two examples of the proscriptive literature available to women are Harland 1882; and of course, Beecher and Stowe 1870, a volume reissued many times.

11. Claney 2004; Wall 1994; Kasson 1987.

12. Foner 1983; Kantrowitz 2006.

13. Kantrowitz 2006.

14. Faust 1996; Fox-Genovese 1988; Smith-Rosenberg 1985.

15. Chudacoff 1999 includes a discussion of San Francisco's bachelor population.

16. Costello 2000; Seifert 1991; Seifert et al. 2000; Yamin 2006.

17. Carnes 1989: 1

18. Kimmel 2006: 114.

19. Carnes 1989; Dunmenil 1984; Clawson 1989.

20. Carnes 1989: 149.

21. Smith-Rosenberg 1985; Ryan 2006; D'Emilio and Freedman 1988; Ullman 1997.

22. Quoted in Robson 1977.

23. Torbenson 2005.

24. Torbenson 2005.

25. Robson 1977: 5–6.

26. Torbenson 2005.

27. Robson 1977: 10.

28. Carnes 1989.

29. Zeta Psi 1899: 19.

30. Zeta Psi 1899: 496.

31. Douglass 2000: 26.

32. Douglass 2000: 32.

33. Douglass 2000: 32.

34. Douglass 2000: 31–42.

35. Ferrier 1930; Stadtman 1970.

36. "California," *College Echo*, April 2, 1858.

37. Nerad 1999; Gordon 1999; Registrar's Office 1919–1947; University of California 1905.

38. Ferrier 1930: 351

39. Ritter 1933: 174.

40. Ritter 1933: 173.

ACT I

1. Ferrier 1930.

2. Ferrier 1930; Zeta Psi 1899.

3. Starr 1981; Bederman 1995; Kimmel 2005, 2006; Kasson 2001.

4. Zeta Psi 1899. The founding of the chapter was encouraged by visiting Zetes from eastern colleges. Charles Allen Sumner, a Zete from Williams College, is cited in fraternity histories as one who encouraged Cal student Brainerd Brown to form a chapter in 1870. The new chapter was formed and recognized at the grand chapter meeting in New Providence, New Jersey, December 27–28, 1871.

5. The *University Echo* was published by a student organization, the Durant Rhetorical Society, which was dedicated to the fine manly art of verbal jousting. *University Echo*, October 1871. Although unnamed, the author of this article was likely F. H. Whitworth or Everett Pomeroy, class of 1871, charter members of Zeta Psi and, coincidently, two of the *University Echo*'s three editors—the third editor, Josephine Lindley, as a woman, would not have been eligible for membership.

6. "Zeta Psi," *University Echo*, October 1871; Zeta Psi 1880, 1926.

7. *University Echo*, October 1871.

8. Zeta Psi 1899: 714.

9. "The Admission of Young Ladies to the University," *University Echo*, April 1871.

10. Bederman 1995; Carnes and Griffin 1990; Rotundo 1993.

11. Douglass 2000.

12. Weber 1992.

13. Starr 1981.

14. Brodkin 1998; Frankenburg 1997; Roediger 2005, 2007; Spelman 1988; Ignatiev 1996.

15. Barrie 1928: 9–10.

16. *The Blue and Gold* yearbooks of the nineteenth century included a feature called the "Senior Record," which gave statistics on student ages at the time of graduation. A reading of this feature in yearbooks published between 1874 and 1890 established that nearly all the graduating students were between twenty and twenty-three years of age.

17. There are, of course, inherent problems in data of this sort. Where we cannot confirm the brothers' biographies from other sources, we can only hope that the brothers were honorable in reporting their accomplishments. Zeta Psi 1926.

18. Zeta Psi 1926.

19. Zeta Psi 1926.

20. *In Memoriam* 1931.

21. *In Memoriam* 1938.

22. Joseph and John LeConte were among the first faculty of the university. The Hittell family included John S. Hittell, recognized by many (including state librarian

emeritus Kevin Starr) as one of California's early important historians. The Dwinelle family included Oakland mayor John Whipple Dwinelle, a key mover in the founding of the University of California.

23. Clark 1915.

24. Stadtman 1970: 27. Verne Stadtman claims that the first house was constructed by former regent Samuel Merritt, but I haven't found corroboration of this assertion. Several Merritt descendants were Zeta Psi brothers in the twentieth century.

25. Zeta Psi 1899: 714.

26. Berkeley Historical Society, plat map, 1884.

27. *Berkeleyan*, September 1880.

28. Barrie 1928, stage directions for act 2.

29. UA, Iota of Zeta Psi, ca. 1892–ca. 1900, UARC Album 15.

30. Lichtenstein 1901.

31. Deutsch 1926; Jones 1901; Sibley and Sibley 1952.

32. *The Occident*, August 18, 1881.

33. For insights on traditions at other colleges, see particularly Horowitz 1987, but also Atkinson and Drugger 1959; Brubaker and Rudy 1968; Keppel 1917; Parsons 1905; Porter 1888; Rice 1915a, 1915b; Sheffield 1889; Lippincott 1919.

34. "Class of 1887" 1886. Kurtz 1943: 101, provides an excellent description of the Bourdon's history. "At the end of each college year the freshman class placed two hated textbooks in a coffin, and in solemn funeral procession bore the coffin across the campus to a little slope that used to be called 'co-ed canyon,' just west of the modern Faculty Club. There, after appropriate ceremonies, the casket was lowered into a grave and covered with earth. A suitable epitaph was erected. The rows of little graves were not molested, and were one of the stock sights of the University. Later, cremation was substituted for burial, with wild processions of devils and priests through the city streets, mock mourning, good natured warring, and scurrilous scoffing, with a truck for a hearse, with weird priests setting off red fires and skyrockets from the trucks, and with a grand finish on the campus where flames at last licked up the coffin while the 'Damnatory' spoke his curses upon the books, and a 'Laudator' sung the praises of the freshman. The date of the first Burial of Bourdon was June 3, 1875, Minto was added at the Burial of May 22, 1886." It is worth noting that the ceremony featured the manly art of rhetoric in the form of the "Damnatory" and "Laudator." The Bourdon Burial ended in 1900, about the same time that the new masculinity was becoming entrenched on campus.

35. "Class of 1877" 1876: 29.

36. Lichtenstein 1901.

37. "Class of 1878" 1877.

38. Jones 1901.

39. Editorial, *Oestrus*, August 11, 1879.

40. Wilkie 1998a.

41. Lichtenstein 1901: 142.

42. Editorial, *Oestrus*, August 11, 1879.

43. "Class of 1880" 1879.

44. Fouke 1928.

45. "Class of 1893" 1892.

46. *University Echo*, June 1873.

47. Lichtenstein 1901: 148.

48. Zeta Psi 1899.

49. Zeta Psi 1899; University of California 1905.

50. Zeta Psi 1899; University of California 1905; "Class of 1883" 1882.

51. Jones 1901; Ferrier 1930; "Class of 1896" 1895.

52. "Class of 1913" 1912.

53. The easiest way to answer this question, of course, would have been to take samples of wood from several of the planks and have the age of the planks determined by means of dendrochronology, or tree-ring dating. This would have been a reasonable way to proceed if I had thought of it while I still had the planks. Unfortunately, after we recorded the planks and finished the 2001 field season, I traveled to Louisiana for a yearlong sabbatical. I learned that the university planned to throw out the panels, despite the current Iota chapter's interest in recovering them. Through a series of hastily transmitted e-mail messages, I was able to get access to the planks for a brother we had worked with during the field school, and they were returned, after nearly fifty years, to the Zetes. I am told they are now housed as sacred objects in the chapter room. Frankly, I don't know that the question warrants the trouble of messing with sacred objects.

54. Wall 1994, 2001; Clarke 1987; Fitts 1999; Kasson 1987; Recknor and Brighton 1999.

55. "Class of 1887" 1886: 101.

56. Wall 1994; Praetzellis and Praetzellis 2004; Rottman 2005; DeCunzo 1995.

57. See in particular contributions to Lawrence 2003.

58. LeConte 1990: 18–19.

59. Israel 1997.

60. To use an ethnographic example to illustrate, through the years my archaeological lab has been the site of a steadily growing population of mugs and Nalgene water bottles. Students who spend enough time in the lab to require hot or cold beverages seem to find the effort of taking these items away too burdensome, and at some point I must either host a tea party or have a garage sale. Another example has a fraternity tie in: a few years back, I was surprised to find in the current kitchen of the Archaeological Research Facility an early-twentieth-century platter with a fraternity insignia on it (not Zeta Psi's). I asked where it had come from, and a staff member of long duration told

me it had been there ever since we had taken over the building in the late 1980s. Based on the manufacturer's mark, the vessel could not have been made after 1971. In 2006, people at the facility decided they were tired of it and gave it to me. Given the number of reported pranks between fraternities, I have to wonder if it was nicked by a Zete brother, brought back to the house, and then left in its place in the china cabinet by multiple generations of scholars. The Zetes' habit of "borrowing" from the campus facilities and other fraternities became widely known in 1953. That this platter is a leftover from the fraternity is not so far-fetched an idea if you consider that literally hundreds of graduate students and dozens of staff and faculty have ignored it for twenty years. Is it really outrageous to think it could have been ignored for the previous thirty years?

61. University of California Regents, Correspondence and Papers, 1877–1887.

62. Armstrong and Armstrong 1991.

63. "Class of 1895" 1894.

64. Kyvig 1985; Aurbach 1930; Franklin 1922.

65. Kyvig 1985, 2000.

66. Paul Mullins 2001.

67. Armstrong and Armstrong 1991; Schwartz 2000: 150.

ACT II

1. Ferrier 1930; Jones 1901; Stadtman 1970; Horowitz 1987.

2. See Bederman 1995; Kimmel 2005, 2006.

3. Kasson 2001.

4. Bederman's 1995 and Kasson's 2001 discussions of boxer Jack Johnson and of the Wild West show phenomenon illustrate the kinds of racial insecurities felt by white men.

5. Kline 2001; Black 2003; and Roberts 1997 discuss the early eugenics movements in the United States in greater detail, while Dalton 2003 gives biographical consideration to Teddy Roosevelt's role in shifting national agendas.

6. Nerad 1999; Deutsch 1926.

7. Douglass 2000.

8. Stone and Stone 2002.

9. The Zetes' earliest neighbors appear to have been Samuel Christy and his family, who built a modest two-story home at 2234 Bancroft Avenue in 1889. Christy taught courses in mining and metallurgy in the school of mining. He would have been a familiar face to the many Zetes who majored in mining, and may have been a sympathetic neighbor. He and his family lived in the house until 1927. In 1885, a young married couple who were Cal alumni, the Cheneys, built a house on a two-lot parcel that was separated by one lot from the Zetes. Warren Cheney had graduated in 1878, and then continued on to earn a law degree. It was during his law education that he met the lovely

May Sheperd, class of 1883. Warren had not belonged to a fraternity himself while at Cal, but Academic Senate records demonstrate that he was in classes with a number of Zetes and involved in some of the same campus organizations. May was one of the few women on campus not to join Kappa Kappa Gamma, the first female fraternity on campus. She also served as the literary editor for the *Occidental*—an antifraternity newspaper founded in 1881. Perhaps her interests were purely literary and she did not share the editorial philosophy of the paper, but it remains intriguing that she and her husband chose to live and raise their three sons so close to a well-established and well-known fraternity house. Warren held a variety of careers, and May ultimately found employment with the university as an appointment secretary, a title that diminishes the importance of her work as the founder of the university's modern career placement center. The Cheney family built additional houses on lots adjacent to their home and rented them out. In 1896, the Zetes acquired their first next-door neighbors, at 2245 College—the widow Harriett J. Lee. In 1903, the Cheney family built another rental home, at 2243 College Avenue, which they rented to James T. Allen, a professor of theater arts, his wife, and their infant son. Eugene Hilgard had long resided at 2728 Bancroft Avenue; this block quickly filled in during the first years of the 1900s. By 1903, the families of E. J. Wicker, another university employee, and Dr. Howison, a professor of philosophy, built homes on lots facing Bancroft that abutted Zeta Psi's land. East of these lots were the homes of Caroline LeConte, widow of John LeConte, and on the corner of Piedmont Avenue and Bancroft, the family of George Day. A member of the LeConte family, nephew Joseph N. LeConte, became a member of Zeta Psi in 1891, so we can assume Caroline LeConte was sympathetic to the fraternity men in that neighborhood. More lots along Piedmont Avenue filled in with residential dwellings during the period of 1903 to 1911. Charles Noble, a math professor, built at 2224 in 1909, and real estate developer Charles Bancroft and his wife built a home at 2222 in 1910.

10. Page and Turnball 2006a, 2006b, 2006c, 2006d, 2006e, 2006f; Sanborn Fire Insurance Maps, Berkeley, California, 1903, p. 516 and 1911, p. 91.

11. My evidence of the Zetes' public lives is drawn mainly from university sources like newspapers, magazines, yearbooks, Academic Senate records, and presidents' and regents' records.

12. Stone 1957 discusses the relationship between education and musical training in the nineteenth-century United States.

13. I have been told that Zeta Psi published its own songbook, but I have not seen it.

14. Torbenson 2005; Piper 1897; and Stevens 1899 all provide histories of the origins of college fraternities. Wills 1992 discusses the importance of the rhetorical arts in the nineteenth century.

15. Zete was represented by brothers E. A. Rix and W. Van Dyke; "Class of 1878," 1877: 17. Zete Godwin McNeil led the Durants to victory that year; "Class of 1879," 1878.

16. "Class of 1882" 1881, as well as the volumes published by the classes of 1883 to 1896.

17. Ferrier 1930; Stadtman 1970 provide histories of student publications on campus.

18. Editorial, *University Echo*, January, June, and July 1873.

19. Editorial, *University Echo*, October 1871.

20. Zeta Psi 1880.

21. "Class of 1880" 1879.

22. Editorial, *University Echo*, April 1871.

23. Editorial, *University Echo*, March 1873.

24. Editorial, *University Echo*, November 1872.

25. "Class of 1913" 1912: 23.

26. Ferrier 1930; Sibley and Sibley 1952: 78.

27. "Class of 1879" 1878; "Class of 1880" 1879; "Class of 1882" 1881; "Class of 1883" 1882; Zeta Psi 1880.

28. Jones 1901.

29. Jones 1901: 116.

30. *Berkeleyan*, November 1875; UA, Academic Senate Record, vol. 1, November 19, 1875.

31. "Class of 1878" 1877.

32. Zeta Psi 1880: 96.

33. Editorial, *Occident*, February 14, 1884; "Class of 1886" 1885; "Class of 1891" 1890.

34. "Class of 1894" 1893: 57.

35. Editorial, *Occident*, May 4, 1882: 3.

36. UA, Academic Senate Record, vol. 2, 1880.

37. Zeta Psi 1880: 52.

38. "Class of 1895" 1894: 266–267.

39. UA, Academic Senate Record, vol. 2, 1880.

40. UA, Iota of Zeta Psi, ca. 1892–ca. 1900, UARC Album 15.

41. Dorsett 1993 provides a useful discussion of the boundaries between men's studies, gay studies, and masculinities studied through feminism of and the implications for understandings of gay history and scholarship. Chauncey 1993, 1995; Sedgwick 1990; Kimmel 2004; and Kinsmen 2004 provide overviews of the history of gay masculinities in the United States.

42. Kasson 2001: 29.

43. A number of publications discuss how homosexuality is perceived and treated in fraternal situations. In addition to Sanday 1990, see Windmeyer and Freeman 1998; Yeung and Stombler 2000.

44. Lazarus 1990.

45. Kasson 2001 describes the importance of the Wild West shows and the concept of the frontier. See also Amory 1969: 167. The 1902 Sears catalog features the sale of an educational stereoscope set about the "extinction" of Native American peoples as a subject for wholesome thought.

46. Dalton 2003.

47. Messner 1992; Green 1986.

48. Starr 1981, 1985; Tsing 2005; Smith 1987; Lankford 1991; and Jesperson 1997 discuss to differing degrees the role of the environmental movement in California and, in some cases, its links to discourses on masculinity; Tsing, for example, ties hypermasculinity to frontier settings in general.

49. LeConte 1990.

50. LeConte 1990: 52.

51. This statue, called *The Football Players*, was sculpted by noted artist Douglas Tilden.

52. Park 1998, 2000.

53. Lichtenstein 1901.

54. Lichtenstein 1901: 84–85.

55. "Class of 1877" 1876; as well as the volumes published by the classes of 1878–1880 and 1882–1890; Zeta Psi 1880.

56. Park 2000; "Class of 1879" 1878; as well as the volumes published by the classes of 1880 and 1882–1885; Zeta Psi 1880.

57. Park 2000.

58. At that time, W. H. Henry held the 120-yard hurdle record, having run that race in 15¾ seconds in 1892 at the Olympic Club grounds on May 30. Edwin Mays in 1892 served as the Athletic Association's president and held school records in the 75-, 100-, 120-, 220- and 440-yard dashes. F. S. Pheby was an accomplished middle-distance runner, holding school records in 1,000-yard, 1-mile, and 2-mile races. "Class of 1894" 1893.

59. "Class of 1893" 1892; as well as the volumes published by the classes of 1894–1900.

60. "Class of 1878" 1877: 6; Ferrier 1930: 426.

61. Blue and Gold 1886: 71.

62. Equipment recommended by Edwards to furnish the men's gymnasium (UA, Records of the Office of the President, Alphabetical Files, 1886).

Type of equipment	Use	Cost in dollars
Shoulder machine	For drooping and rounded shoulders	20
Neck machine with pulley weights and bridle	For strengthening muscles of the neck	15

Type of equipment	Use	Cost in dollars
Eccentric	For developing wrist, forearm and shoulder	25
Eccentric	For inner muscles of the arms and the muscles of the sides and legs	45
Wrist machine with box and brake		25
Finger machine		20
Foot machine	For extension to develop the muscles below the knee	25
Foot machine	For rotation to develop leg muscles not used in former foot machine	30
Twisting machine	Paddle movement calls into action muscles of the arms, chest, back, legs, and abdomen	20
Traveling parallels	For beginners	40
High back pulley	For backs, legs, and arms	15
Low back pulley		20
Rowing machine pneumatic double cylinder		25
8 sets of foils, masks and gloves		56
8 sets single sticks, masks and gloves		44
Transportation costs		75
Total		500

63. Kasson 2001: 223.

64. Kasson 2001: 223.

65. Editorial, *Occident,* October 5, 1882.

66. Editorial, *Occident,* October 20, 1882.

67. The yearbooks and the alumni register of 1905 provided me with the opportunity to compare the Zeta Psi register list of members. And I found that, until 1885, the records of the Academic Senate provided details of student disciplinary matters, including matters of gentlemanly behavior, academic honesty, excessive and unexcused absences,

deficiencies (failing required courses) and remandments (being held back from advancing to the next level with one's class).

68. The Zete brothers do make frequent appearances in the records of the senate. Sometimes it is because a brother, as a representative of the Durant Rhetorical Society, is inviting the faculty to attend an event or asking for permission to use a lecture hall. Other times, the brothers are petitioning to change classes, to waive or substitute electives, to receive leaves of absence, or to change their courses of study. Most of the remaining mentions, however, are related to flagging academic performance or outright disciplinary issues. Mailliard 1924; UA, Academic Senate Record, University Regents 1905; Edwards 1911; Zeta Psi 1899, 1926.

69. UA, Academic Senate Record, 1869–1885, vol. 1, 2, 4. E. C. Frick, another Zete with a checkered career, never graduated. He first showed up in the Academic Senate Records in May of 1881, where it was noted that he was deficient in comportment and history but that he should be allowed to continue. In May 1883, he tried unsuccessfully to have his excess chemistry hours substitute for German so he could get his bachelor of letters degree. His petition was turned down when the faculty realized that Frick did not have any excess hours in chemistry. The ongoing foibles of generations of Zete brothers and the German language may explain the skit about speaking German at the dinner table presented in *The Blue and Gold*.

70. UA, Academic Senate Record, University Regents 1905; UA, Academic Senate Record, vols. 1, 2, 4. 1869–1885.

71. UA, Academic Senate Record, vols. 1, 2, 4, 1869–1885.

72. UA, Academic Senate Record, vol. 1, 1869–1877.

73. UA, Academic Senate Record, vols. 1, 2, 1869–1883.

74. UA, Academic Senate Record, vols. 1, 2, 1869–1883.

75. University of California Regents, Correspondence and Papers, 1880–1889. Eugene Woldeman Hilgard was one of the stars of the early university. He was born in Bavaria and studied in Zurich, earning a PhD in 1853. He became the assistant state geologist of Mississippi in 1857 (later serving in the Confederate Army). He was part of a large geological survey of the Mississippi River Delta, which drew the attention of academics. He taught at the University of Michigan in 1873 and was wooed away to be Cal's professor of agriculture in 1874. Hilgard is viewed by many as the father of modern soil science and chemistry. His authoritative public appearances during the political assault of the Grangers against the university convinced many farmers that the university was serving their community in important ways, despite accusations to the contrary. While he was an important scholar, he also seems to have been a high-maintenance prima donna. The records of the University Archives demonstrate that Hilgard was a regular writer to the regents (and the university president, and the Academic Senate, and so on). His typical letters were demands for additional funding for lab equipment,

reimbursements for supplies, budgets for travel, and the like. It is easy to imagine the secretary of the regents, R. E. C. Strearns, rolling his eyes and sighing when sorting through the mail and finding a letter from Hilgard—which, based on the archival records, seems to have happened as often as once a week. What exactly Hilgard thought the regents could do about faulty plumbing on private property is unclear. However, that he felt he needed to go to the regents rather than the Zetes themselves is perhaps telling.

76. Sanborn Fire Insurance Maps, 1903, p. 376 and 1911, p. 91; Kett's City Directory 1936.

77. "Class of 1901" 1900: 208.

78. "Class of 1904" 1903: 341.

79. "Class of 1905" 1904: 587.

ACT III

The epigraph for this chapter comes from Barrie 1928.

1. Gordon 1990; Fass 1977; Nerad 1999; Ruyle 1998a, 1998b.

2. Editorial, *Oestrus*, October 7, 1878.

3. Ferrier 1930.

4. Editorial, *Oestrus*, April 23, 1878.

5. UA, Academic Senate Record, vol. 2, May 10, 1878. Unfortunately, the University Archives' collections of papers from the Office of the President begin with 1885, long after this incident exploded.

6. *Scylla*, April 1878: 1. The editors go on to state that the "pusillanimous cowards" called Delta Kappa Epsilons were not involved, since they were base knaves and not deserving of the other fraternities' recognition.

7. *Scylla*, May 3, 1878.

8. *Scylla*, May 3, 1878.

9. Ruyle 1998a, 1998b; Ferrier 1930; Stadtman 1970.

10. *Scylla*, September 1878, no. 3.

11. Editorial, *Oestrus*, August 26, 1878; September 9, 1878; September 22, 1878.

12. "A Letter from a Freshman," *Oestrus*, March 31, 1879. The writer states, "Now I ask what claim a certain fraternity, which considers itself the most desirable of the three societies, has upon the name of respectability, when it is a known fact (at least to myself and some others) that the majority of its members are nothing but gamblers. . . . It is truly disgusting to see the want of manliness and self-respect exhibited by some of the students." The freshman is referring to Zeta Psi, who had always declared itself the finest of the fraternities. It was not this section of the letter that led to campus scandal, however, but the second part, where the freshman claims that one of the fraternities stole the election.

13. According to the letter writer, a popular fraternity front-runner, a Mr. H—, stood up to announce that he would not run, since there was such a pervasive feeling among some members of the class that fraternities were trying to take over all aspects of student lives. The freshman class then elected C. E. Hayes, who ran on his credential of not being a fraternity man. Two days later, Hayes showed up on campus wearing a pledge pin. According to *The Blue and Gold* of that year, C. E. Hayes became a member of Delta Kappa Epsilon—the fraternity of "pusillanimous cowards" mentioned in the *Scylla*. The other Mr. H— would have to be F. J. Heney, the only other member of that fraternity with a surname beginning with *H*.

14. *Oestrus*, April 7, 1879, Records of the Academic Senate, vol. 2, April 9, 1879. The records of the Academic Senate report the case as follows:

> The president laid before the faculty a case of assault on the person of Murray Laidlaw and on that of C. M. Davis by F. J. Heney. He read the testimony taken before himself of Messrs. Davis, Heney and Laidlaw and of the following witnesses: Mr. Mahon, Chapline, Josphen and Wilkins. The affair grew out of an article published in the *Oestrus* (a newspaper published by students of the university and of which paper C. M. Davis is the Chief Editor) of March 31, 1879, and signed "A Freshman," the writer being Laidlaw, and the assault on C. M. Davis was with the hands, and that on Laidlaw by means of a cowhide."

Heney was suspended from the university for a year. His departure did not end disciplinary problems on the campus.

15. UA, Academic Senate Record, vol. 2, May 16, 1879.

16. Ferrier 1930; Zeta Psi 1880.

17. UA, Academic Senate Record, vol. 2, August 22, 1879. The committee appointed to draft the resolution was composed of Professors Soule (who had been insulted by a Zete), Joseph LeConte (a Zete neighbor, and ironically, father of a future Zete), Eugene Hilgard (another Zete neighbor), and Bernard Moses.

18. Editorial, *Oestrus*, October 6, 1879.

19. The copy of the *Scylla* in the library may implicate the Zetes. The name C. L. Tilden is penciled at the top of the front page; on the back, in the same hand, someone has penciled in "McGillivray?" and "Henshaw," both of whom were Zetes of the class of 1879. Is this an accusation?

20. In their 1880 description of the *Scylla*, the Zetes misidentified which issue of the *Scylla* was the offensive one. Whether this was an intentional misdirection to create an illusion of innocence, or a legitimate oversight of an innocent fraternity, we are left to ponder.

21. Editorial, *Oestrus*, September 9, 1879: the editors used the phrase "Upper 10th," and the term "sorehead" in an October 7, 1878, editorial. I have not found this terminology

used in any of the articles or opinion pieces written by Zetes in their own publications and student papers.

22. Editorial, *Oestrus*, March 10, 1879.

23. Barrie 1928.

24. UA, Academic Senate Record, vol. 2, December 2, 1879.

25. UA, Academic Senate Record, vol. 2, December 2, 1879.

26. UA, Academic Senate Record, vols. 1, 2, and 4.

27. Zeta Psi 1880: 53.

28. Zeta Psi 1880: 54.

29. Ferrier 1930; Stadtman 1970.

30. Stadtman 1967, 1970.

31. Editorial, *Occident*, May 16, 1883.

32. Stadtman 1967, 1970.

33. Deutsch 1926: 81.

34. Barrie 1928.

35. Barnhart 1986; Fisher 1997; Gentry 1964; Gilfoyle 1992.

36. Birkin 1979; Jack 1991.

37. Wolf 1997.

38. Gordon, 1990; Nerad 1999; Ruyle 1998a, 1998b.

39. Ferrier 1930; Stadtman 1970.

40. Gordon, 1990: 95.

41. Women as a percentage of all graduates of the University of California, 1870–1900.

Year	Number Women	% of graduates
1870	0	0
1871	0	0
1872	0	0
1873	0	0
1874	1	4
1875	0	0
1876	3	8.8
1877	1	3.3
1878	3	10.0
1879	8	12.9
1880	9	21.9
1881	4	13.3
1882	5	11.6

Year	Number Women	% of graduates
1883	10	31.25
1884	9	34.6
1885	8	24.2
1886	5	23.8
1887	7	15.9
1888	3	8.3
1889	5	12.8
1890	8	17.0
1891	6	10.7
1892	20	31.3
1893	19	25.0
1894	33	31.7
1895	38	32.8
1896	53	34.4
1897	70	42.3
1898	100	41.3
1899	100	43.6
1900	90	38.1

42. Gordon 1990; Nerad 1999; Ruyle 1998a, 1998b.

43. Editorial, *University Echo*, March 1871.

44. Unfortunately, Lindley did not graduate from the university, but she was granted an honorable dismission from the university and granted a certificate of proficiency on July 9, 1872. UA, Academic Senate Record, vol. 1, July 9, 1872, note on Lindley.

45. Lindley was a sibling of Zeta Psi brother David Lindley.

46. Editorial, *University Echo*, May 1873.

47. "Class of 1876" 1875: 28.

48. It is beyond the scope of this work to present a complete history of women's experiences on the University of California campus. I focus my efforts here on exploring the changing ways that women would have crossed the paths of the Zeta Psis during their college careers, and the ways that the growing numbers of coeds necessarily reshaped the experiences of Zeta Psi men on campus. Senior surveys included in *The Blue and Gold* during the 1880s provide some insights into the ways that coeducation was perceived on campus and, in particular, into the Zetes' views on the subject.

49. "Class of 1880" 1879: 28.

50. Zeta Psi 1880; "Class of 1878" 1877.

51. "Class of 1882" 1881. Frank Adams, Douglas Lindley, J. J. McGillivray, Hiram Pearson, and William Story were the graduating Zetes included in the survey.

52. "Class of 1882" 1881.

53. Editorial, *Occident*, April 13, 1883.

54. "Class of 1883" 1882.

55. "Class of 1885" 1884. Badger seems to have been a bit of a "card," also putting forward as his favorite beverage "Holy Water."

56. "Class of 1886" 1885.

57. UA, Academic Senate Record, vol. 2. 1880.

58. UA, Academic Senate Record, vol. 2, 1883.

59. MacLachlan 1998; Nerad 1999. Kellogg supported women on campus in a variety of ways. He supported May Sheperd Cheney's university placement service and was responsible for her hiring at the university. While he was university president, Kellogg asked the regents in 1898 to hire a female faculty member, and this lead to the hiring of Dr. Mary Ritter. His compromise was probably his best effort to see Pratt's achievements recognized.

60. University of California Regents, Correspondence and Papers, 1877–1887; UA, Academic Senate Record, vol. 2, May 27, 1881. As a matter of interest, the university's current Web site lists Lindley and Pratt as medal recipients.

61. UA, Academic Senate Record, vol. 2; Ferrier 1930.

62. Zeta Psi 1880; "Class of 1882" 1881; as well as the volumes published by the classes of 1883–1890.

63. Gordon 1990: 72.

64. "Class of 1896" 1895.

65. Nerad 1999.

66. Parsons 1905.

67. Canfield 1909.

68. Hinsdale 1910.

69. Kurtz 1943; Gordon 1990.

70. "No Coeds Need Apply: Professor Gayley Saves His Class for Men Students through Heroic Efforts," *Daily Cal*, January 3, 1903.

71. "Good Mother Supports Cause of Abused Co-Eds," *Sacramento Bee*, republished in *Daily Cal*, February 12, 1904.

72. "Would Have Speech of Professors Censured: Alumna Correspondent Objects to Recent Criticism of 'Co-ed' Conduct," *Daily Cal*, April 18, 1904.

73. "Men and Women Must Not Associate in Clubs," *Daily Cal*, April 29, 1904.

74. "College Actors Need No Aid from Actresses," *Daily Cal*, April 21, 1904.

75. Ferrier 1930.

76. Editorial, *Oestrus*, February 17, 1879.

77. "Class of 1894" 1893: 8, editor's remarks.

78. Park 1998.

79. "Conversion of Hearst Hall to Ladies' Gym," *Daily Cal*, April 11, 1900; Kantor 1998.

80. Sanborn Fire Insurance Maps, Berkeley, 1911.

81. "Feminist Movement Earns Great Victory" *Daily Cal*, October 9, 1916.

82. "Object to Women on Steps," *Daily Cal*, July 6, 1906.

83. "Tit for Tat," *Daily Cal*, August 2, 1906. This issue reprints letters originally published in the *Oakland Tribune*.

84. "Steps for Men Only," *Daily Cal*, March 16, 1904.

85. Ferrier 1930: 499.

86. "Women Stroll into Men's Gymnasium," *Daily Cal*, September 18, 1907.

87. Gordon 1990; Ruyle 1998a.

88. Gordon 1990.

89. Editorial, *Daily Cal*, March 1902; Editorial, *Daily Cal*, April 9, 1906.

90. Editorial, *Daily Cal*, April 11, 1906.

91. "ASUC," *Daily Cal*, October 17, 1907.

92. "Class of 1886" 1885; "Women Form Suffrage Club," *Daily Cal*, February 3, 1908.

93. "Women Students Form the Equal Suffrage League," *Daily Cal*, October 6, 1909; "Professor of Philosophy Talks on Equal Suffrage," *Daily Cal*, November 16, 1910; "New Club Will Study Equal Suffrage Question," *Daily Cal*, August 28, 1911.

94. Nerad 1999; Deutsch 1926.

95. *Pelican*, October 1909: 2. The paper got its name from campus slang for a hard-working and destined-to-be-a-spinster coed. Ironically, the publication was mainly a forum for male students' opinions.

96. *Pelican*, February 1904: 9.

97. "Cal and Stanford Debate Suffrage," *Daily Cal*, April 18, 1909.

98. Clifford 1998; "Class of 1883" 1882. Although founded in 1880, this is the first yearbook in which the Pi chapter of Kappa Kappa Gamma appears. Members included Annie Edmonds, Evelyn Stoddard, Carrie Swyney, Ella Florence Bailey, Flora Beal, Lottie Hollister, Fannie McLean, Elizabeth Blanchod, Helen Shearer, Mary Campbell, Alice Gibbons, and M. Frank Potter.

99. "Class of 1891" 1890; "Class of 1892" 1891; "Class of 1893" 1892; "Class of 1894" 1893; "Class of 1883" 1882.

100. Ritter 1933.

ACT IV

1. Gordon 1990; Kimmel 2006.

2. Moore 1996; Brockman 1996; Hering 1931.

3. "Cornerstone Is Laid for New Zeta Psi Chapter House," *Oakland Tribune*, February 6, 1910.

4. Ibid.

5. Ibid.

6. Ibid.

7. Wilkie and Kozakavich 2003.

8. Wilkie and Kozakavich 2003.

9. Nerad 1999; Kurtz 1943.

10. Moore 1996; Brockman 1996.

11. Stevens 1899.

12. Piper 1897.

13. Piper 1897: 648.

14. Piper 1897: 648.

15. Carnes 1989; Sanday 1990; Martin and Hummer 1989.

16. Sanday 1990: 137–142.

17. "Not Panhellenic . . . but Something Worse," *Pelican*, February 1908. This cartoon depicts fraternity brothers taking pledges, drinking, driving, and tubbing initiates. Zeta Psi alumni claim that, at Cal, only Zetes tubbed initiates, and that it was preferable to other kinds of chastising. To date, I've not found any evidence to contradict this claim. However, tubbing was known on other campuses.

18. UA, Iota of Zeta Psi, ca. 1892–ca. 1900, UARC Album 15.

19. Branding is indicated in a 1940s photograph in the University Archives: Scrapbooks of University of California, Berkeley Students, ca. 1878–1940; University of California, Berkeley Campus Events, ca. 1880–.

20. Sanday 1990; Fass 1977.

21. Berkeley Historical Society, blueprints (photocopies) for Zeta Psi House, 2251 College Avenue, Berkeley.

22. Deutsch 1926; Sanborn Fire Insurance Maps 1911, 1929.

23. Newcomb 1990.

24. The ceremonial garb was apparently composed of white robes that covered the body from head to toe—similar to the notorious robes of the Ku Klux Klan.

25. Over the years, my students and I have had the opportunity to formally and informally chat with many Zetes. See Lorinda Miller 1996, Roberts 2006, Wilkie 2001. Still others have written notes to me describing their experiences or have talked to the media in published or televised accounts. I identify by name only those Zetes who have been named and quoted in newspapers or have signed waivers indicating a willingness to have their oral histories published with their names attached.

26. Clark 1915: 69–70. Thomas Clark, who served as the dean of men at the University of Illinois, wrote frequent essays on fraternity life for *Banta's Greek Exchange*,

a publication that was started in 1901 to serve as a forum for discussion and to relate news about Greek life on different campuses. It was part of a move by Greek letter societies to organize nationally in the early twentieth century.

27. Clark 1915: 72–73.

28. Roberts 2006.

29. Registrar's Office, with particular attention to 1910, 1934–1935, 1946–1947.

30. ASUC 1928–1958. While it was possible to identify relationships between men in the fraternity's first house using the published Zete directory of 1899, a comparable document is not available for the second house. The published directory (Zeta Psi 1926) contains too many members to include the same level of detail provided in the earlier publication. Therefore, *The Blue and Gold* yearbooks were the most important resource for identifying fraternity members during this time.

31. Syracuse China Archive.

32. Schramm 1940.

33. Feinman 1979: 120; Mirkin 1970: 919.

34. For the most part, Zete alumni were less than helpful in recalling tablewares—the only man I found who explicitly remembered the dishes we recovered archaeologically worked as a dishwasher in the house to pay off his dues and expenses. The vast majority of the brothers, no matter their year of graduation, recalled the formality of their meals, particularly the need to dress for Monday chapter meeting dinners.

35. Godden 1964; Lehner 1988.

36. The Zetes went as far as to remove a crest mounted on the southern exterior chimney—no small height from the ground. Archaeologists working in prehistoric settings discuss "killing houses" at the ends of the houses' lifecycles, by burning or abandoning them; see in particular Tringham 1994.

37. Clark 1915: 44.

38. Zeta Psi Iota Archive, 1933–1934 Pledge Diary. The pledge class rotated the responsibility for recording daily events in the diary during the school year. This seems to have been, unfortunately, a practice limited to one pledge year only.

39. Clark 1915; Luong 1996.

40. Lovegren 1995: 160–173.

41. The following publications give a sense of how Prohibition was seen by those who lived during that time: Aurbach 1930; Franklin 1922; National Association of Distillers and Wholesale Dealers 1918; Seibel and Schwartz 1933. Kyvig 1985 and 2000 provide a modern perspective.

42. Wilkie and Farnsworth 1989.

43. Schwartz 2000.

44. ASUC 1920–1933; Zeta Psi Iota Archive, 1923 Photo Album, 1933–1934 Pledge Diary.

45. Kerr 2001.

46. Pendergast 2000; Benwell 2003; and particularly Osgerby 2003.

47. Fike 1988.

48. For a general overview of race, see Roediger 2005, 2007; and Brodkin 1998; for a sense of how race is viewed archaeologically, see Orser 2001, 2007.

49. Espiritu 2003; Sandmeyer 1991.

50. The Zetes' neighbors employed Swedish and Irish women house servants, a contrast to the Asian men consistently hired in the fraternities. Federal Population Census 1900, 1910, 1920.

51. "In the Fraternity," *San Francisco Call*, June 2, 1901.

52. For overviews of archaeological research on Chinese American sites, see Greenwood 1996; Fong 2007; Orser 2007; Voss 2005. Lovegren 1995 provides an overview of American food fads during the twentieth century.

53. "Some Frat Rules," *Pelican*, February 1904.

54. "Class of 1912" 1911.

ACT V

1. For example, Kimmel 2005; Chauncey 1993, 1995; Chudacoff 1999.

2. Horowitz 1987; Ruyle 1998a, 1998b; Gordon 1990.

3. For several perspectives on the social roles of fraternities on American campuses in the first half of the twentieth century, see Fass 1977; Brubaker and Rudy 1968; Deakins 1941; Smith 1905.

4. Notable examples of scholarly publications focused on fraternity life as an administrative issue include Benjamin 1915; Keppel 1917; Onthank 1934; Walton 1915; Warnock 1914.

5. Interfraternity Conference 1928.

6. Kurtz 1943.

7. Deutsch 1926; Stadtman 1967.

8. "Class of 1910" 1909.

9. "Class of 1894" 1893; Stadtman 1967; UA, Iota of Zeta Psi, ca. 1892–ca. 1900, UARC Album 15.

10. Stadtman 1967.

11. Park 2000; Green 1986; Newcomb 1915.

12. ASUC 1928.

13. "Class of 1919" 1920.

14. The following show typical examples of the ways women were excluded from supporting university teams: "Smoker Rally in Harmon Gym Tonight; Women Will Be Banned," *Daily Cal*, November 8, 1906; "Glee Club Limits Audience at Football Show

to Men Students," *Daily Cal,* October 31, 1913. Not until the 1950s were men-only rooting sections abolished; see van Houten and Barrett 2003.

15. Park 1998, 2000.

16. Fass 1977; Lyons 1962; Horowitz 1987.

17. ASUC 1927, 1928, 1929, 1930; "Class of 1921" 1922; as well as the volumes published by the classes of 1922–1924.

18. My stepgrandfather, who attended the University of Pennsylvania during the late 1920s and early 1930s, proudly showed me his various university keys, which he had worn on his watch fob as a student.

19. ASUC 1928: 564.

20. Stone and Stone 2002: 18.

21. Page and Turnball 2006a, 2006b, 2006c, 2006d, 2006e, 2006f; Kett's City Directory Company 1936.

22. "Class of 1912" 1911; "Class of 1923" 1922: 653.

23. "Class of 1913" 1912; "Class of 1923" 1922: 653.

24. Roberts 2006.

25. "Class of 1923" 1922: 664.

26. Ritter 1933: 213. Groups such as Abracadabra, Acacia, and Black Caldron are examples of groups that started as house clubs but later became "local" fraternities.

27. Fass 1977; Horowitz 1987.

28. ASUC 1948: 401.

29. ASUC 1949.

30. "Class of 1923" 1922: 132. A review of *The Blue and Gold* yearbooks revealed a few prominent Zeta Psi athletes. William Norris King ('13) was a varsity footballer, George J. O'Brien ('19) was a varsity swimmer and captain of the swim team, and John Raggio ('22), in addition to playing for the university team, made the Olympic rugby team. Louie LeHane "led the Blue and Gold to one of its best years. LeHane played a heady game of basketball, and his efficient guarding prevented opponents from scoring many points against Cal" ("Class of 1924" 1923: 198). Kent Weaver ('38) was a track star, Samuel Abbott was a varsity rower, and Donn Duerr ('47) played varsity football and rugby.

31. In addition to Jack Witter, Jean C. Witter ('16) played basketball, Willis G. ('17) ran varsity track, Edwin ('22) was a baseball manager, Guy Phelps ('24) played baseball, Wendell ('32) managed basketball, William ('47) played rugby and football, Phelps ('51) played rugby, and Thomas ('51) played football. Ronald ('53) was another rugby-playing Witter.

32. John Chapman ('27) managed baseball and football, and Thomas Proctor ('28), managed track. David White ('32) earned kudos as a crew manager, and George Martin ('34) earned a spot in *The Blue and Gold*'s senior "Hall of Fame" section for his role as

senior football manager. His brother (and sibling) John Martin ('37) also served as a football manager.

33. Ernest George Clewe ('12) was active in drama on campus and was a member of Mask and Dagger, the theater honor society. John Beales ('29) was recognized by the engineering honor society; Temple Clewe ('37) was a member of Blade and Scabbard, the military honor society, and the American Association of Engineers. Chaffee Hall ('38) belonged to Gamma Beta, Pi Delta Epsilon, and the Senior Peace Committee, the group that oversaw the freshman-sophomore brawl to ensure that it stayed safe.

34. A notable number of Zete men answered the call to serve their country in the Great War. In 1918, eight of Zeta Psi's junior and senior men were listed as being "in the service." Two, George Carson and Malin Thomas Langstroth, were identified as serving in the navy, and the others were simply identified as being in the service, presumably meaning the army.

35. Nerad 1999.

36. "What Women Can Do," *Daily Cal,* June 23, 1919.

37. " 'Ladies an Obsolete Term' says Fair One," *Daily Cal,* December 1, 1919.

38. Deutsch 1926.

39. Ritter 1933; Fass 1977.

40. Stone and Stone 2002: 180.

41. ASUC 1928: 565–566.

42. It is worth commenting on the Zetes' reputation as "women haters," referred to in the 1948 *Blue and Gold.* My research shows that this perception is an artifact of the time when the fraternity was founded. At that time, there were no female secret societies—in fact, as mentioned earlier, male fraternal organizations were founded to permit men to escape the stifling influence of the female domestic sphere. But times changed, and while fraternal men might still question whether women students were equal to men, they enjoyed their company. Fraternities founded during the twentieth century, when it was more common for men and women to socialize together as part of the new youth culture, created institutionalized relationships that paired one organization with another. Zeta Psi, however, did not have a formalized relationship with a sorority house. A member of the class of 1958 recalled that he had dated mainly women from Pi Phi and Delta Gamma, which was the result of his knowing several of the women in those houses from high school. He stated that Zeta Psi was never involved in any "exchanges," as they were called, with sororities (Roberts 2006). This man's memory conforms to information provided by Zetes from the 1930s, 1940s, and 1950s whom I have met over the years. The decision of the Zete fraternity to maintain its social emphasis on the relationships between brothers could have contributed to its reputation for being both antisocial and woman hating. This reputation did not hurt the social lives of the Zetes.

43. Robbins 1956.

44. Robbins 1956; for female cross-dressing during Mardi Gras, see Wilkie 1998a.

45. Ullman 1997.

46. Wolf 1997, 2003; Elkins 1997.

47. White and Tarr 2006.

48. "Skull and Keys Entertains," *Daily Cal*, April 26, 1900.

49. "College Actors Need No Aid from Actresses," *Daily Cal*, April 21, 1904.

50. "Running of Skull and Keys," *Daily Cal*, October 30, 1905. Recall that Anna Head was one of the coeds accused by the *Scylla* of being part of a love triangle. The Cal alumna founded a school for girls near the university.

51. "Pseudo Co-eds to Play Gentlemanly Game of Football," *Daily Cal*, March 5, 1908.

52. "Race for Queen Becomes Exciting; Co-eds Poll a Heavy Vote for Their Favorite Candidate," *Daily Cal*, September 9, 1907; "Many Candidates for Queen of Carnival," *Daily Cal*, September 16, 1907.

53. "Class of 1923" 1922: 61.

54. George Chauncey provides important clarification about the ways that homosexual behavior was categorized in the World War I period, based on analysis of an inquiry into "sexual perversion" among navy men in 1919. *Queers* was the term used to label men who took on the perceived feminine role during sexual encounters, and *queens* were effeminate men, typically queers, who donned female clothing. Men who served as penetrants of other men, or "husbands," were apparently still recognized at straight. Straights were perceived as falling into two categories—those who would accept advances from gay men, and those who would not. By portraying themselves in dress as "queeners," perhaps college men were identifying those seen as the most effeminate of men as their mirror image, and therefore stating a form of hyperheterosexuality through these displays.

55. Examples of cross-dressing in the university yearbooks include "Class of 1912" 1911, photographs of Skull and Keys; "Class of 1923" 1922, photographs from an unspecified campus event; and ASUC 1936, montages of photographs from Sirkus celebrations.

56. UA, Scrapbooks of University of California, Berkeley Students, ca. 1878–1940, cu-299; UA, University of California, Berkeley Campus Events, ca. 1880–.

57. "Law to Ban Fraternities," *Daily Cal*, January 28, 1915.

58. Forsyth 1910: 912. The 284 fraternity men surveyed spent $166,725, or an average of $587.05 per person, while the nonfraternity men spent $115,348.25, or an average of $407.56 per person. Forsyth found that, "as a general thing, those fraternities which are national and reputably strong spent the most, while the men of the local organizations incurred no more expense on the average than the non-fraternity men. One strong fraternity had thirty eligible men, of which half spent $800 or more, while seven spent $1000 or more." He noted that dues for most fraternities were about $50 per semester,

and that this accounted for at least $100 of the expenditures not made by the nonfraternity men.

59. Warnock 1914: 545. Warnock's analysis includes a particular consideration of the Illinois chapter of Zeta Psi: "The curve of the average of Zeta Psi is interesting. For five semesters it is very low, then in one semester it takes a sudden rise, and in the next semester assumes the top place, where it remains for a quite-long period. The impetus to scholarship in this chapter was furnished by the planning and activity of one man during the periods of 1910–1911 and 1911–1912. This man thoroughly ruled the chapter and insisted upon careful selection of freshmen pledges" (545). In this sense, Warnock's conclusions illustrate the trend visible in the social activities selected by Zetes in their first house—the interests of a single member could radically shape the activities of the group.

60. Walton 1915.

61. Benjamin 1915: 137. Here Benjamin presented data showing the participation of fraternity men and nonfraternity men in social activities at Purdue and the University of Wisconsin in 1911–1912. Benjamin used categories of social activities that align closely to those I established for Zeta Psi: athletics, publishing, music or drama, holding class office, and honor society. He found that, at Purdue, an average of 32.6 percent of fraternity men were involved in campus activities, compared to 23.6 percent of nonfraternity men. At Wisconsin, 52.7 percent of fraternity men were involved in campus activities, versus 27.3 percent of nonfraternity men. For Zeta Psi, in this same school year, 100 percent of the senior men were involved in campus activities.

62. Harris 1916.

63. "Student Grades," *Daily Cal*, January 11, 1915; "Student Grades," *Daily Cal* January 25, 1915; "Student Grades," *Daily Cal*, January 29, 1915.

64. "Dean of Students Issues New Rules on Initiation," *Daily Cal*, September 14, 1923.

65. Interfraternity Conference, 1928: 3.

66. "Interfraternity Council Formed," *Daily Cal*, January 28, 1915.

67. Fouke 1928: 7.

68. Fouke 1928: 40–41.

69. Fouke 1928: 40–41.

70. "Fraternity Jurisdiction to Be Handled by Intrafraternity Council," *Daily Cal*, April 5, 1928.

71. "Organizations to Be Ranked in New Way," *Daily Cal*, January 23, 1928.

72. "Zeta Psi's Treasure Room 'Borrowed' Loot Found," *Daily Cal*, January 5, 1953.

73. "Initiation Time," *Daily Cal*, March 14, 1947.

74. There is reason to think such traditions remain active. In 2005, the Archaeological Research Facility had a banner reading "ARCHAEOLOGY" hung over the front of

2251 College Avenue that obscured the Zeta Psi letters embedded in the building. The banner was stolen one weekend during spring of that year. We later heard, via several different student sources, that there was reason to believe Zeta Psi's pledges had "borrowed" the banner to restore the dignity of the fraternal letters. I wouldn't be surprised to learn that it is housed in the fraternity's chapter room. Incidentally, I don't take it personally; institutional memories are short in fraternities, and I did not know any of the Zetes at that time.

75. "Fraternity Banned," *Daily Cal*, April 8, 1949.

76. Stone and Stone 2002: 168.

77. "Liquor Violations Puts Four Fraternities on Probation" *Daily Cal*, November 2, 1954.

78. Ibid.

79. Kerr 2001.

80. Page and Turnball 2006a, 2006b, 2006c, 2006d, 2006e, 2006f; Kett's City Directory Company 1936.

81. UA, Records of the Office of the President, Numerical Bound Folders, 1929–1958; UA, University of California, Berkeley, Chancellor Records, 1952–.

82. UA, Records of the Office of the President, Numerical Bound Folders, 1929–1958; UA, University of California, Berkeley, Chancellor Records, 1952–. A January 10, 1955, report by treasurer Richard Harstock states that the fraternity first requested that the university pay them $165,000 in addition to giving them the Hilgard property. The university had countered that its appraisal indicated that the Hilgard lot was worth $2,500 more than the College Avenue lot, leading Zeta Psi to counter with a request for $100,000 instead. The university's appraisal is questionable. Although it used three separate appraisers and generated an average value from the three estimates, one appraiser undervalued the Zeta Psi property to the point that his appraisal dramatically lowered the final appraised value. Of course, the negotiations overlapped with the time when the Zetes were being unruly, a circumstance that surely hurt their bargaining position.

83. If the fraternity was rushed in its move to the new house, this may explain why the planks were left in the second house.

84. Letter from James Corley, June 31, 1954, Records of the Office of the President, Numerical Bound Folders, 1929–1958. This was a threat that remained as recently as the mid-1990s, when it was not clear whether the university would invest in retrofitting the building, which, as an unreinforced masonry building near the Hayward Fault, was then the second-most dangerous on campus.

85. University of California President's "Bound Folders," File 400, 1929–1958. A garbled oral history about this period of the university's use of the building has been passed down to the current occupants. Until the retrofit, people who used the archaeological lab in the former chapter room swore that it smelled like animal urine during the wet season. The more "spiritually sensitive" members of our community told stories of hearing the

screams of ghost monkeys who had been tortured in the basement as part of early space programs. After shifting between a number of different university units, the Archaeological Research Facility acquired the building in 1989 and has remained there since.

86. University of California President's "Bound Folders, " File 400, 1929–1958.

EPILOGUE

1. There are, of course, difficulties in using such publications, some of which have been amply discussed in an earlier chapter. The listings represent a moment in time during a person's life, not the entirety of a career. Different individuals feel compelled to offer different levels of information, resulting in a sizeable proportion of brothers who do not identify their careers. Among those who contributed to a publication close to the time of their graduation, their early professional life may have had no relationship whatsoever to their later careers. The directories capture all alumni at a single moment— those who have just graduated and those who are at the middle or end of their work life. Still, even if they offer only a vague portrait, the documents do provide a portrait of the brothers' lives after leaving the university. The following tables summarize the occupational choices of the men up to 1900.

	Occupation	Number	Percentage
1870–1880	Not given	24	35.3
	Real estate	1	1.5
	Engineer	4	6.0
	District attorney	1	1.5
	Lawyer	9	13.2
	Steamboat	1	1.5
	University	3	4.5
	Wine agriculture	1	1.5
	Astronomer	1	1.5
	Farmer	4	6.0
	Journalist	2	3.0
	Surveyor	1	1.5
	Clerk	5	7.5
	Printing	1	1.5
	Mining	2	3.0
	High school principal	1	1.5
	Bank cashier	2	3.0
	Industry	1	1.5

Occupation	Number	Percentage
Railroad	2	3.0
Paper business	1	1.5
Doctor	1	1.5

	Occupation	Number	Percentage
1881–1890	Not given	21	31.0
	Engineer	4	6.0
	Lawyer	5	7.5
	Journalist	1	1.5
	Clerk	2	6.0
	Mining	16	24.0
	Doctor	4	6.0
	Merchant	2	3.0
	Business	6	9.0
	Banking	1	1.5
	Orchardist	1	1.5
	City worker	1	1.5
	Architect	1	1.5
	Chemist	1	1.5
	Beef-cattle raising	1	1.5

	Occupation	Number	Percentage
1891–1900	Not Given	16	29.6
	Engineer	9	16.6
	Lawyer	6	11.1
	Clerk	6	11.1
	Mining	6	11.1
	College instructor	1	1.8
	Doctor	1	1.8
	Merchant	2	3.6
	Farmer	1	1.8
	Teacher	4	8.0
	Military	2	3.6

2. Zeta Psi 1899.
3. Zeta Psi 1899.
4. Zeta Psi 1899.

5. Zeta Psi 1899; Mailliard 1924.

6. Dean Witter Foundation, "The Foundation," www.deanwitterfoundation.org, provides biographical information on Dean Witter.

7. Zeta Psi 1899, 1926.

8. *In Memoriam* 1950: 20.

9. *In Memoriam* 1950: 20.

10. "Joseph Nesbit LeConte Celebrated 45th Birthday," *Daily Cal,* February 5, 1915.

11. *In Memoriam* 1950: 20.

12. Dean Witter Foundation, "Grant Recipients," www.deanwitterfoundation.org.

13. Witter 1956; Witter 1961.

14. "Class of 1910" 1911: 19–20.

15. *In Memoriam* 1938.

16. Mailliard 1924: 12.

17. UA, Academic Senate Record, vols. 1, 2, 4.

18. Dalton 2003.

19. Miller and Hintilian-Lucero 1996.

20. Miller and Hintilian-Lucero 1996; Wilkie 2001.

21. UA, Iota of Zeta Psi, ca. 1892–ca. 1900, UARC Album 15.

22. Clark 1915.

23. "The Greeks among Us," *Daily Cal,* February 2 and 3, 1956; "An Ugly Concept," *Daily Cal,* February 3, 1956.

24. See Sanday 1990, but also Kalof and Cargill 1991; Martin and Hummer 1989; Stombler 1994; Nuwer 1990; Moffat 1989.

25. Martin and Hummer 1989; Moffatt 1989.

26. Wolf 1997.

27. Front-page articles about the University of California panty raid can be found in the following papers: *San Francisco Chronicle,* May 17, 1956; *Daily Cal,* May 17, 1956; *Oakland Tribune,* May 17, 1956; and *Berkeley Gazette,* May 17, 1956.

28. *San Francisco Chronicle,* May 17, 1956.

29. Ibid.

30. "Masses and Asses," *Daily Cal,* May 17, 1956.

31. In his memoirs, Kerr described the event as follows: "On a warm night in late spring 1956, students from the fraternities went on a 'panty raid.' The incident now seems innocent enough, but at that time it made headlines around the world. One alumnus sent me a newspaper story from Beirut about how naked women had been carried through the streets of Berkeley on the shoulders of men students on their way to an orgy that would match anything the Ancient Romans could have organized. . . . I went to Walter Hass of the Class of 1910 to ask him whether the answer to a warm night in spring might better be a cold dip in a supervised swimming pool. He answered 'yes' and

contributed $300,000" (2001: 103). Apparently, boys will be boys unless they have access to a swimming pool.

32. *Oakland Tribune*, May 17, 1956; *Berkeley Gazette*, May 17, 1956.

33. "Chancellor's Report," *Daily Cal*, May 29, 1956.

34. Ibid.

35. "Ex-Com Abolishes Male Cheer Section," *Daily Cal*, May 17, 1956.

36. "Sororities Tarred and Painted Previous Friday," *Daily Cal*, May 29, 1956.

37. *San Francisco Chronicle*, March to May, 1956.

38. Barrie 1928.

39. Carnes 1989.

40. "Sane Adults Unblushingly Tell Peter Pan They Believe in Fairies," *San Francisco Call*, June 11, 1907.

41. Barrie 1928.

BIBLIOGRAPHY

ARCHIVAL SOURCES

Berkeley Historical Society
    Blueprints (photocopies) for Zeta Psi House, 2251 College Avenue, Berkeley.
    Plat map of lots and owners between Audubon, Piedmont and Bancroft Way.
    Berkeley, 1884.
Syracuse China Archive, Syracuse, New York. Record of China Purchases from Iota
Chapter of Zeta Psi, 1918–1952.
University Archives (UA), University of California
    Academic Senate Record, vol. 1. 1869–1877.
    Academic Senate Record, vol. 2. 1877–1883.
    Academic Senate Record, vol. 4. 1883–1885.
    Academic Senate Record, University Regents, 1905.
    Alphabetical Files, 1886, Col. G. Edwards File.
    Records of the Office of the President
        Numerical Bound Folders, 1886, A-Z.
        Numerical Bound Folders, 1887, A-Z.
        Numerical Bound Folders, 1888, A-Z.
        Numerical Bound Folders, 1900, A-Z.
        Numerical Bound Folders, 1929–1958.
    Scrapbooks of the University of California, Berkeley Students, cu-299.
    University of California, Berkeley Campus Events, c. 1880–.
    University of California, Berkeley, Chancellor Records, 1952–, Bound File 175.

University of California President's "Bound Folders," File 400.
University of California Regents
    Correspondence and Papers, 1877–1887.
    Correspondence and Papers, 1880–1889.
    Iota of Zeta Psi, ca. 1892–ca. 1900. UARC Album 15.
Zeta Psi Iota Archive (Iota Chapter, University of California, Berkeley)
    1923 Photo Album.
    1933–1934 Pledge Diary.

PERIOD NEWSPAPERS AND JOURNALS

Berkeleyan

Berkeley Gazette

College Echo

Daily Californian

Oakland Tribune

Occident

Oestrus

Pelican

San Francisco Call

San Francisco Chronicle

University Echo

BOOKS AND ARTICLES

Alberti, Benjamin. 2006. Archaeology, Men, and Masculinities. In *Handbook of Gender in Archaeology*, edited by Sarah Milledge Nelson, pp. 401–434. Walnut Creek, CA: Alta Mira Press.

Amory, C., ed. 1969. *1902 Edition of Sears, Roebuck Catalogue*. New York: Crown.

Armstrong, D., and E. M. Armstrong. 1991. *The Great Medicine Show: Being an Illustrated History of Hucksters, Healers, Health Evangelists, and Heroes from Plymouth Rock to the Present*. New York: Prentice Hall.

Associated Students of the University of California (ASUC). 1927. *The Blue and Gold*. vol. 54. Berkeley: ASUC.

———. 1928. *The Blue and Gold*, vol. 55.

———. 1929. *The Blue and Gold*, vol. 56.

———. 1930. *The Blue and Gold* vol. 57.

———. 1931. *The Blue and Gold*, vol. 58.

———. 1932. *The Blue and Gold*, vol. 59.

———. 1933. *The Blue and Gold*, vol. 60.

———. 1934. *The Blue and Gold*, vol. 61.

———. 1935. *The Blue and Gold*, vol. 62.

———. 1936. *The Blue and Gold*, vol. 63.

———. 1937. *The Blue and Gold*, vol. 64.

———. 1938. *The Blue and Gold*, vol. 65.

———. 1939. *The Blue and Gold*, vol. 66.

———. 1940. *The Blue and Gold*, vol. 67.

———. 1941. *The Blue and Gold*, vol. 68.

———. 1942. *The Blue and Gold*, vol. 69.

———. 1943. *The Blue and Gold*, vol. 70.

———. 1944. *The Blue and Gold*, vol. 71.

———. 1945. *The Blue and Gold*, vol. 72.

———. 1946. *The Blue and Gold*, vol. 73.

———. 1947. *The Blue and Gold*, vol. 74.

———. 1948. *The Blue and Gold*, vol. 75.

———. 1949. *The Blue and Gold*, vol. 76.

———. 1950. *The Blue and Gold*, vol. 77.

———. 1951. *The Blue and Gold*, vol. 78.

———. 1952. *The Blue and Gold*, vol. 79.

———. 1953. *The Blue and Gold*, vol. 80.

———. 1954. *The Blue and Gold*, vol. 81.

———. 1955. *The Blue and Gold*, vol. 82.

———. 1956. *The Blue and Gold*, vol. 83.

———. 1957. *The Blue and Gold*, vol. 84.

———. 1958. *The Blue and Gold*, vol. 85.

Atkinson, Byron H., and A. T. Drugger. 1959. Do College Students Drink Too Much? Two Deans Reply to This Perennial Question. *Journal of Higher Education* 30 (6):305–312.

Aurbach, Joseph S. 1930. *An Indictment of Prohibition*. New York: Harper and Brothers.

Barile, K. S., and J. C. Brandon, eds. 2004. *Household Chores and Household Choices: Theorizing the Domestic Sphere in Historical Archaeology*. Tuscaloosa: University of Alabama Press.

Barnhart, Jacqueline Baker. 1986. *The Fair but Frail: Prostitution in San Francisco, 1849–1900*. Reno: University of Nevada Press.

Barrie, J. M. 1916. *Peter and Wendy*. New York: Charles Scribner's Sons.

———. 1928. *Peter Pan, or the Boy Who Would Not Grow Up*. London: Hodder and Stoughton.

———. 1957. *When Wendy Grew Up: An Afterthought*. Edinburgh: Nelson.

Beaudry, M., ed. 1988. *Documentary Archaeology in the New World*. Cambridge: Cambridge University Press.

———. 2006. *Findings*. New Haven: Yale University Press.

Beaudry, M., L. Cook, and S. Mrozowski. 1991. Artifacts and Active Voices: Material Culture as Social Discourse. In *The Archaeology of Inequality*, edited by R. McGuire and Paynter, pp. 150–191. Oxford: Basil Blackwell.

Bederman, Gail. 1995. *Manliness and Civilization: A Cultural History of Gender and Race in the United States, 1880–1917*. Chicago: University of Chicago Press.

Beecher, Catherine, and Harriet Beecher Stowe. 1870. *Principles of Domestic Science*. New York: J. B. Ford and Company.

Bell, Catherine. 1992. *Ritual Theory Ritual Practice*. Oxford: Oxford University Press.

Benjamin, C. H. 1915. Fraternity Grades at Purdue. *Science*, n.s., 41(1047):135–138.

Benwell, Nathan, ed. 2003. *Masculinity and Men's Lifestyle Magazines*. Oxford: Blackwell.

Beynon, John. 2002. *Masculinities and Culture*. Buckingham, PA: Open University Press.

Birkin, Andrew. 1979. *J. M Barrie and the Lost Boys*. London: Constable and Company.

Black, Edwin. 2003. *War against the Weak: Eugenics and America's Campaign to Create a Master Race*. New York: Four Walls and Eight Windows.

Black, Tyra, Joanne Belknap, and Jennifer Ginsburg. 2005. Racism, Sexism, and Aggression: A Study of Black and White Fraternities. In *African American Fraternities and Sororities: The Legacy and the Vision*, edited by Tamara L. Brown, Gregory S. Parks, and Clarenda M. Phillips, pp. 363–392. Lexington: University Press of Kentucky.

Blue and Gold. 1886. *The Blue and Gold Handbook of the University of California*. Berkeley, CA: Blue and Gold.

Brockman, C. Lance, ed. 1996. *Theatre of the Fraternity: Staging the Ritual Space of the Scottish Rite of Freemansonry, 1896–1929*. Oxford: University Press of Mississippi.

Brodkin, Karen. 1998. *How Jews Became White Folks and What That Says about Race in America*. New Brunswick: Rutgers University Press.

Brooks, Alasdair. 1997. Beyond the Fringe: Transfer Printed Ceramics and the Internationalization of Celtic Myth. *International Journal of Historical Archaeology* 1:39–55.

Brown, Tamara L., Gregory S. Parks, and Clarenda M. Phillips, eds. 2005. *African American Fraternities and Sororities: The Legacy and the Vision*. Lexington: University Press of Kentucky.

Brubaker, John S., and Willis Rudy. 1968. *Higher Education in Transition: A History of American Colleges and Universities, 1636–1968*. New York: Harper and Row.

Buchli, V., and G. Lucas, eds. 2001. *Archaeologies of the Contemporary Past*. London: Routledge.

Burroughs, Edward. 2003. *Tarzan of the Apes*. New York: Modern Library Classics.

Canfield, A. G. 1909. The Chairman's Address: Coeducation and Literature. *PMLA* 24, *Appendix, Proceedings of the Twenty-Seventh Annual Meeting of the Modern Language Association of America, 1909,* pp. lxvi–lxxxii.

Carnes, Mark C. 1989. *Secret Ritual and Manhood in Victorian America*. New Haven: Yale University Press.

Carnes, Mark C., and Clyde Griffen, eds. 1990. *Meanings for Manhood: Constructions of Masculinity in Victorian America*. Chicago: University of Chicago Press.

Chauncey, George, Jr. 1993. Christian Brotherhood or Sexual Perversion? Homosexual Identities and the Construction of Sexual Boundaries in the World War I Era. In *Gender and American History since 1890*, edited by Barbara Melosh, pp. 72–105. New York: Routledge.

———. 1995. *Gay New York: Gender, Urban Culture, and the Making of the Gay Male World, 1890–1940*. New York: Basic Books.

Chudacoff, Howard P. 1999. *The Age of the Bachelor: Creating an American Subculture*. Princeton: Princeton University Press.

City of Berkeley Liaison Committee. 1957. Report on the Master Plan for the University of California. City of Berkeley, California. Report on file at the Bancroft Library, University of California, Berkeley.

Claney, Rebecca. 2004. *Rockingham Ware in American Culture, 1830–1930: Reading Historical Artifacts*. Hanover, NH: University Press of New England.

Clark, Bonnie, and Laurie A. Wilkie. 2006. Prisms of the Self: Gender and Personhood. In *Handbook of Gender in Archaeology*, edited by Sarah Nelson, pp. 333–364. Walnut Creek, CA: Alta Mira Press.

Clark, Emily. 2006. The Female Figure in J. M. Barrie's Peter Pan: The Small and the Mighty. In *Peter Pan in and out of Time*, edited by Donna R. White and C. Anita Tarr, pp. 23–45. Lanham, MD: Scarecrow Press.

Clark, Thomas Arkle. 1915. *The Fraternity and the College: Being a Series of Papers Dealing with Fraternity Problems*. Menasha, WI: George Banta Publishing.

Clarke, C. E., Jr. 1987. The Vision of the Dining Room: Plan Book Dreams and Middle-Class Realities. In *Dining in America, 1850–1900*, edited by K. Grover. Amherst: University of Massachusetts Press.

Class of 1875. 1874. *The Blue and Gold*, vol. 1. Berkeley, n.p.

Class of 1876. 1875. *The Blue and Gold*, vol. 2. Berkeley, n.p.

Class of 1877. 1876. *The Blue and Gold*, vol. 3. Berkeley, n.p.

Class of 1878. 1877. *The Blue and Gold*, vol. 4. Berkeley, n.p.

Class of 1879. 1878. *The Blue and Gold*, vol. 5. Berkeley, n.p.

Class of 1880. 1879. *The Blue and Gold*, vol. 6. Berkeley, n.p.

Class of 1882. 1881. *The Blue and Gold*, vol. 8. Berkeley, n.p.

Class of 1883. 1882. *The Blue and Gold*, vol. 9. Berkeley, n.p.

Class of 1884. 1883. *The Blue and Gold*, vol. 10. Berkeley, n.p.

Class of 1885. 1884. *The Blue and Gold*, vol. 11. Berkeley, n.p.

Class of 1886. 1885. *The Blue and Gold*, vol. 12. Berkeley, n.p.

Class of 1887. 1886. *The Blue and Gold*, vol. 13. Berkeley, n.p.

Class of 1888. 1887. *The Blue and Gold*, vol. 14. Berkeley, n.p.

Class of 1889. 1888. *The Blue and Gold*, vol. 15. Berkeley, n.p.

Class of 1890. 1889. *The Blue and Gold*, vol. 16. Berkeley, n.p.

Class of 1891. 1890. *The Blue and Gold*, vol. 17. Berkeley, n.p.

Class of 1892. 1891. *The Blue and Gold*, vol. 18. Berkeley, n.p.

Class of 1893. 1892. *The Blue and Gold*, vol. 19. Berkeley, n.p.

Class of 1894. 1893. *The Blue and Gold*, vol. 20. Berkeley, n.p.

Class of 1895. 1894. *The Blue and Gold*, vol. 21. Berkeley, n.p.

Class of 1896. 1895. *The Blue and Gold*, vol. 22. Berkeley, n.p.

Class of 1897. 1896. *The Blue and Gold*, vol. 23. Berkeley, n.p.

Class of 1898. 1897. *The Blue and Gold*, vol. 24. Berkeley, n.p.

Class of 1899. 1898. *The Blue and Gold*, vol. 25. Berkeley, n.p.

Class of 1900. 1899. *The Blue and Gold*, vol. 26. Berkeley, n.p.

Class of 1901. 1900. *The Blue and Gold*, vol. 27. Berkeley, n.p.

Class of 1902. 1901. *The Blue and Gold*, vol. 28. Berkeley, n.p.

Class of 1903. 1902. *The Blue and Gold*, vol. 29. Berkeley, n.p.

Class of 1904. 1903. *The Blue and Gold*, vol. 30. Berkeley, n.p.

Class of 1905. 1904. *The Blue and Gold*, vol. 31. Berkeley, n.p.

Class of 1906. 1905. *The Blue and Gold*, vol. 32. Berkeley, n.p.

Class of 1908. 1907. *The Blue and Gold*, vol. 34. Berkeley, n.p.

Class of 1909. 1908. *The Blue and Gold*, vol. 35. Berkeley, n.p.

Class of 1910. 1909. *The Blue and Gold*, vol. 36. Berkeley, n.p.

Class of 1911. 1910. *The Blue and Gold*, vol. 37. Berkeley, n.p.

Class of 1912. 1911. *The Blue and Gold*, vol. 38. Berkeley, n.p.

Class of 1913. 1912. *The Blue and Gold*, vol. 39. Berkeley, n.p.

Class of 1914. 1913. *The Blue and Gold*, vol. 40. Berkeley, n.p.

Class of 1915. 1914. *The Blue and Gold*, vol. 41. Berkeley, n.p.

Class of 1916. 1915. *The Blue and Gold*, vol. 42. Berkeley, n.p.

Class of 1917. 1916. *The Blue and Gold*, vol. 43. Berkeley, n.p.

Class of 1918. 1917. *The Blue and Gold*, vol. 44. Berkeley, n.p.

Class of 1919. 1918. *The Blue and Gold*, vol. 45. Berkeley, n.p.

Class of 1920. 1919. *The Blue and Gold*, vol. 46. Berkeley, n.p.

Class of 1921. 1920. *The Blue and Gold*, vol. 47. Berkeley, n.p.

Class of 1922. 1921. *The Blue and Gold*, vol. 48. Berkeley, n.p.

Class of 1923. 1922. *The Blue and Gold*, vol. 49. Berkeley, n.p.

Class of 1924. 1923. *The Blue and Gold*, vol. 50. Berkeley, n.p.

Clatterbaugh, Kenneth. 1997. *Contemporary Perspectives on Masculinity*. 2nd ed. Boulder, CO: Westview Press.

Clawson, Mary Ann. 1989. *Constructing Brotherhood: Class, Gender, and Fraternalism*. Princeton, Princeton University Press.

Clifford, Feraldine Jonçich. 1998. "No Man and No Thing Can Stop Me": Fannie McLean, Woman Suffrage, and the University. *Chronicle of the University of California* 1(2):83–94.

Connell, R. W. 1995. *Masculinities*. Berkeley: University of California Press.

———. 2000. *The Men and the Boys*. Berkeley: University of California Press.

Costello, J. G. 2000. Red Light Voices: An Archaeological Drama of Late Nineteenth-Century Prostitution. In *Archaeologies of Sexuality*, edited by R. Schmidt and B. Voss, pp. 160–175. London: Routledge.

Dalton, Kathleen. 2003. *Theodore Roosevelt: A Strenuous Life*. New York: Random House.

Deakins, Clarence. 1941. In Defense of Fraternities. *Journal of Higher Education* 123: 259–264.

DeCunzo, Luann. 1995. Reform, Respite, Ritual: An Archaeology of Institutions. The Magdalene Society of Philadelphia, 1800–1850. *Historical Archaeology* 294. Special issue.

DeCunzo, Luann, and John Jameson. 2005. *Unlocking the Past*. Gainesville: University Press of Florida.

Deetz, James F. 1994. *In Small Things Forgotten*. 2nd ed. New York: Penguin.

Dekker, Rudolf M., and Lotte C. van de Pol. 1989. *The Tradition of Female Transvestism in Early Modern Europe*. London: Macmillan.

D'Emilio, John, and Estelle Freedman. 1988. *Intimate Matters: A History of Sexuality in America*. New York: Harper and Row.

Deutsch, Monroe, ed. 1926. *Benjamin Ide Wheeler: The Abundant Life*. Berkeley: University of California Press.

Dorsett, G. W. 1993. I'll Show You Mine, If You'll Show Me Yours: Gay Men, Masculinity Research, Men's Studies, and Sex. *Theory and Society* 22:697–709.

Douglass, John Aubrey. 2000. *The California Idea and American Higher Education: 1850–1960 Master Plan*. Stanford: Stanford University Press.

Dunbar, Janet. 1970. *J. M. Barrie: The Man behind the Image*. Boston: Houghton Mifflin.

Dunmenil, Lynn. 1984. *Freemasonry and American Culture*. Princeton: Princeton University Press.

Edwards, G. 1911. Remembrances of the University. In *The Blue and Gold*. Berkeley, CA: Class of 1912.

Elkins, Richard. 1997. *Male Femaling: A Grounded Theory Approach to Cross-Dressing and Sex Changing*. London: Routledge.

Emeryville Historical Society. 2005. *Images of America: Emeryville*. San Francisco: Arcadia Publishing.

Espiritu, Yen Le. 2003. All Men Are Not Created Equal: Asian Men in U.S. History. In *Men's Lives*, edited by Michael Kimmel and Michael Messner, pp. 35–44. Boston: Allyn and Bacon.

Executive Committee. 1937. *A Preliminary Report on Revitalizing Fraternity Life at Dartmouth College*. Hanover, NH: Intrafraternity Dartmouth Committee, Dartmouth College.

Fass, Paula S. 1977. *The Damned and the Beautiful: American Youth in the 1920s*. New York: Oxford University Press.

Faust, Drew Gilpin. 1996. *Mothers of Invention: Women of the Slaveholding South in the American Civil War*. Chapel Hill: University of North Carolina.

Federal Population Census. 1900. *Population Schedule of the Twelfth Census of the United States, Berkeley, California*. Washington, DC.

————. 1910. *Population Schedule of the Thirteenth Census of the United States, Berkeley, California*. Washington, DC.

————. 1920. *Population Schedule of the Fourteenth Census of the United States, Berkeley, California*. Washington, DC.

Feinman, Jeffrey. 1979. *The 1909 Fall Sears, Roebuck and Company Catalog*. New York: Ventura Books.

Ferrier, William Warren. 1930. *Origin and Development of the University of California*. Berkeley, CA: Sather Gate Book Shop.

Fike, Richard E. 1988. *The Bottle Book*. Caldwell, NJ: Blackburn Press.

Fisher, Trevor. 1997. *Prostitution and the Victorians*. New York: St. Martin's Press.

Fitts, R. 1999. The Archaeology of Middle-Class Domesticity and Gentility in Victorian Brooklyn. *Historical Archaeology* 33(1):39–62.

Foner, Eric. 1983. *Nothing but Freedom: Emancipation and Its Legacy*. Baton Rouge: Louisiana State University Press.

Fong, Kelly. 2007. Laundering the Past: Reexamining Race in the Chinese American Historic Archaeological Record. Interdepartmental Archaeology Program Masters of Arts in Archaeology paper, University of California, Los Angeles.

Forsyth, C. H. 1910. A Comparison between Fraternity and Non-fraternity Expenses at the University of Illinois. *Science*, n.s., 32(834):911–913.

Foucault, Michel. 1990. *The History of Sexuality*. Vol. 1: *An Introduction*, translated by Robert Hurley. New York: Penguin.

Fouke, Robert H., ed. 1928. *Fraternity Manual*. Berkeley, CA: Fraternity Manual Company, James J. Gillick and Company.

Fowler, Christopher. 2004. *The Archaeology of Personhood*. London: Routledge.

Fox, Paul. 2006. The Time of His Life: Peter Pan and the Decadent Nineties. In *Peter Pan in and Out of Time*, edited by Donna R. White and C. Anita Tarr, pp. 23–45. Lanham, MD: Scarecrow Press.

Fox-Genovese, E. 1988. *Within the Plantation House: Black and White Women of the Old South*. Chapel Hill: University of North Carolina Press.

Frankenburg, Ruth, ed. 1997. *Displacing Whiteness: Essays in Social and Cultural Criticism*. Durham: Duke University Press.

Franklin, Fabian. 1922. *What Prohibition Has Done to America*. New York: Harcourt, Brace and Company.

Fried, R., and W. Vandereychken. 1989. The Peter Pan Syndrome: Was James M. Barrie Anorexic? *International Journal of Eating Disorders* 8(3):369–376.

Galle, J. E., and A. L. Young, eds. 2006. *Engendering African American Archaeology: A Southern Perspective*. Knoxville: University of Tennessee Press.

Garber, Marjorie. 1992. *Vested Interests: Cross-Dressing as Cultural Anxiety*. New York: Routledge.

Gentry, Curt. 1964. *Madams of San Francisco*. Garden City, NY: Doubleday and Company.

Gilchrist, Roberta. 1999. *Gender and Archaeology: Contesting the Past*. London: Routledge.

———. 2000. Archaeological Biographies: Realizing Human Lifecycles, -Courses, and -Histories. *World Archaeology* 31(3):325–328.

Gilfoyle, Timothy J. 1992. *City of Eros: New York City, Prostitution, and the Commercialization of Sex, 1790–1920*. New York: Norton.

Godden, Geoffrey. 1964. *Encyclopaedia of British Pottery and Porcelain Marks*. London: Barrie and Jenkins.

Gordon, Lynn D. 1990. *Gender and Higher Education in the Progressive Era*. New Haven: Yale University Press.

Grant, Cecil, and Norman Hodgson. 1913. *The Case for Co-Education*. London: Grant Richards.

Green, Harvey. 1986. *Fit for Life: Health, Fitness, Sport, and American Society*. New York: Pantheon.

Greenwood, Roberta. 1996. *Down by the Station: Los Angeles Chinatown, 1880–1933*. Los Angeles: Institute of Archaeology University of California.

Hall, Martin. 2000. *Archaeology and the Modern World: Colonial Transcripts of South Africa and the Chesapeake*. London: Routledge.

Hardesty, D. L. 1994. Class, Gender Strategies, and Material Culture in the Mining West. In *Those of Little Note: Gender, Race, and Class in Historical Archaeology*, edited by E. M. Scott, pp. 129–145. Tucson: University of Arizona Press.

Harland, M. 1882. *Common Sense in the Household: A Manual of Practical Housewifery*. New York: Charles Scribner's Sons.

Harris, George. 1916. The Ethics of College Students. *Harvard Theological Review* 98:190–200.

Harrison, Rodney. 2002. Archaeology and the Colonial Encounter: Kimberley Spearpoints, Cultural Identity, and Masculinity in the North of Australia. *Journal of Social Archaeology* 2(3):352–377.

Heneghan, Bridget. 2003. *Whitewashing America: Material Culture and Race in the Antebellum Imagination*. Jackson: University Press of Mississippi.

Hering, Oswald C. 1931. *Designing and Building the Chapter House*. Menasha, WI: Collegiate Press, George Banta Publishing.

Hicks, Dan, and Mary Beaudry, eds. 2006. *Historical Archaeology*. Cambridge: Cambridge University Press.

Hinsdale, Ellen C. 1910. Coeducation Again. *School Review* 18(1):36–39.

Hogg, Michael A., Deborah J. Terry, and Katherine M. White. 1995. A Tale of Two Theories: A Critical Comparison of Identity Theory with Social Identity Theory. *Social Psychology Quarterly* 58(4):255–269.

Holdsworth, Deryck W. 1995. "I'm a Lumberjack and I'm OK": The Built Environment and the Varied Masculinities in the Industrial Age. In *Gender, Class, and Shelter: Perspectives in Vernacular Architecture, V,* edited by Elizabeth Collins Cromley and Carter L. Hudgins, pp. 11–25. Knoxville: University of Tennessee Press.

Hollindale, Peter. 2005. A Hundred Years of Peter Pan. *Children's Literature in Education* 36(3):197–215.

hooks, bell. 2004. *The Will to Change: Men, Masculinity, and Love.* New York: Atria Books.

Horowitz, Helen Lefkowitz. 1987. *Campus Life: Undergraduate Cultures from the End of the 18th Century to the Present.* New York: Knopf.

Ignatiev, Noel. 1996. *How the Irish Became White.* New ed. New York: Routledge.

Igra, Anna R. 1996. Male Providerhood and the Public Purse: Anti-Desertion Reform in the Progressive Era. In *The Sex of Things,* edited by Victoria de Grazia and Ellen Furlough, pp. 188–211. Berkeley: University of California Press.

In Memoriam. 1931. George Cunningham Edwards: Mathematics, Berkeley. Berkeley: University of California.

———. 1938. Joseph Cummings Rowell, 1853–1938. Special booklet. 60 pp. Berkeley: University of California.

———. 1950. Joseph Nisbet LeConte, Mechanical Engineering, Berkeley, pp. 17–20. Berkeley: University of California.

Interfraternity Conference. 1928. *The Interfraternity Conference: What It Is and What It Does.* New York: Interfraternity Conference.

Israel, F., ed. 1997. *1897 Sears, Roebuck Catalogue.* New York: Chelsea House.

Jack, R. D. S. 1991. *The Road to Neverland: A Reassessment of J. M. Barrie's Dramatic Art.* Aberdeen, Scotland: Aberdeen University Press.

Jenkins, Richard. 2000. Categorization: Identity, Social Process, and Epistemology. *Current Sociology* 48(3):7–25.

Jesperson, Christine. 1997. Engendering Adventure: Men, Women, and the American "Frontier," 1880–1927. PhD diss., Rutgers University.

Johnson, M. 1996. *An Archaeology of Capitalism.* Oxford: Blackwell.

Jones, William Carey. 1901. *Illustrated History of the University of California.* Berkeley: Students Cooperative Society.

Joyce, Rosemary. 2000. A Pre-Columbian Gaze: Male Sexuality among the Ancient Maya. In *Archaeologies of Sexuality,* edited by Robert A. Schmidt and Barbara Voss, pp. 263–283. London: Routledge.

———. 2001. *Gender and Power in Prehispanic Mesoamerica.* Austin: University of Texas.

———. 2002. *The Languages of Archaeology: Dialogue, Narrative, and Writing.* Oxford: Blackwell.

———. 2006. Writing Historical Archaeology. In *Historical Archaeology,* edited by Dan Hicks and Mary C. Beaudry, pp. 48–65. Cambridge: Cambridge University Press.

Kalof, Linda, and Timothy Cargill. 1991. Fraternity and Sorority Membership and Gender Dominance Attitudes. *Sex Roles* 25:417–423.

Kantor, J. R. K. 1998. Cora, Jane, and Phoebe: Fin-de-Siècle Philanthropy. *Chronicle of the University of California* 1(2):1–8.

Kantrowitz, Stephen. 2006. Fighting Like Men: Civil War Dilemmas of Abolitionist Manhood. In *Battle Scars: Gender and Sexuality in the American Civil War,* edited by Catherine Clinton and Nina Silber, pp. 19–40. Oxford: Oxford University Press.

Kasson, John F. 1987. Rituals of Dining: Table Manners in Victorian America. In *Dining in America, 1850–1900,* edited by K. Grover. Amherst: University of Massachusetts Press.

———. 2001. *Houdini, Tarzan, and the Perfect Man: The White Male Body and the Challenge of Modernity in America.* New York: Hill and Wang.

Kasson, Joy S. 2000. *Buffalo Bill's Wild West: Celebrity, Memory, and Popular History.* New York: Hill and Wang.

Keppel, Frederick P. 1917. *The Undergraduate and His College.* Boston: Houghton Mifflin.

Kerr, Clark. 2001. *The Gold and the Blue: A Personal Memoir of the University of California, 1947–1967.* Vols. 1 and 2. Berkeley: University of California Press.

Kett's Directory Company. 1936. *Geographical Directory: Oakland and East Bay Cities.* Oakland, CA: Kett's Directory Company.

Kimbrough, Walter M. 2003. *Black Greek 101.* London: Fairleigh Dickenson University Press.

Kimmel, Michael S. 2004. Masculinity as Homophobia: Fear, Shame, and Silence in the Construction of Gender Identity. In *Feminism and Masculinities,* edited by Peter F. Murphy, pp. 182–199. Oxford: Oxford University Press.

———. 2005. *The History of Men: Essays on the History of American and British Masculinities.* Albany: State University of New York Press.

———. 2006. *Manhood in America: A Cultural History.* 2nd ed. Oxford: Oxford University Press.

Kinsman, Gary. 2004. Men Loving Men: The Challenge of Gay Liberation. In *Feminism and Masculinities,* edited by Peter F. Murphy, pp. 165–181. Oxford: Oxford University Press.

Kline, Wendy. 2001. *Building a Better Race: Gender, Sexuality, and Eugenics from the Turn of the Century to the Baby Boom.* Berkeley: University of California Press.

Knapp, A. Bernard. 1998a. Boys Will Be Boys: Masculinist Approaches to a Gendered Archaeology. In *Reader in Gender Archaeology*, edited by Kelley Hays Gilpin and David S. Whitley, pp. 365–373. London: Routledge.

———. 1998b. Who's Come a Long Way Baby? Masculinist Approaches to a Gendered Archaeology. *Archaeological Dialogues* 5(2):91–106.

Knapp, A. Bernard, and Lynn Meskell. 1997. Bodies of Evidence on Prehistoric Cyprus. *Cambridge Archaeological Journal* 7(2):183–204.

Kuchta, David. 1996. The Making of the Self-Made Man: Class, Clothing, and English Masculinity, 1688–1832. In *The Sex of Things: Gender and Consumption in Historical Perspective*, edited by Victoria de Grazia and Ellen Furlough, pp. 54–78. Berkeley: University of California Press.

Kurtz, Benjamin P. 1943. *Charles Mills Gayley*. Berkeley: University of California Press.

Kyvig, David E. 1985. Law, Alcohol, and Order: Perspectives on National Prohibition. Westport, CT: Greenwood Press.

———. 2000. *Repealing National Prohibition*. 2nd ed. Kent, OH: Kent State University Press.

Lankford, Scott. 1991. John Muir and the Nature of the West: An Ecology of American Life, 1864–1914. PhD diss., Stanford University.

LaRoche, C., and M. Blakey. 1997. Seizing Intellectual Power: The Dialogue at the New York African Burial Ground. *Historical Archaeology* 31(3):84–106.

Lawrence, Susan., ed. 2003. *Archaeologies of the British: Explorations in Identity in the United Kingdom and Its Colonies, 1600–1945*. New York: Routledge.

Lazarus, Edward. 1990. *Black Hills White Justice: The Sioux Nation versus the United States, 1775 to Present*. New York: Harper Collins.

LeConte, Joseph N. 1990. *A Yosemite Camping Trip, 1889*. Friends of the Bancroft Library 38. Berkeley: University of California.

Lehner, Lois. 1988. *Lehner's Encyclopedia of U.S. Marks of Pottery, Porcelain, and Clay*. Paducah: Schroeder.

Leone, M., and P. Potter, eds. 1999. *Historical Archaeologies of Capitalism*. New York: Kluwer Academic/Plenum.

Lichtenstein, Joy. 1901. *For the Blue and Gold: A Tale of Life at the University*. San Francisco: A. M. Robertson.

Limerick, Patricia. 1987. *Legacy of Conquest*. London: Norton.

Lippincott, Horace Mather. 1919. *The University of Pennsylvania, Franklin's College: Being Some Accounts of Its Beginnings and Development, Its Customs and Traditions, and Its Gifts to the Nation*. Philadelphia: J. B. Lippincott.

Little, B. J., ed. 1992. *Text-Aided Archaeology*. Boca Raton: CRC Press.

London, Jack. 1988. *The Call of the Wild*. New York: Aerie Books.

———. 2001. 1901. *White Fang*. New York: Scholastic.

Lovegren, Sylvia. 1995. *Fashionable Food*. New York: Macmillan.

Ludlow Collective. 2001. Archaeology at the Colorado Coal Field War, 1913–1914. In *Archaeologies of the Contemporary Past*, edited by V. Buchli and G. Lucas, pp. 94–107. London: Routledge.

Luong, Carolyn. 1996. Food Containers and Other Related Items. Manuscript, Historical Archaeology Laboratory, Department of Anthropology, University of California, Berkeley.

Lyons, John O. 1962. *The College Novel in America*. Carbondale: Southern Illinois University Press.

MacDill, David, Jonathon Blachard, and Edward Beecher. 1868. *Secret Societies: A Discussion of the Character and Claims*. No. 28. N.p., Cincinnation Western Tract and Book Society.

MacLachlan, Anne J. 1998. May Cheney's Contribution to the Modern University. *Chronicle of the University of California* 1(2):75–81.

Mailliard, Joseph. 1924. Autobiography of Joseph Mailliard. *Condor* 26(1):10–29.

Martin, Patricia Yandcy, and Robert Hummer. 1989. Fraternities and Rape on Campus. *Gender and Society* 3(4):457–473.

McLaren, Angus. 1997. *The Trials of Masculinity: Policing Sexual Boundaries, 1870–1930*. Chicago: University of Chicago Press.

Mechling, Jay. 2001. *On My Honor: Boy Scouts and the Making of American Youth*. Chicago: University of Chicago Press.

Melosh, Barbara, ed. 1993. *Gender and American History since 1890*. New York: Routledge.

Meskell, Lynn. 2002. *Private Life in New Kingdom Egypt*. Princeton: Princeton University Press.

Meskell, Lynn, and Rosemary Joyce. 2003. *Embodied Lives*. New York: Routledge.

Messner, Michael. 1992. *Power at Play: Sports and the Problem of Masculinity*. Boston: Beacon.

Miller, Lorinda, and Persephone Hintilian-Lucero. 1996. Oral History and Ethnography of Zeta Psi. Manuscript, Historical Archaeology Laboratory, Department of Anthropology, University of California, Berkeley.

Mirkin, Alan, ed. 1970. *The 1927 Edition of the Sears, Roebuck Catalogue*. New York: Crown.

Moffatt, Michael. 1989. *Coming of Age in New Jersey: College and American Culture*. New Brunswick: Rutgers University Press.

Moore, William D. 1996. The Masonic Lodge Room, 1870–1930: A Sacred Space of Masculine Spiritual Hierarchy. In *Gender, Class, and Shelter: Perspectives in Vernacular Architecture, V*, edited by Elizabeth Collins Cromley and Carter L. Hudgins, pp. 26–39. Knoxville: University of Tennessee Press.

Moreland, J. 2001. *Archaeology and Text*. London: Gerald Duckworth and Company.

Morse, M. Joy. 2006. The Kiss: Female Sexuality and Power in J. M. Barrie's Peter Pan. In *Peter Pan in and out of Time*, edited by Donna R. White and C. Anita Tarr, pp. 281–302, Lanham, MD: Scarecrow Press.

Mullins, Paul. 2001. Racializing the Parlor: Race and Victorian Bric-a-Brac Consumption. In *Race and the Archaeology of Identity*, edited by Charles E. Orser, pp. 158–176. Provo: University of Utah Press.

Murphy, Peter F., ed. 2004. *Feminism and Masculinities*. Oxford: Oxford University Press.

National Association of Distiller and Wholesale Dealers. 1918. *The Anti-Prohibition Manual: A Summary of Facts and Figures Dealing with Prohibition*. Cincinnati, OH: Publicity Department of the National Association of Distillers and Wholesale Dealers.

Nelson, Dana D. 1998. *National Manhood: Capitalist Citizenship and the Imagined Fraternity of White Men*. Durham: Duke University Press.

Nerad, Maresi. 1999. *The Academic Kitchen: A Social History of Gender Stratification at the University of California, Berkeley*. Albany: State University of New York Press.

Nevius, C. W. 2007. Can Death Dent Media's Humiliation Fad? *San Francisco Chronicle*, January 21, 2007, p. 2.

Newcomb, Rexford. 1990. *Spanish Colonial Architecture in the United States*. Minneola, NY: Dover.

Newcomb, Simon. 1915. University Athletics. In *College and the Future*, edited by Richard Rice, pp. 115–130. New York: Charles Scribner's Sons.

Nuwer, Hank. 1990. *Broken Pledges: The Deadly Rite of Hazing*. Atlanta: Longstreet Press.

Oakley, Anne. 1984. *The Captured Womb: A History of Medical Care of Pregnant Women*. New York: Basil Blackwell.

Onthank, Karl W. 1934. Fraternity Choices. *Journal of Higher Education* 5(8):422–425.

Orser, Charles, ed. 2001. *Race and the Archaeology of Identity*. Salt Lake City: University of Utah Press.

———. 2007. *The Archaeology of Race and Racialization in Historic America*. Gainesville: University Press of Florida.

Osgerby, Bill. 2003. A Pedigree of the Consuming Male: Masculinity, Consumption, and the American "Leisure Class." In *Masculinity and Men's Lifestyle Magazines*, edited by Bethan Benwell, pp. 57–85. Oxford: Blackwell.

Page and Turnball. 2006a. 2222 Piedmont Ave. Historic Structure Report Prepared for the University of California, Berkeley. Report on file, Capital Projects, University of California, Berkeley.

———. 2006b. 2224 Piedmont Ave. Historic Structure Report Prepared for the University of California, Berkeley. Report on file, Capital Projects, University of California, Berkeley.

———. 2006c. 2232 Piedmont Ave. Historic Structure Report Prepared for the University of California, Berkeley. Report on file, Capital Projects, University of California, Berkeley.

———. 2006d. 2240 Piedmont Ave. Historic Structure Report Prepared for the University of California, Berkeley. Report on file, Capital Projects, University of California, Berkeley.

———. 2006e. 2241 College Ave. Historic Structure Report Prepared for the University of California, Berkeley. Report on file, Capital Projects, University of California, Berkeley.

———. 2006f. 2243 College Ave. Historic Structure Report Prepared for the University of California, Berkeley. Report on file, Capital Projects, University of California, Berkeley.

Park, Roberta J. 1998. A Gym of Their Own: Women, Sports, and Physical Culture at the Berkeley Campus, 1876–1976. *Chronicle of the University of California* 1(2):21–47.

———. 2000. Athletics and Berkeley. *Chronicle of the University of California* 4(1): 175–188.

Parsons, Edward S. 1905. The Social Life of the Coeducational College. *School Review* 13(5):382–389.

Pendergast, Tom. 2000. *Creating the Modern Man: American Magazines and Consumer Culture, 1900–1950.* Columbia: University of Missouri Press.

Piper, P. F. 1897. College Fraternities. *Cosmopolitan Magazine* 22:641–648.

Porter, John Addison. 1888. College Fraternities. *Century* 36:759–760.

Praetzellis, A., and M. Praetzellis, eds. 1998. Archaeologists as Storytellers. *Historical Archaeology* 3225. Special issue.

———, eds. 2004. *Putting the "There" There: Historical Archaeologies of West Oakland: I-880 Cypress Replacement Project.* Rohnert Park, CA: Anthropological Studies Center, Sonoma State University.

Purser, M. 1991. "Several Paradise Ladies Are Visiting in Town": Gender Strategies in the Early Industrial West. *Historical Archaeology* 25(4): 6–16.

Recknor, P. E., and S. A. Brighton. 1999. Free from All Vicious Habits: Archaeological Perspectives on Class Conflicts and the Rhetoric of Temperance. *Historical Archaeology* 3327:63–86.

Registrar's Office. 1910, 1919–1947. *Statistical Appendum*. Berkeley: University of California.

Rice, Richard, Jr., ed. 1915a. *College and the Future: Essays for the Undergraduate on Problems of Character and Intellect*. New York: Charles Scribner's Sons.

———. 1915b. Panem et Circenses. In *College and the Future*, edited by Richard Rice Jr., pp. 131–142. New York: Charles Scribner's Sons.

Riddle, J. M. 1997. *Eve's Herbs: A History of Contraception and Abortion in the West*. Cambridge, MA: Harvard University Press.

Ritter, Mary Bennett. 1933. *More Than Gold in California*. Berkeley, CA: Professional Press.

Robbins, Alexandra. 2004. *Pledged: The Secret Life of Sororities*. New York: Hyperion.

Robbins, Phyllis. 1956. *Maude Adams: An Intimate Portrait*. New York: G. P. Putnam's Sons.

Roberts, Dorothy. 1997. *Killing the Black Body*. New York: Pantheon.

Roberts, Sujata. 2006. Oral history of A. Douglas Hobson. Manuscript, Historical Archaeology Laboratory, University of California, Berkeley.

Robson, John, ed. 1977. *Baird's Manual of American College Fraternities*. 19th ed. Menasha, WI: Baird's Manual Foundation.

Roediger, D. 2005. *Working toward Whiteness: How American's Immigrants Became White*. New York: Basic Books.

———. 2007. *The Wages of Whiteness: Pace and the Making of the American Working Class*. 2nd ed. London: Verso.

Rose, Jacqueline. 1984. *The Case for Peter Pan, or, the Impossibility of Children's Fiction*. London: Macmillan.

Roth, Christine. 2006. Babes in Boy-Land: J. M. Barrie and the Edwardian Girl. In *Peter Pan in and out of Time*, edited by Donna R. White and C. Anita Tarr, pp. 47–67. Lanham, MD: Scarecrow Press.

Rothman, Sheila. 1978. *A Woman's Proper Place: A History of Changing Ideals and Practices, 1870 to the Present*. New York: Basic Books.

Rottman, Deborah. 2005. Newly Weds, Young Families, and Spinsters: A Consideration of Developmental Cycle in Historical Archaeologies of Gender. *International Journal of Historical Archaeology* 9(1):1–36.

Rotundo, E. Anthony. 1993. *American Manhood: Transformations in Masculinity from the Revolution to the Modern Era.* New York: Basic Books.

Routh, Chris. 2001. "Man for the Sword and the Needle She": Illustrations of Wendy's Role in J. M. Barrie's Peter and Wendy. *Children's Literature in Education* 32(1): 57–75.

Ruyle, Janet, ed. 1998a. The Early Prytaneans. *Chronicle of the University of California* 131:49–56.

———. 1998b. Ladies Blue and Gold. *Chronicle of the University of California* 1(2): 1–172.

Ryan, Mary. 2006. *Mysteries of Sex: Tracing Men and Women through American History.* Chapel Hill: University of North Carolina Press.

Sanborn Fire Insurance Maps. Maps from the Sanborn Map Company Archives, late nineteenth century to 1990. Bethesda, MD: California University Publications of America.

Sanday, Peggy Reeves. 1990. *Fraternity Gang Rape: Sex, Brotherhood, and Privilege on Campus.* New York: New York University Press.

Sandmeyer, Elmer Clarence. 1991. *The Anti-Chinese Movement in California.* Urbana: University of Illinois Press.

Sanua, Marianne R. 2003. *Going Greek: Jewish College Fraternities in the United States, 1895–1945.* Detroit: Wayne State University Press.

Schmidt, Robert, and Barbara Voss, eds. 2000. *Archaeologies of Sexuality.* London: Routledge.

Schott, Penelope Scamby. 1974. The Many Mothers of Peter Pan: An Exploration and Lamentation. *Research Studies* 42(1):1–10.

Schramm, Edward S. 1940. Chinaware: Its Selection and Maintenance. *Fraternity House Management* (March):13–15, 35.

Schroeder, J., ed. 1970. *1900 Sears, Roebuck Catalogue.* Northfield, IL: DBI Books.

———, ed. 1971. *1908 Sears, Roebuck Catalogue.* Northfield, IL: DBI Books.

Schwartz, Richard. 2000. *Berkeley, 1900: Daily Life at the Turn of the Century.* Berkeley, CA: RSB Books.

Scott, Elizabeth. 1997. "A Little Gravy in the Dish and Onions in a Teacup": What Cookbooks Reveal about Material Culture. *International Journal of Historical Archaeology* 1(2):131–155.

Scott, William A. 1965. *Values and Organizations: A Study of Fraternities and Sororities.* Chicago: Rand McNally.

Sedgwick, Eve Kosofsky. 1990. *Epistemology of the Closet.* Berkeley: University of California Press.

Seibel, John E., and Anton Schwarz. 1933. *History of the Brewing Industry and Brewing Science in America*. Chicago: G. L. Peterson.

Seifert, D. J. 1991. Within Sight of the White House: The Archaeology of Working Women. *Historical Archaeology* 25(4): 82–108.

Seifert, D. J., E. B. O'Brien, and J. Balicki. 2000. Mary Ann Hall's First-Class Brothel: The Archaeology of a Capital Brothel. In *Archaeologies of Sexuality*, edited by R. Schmidt and B. Voss, pp. 117–128. London: Routledge.

Seldes, Gilbert. 1930. *The Future of Drinking*. Boston: Little, Brown.

Sharer, Robert, and Wendy Ashmore. 2000. *Discovering Our Past: A Brief Introduction to Archaeology*. New York: Mayfield Press.

Sheffield, Edith L. 1889. Student Life in the University of Michigan. *Cosmopolitan Magazine* 72:107.

Sibley, Robert, and Carol Sibley. 1952. *California Pilgrimage: A Treasury of Tradition, Lore, and Laughter*. N.p., self-published.

Smart, C., ed. 1992. *Regulating Womanhood: Historical Essays on Marriage, Motherhood, and Sexuality*. London: Routledge.

Smith, Michael. 1987. *Pacific Visions: California Scientists and the Environment, 1850–1915*. New Haven: Yale University Press.

Smith, Spencer. 1905. Report of the Committee on the Influence of Fraternities in Secondary Schools. *School Review* 13(1):1–10.

Smith-Rosenburg, Carroll. 1985. *Disorderly Conduct: Visions of Gender in Victorian America*. New York: Knopf.

Spelman, E. 1988. *Inessential Woman: Problems of Exclusion in Feminist Thought*. Boston: Beacon.

Stadtman, Verne A., ed. 1967. *The Centennial Record of the University of California*. Berkeley: University of California Printing Department.

———. 1970. *The University of California, 1868–1968*. New York: McGraw-Hill.

Starr, Kevin. 1981. *Americans and the California Dream, 1850–1915*. Santa Barbara, CA: Peregrine Smith.

———. 1985. *Inventing the Dream: California through the Progressive Era*. Oxford: Oxford University Press.

Stevens, Albert C. 1899. *The Cyclopedia of Fraternities*. Paterson, NJ: Hamilton Printing and Publishing.

Stevenson, Robert Louis. 1948. *Kidnapped*. New York: Grosset and Dunlap.

———. 1967. *Dr. Jekyll and Mr. Hyde*. New York: Bantam.

———. 1999. *Treasure Island*. New York: Penguin.

Stombler, Mindy. 1994. "Buddies" or "Slutties": The Collective Sexual Representation of Fraternity Little Sisters. *Gender and Society* 8(3):293–296.

Stone, Irving, and Jean Stone, eds. 2002. *There Was Light: Alumni Essays.* Berkeley: University Press of California.

Stone, James H. 1957. Mid-nineteenth-century American Beliefs on the Social Value of Music. *Musical Quarterly* 43(37):38–49.

Summers, Leigh. 2001. *Bound to Please: A History of the Victorian Corset.* Oxford: Berg Press.

Tarlow, S., and S. West, eds. 1999. *The Familiar Past? Archaeologies of Later Historical Britain.* London: Routledge.

Thomas, David Hurst. 1991. *Archaeology: Down to Earth.* New York: Harcourt Brace Jovanovich College Publications.

Thwing, Charles F. 1920. *The American Colleges and Universities in the Great War, 1914–1919.* New York: Macmillan.

Torbenson, Craig L. 2005. The Origin and Evolution of College Fraternities and Sororities. In *African American Fraternities and Sororities: The Legacy and the Vision,* edited by T. Brown, G. Parks, and C. Phillips, pp. 37–66. Lexington: University Press of Kentucky.

Tringham, Ruth. 1994. Engendered Places in Prehistory. *Gender, Place, and Culture* 1(2):169–203.

Tsing, Anna Lowenhaupt. 2005. *Friction: An Ethnography of Global Connection.* Princeton: Princeton University Press.

Ullman, Sharon R. 1997. *Sex Seen: The Emergence of Modern Sexuality in America.* Berkeley: University of California Press.

University of California. 1905. *Directory of Graduates.* Berkeley: University of California.

Van Houten, Peter S., and Edward L. Barrett Jr. 2003. *Berkeley and Its Students, Days of Conflict, Years of Change, 1945–1970.* Berkeley: Berkeley Public Policy Press, Institute of Governmental Studies, University of California.

Voss, B. 2000a. Colonial Sex: Archaeology, Structured Space, and Sexuality in Alta California's Spanish-Colonial Missions. In *Archaeologies of Sexuality,* edited by R. A. Schmidt and B. L. Voss, pp. 35–61. London: Routledge.

———. 2000b. Feminisms, Queer Theories, and the Archaeological Study of Past Sexualities. *World Archaeology* 37(3): 424–439.

———. 2005. The Archaeology of Overseas Chinese Communities. *World Archaeology* 3740:424–439.

Wall, D. 1994. *The Archaeology of Gender: Separating the Spheres in Urban America.* New York: Plenum.

————. 2000. Family Meals and Evening Parties: Constructing Domesticity in Nineteenth-Century Middle-Class New York. In *Lines That Divide,* edited by J. A. Delle, S. A. Mrozowski, and R. Paynter. Knoxville: University of Tennessee.

Walton, L. B. 1915. Fraternities and Scholarship. *Science,* n.s., 41(1045):63–64.

Warnock, Arthur Ray. 1914. Fraternities and Scholarship at the University of Illinois. *Science,* n.s., 40(1033):542–547.

Wasinger, Carrie. 2006. Getting Peter's Goat: Hybridity, Androgyny, and Terror in Peter Pan. In *Peter Pan in and out of Time,* edited by Donna R. White and C. Anita Tarr, pp. 217–236. Lanham, MD: Scarecrow Press.

Weber, David J. 1992. *The Spanish Frontier in North America.* New Haven: Yale University Press.

Whaley, Deborah Elizabeth. 2005. The Empty Space of African-American Sorority Representation: Spike Lee's School Daze. In *African American Fraternities and Sororities: The Legacy and the Vision,* edited by Tamara L. Brown, Gregory S. Parks, and Clarenda M. Phillips, pp. 417–436. Lexington: University Press of Kentucky.

White, Donna, and C. Anita Tarr, eds. 2006. *Peter Pan in and out of Time.* Lanham, MD: Scarecrow Press.

White, Hayden. 1975. *Metahistory: The Historical Imagination in Nineteenth-Century Europe.* Baltimore: Johns Hopkins University Press.

Wilkie, Laurie A. 1998a. Beads and Breasts: The Negotiation of Gender Roles and Power at New Orleans Mardi Gras. In *Beads and Beadmakers,* edited by Lidia Sciama and Joanne Eicher, pp. 193–211. London: Berg Publishers.

————. 1998b. The Other Gender: The Archaeology of an Early 20th Century Fraternity. *Proceedings of the Society for California Archaeology* 11:7–11.

————. 2000a. *Creating Freedom: Material Culture and African-American Identity at Oakley Plantation, Louisiana, 1845–1950.* Baton Rouge: Louisiana State University Press.

————. 2000b. Not Merely Child's Play: Creating a Historical Archaeology of Children and Childhood. In *Children and Material Culture,* edited by Joanne Sofaer-Derevenski, pp. 100–113. London: Routledge.

————. 2001. Black Sharecroppers and White Frat Boys: Living Communities and the Construction of Their Archaeological Pasts. In *The Archaeology of the Contemporary Past,* edited by Victor Buchli and Gavin Lucas, pp. 108–118. London: Routledge.

————. 2003. *The Archaeology of Mothering: An African-American Midwife's Tale.* New York: Routledge.

Wilkie, Laurie A., and Paul Farnsworth. 1989. Analysis of Materials from CA-LAn-1134H, Malibu Creek State Park. Manuscript. California Department of Parks and Recreation, Los Angeles.

————. 2005. *Sampling Many Pots: An Archaeology of Memory and Tradition at a Bahamian Plantation*. Gainesville: University Press of Florida.

Wilkie, Laurie A., and Katherine Howlett Hayes. 2006. Engendered and Feminist Archaeologies of the Documented and Recent Pasts. *Journal of Archaeological Research* 14(3):243–264.

Wilkie, Laurie A., and Stacy Kozakavich, eds. 2003. Archaeological Field Research at the Conservatory/Observatory Hill Sites. Manuscript, Historical Archaeology Laboratory, University of California, Berkeley.

Wills, Garry. 1992. *Lincoln at Gettysburg: The Words That Remade America*. New York: Simon and Schuster Paperbacks.

Windmeyer, Shane L., and Pamela Freeman. 1998. *Out on Fraternity Row: A Personal Account of Being Gay in a College Fraternity*. New York: Alyson.

Witter, Dean. 1956. *Meanderings of a Fisherman*. San Francisco: James H. Barry.

————. 1961. *Shikar*. San Francisco: James H. Barry.

Wolf, Stacy. 1997. "Never Gonna Be a Man/Catch Me If You Can/I Won't Grow Up": A Lesbian Account of Mary Martin as Peter Pan. *Theatre Journal* 49(4):493–509.

————. 2003. *A Problem Like Maria: Gender and Sexuality in the American Musical*. Ann Arbor: University of Michigan Press.

Yaeger, Jason, and Marcello A. Canuto, eds. 2000. *The Archaeology of Communities: A New World Perspective*. London: Routledge.

Yamin, Rebecca. 2006. Wealthy, Free, and Female: Prostitution in Nineteenth-Century New York. *Historical Archaeology* 39(1):4–18.

Yentsch, A. E. 1994. *A Chesapeake Family and Their Slaves: A Study in Historical Archaeology*. Cambridge: Cambridge University Press.

Yeung, King-to, and Mindy Stombler. 2000. Gay and Greek: The Identity Paradox of Gay Fraternities. *Social Problems* 47(1):134–152.

Zeta Psi. 1880. *The Blue and Gold*. Vol. 7. Berkeley, CA: Zeta Psi.

————. 1899. *Semi-Centennial Biographical Catalogue of the Zeta Psi Fraternity of North America*. New York: Zeta Psi Fraternity of North America.

————. 1926. *Directory of the Zeta Psi Fraternity*. New York: Zeta Psi Fraternity of North America.

INDEX

Text:	10.25/14 Fournier
Display:	Fournier
Compositor:	Westchester Book Group
Printer and Binder:	Maple-Vail Book Manufacturing Group